# R U N N I N G

# UNIX

# R U N N I N G
# UNIX

JoAnne Woodcock, Michael Halvorson,
and Robert Ackerman

*An Introduction to*
*SCO™ UNIX System V/386 and*
*XENIX® Operating Systems*

• • •

PUBLISHED BY
Microsoft Press
A Division of Microsoft Corporation
One Microsoft Way
Redmond, Washington 98052-6399

Library of Congress Cataloging-in-Publication Data
Woodcock, JoAnne.
    Running UNIX : an introduction to SCO UNIX/XENIX / JoAnne
Woodcock, Michael Halvorson, Robert Ackerman.
        p.    cm.
    ISBN 1-55615-270-1 : $24.95
    1. UNIX (Computer operating system)    2. XENIX (Computer operating
system)    I. Halvorson, Michael.    II. Ackerman, Robert, 1942-
III. Title.
QA76.76.O63W662      1990                                    90-5791
005.4'3--dc20                                                CIP

Printed and bound in the United States of America.

1 2 3 4 5 6 7 8 9    MLML    4 3 2 1 0

Distributed to the book trade in Canada by General Publishing Company, Ltd.

Distributed to the book trade outside the United States and Canada by Penguin Books Ltd.

Penguin Books Ltd., Harmondsworth, Middlesex, England
Penguin Books Australia Ltd., Ringwood, Victoria, Australia
Penguin Books N.Z. Ltd., 182–190 Wairau Road, Auckland 10, New Zealand

British Cataloging in Publication Data available

AT&T® and UNIX® are registered trademarks of American Telephone and Telegraph Company.
Apple® and A/UX® are registered trademarks of Apple Computer, Incorporated. COMPAQ® is
a registered trademark of Compaq Computer Corporation. DEC,® Ultrix,® VAX,® and VMS® are
registered trademarks of Digital Equipment Corporation. CP/M® is a registered trademark of
Digital Research Incorporated. HP-UX® is a registered trademark of Hewlett-Packard Company.
386™ is a trademark of Intel Corporation. IBM® is a registered trademark of International Busi-
ness Machines Corporation. Microsoft,® MS-DOS,® Multiplan,® and XENIX® are registered trademarks of Microsoft Corporation. Tandy® is a registered trademark of Radio Shack, a division of
Tandy Corporation. SCO™ is a trademark of the Santa Cruz Operation, Incorporated.

**Acquisitions Editor:** Marjorie Schlaikjer
**Project Editor:** Ron Lamb
**Technical Editor:** Jim Johnson

# Contents

---

## SECTION II
## FOR THE SYSTEM ADMINISTRATOR

---

---

## SECTION III
## APPENDIXES

---

# Acknowledgments

A Microsoft Press book represents the talent and dedication of many skilled professionals. The following individuals deserve specific mention for their efforts on *Running UNIX*: Ron Lamb, for his skillful editing and project management; Jim Johnson and Mary DeJong, for their technical editing and insight; Marjorie Schlaikjer, for keeping us on track; Debbie Kem and Cathy Thompson, for word processing; Cynthia Riskin, Brianna Morgan, Alice Copp Smith, Jean Zimmer, and Kathleen Atkins, for proofreading; Carolyn Magruder, for typesetting; Peggy Herman, for pasteup; Becky Geisler-Johnson, for artwork; Darcie Furlan, for interior design; and Mark Souder and Susan McRhoton, for scheduling and keeping all those pink folders moving. Many thanks also to Bill O'Brien for getting us started last time.

A special acknowledgment and thank-you also go to Brigid Fuller, Allen Ginzburg, John Harker, and Mark Taub of the Santa Cruz Operation. Their direction and quick response to questions large and small kept us moving and helped us focus on the needs of users new to the UNIX operating system.

*JoAnne Woodcock*
*Michael Halvorson*
*Robert Ackerman*
*April, 1990*

# Introduction

Welcome to SCO UNIX. You might already know that SCO UNIX is an operating system, but you might not know how to use it and what it does. In this book, you will learn what SCO UNIX can do for you and some of the many ways in which you can use it to make your work easier and more productive.

As you'll learn in Chapter 1, any operating system is a set of programs that work closely with your computer, enabling it to perform a variety of important tasks—from displaying characters on the screen to storing and tracking your data.

SCO UNIX performs these tasks efficiently and for the most part invisibly. SCO UNIX is designed not only to perform work for many users (multiuser) but also to perform many tasks at the same time (multitasking). As a result, SCO UNIX lets you and your coworkers share files, send messages, print one letter while working on another, add and contribute to a single document or information base—all without leaving the keyboard and screen on your desktop. Although SCO UNIX is a multiple-user environment, you can protect those documents you want to keep private. In addition, SCO UNIX functions equally well as a dedicated, single-user system (or as a programmer's environment, although that aspect of SCO UNIX is not covered in this book).

## THE TWO SIDES OF SCO UNIX

Depending on the role SCO UNIX will play in your day-to-day work, either you will use it simply as a tool to "get things done" or you will take responsibility for ensuring that your SCO UNIX system runs smoothly for you and for the other users on your system.

If you use it primarily as a tool, you will want to learn how SCO UNIX can help you accomplish your work. If you have the responsibility of administering the system, you will also want to know when and how to install SCO UNIX on a computer, how to make SCO UNIX aware of new users, how to manage files and disks, and so on.

Because these two approaches to SCO UNIX are based on different goals and different priorities, we've divided this book into two sections. The first, Chapters 1 through 11, concentrates on what you can do with SCO UNIX. These chapters are dedicated to everyone who uses SCO UNIX, but they concentrate on the needs of those who are not computer professionals and simply want to make the best use of a flexible tool for data management.

The second section, Chapters 12 through 15, deals primarily with the needs of the system administrator—the person responsible for maintaining the SCO UNIX system and keeping it running. However, these chapters are not for the system administrator alone; they are for anyone interested in learning some of the "behind-the-scenes" details of their system.

## WHAT YOU WILL FIND

As you read this book, you will find many examples that illustrate the details and concepts outlined in each chapter. You can practice these examples if you want, but we did not intend this book to be simply a workbook. Assuming that you will not always have a computer or terminal handy, we provide graphics to show you what you should or would see on your own screen as the examples progress.

In addition, we present topics in the order in which we feel you will be most comfortable learning about SCO UNIX. But no one way is the only right way. Read or reread these chapters as you want. You might, for example, want to learn about the SCO UNIX *mail* system, which is covered in Chapter 7. If you stumble over a concept you don't understand, simply back up to the chapter in which it is covered. Here is a brief summary of the book's contents:

- Chapter 1: an introduction to SCO UNIX.
- Chapter 2: logging in (making SCO UNIX aware of your presence) and taking a quick look at some interesting features.
- Chapter 3: creating, using, and removing SCO UNIX directories.
- Chapter 4: managing data files and using *ed*, the SCO UNIX line editor.
- Chapters 5 and 6: using *vi*, the SCO UNIX visual text editor.

- Chapter 7: using the SCO UNIX *mail* system.

- Chapter 8: using advanced file-handling commands and techniques.

- Chapters 9 and 10: using the SCO UNIX shells (the command interpreters that translate your commands into a form that SCO UNIX can understand).

- Chapter 11: taking a look at Open Desktop, the SCO UNIX graphical environment.

- Chapter 12: installing SCO UNIX (the first of the chapters on system administration).

- Chapter 13: managing the system—adding user accounts and terminals.

- Chapter 14: managing disks and disk drives.

- Chapter 15: networking SCO UNIX systems.

Appendix A briefly lists and describes the SCO UNIX commands discussed in this book, and Appendix B lists the most commonly used SCO UNIX directories and files.

# TYPOGRAPHICAL CONVENTIONS

Because many SCO UNIX features described in this book are presented in an "If you do this, you see that" format, we've adopted certain conventions to help you recognize SCO UNIX commands and their results.

A command that you can type as it is shown is on a separate line, like this:

```
mail johnd
```

The format for a command is shown like this:

```
copy file1 file2
```

The items in italics indicate entries that you provide, according to your own needs and situation.

The results that appear on your screen look like this:

```
$ pwd
/usr/danh
$_
```

Not all SCO UNIX systems are exactly the same, so bear in mind that your system's responses and displays might differ from those shown in this book. Aside from possible differences in installation, the differences will not be substantial.

# A WORD ABOUT SPECIFICS

UNIX is available in a number of different versions. Some come from different manufacturers or are for different brands of microcomputer. This book is based on SCO (The Santa Cruz Operation, Inc.) UNIX System V/386 and on UNIX System V from AT&T.

# I

# FOR THE
# SYSTEM USER

# 1

# The Flexibility of SCO UNIX

SCO UNIX is an electronic file cabinet, a text processor, a calculator, a calendar, a messenger, a programming environment, and much more. You will discover how much more as you learn to use SCO UNIX for such tasks as building and organizing a file system, creating and printing documents, sharing information, sending and receiving electronic mail, and safeguarding valuable data. Important as these capabilities are, however, each is but one feature among many others. To appreciate how much you can do with SCO UNIX, you need to see SCO UNIX as a whole: to know what it is and why you're using it.

Let's begin with the question "What is SCO UNIX?"

## SCO UNIX IS AN OPERATING SYSTEM

From the lap-sized portables you can tuck under your arm to the giant mainframes that can put a rocket on the moon, all computers need an operating system. The operating system coordinates the multitude of activities going on within the machine itself—activities that take place at electronic speeds and, at times, almost simultaneously. At all times, the operating system must ensure that characters are correctly displayed on the screen, that data is saved and retrieved without error, that instructions are processed in an orderly way, and that you are informed if a problem occurs.

Think of an operating system as a housekeeper, a traffic cop, an administrator, or any other type of coordinator, and you have defined its basic function: to keep all parts of the system functioning smoothly and in harmony.

On a more elemental level, an operating system is a set of computer programs (software) designed to work with a particular type of computer or computer system (hardware). On your computer, the operating system is UNIX.

# THE UNIX ENVIRONMENT

All operating systems manage data, as well as coordinate the various pieces of equipment that make up a computer system. Why, then, use SCO UNIX—especially if you are already familiar with another microcomputer operating system, such as MS-DOS or Apple DOS, or with a minicomputer operating system, such as VAX/VMS?

To answer this question, we'll approach it from two sides: the computer or computers on which you run SCO UNIX and SCO UNIX itself.

## The Computer System

Part of the answer to "Why SCO UNIX?" lies with the type of computer you have. As mentioned earlier, the operating system is the software that runs a computer's hardware. Each hardware setup, or configuration, can only recognize and function with software specifically designed for it. Thus, an Apple IIe computer cannot use an operating system intended for an IBM Personal Computer, nor can the IBM use the operating system intended for the Apple. The hardware and software are incompatible—they can't work together. SCO UNIX System V/386 is designed to run on computers that use the Intel 80386 processor or the Intel 80486 processor, such as the IBM PS/2 Model 80 or the Tandy 4000.

Although the details might vary, a typical SCO UNIX computer system is put together in one of the following three arrangements:

■ Somewhere in your office building or buildings is one main computer, which we'll call the host computer. It is the computer on which SCO UNIX itself is installed, and quite likely there is at least one powerful printer attached to it. You are one of several SCO UNIX users who gain access to the host computer through a dumb terminal—a computer-like device with a keyboard and a monitor but no built-in computing ability—or through a microcomputer, such as an IBM PC or an Apple Macintosh, together with some communication software.

■ Alternatively, you might be using SCO UNIX by yourself, on a microcomputer of your own. In this case, your machine is the host computer and you are, effectively, the only SCO UNIX user of your system.

■ Finally, you might have SCO UNIX installed on your own computer, as in the preceding instance, but be linked by a network to other SCO UNIX users, all of whom might also have SCO UNIX installed on their computers. Here, each person in your network can communicate with the others. Essentially, you belong to one of several host computers that are joined by the network.

There are variations on these three setups. You might, for example, be using a call-in device—a modem—to dial in to the SCO UNIX computer from your home or from another office. We won't be concerned with such variations unless they affect your use of SCO UNIX. In that case, you'll be given special instructions.

## UNIX Itself

The computer installation is only one reason you need SCO UNIX. Another, with far more impact on the work you do, is how the operating system itself does its job. Unlike many others, SCO UNIX is a multiuser, multitasking operating system. That means it can handle the needs of more than one person and, when necessary can work on more than one task at a time. These are two enormous benefits wherever a number of people need to share resources and data.

For example, in a multiuser environment, several people can share a printer. Several people can use the same set of data. Several people can respond to a single message. And each can do so without carrying a floppy disk or a bundle of papers from one place to another. In addition, people can interact from across the country almost as easily as they can from across the hall. For managing, distributing, updating—even creating—customer reports, memos, messages, inventories, phone lists, or any other type of shared information, SCO UNIX is ideal.

Then, too, SCO UNIX has multitasking capability. Whether you are one user among many or the only user on a SCO UNIX system, you have the ability to tell SCO UNIX to handle a task either in the foreground (that is, while you wait) or in the background (while you do something else). Suppose, for example, you have a lengthy list of prospective customers and you want SCO UNIX to sort them for you—alphabetically, perhaps, or by zip code. You'd like to distribute copies of the sorted list at a meeting later in the day, but you also have a variety of memos to compose and send through SCO UNIX to others in the office. You can do it all by having the sorting and printing job run in the background while you work on your memos. SCO UNIX does this with all the requests from all the devices that require its attention at the same time. More important, you get all this and more at microcomputer prices.

# THE EVOLUTION OF SCO UNIX

In many ways, SCO UNIX's capabilities resemble those you would expect to find on a much larger computer system. The resemblance is not accidental. SCO UNIX System V/386 is an operating system with an intriguing history in which the mainframe world (in the form of an operating system called UNIX) and the microcomputer world (through the efforts of Microsoft Corporation) were joined.

# UNIX

In the late 1960s, Ken Thompson—a programmer at Bell Laboratories, a research institution known in the computer world as a source of innovation and new technology—had a program named Space Travel, which worked out the motions of the planets in our solar system. To run this program, Thompson used a time-sharing system, renting time on a large mainframe computer belonging to General Electric. Like renting a car, time-sharing works quite well until the amount of time you use begins to increase. Thompson had that problem: Space Travel required a lot of computer time.

His solution was the PDP-7, a minicomputer manufactured by Digital Equipment Corporation (DEC). One step down from a mainframe, a minicomputer costs quite a bit less but loses relatively little computing power. The PDP-7 became Thompson's in-house system for running Space Travel and the machine on which he developed his own operating system—UNIX.

During the following year or two, UNIX caught the attention of other programmers at Bell Labs and became a functional entity there in 1971.

## The Translation to B

Thompson's original UNIX was written in a programming code known as assembly language. Not too long after developing UNIX, however, Thompson also developed a new language for writing programs. He called this language B and soon rewrote UNIX in the new language, along the way incorporating some new program routines written in B.

## From B to C

Dennis Ritchie, another Bell programmer, refined Thompson's B, added a few routines of his own, and called it C. The development of C might seem unrelated to our story, but it isn't: Today UNIX is almost entirely written in C, and with good reason.

To understand the connection, you need to know a little about how programs (including operating systems) work. Programs such as Thompson's original UNIX are not generated in a single-step process. The programmer originally codes the program in a form that he or she can read. This form of the program is called source code, and it's written in a programming language, such as assembly language. It is not, at this stage, usable by the computer. Only later, in an entirely separate step, is the source code transformed into executable, or machine-readable, form. This transformation is performed by a program known as a compiler.

The limitation of assembly-language programs is that each type of computer can use a different assembly-language dialect. If you wanted to move an assembly-language program from one computer to another that used a different dialect, you would first need to modify the assembly-language source code.

C programs are generated in the same two-step process, with one important difference: C is universal. The instructions you write to perform the function you want accomplished are the same, no matter what computer you're using. The C compiler is machine specific, so it's the compiler that is responsible for translating C's universal code into the dialect required by a particular computer. Thus, if a C compiler exists for any given computer and the hardware is compatible with the machine on which the code originated, a C program—like UNIX—can be moved (or ported) to it.

Being rewritten in C, then, meant that UNIX became accessible to a great variety of computers.

## Refinement

Over the years, UNIX has achieved great popularity in the world of mainframes and minicomputers. At the University of California at Berkeley, new UNIX utilities (tools) were developed. Programmers there created a text editor, *vi*, that used the newer cathode-ray display technologies rather than the teletype technology for the editor originally built into UNIX, and programmers enhanced UNIX's file-management capabilities. They also created a better environment, called the C shell, for C programmers.

## Proliferation

UNIX proliferated, and in the process a certain number of nonstandard features crept into the various versions. *The* version was still the one licensed from AT&T, but manufacturers were free to add new features to it as and when they thought such features would benefit the computer that a particular version was designed for.

Eventually, UNIX existed in several versions. The first licensed version was version 6, aimed at the education market. Then came version 7, for commercial uses.

That was followed by PWB/UNIX (Programmer's WorkBench UNIX), with a concentration on programming tools. Then came System III, which was superseded but not necessarily replaced by System V. And there's still Berkeley's UNIX, which has achieved popularity in engineering fields.

Third-party licensed versions of UNIX exist and you can also find UNIX called CPIX, HP-UX, PC/IX, UNX/VS, AUX, Ultrix, Zeus, and a host of other names.

If an operating system is to become truly popular, especially when it's meant for use on a variety of different computers, it must possess a high degree of standardization. People who use the system must be free to wander from machine to machine without needing to learn new commands and procedures for each.

To tie up UNIX's loose ends, a group of users and vendors called /usr/group met in 1981 and began work on defining a standard version of UNIX. In January of 1985, AT&T announced the System V Interface Definition, which helps to define a standard UNIX version. With the approval of the UNIX community, this System V has become the version of choice today.

And that's the history of UNIX in a nutshell. How does all this tie in with SCO UNIX and with you?

# ENTER MICROCOMPUTERS

The obvious place to begin is with the advent of the microcomputer—the machine on which SCO UNIX is installed in your system and quite possibly the machine from which you gain access to SCO UNIX.

UNIX and microcomputers developed more or less at the same time. The first microcomputers appeared in the early 1970s but were too low on the technological ladder to use UNIX. They were much slower than their larger cousins and had a very limited amount of memory—nothing like the microcomputers so prevalent today and even less like those that will appear in the near future.

Like other computers, however, microcomputers need an operating system. If not UNIX, then what?

Through about 1980, the dominant microcomputer operating system was CP/M (Control Program for Microprocessors) from Digital Research Incorporated. The bulk of the microcomputers available at that time were based on processors that handled information eight bits at a time. Eight pieces of information (roughly equivalent to one character) could be passed from the central processing unit into the rest of the computer and back again. Although that might not sound like much, because the processor worked at electronic speeds, the overall performance really wasn't poor at all.

CP/M addressed this 8-bit world very well. It was relatively inexpensive (if the computer manufacturer did not actually supply it with the machine), and because of its availability, programs such as word processors and spreadsheets were written to run in its environment. With a large number of available programs, the operating system became even more popular.

In 1978, Onyx Systems licensed UNIX for a 16-bit microcomputer designed for multiple users, but all in all, UNIX seemed to enter a dormant phase as far as microcomputers were concerned.

## Enter Microsoft

Now we come to the second part of our SCO UNIX equation: Microsoft Corporation. Best known at that time for its implementation of the BASIC programming language, Microsoft announced in 1980 a faster, smoother, trimmer version of UNIX based on UNIX version 7. This enhanced version was called XENIX, and it was designed especially for a microcomputer environment.

This announcement came at a very hectic time. Microcomputers were in the throes of evolving from 8-bit machines to 8/16-bit computers that offered the double advantage of being able to use 8-bit programs while processing information at increased (16-bit) speed.

XENIX began to generate interest within the microcomputer world, but as yet this was a very small world. Then in August 1981 came the IBM PC, supported by Microsoft's MS-DOS operating system. Within a year, the PC and the MS-DOS single-user operating environment had captured a large share of the market. XENIX, which was aimed primarily at the multiuser, multitasking environment, was momentarily forgotten.

Microsoft followed AT&T's move and revised XENIX from version 7 to System III and then to System V, the current and accepted version. System V incorporated enhancements of the *vi* editor; the C shell for programming ease; and Microsoft's own invention, the Visual shell, which provides a simple, easy-to-use system of menu choices for the beginner. Versions of XENIX came from manufacturers such as The Santa Cruz Operation, Altos, Tandy, COMPAQ, and IBM. At that time, too, microcomputers with even faster processors, such as the Intel 80286 and 80386, began to appear. Further development by Microsoft in conjunction with The Santa Cruz Operation combined the essential elements of both SCO XENIX System V and UNIX System V from AT&T. This book is based on SCO UNIX System V/386 Release 3.2, which is the first operating system licensed by AT&T to carry the UNIX trademark.

And now, knowing what SCO UNIX is and where it came from, let's take one more look at SCO UNIX as a whole. But this time, we'll approach it from the "Who needs to use it?" angle.

# WORKING

There they sit: computer, screen, printer, and maybe a few other accessories. All told, you see perhaps $7,000 to $10,000 worth of hardware. But what happens when the workload increases? Or more than one person needs to use it? You add another computer, and another after that, and another still. There is, literally, no end to the amount of money you can spend. In addition, you might need to duplicate printer costs or add extra dollars for hard disks with each new system. You might have to do all this if you didn't have SCO UNIX.

In a multiuser environment like SCO UNIX, several terminals share the processor time of the host computer. Any computing that is done originates and is controlled from that computer.

This situation is as cost-effective as it sounds. Terminals cost $400 to $500 each, and a four-user system can be bought for as little as $9,000. So where's the catch? There isn't any, simply a warning: In a multiuser system, both the hardware and the software need to be fully integrated to produce the best results, and both must be proven performers.

Microcomputers today are running at speeds that are 10 to 20 times faster than those of the late 1970s, when these machines were far too limited to handle an operating system as sophisticated as SCO UNIX. Now, too, memory and storage capacity can both be measured in millions of characters—far removed from the mere thousands available only a few years ago.

The hardware stage is set. As far as the software goes, UNIX is a recognized success in the minicomputer and mainframe markets. In the past 19 years, it has been forged into a very precise tool. Microsoft has done an excellent job of maintaining the UNIX environment while making it compatible with a variety of microcomputers. What do you get? A precise, flexible, proven multiuser operating system.

And you get multitasking. Multitasking normally happens in a multiuser system because each person's use of the system is, in effect, a "task" being performed at the same time as all the others. Beyond this, in SCO UNIX each person using the system has the ability to make things happen in the foreground (where computers normally process information) or in the background, where they can be completed on their own while some other task is being handled in the foreground.

# IN SHORT

As other operating systems evolve, they will begin to emulate more of the UNIX features than they do now. As in any commercial environment, it's the nature of the beast to turn toward whatever is working best. But SCO UNIX—your SCO UNIX—is already a faithful implementation of UNIX, in form, format, and command. For the multiuser, multitasking environment, tomorrow is here today. SCO UNIX is now what most other operating systems will become.

# 2

# Looking Around

Now that you have been introduced to SCO UNIX, it's time to put it to work. You'll log in, try a few commands, and log out. (You begin a session with SCO UNIX by logging in, and you end it by logging out.) Whether your system is operational a few hours a day or around the clock, and whether you are the only user on your system or one of many, you must still log in and log out whenever you use SCO UNIX.

## A LOOK

Let's pause for a moment and look at the setup of the computer system you are using. Recall that an SCO UNIX installation can be put together in one of the following ways:

- A host computer with one or more terminals, computers acting as terminals, or a combination of terminals and computers connected to it.

- A single computer operated as an independent SCO UNIX system.

- A series of independent SCO UNIX computers networked together so that their users can communicate with one another.

Of these three setups, a host computer with terminals, microcomputers acting as terminals, or a combination of terminals and microcomputers is the most common type of computer system on which SCO UNIX runs. For that reason, it is the type assumed in this book. This book also assumes that, as a user, you gain access to the SCO UNIX computer from a terminal or from another microcomputer and that, as is the case in most multiuser environments, a single system administrator runs and maintains the SCO UNIX computer.

Although SCO UNIX is designed for a setup that includes a host computer with ter-minals, microcomputers, or a combination of terminals and microcomputers, it can be used as easily and effectively by one person. If you are the only user on your system, however, you gain access to SCO UNIX from the host computer, and that means you play the dual role of system user and system administrator. Refer to Section II of this book before continuing if either of the following conditions apply:

■ SCO UNIX is or must be installed on your computer. (This applies to either a single computer operated as an independent SCO UNIX system or a series of independent SCO UNIX computers networked together.)

■ You are the system administrator.

Section II contains information on the necessary procedures for starting and main-taining SCO UNIX on your computer.

# STARTING WITH THE MANUALS

If you unpacked your system or consulted your library, you saw that SCO UNIX comes with an extensive set of manuals. The set has two basic groups: manuals for system users and manuals for system administrators. Let's take a brief tour of the manuals so that you can determine the best place to look when you have a question or need information. We'll look first at the user's manuals and then at the system administrator's manuals.

## The User's Manuals

The following three manuals are for SCO UNIX users:

■ *Tutorial*

■ *User's Reference*

■ *User's Guide*

*Tutorial* is a brief introduction to using the SCO UNIX operating system.

*User's Reference* has four parts: Commands, Miscellaneous, File Formats, and Permuted Index.

The Commands section contains, in alphabetic sequence, all the commands that all users of the system can access. Each entry begins with a description of the syntax for a command—that is, what you type on your keyboard to execute the command and its options.

The Miscellaneous section has entries of various types, all in alphabetic order, ranging from user commands, such as *login*, to function calls, which programmers use to develop application programs. The entry titled "Messages" lists all the system messages that might appear on your display. For instance, if you attempt to read a data file but you don't have system permission to do so, the message *Not owner* appears on your display. If you turn to the subsection "System Services Messages," you will find an entry for this message followed by a brief description of its meaning.

The File Formats section describes the contents and layout of various standard data files that the SCO UNIX operating system uses.

The last section of the *User's Reference* is the Permuted Index. Each entry in this index consists of a command name followed by a description of the command and the command name again. The index entries are not in standard alphabetic order, beginning with the first letter of the command, but in alphabetic order by a keyword somewhere within the command description. A command might appear under several different letters of the alphabet if its description contains several keywords. For instance, the following entry appears under both D, N, P, and W:

```
pwd: Prints working directory name ....... pwd(C)
```

In the preceding example, the keywords are *directory, name, prints* and *working.*

Following the second instance of the command name, at the end of the index entry, is a letter in parentheses, such as *(C)* in the previous example. This part of the entry tells you which section of the manual has the command description. For instance, *(C)* refers to the Commands section of *User's Reference.* These letters in parentheses might also direct you to sections of the *System Administrator's Reference* or the *Programmer's Reference* manual.

Segments titled "See Also" at the end of the command descriptions might contain cross references to other commands as well. If you look in the Commands section of the *User's Reference* under *pwd*, you'll find that the "See Also" segment refers you to the description of *cd* in the Commands section of *User's Reference*, which describes how to change the working directory.

*User's Guide* contains task descriptions. Chapter 2 of the *User's Guide*, for example, covers the use of *vi* (the visual editor) to create or alter a text file. In contrast, the description in *User's Reference* consists only of a list of all options, keys, functions, and mnemonic commands within *vi.*

# The System Adminstrator's Manuals

The following three manuals are for system administrators:

- *Release Notes*
- *System Administrator's Reference*
- *System Administrator's Guide*

They cover the system characteristics, system installation, and ongoing system administration.

*Release Notes* contains information about the particular software release of SCO UNIX. You need to know this information when you install SCO UNIX.

The *System Administrator's Reference* comprises three sections: Installation Guide, ADM (System Administration), and HW (Hardware Dependent).

The Installation Guide section contains the instructions for installing the operating system either in whole or in part. It also covers removal of parts of the system, reinstalling the system, and troubleshooting the installation. The ADM (System Administration) section contains an alphabetic list of all the commands that authorized system administrators can access. Each command begins with a syntax description—what you type on your keyboard to execute the command and its options. The HW (Hardware Dependent) section has entries of various types, all in alphabetic order. For example, the entry *hd* provides information relating to internal hard disk drives.

*System Administrator's Guide* contains descriptions of system administration tasks. Chapter 3 of *System Administrator's Guide,* for example, describes how to start and stop the system, as well as how to customize the startup procedure.

# THE HARDWARE

Assuming that you are one of a group of people who gain access to SCO UNIX through a terminal or a microcomputer, let's begin your work with SCO UNIX by looking at the equipment you use. It's your window into the SCO UNIX world.

A terminal consists of a keyboard and a monitor, which together look a little like a microcomputer. A terminal does not, however, have any innate computing ability. The only real difference between a microcomputer and a terminal is that a microcomputer can compute. To use your microcomputer with SCO UNIX, you need communication software that makes it act like a terminal. (Even though two computers running SCO UNIX can communicate with one another, the current version of SCO UNIX does not recognize your microcomputer itself as a device with its own disk drives and operating system, hence the need for communication software.)

No matter what kind of device you're using, this book calls your device a terminal for simplicity's sake.

Elsewhere—in sight, in another room, or even in another building—is the computer that runs SCO UNIX. Typically, the SCO UNIX computer is accompanied by a printer that all the SCO UNIX users can share.

Your terminal and the SCO UNIX computer are connected so that they can communicate. Your terminal might be connected to your SCO UNIX system in one of two ways: through local access or through remote access.

If your terminal (or equivalent) is hardwired to the system—that is, if the terminal is connected directly to the system by a cable—you have local access. In an office environment, this is the typical means of accessing the SCO UNIX system.

On the other hand, you might dial into the system. The dial-in method is called remote access. In this case, your terminal is at some other location, and you use a communications device—a modem—to contact the computer through the phone lines. If you use remote access, the SCO UNIX computer must also be equipped with a modem so that it can answer your call and understand your transmissions.

# Your Terminal

As with all operating systems, when you use SCO UNIX, you interact with it. You type a command, and SCO UNIX either responds or requests further information.

### The Enter key

Answering any SCO UNIX question or prompt requires that you type a reply, so you must have a way of telling SCO UNIX to recognize and accept your reply. You do so by using the Enter key on your terminal's keyboard. SCO UNIX requires that you press Enter after you type most commands. For that reason, this book refers to typing a command and then pressing Enter as "entering" a command.

Not all terminals have a key labeled *Enter*. On a few devices, this key is labeled *RETURN*. On some IBM products, the Enter key bears an arrow pointing left, with a right-angled bend in its shaft. Some devices have *both* an Enter key and a Return key. If your terminal is in this group, you can press either as the Enter key; SCO UNIX ordinarily makes no distinction between the two.

### The importance of case

Most of what you type contains a mixture of uppercase and lowercase letters. SCO UNIX distinguishes between uppercase and lowercase letters when you communicate with it, so be sure to enter commands and other information *exactly* as described.

If your terminal has a Shift Lock key, a Caps Lock key, or an Alpha Lock key, which causes all letters to appear in uppercase when you press it, be sure that it's not engaged when you begin your work with SCO UNIX. On some terminals, the Shift Lock key lights up when it's active. On others, it can be physically locked in a down position. No matter which case is true for your keyboard, pressing the key is usually all you need do to deactivate it.

## Changing Your Terminal

In most local-access situations, your system administrator will have correctly configured (set up) the terminal to which you're assigned to work with SCO UNIX as well as SCO UNIX itself to let it know what type of terminal you have. If you're dialing into SCO UNIX, notify your system administrator so that he or she can modify the SCO UNIX files that contain information about the type of terminal you're using. If at any time your SCO UNIX terminal behaves improperly, notify your system administrator.

# YOUR KEYS TO SCO UNIX

In identifying you to SCO UNIX, your system administrator should already have supplied you with two vital pieces of information: your login name and your private password. If you haven't been told what these are, find out. You can't log in without them.

# LOGGING IN

Now it's time to combine theory and practice. Let's log in.

If you're connected to the system by means of a terminal, switch it on. From a remote location, dial your system's access telephone number and wait for a "connect" message from your modem. If you're using a computer and communication software, start the software by using the communication parameters that your system administrator has supplied. From either starting point, you'll soon see a message like the following:

```
bifrost

Welcome to SCO System V/386

bifrost!login:
```

The name of the computer on which you're logging in (in this case, *bifrost*) might appear as a part of the login prompt (as it does here).

If the *login:* message does not appear immediately, press the Enter key a few times. If you still see nothing, check the schedule of your SCO UNIX system, or contact your system administrator. If you are a dial-in user, you might need to verify the transmission speed and other telecommunication settings.

When you see the login prompt, type your login name (remember the importance of uppercase and lowercase), and press the Enter key. For example, if your login name were *danh*, you would see the following before pressing Enter:

```
bifrost!login: danh_
```

After you press Enter, you see the following prompt:

```
bifrost!login: danh
Password: _
```

At this point, enter the secret password that lets you access the system. Type your password carefully. Although SCO UNIX displays the characters you type for your login name, to protect your privacy it does not show those you enter for your password.

If you make a mistake in typing either your login name or your password, SCO UNIX will print a message on the screen, telling you something like *Login incorrect*, and will prompt you to start over again by redisplaying the *login:* message.

> **NOTE:** *SCO UNIX has security features that prevent unauthorized persons from entering the system by trying combinations of names and passwords, one after another. The system allows three incorrect attempts; after that, it prevents any further login attempts on that terminal. If you make a mistake on three successive login attempts, contact your system administrator to make the terminal available again.*

# Greetings from SCO UNIX

Depending on the type of terminal you have, after you have successfully logged in, the screen will either clear or advance a few lines. You'll see something like the following:

```
Last    successful login for danh: NEVER
Last unsuccessful login for danh: NEVER
UNIX System V/386 Release 3.2
Copyright (C) 1984, 1986, 1987, 1988 AT&T
Copyright (C) 1987, 1988 Microsoft Corp.
Copyright (C) 1988, 1989 The Santa Cruz Operation, Inc.
All Rights Reserved

/       :    Disk space:   9.06 MB of  36.17 MB available (25.05%).

Total Disk Space:   9.06 MB of  36.17 MB available (25.05%).


              Welcome to SCO System V/386

                        From

              The Santa Cruz Operation, Inc.
You have mail.

Terminal type is ansi
$ _
```

> **NOTE:** *Don't worry if your SCO UNIX system does not display a letter-for-letter match with what is shown in examples throughout this book. Certain details, such as terminal type, messages from the system administrator, and login name, can and will vary from person to person and from system to system.*

Right now, you might see a different opening line (although that would be an extreme example of variability), and SCO UNIX might even be telling you that you have no mail. Neither difference is cause for concern. Remember: Your SCO UNIX reflects your environment and is under the control of your system administrator. What you see here is a "generic" display.

The opening line, for instance, is often referred to as "the message of the day." The system administrator can change this line, so it is often used as a type of bulletin board, to pass along information that is bound to be seen by everyone who logs in. Likewise, the mail SCO UNIX is referring to is a message that is automatically generated when a new user is added to the system. Your system administrator might already have deleted the message as an unnecessary use of storage space.

Either way, don't become preoccupied with screen variations or with the concept of having mail in your account. You'll be told of possible differences, and mail will be covered in detail in Chapter 7.

Right now, let's look at what you see after you log in. It's one of three sources that provide intrinsic information about your use of SCO UNIX.

It's possible that your screen might scroll up a few lines and show you something like the following:

```
Terminal type is vt100
$ _
```

Or, your screen might clear and display something like the following:

```
Terminal type is vt100
1% _
```

The dollar sign ($) in the first example and the percent symbol (%) in the second indicate the shell in which you're operating. The dollar sign prompt indicates that you are in the Bourne shell. The percent symbol indicates that you are in the C shell. (The number that appears in front of the percent symbol is an event number.)

Like mail, both SCO UNIX shells are discussed later in this book, but your involvement with one of those shells has become immediate, so some discussion is in order.

# UNDERSTANDING THE SCO UNIX ENVIRONMENT

When you use SCO UNIX, any typing you do at your terminal quite likely will fall into one of the following two categories:

- A request to initiate some action.

- A response to a query or situation.

You saw the second possibility when you logged in: Your responses to the queries *login:* and *Password:* provided SCO UNIX with the information it needed to permit you to access the system.

The problem faced by any operating system, however, is one of interpretation. The operating system must understand what you're typing and how the entry applies to present conditions. If it didn't understand, the text you enter while word processing could be mistaken for operating system commands, random mental notes...anything. SCO UNIX accomplishes this interpretation by using a somewhat modular approach incorporating the following three main components:

- The kernel

- Built-in utilities

- The shell

Each of these components performs a specific function.

## The Kernel

The kernel is a series of SCO UNIX software instructions that control and monitor all devices connected to the system. The kernel acts as a link between you and the hardware. Among its functions, the kernel does the following:

- Ensures all terminals have equal access to the system.

- Organizes the flow of information to the printer and all other attached devices. (In a multiuser system, two or more people might try to print different documents at the same time. SCO UNIX's kernel acts as a traffic cop, preventing head-on collisions.)

- Oversees operations so that information is always retrieved from and returned to its proper place on the disk no matter how many people are attempting to use information stored on the system's hard disk.

The kernel also manages the memory in your system, judging how to allocate it effectively so that each user receives the most benefit. It even controls the flow of error messages and the system's reactions to them.

## Built-in Utilities

SCO UNIX has several built-in utilities, including *vi* and separate sets of information that describe the system, the equipment attached to it, and the people who have access to it. Your login name and password, for instance, are examples of a utility that contains information; they're kept with other information that forms the profile of you as a user that was given to SCO UNIX.

## The Shell

Now we return to the shell. No matter which shell you're using, this SCO UNIX component is called a command interpreter. Its function is to examine everything you type and then route it appropriately, calling on or responding to the kernel and the utility programs as required.

The shell you are using might be the result of discussions between you and your system administrator, or you might simply have been assigned the one that is best for you. In any case, you're not locked into the shell to which you've been assigned. SCO UNIX is structured to permit you to travel among them all.

The Bourne shell is the one most frequently assigned. In it, you type your commands after the $ prompt and SCO UNIX responds as needed. The Bourne shell lets you interact quickly and efficiently with SCO UNIX, so it is suitable if you rely frequently on SCO UNIX and use it for more than one or two main tasks.

The C shell, too, is quick and efficient. It was originally designed with programmers in mind (specifically, those who have used the C programming language). The event numbers preceding each occurrence of the % prompt make it easy to specify commands that you want to reuse in repetitive tasks.

## Moving from One Shell to Another

Earlier we mentioned that you can move from one shell to another. Here's your chance to try it out. The commands are very similar.

To enter the C shell from the Bourne shell, enter the following command at the $ prompt (type it and then press the Enter key):

```
csh
```

When you want to return to the Bourne shell, at the % prompt hold down the Control (Ctrl) key and then press the letter D key. (The D for the D key is shown as uppercase here, but you don't press the Shift key—only Ctrl and D.) This key combination, usually printed as Ctrl-D, tells SCO UNIX you want to exit the environment in which you're currently working and return to the one from which you came. Because you were originally in the Bourne shell, your terminal will have no problem returning you to it.

To enter the Bourne shell from the C shell, enter the following at the $ prompt:

```
sh
```

When you want to return to the C shell, at the $ prompt hold down the Control (Ctrl) key and then press the letter D key. This will return you to the C shell.

If you are a C shell user, you might want to make use of this ability to move in and out of your normal shell environment. The examples in this book are based on the Bourne shell, and they will be much easier for you to step through if you can see and respond to the same prompts and messages that are illustrated in the examples.

## Working Together

The kernel, the SCO UNIX utilities, and the shell are not independent of each other. They interact to provide you with a cohesive system that responds to your requests. They also give SCO UNIX universality. Regardless of the brand of computer on which you use SCO UNIX, the commands and procedures usually run in the same way. The only place you are likely to find differences is in the kernel, because it is customized to make optimum use of the particular computer system and its related hardware.

But you never become directly involved with the kernel. The SCO UNIX commands you use are passed through the shell, and it's the shell—the command interpreter—that handles their translation.

Now that you've been introduced to the SCO UNIX components, let's put them to work and see a little of what SCO UNIX can do. Right now, you'll try out a few commands to develop a feel for the system. Don't worry about understanding everything you do. That understanding will come later.

To begin, enter the Bourne shell if you are in the C shell. (From the C shell, simply enter *sh* after the % prompt.)

## WHO'S THERE?

First you might be interested in seeing how SCO UNIX "sees" you as one user among others. How will it know who you are and what messages and information belong to you? One easy way to find out is with the *pwd* (print working directory) command. Enter the following at the $ prompt:

```
pwd
```

SCO UNIX will reply with a line something like the following:

```
$ pwd
/usr/danh
$ _
```

You'll learn the details in the next two chapters, but right now, in that brief response, you've seen two important features of SCO UNIX's method of managing information. First SCO UNIX keeps track of you and your work by name—specifically, the name by which you identify yourself when you log in. Second, as you can tell from the command you used, you have a directory. Think of a directory as a card file or a table of contents. SCO UNIX uses directories to find the storage locations of all memos, letters, and other information you send and receive through the system.

Now try another command. At the $ prompt, enter the following:

```
who
```

SCO UNIX responds with a display like the following:

```
$ who
root        console     Apr  9 08:57
danh        tty00       Apr  9 09:09
stanb       tty01       Apr  9 09:02
$ _
```

SCO UNIX is telling you who else is currently logged into the system (*root* is the superuser, or system administrator). Note that it identifies other users by their login names. In addition, SCO UNIX is telling you which terminal (tty00 and so on) each person is using, as well as the date and time of their logins.

# A FEW USEFUL COMMANDS

The first paragraph of this book mentioned that SCO UNIX is many things—among them, a calendar and a calculator. Let's take a quick look at these two features now.

SCO UNIX automatically keeps track of the date and time. As you'll see in Chapter 7, you can use its timekeeping ability to create a "tickler" file as a reminder of upcoming events. But you can also check on the day, date, and time whenever you want. At the $ prompt, enter the following:

```
date
```

SCO UNIX responds with a display like this:

```
$ date
Wed Apr 11 09:09:53 PDT 1990
$ _
```

This display tells you: the day of the week, the month and day, the time (to the second) for the time zone you are in, and the year. It's a handy command. (If you are the system administrator, you might also use the *date* command to modify the existing settings. To do this, consult the appropriate section in Appendix A.)

Then, too, SCO UNIX can act as a desktop calculator. When you want SCO UNIX to perform math calculations, you can call on a special utility program called *bc*. To try it, enter the following:

```
bc
```

This time notice that SCO UNIX's only response is a flashing underline. That underline is telling you that *bc* is waiting for you to type something. So enter the following:

```
1234+6789
```

SCO UNIX responds with the following:

```
$ bc
1234+6789
8023
_
```

Much more sophisticated calculations are possible with *bc*, of course, but right now you can try it out on some more arithmetic. Feel free to use the calculator whenever it's convenient for you. All you need remember is that to divide, you must use the / symbol (as in 4/2), and to multiply, you must use the * symbol (as in 2*2). When you are finished with *bc*, tell SCO UNIX to return you to the shell by entering the following:

```
quit
```

The $ prompt will quickly reappear. If you are not in your home shell, you can return to it by pressing Ctrl-D. For a more in-depth discussion of *bc*, see the related sections in the Command Reference portion of your SCO UNIX documentation.

# READING YOUR MAIL

Now that you've stepped through a few exercises with SCO UNIX, let's go back to where we began: the mail message you received when you first logged in. If you don't have the message, you should read this section anyway. It will introduce the topics of our next two chapters.

From the $ or % prompt, enter the following:

```
mail
```

You'll soon see something like the following appear on your screen:

```
$ mail
SCO System V Mail (version 3.2) Type ? for help.
"/usr/spool/mail/danh": 1 message 1 new
>N  1 root@bifrost.UUCP   Sun Aug 20 19:37   12/370   Welcome to bifrost
? _
```

As mentioned earlier, we'll cover mail in a later chapter. Right now, all we're concerned with is SCO UNIX's indication that you have one message. To see it, press the Enter key. SCO UNIX's mail system responds with the following:

```
Message  1:
From root Sun Aug 20 19:37:20 1989
From: root@bifrost.UUCP (Superuser)
X-Mailer: SCO System V Mail (version 3.2)
To: danh
Subject: Welcome to bifrost
Date: Sun, 20 Aug 89 19:37:14 GMT
Message-ID:  <8908201237.aa00314@bifrost.UUCP>
Status: R

        Welcome to SCO System V/386 !

Your login shell is Bourne shell; please contact the
system Accounts Administrator if you wish this changed.
? _
```

This is the message that was automatically generated by SCO UNIX when the system administrator created your account on the system. Notice the question mark at the bottom left of your display. This character is a prompt from the SCO UNIX mail system, which is now waiting for you to issue another command. Issue the quit command by entering the following:

```
q
```

On your screen, you'll see something similar to this:

```
? q
Saved 1 message in /usr/danh/mbox
Held 0 messages in /usr/spool/mail/danh.
$ _
```

Because you didn't delete the message, SCO UNIX has stored it away for you. But where? There are quite a few slashes (/) distributed between an equal number of words in the last line (the last is probably your own login name).

Recall SCO UNIX's response when you used the command *pwd*. You saw words interspersed with slashes. At that time, you were looking at the name of your working directory—the "table of contents" SCO UNIX uses to locate stored information. Here, those words and slashes indicate the storage place SCO UNIX has used for your mail. Taken as a whole, both collections of words and slashes describe a path leading to a location on the hard disk where SCO UNIX keeps information. That path also points to the topic of the next two chapters: the SCO UNIX file system.

# CHANGING YOUR PASSWORD

Passwords originated as a means of maintaining system security by keeping unauthorized users out of a system. That is why you need to keep your password private, and it is why SCO UNIX never echoes on-screen the password characters you type in. Other than the system administrator, no one should know your password.

One of the best ways to maintain system security is to change your password periodically. In fact, after a certain period of time set by your system adminstrator, SCO UNIX requires you to change your password. When you attempt to log in with your current password, SCO UNIX prevents you from logging in until you change your password. In addition, your system administrator might set a minimum change time. You cannot change your password before that time is up. If your password should somehow become known to an unauthorized user, notify your system administrator and have the system administrator change your password as soon as possible.

If the minimum change time has expired and you have permission to specify your own password, you should immediately change it. The procedure itself is simple. From the shell prompt, enter the following:

```
passwd
```

SCO UNIX responds with a message telling you it is changing the password for your user name and will prompt for your old password. (The root user won't be prompted for this.) Enter the old one. SCO UNIX next prompts for the new password. As with your old password, make the new one easy for you to remember but difficult for others to guess.

After you enter the new password, SCO UNIX prompts you to confirm by retyping it. If you make a mistake at this point, SCO UNIX responds *They don't match; try again.* If this happens, enter and verify your new password again. If you forget your password, notify your system administrator so that you can get a new one.

# GETTING ONLINE HELP

At times when using SCO UNIX, you might need to refresh your memory on some aspect of a command: its exact function, its parameters, its output, and so on. With SCO UNIX, you can have the operating system display information about its commands on your screen. The information displayed is exactly what you would find if you looked in *User's Reference,* and the description is in nearly the same format. In fact, the online help command, *man,* has that name because it displays reference manual pages.

To use the online help, type *man* followed by the name of a command. For instance, to get information about the *who* command, enter the following:

```
man who
```

SCO UNIX responds with the following display:

```
Name
   who -lists who is on the system

Syntax
   who [-uATHldtasqbrp] [ file ]

   who am i

   who am I

Description
   Who can list the user's name, terminal line, login time,
   elapsed time since activity occurred on the line; it
   also lists the process ID of the command interpreter (shell)
   for each current user.  It examines the /tcb/files/inittab
   file to obtain information for the Comments column, and
   /etc/utmp to obtain all other information.  If file is
   given, that file is examined.  Usually, file will be
   /etc/wtmp, which contains a history of all the logins since
   the file was last created.

   who with the am i or am I option identifies the invoking
   user.
:_
```

The entries in square brackets ([ ]) are optional. In this case, they indicate that you can enter only *who,* as you saw in a previous section.

The colon at the bottom of the display is a prompt for paging and search commands. You can page through the manual pages for the *who* command simply by pressing the Enter key. If you find the information you need before the end of the manual pages for that command, you can issue the *q* command by entering the following:

```
q
```

If the entry for a command is long, you can also search for a keyword in the description by enclosing it in slashes. For instance, to search for *clock,* enter the following:

```
/clock/
```

The next page of the description containing the word *clock* appears on your screen.

You use another command, the *pg* command, with the *man* command to page through the descriptions. The colon at the bottom of the screen is the command prompt for the *pg* command. At the Bourne shell $ prompt, you can enter the following to see the manual pages for the *pg* command:

```
man pg
```

Note that where the command description for the *pg* command indicates that you can use a positive number in parentheses for some commands—*(+1)l*, for instance—to move a certain number of lines or pages forward, you can also use a negative number to move backward that same number of lines or pages.

# LOGGING OUT

When you won't be using SCO UNIX for a while—for example, when you go home at night or when you want to disconnect from the system—you tell SCO UNIX you're through by logging out.

If you want to log out now, the procedure is simple, although it might differ depending on the shell you're using.

From the Bourne shell, press Ctrl-D. Recall from earlier in this chapter that Ctrl-D is the key combination you use to exit the environment you're working in. If your home shell is the Bourne shell and that's where you are now, pressing Ctrl-D will log you out of SCO UNIX.

If the C shell is your home shell, enter the following at the % prompt to exit:

```
logout
```

In all cases, a login prompt such as *bifrost!login:* appears on the screen, and you'll be back where you were at the start of this chapter. If you use SCO UNIX from a terminal, you can safely turn it off when you see the *login:* message. If, for some reason, you are using SCO UNIX from the host computer (console) itself, do *not* turn the computer off, because...

## A Word of Warning

Logging out is *not* the same as turning off the SCO UNIX computer. When you log out, you tell SCO UNIX that you—and you alone—are through for a while. SCO UNIX, however, keeps on running. In contrast, turning the system off turns SCO UNIX off, too. No one remains on SCO UNIX—even if they have unfinished work in progress. If, for whatever reason, you are using SCO UNIX from the host computer itself, *never* turn the computer off simply because you have finished. You must follow a special shutdown procedure before you can safely turn the SCO UNIX computer off. If the system is not shut down properly, any unsaved work will be lost beyond recall. Leave the shutdown procedure to your system administrator.

# 3

# Directory Files

On a computer, as in a desk drawer, a file is a repository of information. A computer file exists on a disk in one of three varieties: a data file, a program file, or a directory file. These three types of files provide the framework for everything you do in SCO UNIX. Understanding their differences is essential. Let's begin with the one most likely to be familiar to you.

## DATA FILES

Data files are conceptually the most obvious and the easiest to envision. They contain information that you can save, recall, and manipulate according to your needs. For example, mail messages on your SCO UNIX system are stored in a data file.

## PROGRAM FILES

Program files (usually called simply programs or applications) contain the instructions that enable a computer to perform a task. Depending on the task involved, such a file can range from one or two lines up to many thousands of lines. Thus, a program file can be a simple C program that prints *HELLO* on your screen, a word processor, a database-management application, or the SCO UNIX mail system.

# DIRECTORY FILES

Directory files keep information about all the files on a disk. Directory files keep track of where data files and program files are, how big they are, and what they're called. In general, directory files ensure that you can always find and use these other types of files whenever you want them.

Because the SCO UNIX system's hard disk is responsible for keeping track of your data files (and everyone else's), let's use this chapter to see what it does and how you can use it to your advantage.

## Linear vs. Hierarchical Structure

Before your account was installed on SCO UNIX—indeed, before SCO UNIX itself was installed—your system's hard disk was a vast, vacant expanse of available storage area. Microcomputers and their operating systems condition (format) that space and, as it's used, place file after file into it.

### Linear directories

Early microcomputer directory systems kept track of files simply by keeping a list of them. Perhaps that list was in alphabetic order, or perhaps it was simply in the order in which the files were stored. No matter what the arrangement was, the filenames were listed one after the other like the items on a grocery list. Appropriately, this scheme is called a linear directory system.

When microcomputers relied on floppy disks, linear systems were adequate. Floppy disks can store only a limited number of files, so a linear list would be relatively short. Finding a particular file was easy.

But today, a microcomputer's hard-disk storage system is hundreds of times larger than a floppy disk, and the list of filenames that you can store on such a disk can be enormous. Searching through 500 or 1000 entries for a single filename would be confusing.

Also, with more available storage space, often more than one person works from the same hard disk. To accomplish that, a multiuser environment such as SCO UNIX is installed, or several people simply use the same computer. Whatever the method, in a linear directory system your files, the next person's files, and files created by everyone else using the equipment are all lumped together on the disk. But when you want to use the system, it's *your* work and *your* files that are important, not everyone else's.

Also a linear directory doesn't afford privacy or security—anyone using the system can access your files.

## Hierarchical directories

SCO UNIX supports a hierarchical directory structure. A hierarchical structure consists of a series—a hierarchy—of directory "levels" that let you be quite specific in locating or placing a data file. Let's rely on a familiar analogy to trace our way through a hierarchical system.

At the front of this book is a table of contents. In effect, this table, in its entirety, is a directory to the contents of the pages that follow, providing references to the places in the book you want to find. That's the way a disk's directory system works—whether it's linear or hierarchical. Within the table of contents are subdivisions—chapter titles— that point out separate sections of the book. Often, under each chapter heading is a description of what that chapter contains. These three components—the table of contents itself, the chapter titles, and the description of each chapter—constitute a three-level hierarchical system that provides you with a reference for finding "data files" in a book.

SCO UNIX manages the files on your system's hard disk in much the same way, using one "table of contents," the directory file, for your entire disk to keep track of where every file is.

Within that directory file are other descriptions that refine SCO UNIX's ability to find information on the disk. These descriptions are called subdirectories, and they are files, as well. To go back to the table-of-contents analogy, other subdirectories that further describe the contents of the disk can be "underneath" this first subdirectory level.

# DEFINING A PATH

A table of contents is an independent section of a book. It does not include the contents of the chapters it describes, only their descriptions and locations. The chapters themselves are separate parts of the book. Convention places the table of contents at the front of a book, but its function would be the same no matter where it were positioned.

Under SCO UNIX, the directory file on the system's hard disk works the way a table of contents works. It provides a path that SCO UNIX can follow to get from one place on the hard disk to another place.

Also, like a table of contents, the directory file itself occupies its own space on the disk. To carry through our analogy, both the table of contents and the directory file are data files of a sort because they contain information. That information, however, tells SCO UNIX the path to follow to locate the actual data that you seek.

In our table-of-contents analogy, you can think of the path to a section of a chapter as something like this: */table of contents/Chapter 3/Using Directories*.

This path tells you to start at the table of contents, find Chapter 3, and then find the section titled "Using Directories." In the case of SCO UNIX, think of the path to a file in the same way: */Directory File/Subdirectory File/Data File*. (Recall from Chapter 2 that SCO UNIX informed you that it had saved a mail message by displaying something like *Saved 1 message in /usr/danh/mbox*.) Now let's take a look at some real-life directories.

# USING DIRECTORIES

If you logged out after the last chapter, log in again. Remember: You're in the Bourne shell if a $ prompt appears at the left side of your screen; you're in the C shell if that prompt is a % symbol (usually preceded by a number).

## Finding Your Working Directory

Let's start with the command we saw briefly in Chapter 2—*pwd* (short for print working directory). Your working directory is whatever directory you happen to be in at the time you use the *pwd* command.

When the system administrator created your user account, your personal subdirectory was added to the system. That subdirectory was probably given your login name. It's also called your home directory, and you're automatically deposited there whenever you log in.

Because you've just logged in, your working directory and your home directory are one and the same. Keep in mind, though, that because SCO UNIX uses a hierarchical directory system, you can create directories on different levels. As you grow more experienced with SCO UNIX and, presumably, create more directories to organize your information, you might sometimes want to check on the directory in which you're currently working—hence the command to print the working directory.

To check your working directory, enter the following (in lowercase letters):

```
pwd
```

(Recall that "enter" means type the command and then press the Enter key.) In response, SCO UNIX prints a line like the following on your screen:

```
$ pwd
/usr/danh
$ _
```

In actuality, *pwd* is giving you more information than simply the name of your working directory. It's telling you the name of the path it follows to reach your working directory. That name is the pathname.

### Defining a path

When SCO UNIX is installed on any system's hard disk, part of that installation involves physically putting all of the SCO UNIX programs, data files, and related information on the disk. All of the space that SCO UNIX, in its entirety, occupies is referenced by the root directory, so called because it is the main, or source, directory for the operating system as a whole. As you saw in the actual response, SCO UNIX uses the slash character (/) as the name of the root directory. Within the context of SCO UNIX's directory structure, this slash indicates movement in a (relative) downward direction through the hierarchy. Root being the highest level of directory, the working directory */usr/danh* can be interpreted as "down (from root) to *usr* and then down from *usr* to *danh*."

In our example (and probably on your system as well), a subdirectory called *usr* was created within the SCO UNIX root directory. Whenever a new user is added to SCO UNIX, that person's subdirectory is created within the *usr* directory.

In that light, you can see that */usr/danh* really means this:

/(root)

usr

danh

You can also see that it reveals the path from the root to *usr* and then to *danh*.

In this illustration, we've displayed SCO UNIX's reply on separate lines for clarity.

# CREATING DIRECTORIES

Now let's create a few subdirectories to develop a feel for the system. To put this session into a "real-world" framework, let's assume the following scenario.

It's your first day on the job. You work for a management agency, and you've been assigned three clients. One is in California, another is in Boston, and the third is in New York. You've been assigned the Bourne shell. For each client, you'll want to keep any memos of your own that discuss topics you feel concern that client. You'll also be using SCO UNIX to generate correspondence to your clients and to monitor your clients' accounts.

You have your whole home directory in which to do all this, but let's use SCO UNIX's directory capabilities to create a separate directory for each type of information. You sit down and log into the system. SCO UNIX places you in your home directory. To begin, you decide to create a subdirectory for your California client. You enter the following:

```
mkdir California
```

The *mkdir* command is the SCO UNIX command to make a directory, and you've just created one called *California*. The name you gave it is simple and descriptive. It also is well within the 14-character name limit that SCO UNIX allows.

> **NOTE:** *Remember this 14-character limit. When naming either directories or document files, if you try to use a name longer than the legal limit, SCO UNIX will refuse to accept the extra characters. SCO UNIX also won't accept a blank space in the name or accept any of the following characters:*

| | |
|---|---|
| # | ' |
| $ | / |
| % | [ |
| * | ] |
| \| | " |
| ; | ? |

Within SCO UNIX's environment, the directory you created is one level below the directory from which you're working (your home directory, in this example).

# ADDING MORE DIRECTORIES

Let's make two more subdirectories to cover the other clients. From the shell prompt, enter the following:

```
mkdir Boston New_York
```

Here, you've taken advantage of SCO UNIX's ability to deal with more than one element on a command line. Using a space as a delimiter (a character used to separate items in a list), you've made the directories *Boston* and *New_York* with a single command.

You can also see why you cannot use a blank space in the name of a directory or a file. Because a space is recognized as a delimiter, typing *mkdir Boston New York* would have told SCO UNIX to create three directories, *Boston*, *New*, and *York*. However, because SCO UNIX accepts the underline character as part of a name, you were able to use an underline between the words *New* and *York* to create a valid directory name. You could also have used a period to create a subdirectory named *New.York*.

And finally, notice that each directory name begins with an uppercase letter. In Chapter 4, you'll see how this can help you distinguish between directory files and data files or program files within the same subdirectory.

# LISTING DIRECTORIES

You've seen the system prompt reappear twice, but beyond that, you've been given no hard evidence that anything at all has happened. Perhaps you're skeptical, or you're wondering whether you did everything correctly. If so, enter the following command:

```
ls
```

SCO UNIX responds with the following:

```
$ ls
Boston
California
New_York
$ _
```

That's the least you'll see. If there are any other files in your working directory, they'll be listed as well, because the *ls* command is SCO UNIX's instruction to alphabetically list all files in the current directory. The results are your proof that you really did create the three subdirectories.

# CHANGING DIRECTORIES

Creating and listing subdirectories is only the beginning. In our scenario, you're dealing with three types of information for each of your clients. To help you keep track of which is which, you'll again refine a directory, but this time you'll refine each of the client subdirectories you just created. From the shell prompt, enter the following:

```
cd California
```

The *cd* command is the command to change directories.

The *cd* command, used with the name of a directory and no other symbols, presumes that you want to move in a downward direction. It looks "below" the current directory for the one you've specified.

# MAKING ADDITIONAL SUBDIRECTORIES

From either of SCO UNIX's shells, you're now ready to add some subdirectories to *California*. You can accomplish the additions to the *California* directory in one bold stroke by entering the following:

```
mkdir Memos Letters Accounts
```

Just as you created the *Boston* and *New_York* subdirectories at the same time, you've now created three new subdirectories—*Memos*, *Letters*, and *Accounts*, under *California*.

# A LOOK AT YOUR DIRECTORY STRUCTURE

Altogether, you've created six subdirectories. If you consider what your directory system now looks like, you can diagram it this way:

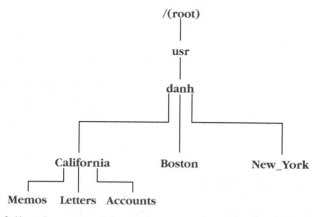

The full pathname to *Memos*, for example, is */usr/danh/California/Memos*.

# MOVING ON THE SAME DIRECTORY LEVEL

Because you also have clients in Boston and New York, you need to move to the *Boston* directory and then to *New_York* to create for those clients the same subdirectories you created under the *California* directory. However, neither the *Boston* directory nor *New_York* is below *California*. They were both created on the same directory level as *California*. From where you are in your directory structure, you need to move sideways to go to either of them.

Although SCO UNIX has no "sideways" directional indicator, it does have one that indicates upward movement through a directory system: the double dot, or dot dot (..), which stands for the directory directly above the current directory (often called the parent directory). If you combine the up (..) and down (/) movement indicators, you can reach your goal. To move to the *Boston* directory from the *California* directory, enter the following:

```
cd ../Boston
```

Effectively, you've moved up one directory level (to *danh*, in this example) and then down one level to *Boston*. The net effect has been to move sideways—your intent.

You could, if you wanted, include a series of double dots and slashes to indicate a more extensive move. SCO UNIX is very intuitive about your instructions, provided you don't try to send it along an incomplete or incorrect path. If you do, SCO UNIX will display the message *No such file or directory*. If you simply make a typing mistake and if the path isn't too garbled, SCO UNIX will display its guess as to your intent and will request that you confirm its guess. For example, if you intended to change to the directory */usr/danh/Boston* but instead typed */usr/danh/Bostom*, SCO UNIX would reply with the following:

```
$ cd /usr/danh/Bostom
cd /usr/danh/Boston?
```

If you respond by typing *y* and pressing the Enter key or by only pressing the Enter key, SCO UNIX will respond with *ok* and will change to the directory it suggested. If you respond by typing *n* and pressing the Enter key, SCO UNIX will cancel the command.

## Absolute Pathnames

In addition to the slash and double-dot "elevator operators," SCO UNIX offers another way to move sideways, still using a single command, as follows:

```
cd /usr/danh/Boston
```

(Remember to substitute your equivalent of */usr/danh* in the pathname.)

In this instance, you've instructed SCO UNIX to take you to the top of the directory structure and then follow the pathname you've supplied to deposit you in the specified directory. With this method, you make an absolute reference to the pathname, as opposed to a relative reference with the directional indicators.

Why use relative references when absolute references are available? "Simplicity" is the best answer. You're currently not very deep within your directory system (*Boston* is only one level below your home directory), so an absolute reference might not seem too imposing. But as you create more levels, or even if you start to use the full 14 characters available for each of the names you assign, typing the absolute reference, from the root directory through the destination directory, can become tedious.

## Varying the Pathname

SCO UNIX offers another way to lighten your work when you need to specify the entire pathname for an SCO UNIX command. SCO UNIX stores the pathname to your home directory (*not* necessarily your working directory) under a special name called *$HOME*.

(The dollar sign is a part of the name, not a prompt symbol, and you must type the name in uppercase letters.) *$HOME* exists for everyone who is on the system, but even though everyone can type *$HOME*, in each instance SCO UNIX interprets *$HOME* to refer uniquely to that user's home directory.

Thus, whenever you need to use an absolute pathname that includes a reference to your home directory, you can substitute *$HOME* for the name of your home directory. The pathname */usr/danh/California*, for example, can also be typed as *$HOME/ California*.

### Going home

You can also go straight to your home directory from anywhere in the SCO UNIX directory system simply by entering the following command:

```
cd
```

When you use *cd* by itself on a command line, SCO UNIX presumes that what you actually mean is *cd $HOME*.

# COPYING DIRECTORY FILES

If you've been following along on your terminal, you're now in the *Boston* subdirectory. You can make new directories here for your three subtopics, move on to *New_York*, and make the same additions there. But there's a quicker way. At the shell prompt, enter the following:

```
copy -r ../California .
```

(Note the space and the dot after *California*.) And then type the following:

```
copy -r ../California ../New_York
```

These two commands, issued from within the *Boston* subdirectory, have actually done all the work you wanted by copying the three *California* subdirectories to *Boston* and *New_York*. Let's see how it happened.

SCO UNIX gives you quite a few ways to copy files, among them the *copy* command, which you can use to copy groups of files from one directory to another and to copy more than one directory at a time when it is typed in the following format:

```
copy -r source destination
```

The *-r* option tells SCO UNIX to take all the directories in the source you specify and duplicate them in the destination you specify. The *r* stands for recursive, which, in this command, simply means, "repeat the copy procedure again and again until all directories have been copied." The hyphen (-) is a lead-in character that is used with SCO

UNIX options. You can sometimes include more than one option in a single command; in those instances, the hyphen precedes only the first option in the series.

Notice that because you were in the *Boston* subdirectory when you issued the commands, the pathname you used (*../California*) for the source of the first procedure directed *copy* to go up one directory level (..) to your home directory and then down one level (/) to *California* to find what it was to copy. The single dot (.) at the end of the command line for the destination indicates your working directory (*/usr/danh/Boston*). The single dot always means "here"—your current working directory. And that's where *copy* duplicated what it found in *California*.

The second *copy* command duplicated the first until it reached the destination pathname. Here, you sent *copy* to a different destination by telling it to go up one level (again, to your home directory) and then down one level into *New_York*.

# CREATING A DIRECTORY WHILE COPYING

Suppose you had not already created the subdirectories *Boston* and *New_York* before you used the *copy* procedure. Suppose you had created only *California* and its three subdirectories. Because you wanted to duplicate the contents of *California* exactly, you wouldn't have needed to create the other directories before you began the copy. Instead, from your home directory, you could have used the following two forms:

```
copy -r California Boston
```

and

```
copy -r California New_York
```

These commands would first have created the subdirectories *Boston* and *New_York* and then have copied the contents of the *California* subdirectory into them.

# USING WILDCARDS

You've already used the *ls* command to list the contents of a single directory. You can also use *ls* to display the contents of several directories without having to retype the command for each new directory name—if you can find something that all the names have in common. Look at the subdirectories that you've created so far: *California*, *Boston*, and *New_York*. They all contain the letter *o*. If you were in your home directory, you could enter the following:

```
ls *o*
```

SCO UNIX would respond with the following:

```
$ ls *o*
Boston:
Accounts
Letters
Memos

California:
Accounts
Letters
Memos

New_York:
Accounts
Letters
Memos
$ _
```

Each of the asterisks in this example is a wildcard character. If you play poker, you already know that a wild card is a particular card that can be used to represent any other in the deck. In SCO UNIX, you use a wildcard character in much the same way: as a special character that you can use to represent all other characters. A wildcard character offers you a way to make relative references to filenames. It's a way of specifying a range of filenames (or only one if a single file matches the criteria) even if you don't know the actual names. As such, it permits relative references on the *filename* level. SCO UNIX supports two wildcard characters: the asterisk and the question mark. You might also see them referred to as metacharacters, a term partially derived from the Greek word *meta* meaning "change."

## The Asterisk

In our preceding example, we used the asterisk. Within the context of what we did, we told SCO UNIX to list the contents of any directory it found that had an *o* in its name, *no matter what or how many* characters preceded or followed that *o*.

Literally, any directory name that met the criterion was acceptable. When SCO UNIX looked at the directories beneath */usr/danh*, it found that *Boston, California*, and *New_York* matched our criterion, so it listed their contents.

Neither of the following would have produced that result:

```
ls *o
```

or

```
ls o*
```

For the former condition (*ls* *o*), only those directories *ending* in *o* would satisfy the criterion. For the latter (*ls* *o*), SCO UNIX would consider only those directory names *beginning* with an *o*. And none of our directories meet either of those two conditions.

## The Question Mark

Unlike the asterisk, which can be used to represent more than one character, the question mark is the substitute for any *single* character within a filename. Because it can take the place of only one character, you couldn't use the question mark to produce the same results we got with the asterisk. If, for example, you entered the following command, SCO UNIX would list the contents of the *California* subdirectory and no others:

```
ls Cal?fornia
```

(Although, if you happened to have additional directories named *Calofornia*, *Calafornia*, and *Callfornia*, this command would list their contents because these additional directory names conform to your criterion, which says that the fourth letter of the filename can be any character.) Likewise, *???_York* would match *New_York*, *Old_York*, or any other directory name beginning with any three letters, whether uppercase or lowercase, provided the name ended in *_York*.

Wildcards play an important role in file handling. Like a book of matches, they can be helpful, but they can also be dangerous if not used with proper care. Sometimes you might find (too late) that a file matching your wildcard criteria wasn't quite the one you wanted to move, copy, or delete. When we look at wildcards again in the next chapter, you'll see more of both the asterisk and the question mark as well as some enhancements and safeguards you can use to refine their search capabilities.

# LOOKING AT DIRECTORIES

The *ls* command is versatile. Like several other SCO UNIX commands, it has a group of options that you can include when you use it. For instance, entering the following command would again produce a complete listing of the subdirectory files in your *California* directory:

```
ls -l California
```

The same subdirectory files would be listed, but this time the list would look as follows:

```
$ ls -l California
total 6
drwx------   2 danh      group        32 Apr  13 21:21 Accounts
drwx------   2 danh      group        32 Apr  13 21:21 Letters
drwx------   2 danh      group        32 Apr  13 21:21 Memos
```

The *-l* (for long) option produces an expanded list containing additional information about your subdirectory files. Although the list might look cryptic at first glance, it's easily deciphered. Each line actually contains seven fields of information, and those fields tell you almost everything you need to know about each file.

The first field in our example, *drwx------*, is the one most likely to seem difficult, so let's go over it in detail. This field is composed of a group of 10 characters—one initial character and three groups of three characters each. The hyphens here are not dividers; they have meanings of their own.

The first of the 10 characters indicates the type of file. In this case, the character is a *d*, denoting a directory file. If the file were a data file, the initial character would be a hyphen. If the file were what SCO UNIX refers to as a device-type file, the initial character in this group would be *b* or *c*.

The remaining nine characters in this field define the access permissions to the file. The first three characters represent the owner's permissions, the second three represent the group's permissions, and the last three represent the permissions of the public. Within each group of three characters, the first position is for *r* (read), the second is for *w* (write), and the third is for *x* (execute). If any of these privileges is denied, the position the letter would otherwise occupy is held by a hyphen, as in our example.

The owner of the file is you if you're the person who created it.

The group is a predefined selection of individuals who have been identified as a group to SCO UNIX. Perhaps the group would consist of people working on the same projects and having access to your directory. You were assigned a group by the system administrator when your user account was added to the system.

The public represents any other people who are also on the system but who haven't been specifically granted access to your directory area.

Thus, as you can see in the following diagram, the file's owner can read, write to, or execute the file (*rwx*). But both the group to which the owner has been assigned and the public in general have no access permission (---) to the file. This is the typical permission for a file when it is initially created.

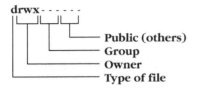

The second field in our long listing, the number *2*, indicates the number of links to this file that exist. Linking is an incredible SCO UNIX feature that deserves more than one paragraph of explanation, so it has its own section in the next chapter. For now, suffice it to say that links are connections between and among files; all files have at least one link, and all directory files have at least two. The line *total 6* in the example tells you how many links to the current directory exist in all.

Field 3, *danh* in the example, is the owner's name. That's followed by field 4, the name of the group to which the person belongs; field 5, the size of the file in bytes (roughly, characters); field 6, the date and time the file was created or last modified; and finally, field 7, the filename. SCO UNIX can provide even more information than we just saw. We can also combine list options to realign or expand what we see. For example, try entering the following:

```
ls -lr California
```

SCO UNIX replies with the following:

```
$ ls -lr California
total 6
drwx------    2 danh      group         32 Apr  13 21:21 Memos
drwx------    2 danh      group         32 Apr  13 21:21 Letters
drwx------    2 danh      group         32 Apr  13 21:21 Accounts
```

Here we have joined the *l* (long) and *r* (reverse) options to produce a new response. This time the contents of the *California* directory are listed in reverse alphabetic order. Note that a single hyphen precedes the two options and that they are *not* separated by a space or by any other character.

# RENAMING AND DELETING DIRECTORIES

Often you'll find you have files that are no longer current. For instance, suppose your Boston client was replaced by one from Cleveland. The *Boston* directory (and any files it might contain) would no longer be active. You might need it at some future time for reference, but right now the *Boston* directory would only clutter the directory system. Then again, even if you maintain the same client base, data files themselves can become outdated—inactive, yet still needed.

The ideal solution is to save these files somewhere out of the way, perhaps with others of their kind. In the paper-and-file-folder world, such storage is called archiving. In the SCO UNIX world, you also have archiving capability. Even though you've already created quite a directory system for your first exercise in using SCO UNIX commands, let's add one more directory to it.

If you're not already in it, return to your home directory (enter *cd*).

Now create the new directory, deliberately typing *Archeve* rather than *Archive*:

```
mkdir Archeve
```

Now change directories to *Archeve*. From the shell prompt, enter the following:

```
cd Archeve
```

Now, under *Archeve*, create three additional directories. From the shell prompt, enter the following:

```
mkdir California Boston New_York
```

These new directories will hold archived material from the individual clients. You're done, so return to your home directory as you did earlier. But wait. You've made an error and misspelled "Archive." Let's remove it and start again.

From your home directory use the SCO UNIX command *rmdir* (remove directory) by entering the following:

```
rmdir Archeve
```

Surprisingly, SCO UNIX replies with the following:

```
$ rmdir Archeve
rmdir: Archeve: Directory not empty
$ _
```

*Archeve*, mistake though it is, is not an empty directory, and therefore SCO UNIX will not remove it. We complicated the situation by creating *California*, *Boston*, and *New_York* under *Archeve*. It doesn't matter that they, like *Archeve*, contain no information. As soon as SCO UNIX finds any files or subdirectories in a directory, it puts a stop to an *rmdir* operation. This automatic braking is a valuable fail-safe device, although, as you can see now, it can be somewhat frustrating.

You could erase the three individual directories and then go back and remove *Archeve*. But that's a roundabout approach. Instead, try the following approach.

## The *mv* Command

From the shell prompt, use the SCO UNIX *mv* (move) command. Enter the following:

```
mv Archeve Archive
```

You've already seen *copy*. The *mv* command is its complement. Ordinarily, you use *mv* to relocate a file, putting it in some other portion of the directory (or in another directory entirely), but in this case, we are applying the command to an entire directory, including all the directories under it. Moving does *not* create a new copy; rather, it transfers what already exists, leaving nothing behind. Like *copy*, *mv* must be balanced: It needs both a source and a destination.

If you look at our example, you can see that you indicated a brand-new directory name as the destination. Because you did not move *Archeve* to an already existing directory, you did not alter the file's location in your directory structure, and the net effect of the *mv* command was simply to change the directory's name. Unlike *rmdir*, *mv* can be used whether or not a directory is empty.

# ORCHESTRATING DIRECTORIES

You may or may not have created the directories outlined in this chapter. Except for the purpose of following along and gaining experience using SCO UNIX, that's relatively unimportant (although we'll be using the file structure we've created in the next chapter too). What is important is that you can now see through the exercises to the concepts underlying what we have done.

On the theoretical level, you've taken your first steps toward understanding SCO UNIX—not only what it does but why. Rather than simply creating subdirectories and guessing at how they are related, you've been able to follow SCO UNIX into and among subdirectories that reflect the logic of your own needs. Perhaps you are beginning to appreciate the SCO UNIX directory system as a flexible tool that, when you are comfortable with it, will enable you to keep a file system that is as accessible and as orderly as any you've kept in drawers or cabinets.

On a more practical level, notice that the names we've used have been chosen with one goal in mind: simplicity. We've kept names as short and as descriptive as possible. Don't overextend yourself by creating subdirectories when none are really needed. And when they are required, make each one a logical branch from the next higher level.

# 4

# Data Files

If you followed along with the examples in Chapter 3, you've created a directory system. At the moment, it's still empty, much like a file drawer neatly divided into categories. Now you can add data files to your directories, filing information wherever it's most useful to you. You'll create your own data file in this chapter with *ed*, the SCO UNIX text editor, and you'll learn some powerful commands that you can use with all data files.

## A SHORT DETOUR

If you're unfamiliar with text editors or have never used one, let's take a quick look at *ed* to set the stage for your work in this chapter.

Almost every operating system has a text editor similar to *ed*. MS-DOS has Edlin; the CP/M operating system has one called Ed. All of them let you enter text from the keyboard, but they have no inherent formatting capability that lets you set margins, page length, and so on, as a word processor does.

Typically text editors are designed to give programmers a quick means of entering and correcting program lines. But they're not meant for prolonged typing activity. The SCO UNIX visual editor, *vi*, is better at that, and we'll be looking at it in the next chapter. But for the quick work we'll be doing in this chapter, *ed* is fine.

SCO UNIX includes another text editor, *ex*. We'll use *ed*, which is a subset of *ex*, but you won't find any major differences between the two in doing the simple tasks described in this book.

> **NOTE:** *This chapter assumes that you have the subdirectory structure we created in Chapter 3. If you don't and you want to try the following exercises, first create the directories* Boston, California, *and* New_York *from your home directory and in each one create the subdirectories* Memos, Letters, *and* Accounts.

# CREATING TEXT WITH *ed*

If you haven't already done so, log into the system, move to your home directory, and be sure the Bourne shell prompt ($) is displayed on your screen. Then enter the following command:

```
ed
```

("Enter" means type the command and then press the Enter key.)

After *ed* is loaded into the computer's memory, you can begin using *ed* commands.

You want to enter text, so enter the following command:

```
a
```

The *a* (append) is the *ed* command to enter insert mode and to append new text to whatever you've already typed.

After you use the *a* command, the cursor advances to the next line on the screen. The line is blank, but everything you type from this point on will be entered into *ed*.

Now enter the following line:

```
This is the first data file I've created with ed.
```

The cursor moves to the next line. On this line, type a period and press Enter again. The period is a special symbol to *ed*. When you type it on a line of its own, *ed* understands that you have finished inserting text and want to return to *ed*'s command mode. The characters you enter next will be interpreted as instructions concerning the text that you inserted.

A data file need not be large. It can be as small as a single character. This particular data file will contain only that one line you typed. Now you want to save the file, so enter the following on a new line:

```
w California/Memos/memo1
```

The *w* (write) command tells *ed* to write the text on disk using the path *California/ Memos* and to place the text in a data file called *memo1*. Now *ed* prints on your screen the number *50* (the number of characters it wrote on disk) and then returns to the command prompt.

Notice that you didn't begin the pathname with a slash. Omitting the slash is a cue to SCO UNIX to look for the *California* subdirectory immediately below the one in which you're working. (The opening slash is needed only when it precedes an absolute pathname.)

Also notice that you began the filename with a lowercase character rather than an uppercase letter as you did in naming your subdirectories. We'll cover the rationale behind that decision shortly. First, however, let's see how to go about making alterations to a data file.

# EDITING YOUR FILE

You can edit with *ed* by means of text substitution. Let's change some of the text in our document. You haven't left *ed* yet, so enter the following command:

```
s/first/second
```

The *s* portion of this command instructs *ed* to make a substitution within the text.

Had your document contained more than one line, you'd have also needed to specify the number of the line in which you wanted the change to occur. You would have typed immediately prior to the *s* the number of the line. Thus, *1s* would have indicated the first line, *5s* the fifth line, and so on. Used without a line number, *s* tells *ed* to make the substitution in the current line (usually the last one you worked on). You can omit the line number in this case because the document contains only one line.

Within the context of *ed*'s editing features, the slashes you typed are delimiters separating the two command parameters. The first parameter tells *ed* what to change ( *first* in our example). The second parameter (*second* in our example) is the substitute word. For our example, *ed* responds by redisplaying the line, with the substitution it has made, as follows:

```
$ ed
a
This is the first data file I've created with ed.
.
w California/Memos/memo1
50
s/first/second
This is the second data file I've created with ed.
—
```

Save this new version on disk by entering the following:

```
w California/Memos/memo2
```

Now create a third data file by entering the following:

```
s/second/third
```

Save it once more by entering the following command:

```
w California/Memos/memo3
```

Next make a data file that's a combination of the three you've just completed. Enter the following two commands:

```
r California/Memos/memo2
r California/Memos/memo1
```

You've told *ed* to read in the contents of *memo1* and *memo2* and append them to the end of the document on which you're working. (The append is automatic when you have existing text and tell *ed* to read in the contents of another file.)

Finally, use the command again to add one more line to the document. Enter the following (note the period on the third line):

```
a
These are the data files I've created with ed.
.
```

# DISPLAYING YOUR FILE

You can look at this new document by entering the following:

```
1,$p
```

The *p* (print) tells *ed* to print text to the screen. When you use this command, you also need to tell *ed* which lines of your document you want it to print. Your document is still short, with only four lines. To print this document, you could also use the following command:

```
1,4p
```

You know how many lines this file contains. But you might sometime work with a file of unknown length. SCO UNIX offers a way to deal with that.

You can take the shortcut you used in the first example. Here, you included an *ed* wildcard character, the dollar sign ($), which tells *ed* to print all lines of the file, from first (1,) to last ($). This is what you see:

```
1,$p
This is the third data file I've created with ed.
This is the second data file I've created with ed.
This is the first data file I've created with ed.
These are the data files I've created with ed.
—
```

These are the only four data files you'll be using for a while, so you can save this last one under the filename *final* by entering the following:

```
w California/Memos/final
```

We're finished for now, so exit *ed* by entering *q* (quit). Your shell prompt reappears.

# COPYING DATA FILES

Now that you have created and saved your data files, you can reassure yourself that everything worked correctly by listing the contents of your *Memos* subdirectory. Enter the following command:

```
ls California/Memos
```

SCO UNIX responds with this:

```
$ ls California/Memos
final
memo1
memo2
memo3
$ _
```

After you've assured yourself that everything's where it belongs, you can copy those files into any other directory. As you saw in the previous chapter, you can do that with the SCO UNIX *copy* command. For example, you could enter the command *copy California/Memos Boston/Memos*, which would cause all four files to be duplicated in the *Boston/Memos* directory.

But what if you wanted to copy only *memo1*? Because the *copy* command affects all files in a directory, use an alternative command, *cp*, to duplicate selected files. Thus, you would enter the following command to copy *memo1* into the *Boston/Memos* directory:

```
cp California/Memos/memo1 Boston/Memos
```

## The *cp* Command and Wildcard Characters

What if you wanted to copy the three files with *memo* in their names? Rather than typing the command three times to duplicate each of the three memo files, you could use wildcard characters, as you did with directory names in Chapter 3.

For example, you could use the asterisk, in which case you might enter your command like this:

```
cp California/Memos/memo* Boston/Memos
```

This instruction tells SCO UNIX to look in the *California/Memos* subdirectory, select all files that begin with the word *memo*, and copy them into the *Boston/Memos* subdirectory.

You could also specify the same files as follows:

California/Memos/m*

In either case, because you have a limited number of files, your memo files would be the only ones that matched your criterion. In a directory containing more files, however, either *memo* or *m*  might cause the following problems:

- Because *memo* would specify all files beginning with *memo*, using that designation in an extensive collection of files might include files with such names as *memoryinfo* or *memo123* as well as those you actually wanted to copy.

- Because *m*  would specify all files beginning with the lowercase letter *m* , using that designation in a large collection of files would apply to any file beginning with *m* in that subdirectory.

As you can see, the wide-ranging coverage afforded by the asterisk wildcard character can be more than you need. To limit the scope of your command, you can use the question mark (?) wildcard character just as you can with directories. Copying only the files that begin with *memo* and that have only one additional character in their names means entering the following command:

cp California/Memos/memo? Boston/Memos

The question mark is the wildcard symbol for a single character, so keep in mind that the file specification *memo?* will work only with filenames that are five characters long and in which the fifth character is unspecified. (The question mark is holding that fifth position.) Thus, if your filenames were *memo00*, *memo01*, and *memo03*, you would need to use *memo??* as the specification. (If you had fewer than 10 *memo* files, you could also use *memo0?* as the specification.)

## Specifying Ranges

SCO UNIX gives you a way to refine wildcard usage. You can specify a range of single character wildcard values to which SCO UNIX will respond. Thus, to copy only the files *memo1* and *memo2* when you also have *memo3*, you can enter the following:

cp California/Memos/memo[1-2] Boston/Memos

The values enclosed in the brackets ([]) comprise a literal wildcard that tells SCO UNIX to consider files only if their names begin with the word *memo* and their fifth character falls in the range of numbers from 1 through 2. The hyphen indicates that 1 and 2 are a range.

SCO UNIX examines each character within the brackets individually rather than as part of a group of characters. If you wanted to copy *memo1* and *memo3* only, the correct command syntax would be as follows:

```
cp California/Memos/memo[13] Boston/Memos
```

This command would match any five-character filename beginning with *memo* and having either a 1 or a 3 as the fifth filename character. Because you've specified only single-character values, you wouldn't copy a file named *Memo13* if one existed.

You can also specify a range of letters rather than numbers. For example, suppose you file employee salary records alphabetically by the first letter of the individual's last name. If your files all begin with *salary*, you can refer to the files for employees whose last names begin with A through M with the following file specification:

```
salary[A-M]
```

Or you can specify the A through D files for employees whose last names begin with the following file specification:

```
salary[ABCD]
```

## Ordered treatment

When you specify ranges, you must remember that SCO UNIX translates characters into code numbers in a certain order. These code numbers follow the standardized order known as ASCII. In ASCII order, the digits 0 through 9, certain punctuation marks, and the uppercase and lowercase letters of the alphabet are assigned the code numbers 48 through 122. The numbers 0 through 9 are at the low end of this range, capital letters A through Z come next, and lowercase letters a through z are at the high end of this range. Thus, although you might consider A and a to be equivalent, SCO UNIX does not. Recall that SCO UNIX differentiates between uppercase and lowercase. This is because the code numbers for the uppercase and lowercase letters fall at different points in the ASCII coding system.

You don't need to become familiar with ASCII numbers—these code numbers remain invisible to you. If you are going to specify ranges, however, bear in mind that, for example, the character range 0-Z includes all numbers and uppercase letters but no lowercase letters. Similarly, the range A-z includes all uppercase and lowercase letters but no numbers. And 0-z includes all numbers, all uppercase letters, and all lowercase ones too. The ASCII values of some special characters are lower than numbers and letters, and the values of others are higher. Because these values are outside the normal range descriptions, you should avoid using them in filenames and directory names.

## Using Wildcards to Distinguish Files

In Chapter 3 we used the convention of beginning directory-file names with uppercase characters. In this chapter, we've used lowercase characters to begin data-file names. Now that you've had a chance to see how you can use ranges, you're in a position to take advantage of that distinction.

Let's look at what you've created so far. You have three subdirectories—*Memos*, *Letters*, and *Accounts*—in your *California* directory. As time goes on, you will probably have more subdirectories of your own and related data files as well. What if you want a listing of only the data files in *California*? The *ls* command ordinarily lists both directories and data files if you don't take advantage of SCO UNIX's range specifications and case sensitivity. If you've begun all directory names with uppercase letters and all data files with lowercase letters, you could enter the following:

```
ls [a-z]*
```

SCO UNIX would interpret your command as an instruction to list all filenames that begin with lowercase letters (the *[a-z]* portion). Likewise, if you wanted to see the names of only the directories, you could enter the command:

```
ls [A-Z]*
```

This command would be interpreted as "List all filenames that begin with uppercase letters." And because you organized your system so that only directory names begin with uppercase letters, those are the only names SCO UNIX would list.

# PREVIEWING A COMMAND WITH *echo*

If you're not quite sure what a specific wildcard might do when you use it, or if you'd simply like to know what the results of a command will be *before* you actually try it, you can use the SCO UNIX *echo* command. For example, if you wanted to copy all data files from your *California/Memos* directory to the *California/Accounts* directory, you could preview the results by entering the following:

```
echo cp California/Memos/m* California/Accounts
```

SCO UNIX would print (echo) to the screen all the filenames that match your criterion, but without really copying them.

```
$ echo cp California/Memos/m* California/Accounts
cp California/Memos/memo1 California/Memos/memo2
California/Memos/memo3 California/Accounts
```

Reading through that screen list would help you determine whether your wildcard criterion would do the job or whether you need to broaden or narrow its scope to achieve the results you want. Specifying *m** would work well for copying the examples in this book, but you might find that using such a wide-ranging wildcard specification might remind you of a few forgotten *m* files—perhaps *mynotes*, *meetings*, *miscellany*, *musings*, or *museums*. If you think this might happen, it's a good idea to use *echo* first.

# COPYING A FILE TO ITSELF

SCO UNIX does not allow two identically named files to exist in the same directory, nor does it allow you to copy an existing file onto itself. This means you cannot copy a file from and to its source directory unless the source and destination filenames are different. For example, entering the following will not work because you are trying to copy the file onto itself:

```
cp California/Memos/memo1 California/Memos/memo1
```

Similarly, entering the following will not work:

```
cp California/Memos/memo1 California/Memos
```

But the following example will work because the name of the destination file differs from the name of the source file:

```
cp California/Memos/memo1 California/Memos/memo4
```

In this case, however, if you specify the name of a destination file that already exists in the directory, SCO UNIX will overwrite (destroy and replace) the contents of the existing file with the incoming data.

# MOVING DATA FILES

Your *California* directory currently contains the following four data files:

- *memo1*
- *memo2*
- *memo3*
- *final*

Your *Boston* subdirectory contains the following two data files:

- *memo1*
- *memo2*

In the previous chapter, you saw how you can use SCO UNIX's *mv* command to change a filename. (That example used a directory file named *Archeve.*) Now we'll use the same command to move files between two directories. To do so, enter the following:

```
mv California/Memos/final Boston/Memos
```

Using the command as you've done here preserves the filename *final* but moves the file you specify from one directory (*California/Memos*) to another (*Boston/Memos*).

To see the result for yourself, give SCO UNIX more than one command parameter on a single command line. Enter the following:

```
 lc California/Memos Boston/Memos
```

SCO UNIX replies with this:

```
$ lc California/Memos Boston/Memos

Boston/Memos:
final   memo1   memo2

California/Memos:
memo1   memo2   memo3
$ _
```

As we planned, *final* is now in *Boston/Memos.* Note that this time we used *lc,* a variation of *ls,* to list the contents of the directories in column format. Using wildcards, we could also have entered one of the following variations:

```
lc Cal*/M* Bos*/M*
```

or

```
lc [BC]*/Memos
```

or

```
lc [BC]*/M*
```

The one you choose depends on the amount of control you want over the arguments for the command.

# DISPLAYING DATA FILES

After you create data files, sometimes you want simply to view them on the screen without entering an editor such as *ed.* In SCO UNIX, you can use the *cat* command to view them. For example, view the file *California/Memos/memo1* by entering the following command:

```
cat California/Memos/memo1
```

That command prints the following on your screen:

```
$ cat California/Memos/memo1
This is the first data file I've created with ed.
$ _
```

This is exactly what you entered when you created the file with *ed*.

# COPYING WITH THE *cat* COMMAND

When you use the *cat* command to view the contents of a data file, you are telling SCO UNIX to send the contents of the file to the standard output. The standard output is normally your screen. You can also use the *cat* command to create another data file and to put the contents of an existing file into the newly created data file. To do so, you redirect the output of the *cat* command from its standard destination, your screen (the standard output) to a file by using the redirection symbol, the greater than sign (>).

To copy the file *California/Memos/memo1* into the file *new_memo* in the *New_York/Memos* directory, enter the following:

```
cat California/Memos/memo1 > New_York/Memos/new_memo
```

The greater than sign instructs SCO UNIX either to create a new file named *New_York/Memos/new_memo* or, if the file already exists, to erase and re-create it. You can use the *ls* command to verify that the new file has been created and the *cat* command to verify its contents. Redirection is an important concept that we'll return to in later chapters.

# ADDING TO A DATA FILE

After you create a data file, you can also use the *cat* command to add the contents of other data files to the end of your data file. You use two greater than signs (>>) with the *cat* command to append data to the end of a data file. Add the file *California/Memos/memo2* to the end of *New_York/Memos/new_memo* by entering the following:

```
cat California/Memos/memo2 >> New_York/Memos/new_memo
```

The two greater than signs either create a new file named *New_York/Memos/new_memo* if it doesn't exist or add to the already existing file. The word "cat" is short for catenate, meaning "join," but that definition covers a wider range of activities than you might at first suspect.

# CREATING DATA FILES AT THE KEYBOARD

You used *ed* to create your practice files, but at times you might find that using a text editor to create only a small data file is impractical. You might, perhaps, simply want to leave yourself a note or a reminder. The *cat* command is also suited to this task.

To create a note to yourself with *cat*, enter the following:

```
cat > itinerary
```

Literally, this command tells SCO UNIX to join something to the file that you named *itinerary*. (The filename could be one of your own choosing, of course.)

What you've left out of the command line is as important as what you've included: You haven't specified what you want catenated. Because you haven't, SCO UNIX assumes that what you want catenated is the standard input, which is normally what you type at your keyboard. Remember that when you didn't use a redirection symbol to give *cat* a destination for its output, it sent the output to the standard output. Similarly, when you don't give *cat* a source, it considers the source to be the standard input. SCO UNIX accepts whatever you type at the keyboard, and it joins that input to *itinerary*. Notice also that your shell prompt did not reappear. The line with the cursor on it remains blank, as SCO UNIX and *cat* wait for you to do your typing. Try entering the following text, pressing the Enter key at the end of each line:

```
June 2
United Airlines Flight #2622
Leave Seattle/Tacoma 7:00am
Arrive Sun Valley 10:45am
```

After you press Enter at the end of the last line, press the Ctrl-D key combination. Ctrl-D ends the command sequence and returns you to your normal shell prompt. If your system doesn't respond immediately, wait. As you know, Ctrl-D is also the key combination SCO UNIX understands as your request to log out. The *cat* command will trap the first occurrence of Ctrl-D as its own signal to end, but a second occurrence will log you out of the system (if you're in your home shell), and you might need to log in again.

# ADDING TO A DATA
# FILE FROM THE KEYBOARD

Now suppose you suddenly realize your *itinerary* file is incomplete. You forgot to include some necessary information in your reminder. The remedy is simple; try entering the following command:

```
cat >> itinerary
```

Then enter the following:

```
Don't forget the sales projections.
```

Press Ctrl-D to return to the shell prompt.

This form of the *cat* command is different from the form you used to create your original *itinerary* file: This time, you used two greater than signs.

Rather than creating a new data file named *itinerary* (overwriting the one that already exists), the double greater than signs instructed SCO UNIX to append text to the end of the existing file. You can verify that SCO UNIX has done so by entering the following:

```
cat itinerary
```

# JOINING TWO DATA FILES

Just as you can add to an existing file, you can use a similar technique to join two data files. Enter this command:

```
cat Boston/Memos/final >> itinerary
```

This command tells SCO UNIX to add a copy of the file named *final* to the end of *itinerary*. (The "original" remains in your *Boston/Memos* subdirectory.)

If you had used a single greater than sign in this command, SCO UNIX would have erased the original *itinerary* file and replaced it with a new *itinerary* that was identical to *final*. Just as when you added a line to *itinerary*, if you told SCO UNIX to add the contents of *final* to a file named *itinerary* that didn't yet exist, SCO UNIX would create the file and then copy the contents of *final* into it.

## Joining Several Data Files

The *cat* command doesn't limit you to joining only two files. Suppose you have a number of files you want to join—perhaps all the memos relating to a particular contract or client. Let's use your *memo* files to see how you can join them using one command.

First, to move down to the *Memos* subdirectory, enter the following command:

```
cd California/Memos
```

Then, to create a file called *big_file* in *California/Memos* and fill it with the contents of *memo1*, *memo2*, and *memo3*, enter the following command:

```
cat memo1 memo2 memo3 > big_file
```

As in all other cases, the source files remain undisturbed. The *cat* command reads their contents and adds them to the file you've specified.

Note that for purposes of illustration, you typed the name of each *memo* file. You could also have used wildcards in the command by typing it in the following two forms:

```
cat memo? > big_file
```

or

```
cat m* > big_file
```

Likewise, instead of changing directories, you could have used both pathnames and wildcards, entering something like the following while still in your home directory:

```
cat California/Memos/memo? > California/Memos/big_file
```

Anytime you decide to use wildcards, be certain that you know which files you are catenating. If you are uncertain, use the *echo* command first.

# VIEWING LONG FILES

So far, all the data files you've worked with have been short. But what if you had a text file that was 40 or 50 lines long? How would you go about viewing it all? Your terminal can probably display at most 25 lines at a time.

One good way to view the contents of a file, especially a long one, is to use the *more* command. The *more* command displays the contents of a file one screen (24 lines) at a time. To use the *more* command to view *big_file*, enter the following:

```
more big_file
```

If your file is longer than one complete screenful, you can press the Enter key to advance the display of the file one line at a time and press the Spacebar to advance one screenful of text at a time. To escape from the *more* command, press the Delete key.

SCO UNIX offers two additional commands, *head* and *tail*, to help you view long files. Suppose you want to see only the first three lines of *big_file*. Enter the following:

```
head -3 big_file
```

SCO UNIX displays only the first three lines. Now enter the following:

```
tail -2 big_file
```

SCO UNIX shows you the last two lines of the file.

You can use any number with either *head* or *tail*. If you don't specify a number, SCO UNIX displays 10 lines. Conversely, if you specify a number greater than the number of lines in the file, SCO UNIX simply prints the entire file. Remember, however, that in both *head* and *tail*, the number you specify is considered a command option. As with all the SCO UNIX command options you've seen so far, you must precede the number with a hyphen.

# BINARY FILES

Regardless of which shell you use, you should know in advance that not all files can be displayed on your screen. The examples we've used are data files that have been stored in text format: The information is placed on disk exactly as you entered it.

Another form of data file is a binary file. In a binary file, information is stored in a special format. Rather than keeping words or characters as they're entered, SCO UNIX translates them into special symbols, some of which indicate a single character, others an entire word.

Usually binary files are program files. If you were to try to display a binary file, most likely you would see only a peculiar-looking, scattered assortment of random characters—whichever ones your terminal is capable of displaying—often accompanied by insistent bell tones.

You usually won't do any harm by trying to display a binary file. However, your terminal might act strangely afterward, displaying characters in reverse video or perhaps changing the size or line length of the display. At worst, your terminal might lock up, preventing you from using it. If that should happen, consult your system administrator. Simply turning the device off and then back on again will usually clear the condition, but check with the administrator to be sure.

## Removing Files

Now that you know how to create and duplicate files, you need to know how to remove them. When we worked with directories in the previous chapter, you tried to use the *rmdir* command to remove your purposely misspelled *Archeve* directory file. The complementary command for data files is *rm*. You can apply this command directly to a file, as in the following:

```
rm California/Memos/memo1
```

Or you can apply it globally by using wildcards to establish criteria for the files you want to remove. For example, you could use this command:

```
rm California/Memos/memo?
```

Remember: After it is removed, a file cannot be recovered. Thus, *rm* is not a command you should use lightly. This is especially true if you use wildcards—you run the risk that the criteria you specify might result in unexpected matches that remove files you actually want to retain.

However, SCO UNIX does give you a way to protect your files from accidental removal when you're using wildcards—by using the *i* (interactive) option you can include in your *rm* command. Before SCO UNIX deletes a file that matches your criteria, it will ask you to confirm the deletion by displaying the filename on the screen and waiting for a *y* (for yes) or an *n* (for no).

For example, suppose you entered this command:

```
rm -i California/Memos/m*
```

SCO UNIX would print to the screen the name of each file that matched *m* and would wait for your response before deleting or retaining that file, as follows:

```
$ rm -i California/Memos/m*
California/Memos/memo1: ? n
California/Memos/memo2: ? n
California/Memos/memo3: ? _
```

Alternatively, as you saw in the discussion of the *cp* command earlier, you can preview the results of a deletion by using the *echo* command. For our example here, you would enter the following:

```
echo rm California/Memos/m*
```

SCO UNIX would print to the screen a list of all the files that matched your wildcard criterion. Reading through that list, you could then determine whether it was safe to use the wildcard specification to achieve the results you want.

Both the *echo* command and the *i* option of the *rm* command are your faithful allies, especially in situations that might cause inadvertent deletion of valuable files.

# SHARING INFORMATION

Up to this point, we've been looking at how SCO UNIX applies to you and your own files. But SCO UNIX is a multiuser operating system, and one of its key features is the ability to make information accessible to more than one individual. It's time now for you to leave your own backyard and begin to look around the neighborhood.

To start, let's obtain a detailed listing of the data files and directory files immediately below your home directory. If you've been entering the practice examples so far, you are in your home directory. If you're not there, return to your home directory by entering the following:

```
cd
```

To request a long directory listing, enter the following command:

```
ls -l
```

SCO UNIX replies with this:

```
$ ls -l
total 10
drwx------    5 danh      group         80 Oct  7 10:50 Archive
drwx------    5 danh      group         80 Oct  7 10:45 Boston
drwx------    5 danh      group         80 Oct  7 10:43 California
drwx------    5 danh      group         80 Oct  7 10:45 New_York
-rw-------    1 danh      group        324 Oct  7 11:19 itinerary
$ _
```

As with all of the examples in this book, the displays you see on your terminal reflect the status of your own files and directories. Even if they differ from what you see here, don't be concerned. The principles behind the actions still apply.

Remember from Chapter 3 that seven fields are represented in this display and that the second field tells you the number of links associated with the file. Now we'll see why those links are so important. To do so, we'll need to backtrack briefly.

In describing the SCO UNIX directory system, we compared it to the table of contents in a book. Just as the chapters listed in a table of contents are not physically contained within it, your SCO UNIX files are not physically located within your directory. The directory simply provides information about, and points to, the actual locations of those files on the system's hard disk.

Not only are your files kept on the hard disk, but everyone else's are too—in whatever space SCO UNIX finds available. So why don't these files get all mixed up? Why can you request a list of your files and SCO UNIX show you your files and not anyone else's? SCO UNIX recognizes the individuality of the subdirectory associated with your user account. Sharing information also means copying information and distributing the copies.

In the paper environment, copies of memos must often go to several people for approval or simply for information. When you move from the paper environment into a computer environment, that requirement doesn't disappear. Information must still be accessible to more than one individual. And because the operating system files that information, the operating system must help us share it.

Whether we distribute memos to one person or to several, the principles remain the same. So, for the sake of simplicity, let's imagine that there is only one person to whom those memos must be passed and that the user name of that person is *boss*. (Therefore, *boss*'s home directory is */usr/boss*.)

# Checking File Permissions

Your overall concern now is how to transfer your memos from the directory they are in to the *boss* account. There is more than one method, but before we cover any of them we must consider one potential stumbling block that is common to all: access permissions.

If you check the file-permission fields in the long file listing of your home directory, you'll notice that in all cases, people in your group and those who are classified as "public" cannot read, write, or execute any of your files or directories. The access permissions for both groups are listed as ---.

Those settings are SCO UNIX's default permission levels for everyone on the system. No one but you can write anything into any of your directories, and the same condition applies to everyone else's directories unless the permissions have been intentionally changed. (Changing access permissions is covered in Chapter 9. At this point, you need to know that access permissions exist and that they determine whether you can modify information in another person's directory. How they can be changed, however, is not relevant to our discussion here.)

Because you need permission to write to another directory, the practice session we'll use assumes the following condition:

■ An account named */usr/boss*, in which there is a special subdirectory to receive your memos. In the examples, this directory is called *Tom*, so the absolute pathname to that directory is */usr/boss/Tom*.

Unless your system administrator has created a directory named */usr/boss* and has modified the access permissions so that you can write into that directory, you cannot follow the instructions without first creating your own local subdirectory system.

To create a subdirectory named *boss* from your home directory, enter the following command:

```
mkdir boss
```

Then create your equivalent of *Tom* under it. Enter the following command:

```
mkdir boss/danh
```

Now you will be able to step through the following examples. Remember, though, that you are not actually writing to another person's directory, so don't include the */usr/* portion of the destination pathnames that you see here. Save */usr/* for later work.

## Making Subdirectories in Another User Account

Although you can place copies of your memos in */usr/boss/Tom*, suppose you prefer to keep those related to your California, Boston, and New York accounts in separate subdirectories within */usr/boss/Tom*. That way you can easily distinguish one from another. To do so, you can use the *mkdir* command and specify the absolute pathname to each directory, as follows:

```
mkdir /usr/boss/Tom/California
mkdir /usr/boss/Tom/Boston
mkdir /usr/boss/Tom/New_York
```

Now, with the destination set up, you have several options for passing your memo files to */usr/boss*.

The most obvious, of course, is to use either *cp* or *copy* to copy files one at a time or in groups (with wildcards) into the directory of your choice. You could also use the *cat* command to copy your memos into one large file in the appropriate directory. Before you choose either approach, however, you should think about one consideration.

Hard disks provide large areas for file storage, but they are finite. You can fill one more easily than you might anticipate. In terms of storage space, you can see that although creating additional copies of your data files might be the simplest way to share information, it is not necessarily the best. And that brings us to a subject mentioned briefly in Chapter 3—linking, one of SCO UNIX's most impressive features. When you understand the concepts behind linking, you will have gone a long way toward fully appreciating SCO UNIX's strength as a multiuser, multitasking operating system.

# MAKING A LINK

To avoid duplication of files, SCO UNIX gives you an *ln* (link) command. With linking, you can connect files instead of copying them. The files will be available to whichever directory they are linked to, just as if you had copied them there, but they will take storage space only in the directory from which they originate.

To see how SCO UNIX makes these connections, try linking the files in your *California/Memos* directory to the new directory */usr/boss/Tom/California*. Enter the following command:

```
ln California/Memos/* /usr/boss/Tom/California
```

That was easy. But what have you really done? To see, we'll request a listing of both your source and destination directories, in each case using an *ls* command option called *i* (inode) to make the results of your linking visible on the screen. First enter the following command:

```
ls -i California/Memos
```

You'll see this:

```
$ ls -i California/Memos
   636 memo1
   640 memo2
   641 memo3
$ _
```

The numbers on the left are known as inode numbers. (You probably won't see the same numbers that are shown here, but don't be concerned—it's the similarity between the numbers and the files you linked that's important.) Whenever you create a file in SCO UNIX, that file is assigned a unique inode number. Your directories are themselves simply files that contain a list consisting of the name of a file that you have created and the inode number for that file (along with access permissions, date of creation, and so on). You need not worry about remembering the inode numbers of your files, nor is it necessary for you to keep track of them—SCO UNIX does it for you. But to see the significance of those numbers, request the same type of listing for your destination directory by entering the following command:

```
ls -i /usr/boss/Tom/California
```

SCO UNIX prints the results to your screen as follows:

```
$ ls -i /usr/boss/Tom/California
   636 memo1
   640 memo2
   641 memo3
$ _
```

Notice that the inode numbers for the files in your home directory and those in the destination directory are identical. Although SCO UNIX has not created exact duplicates of your source files and placed them in */usr/boss/Tom/California*, it has added a copy of the directory file (*Memos*) to the directory file */usr/boss/Tom/California* specified in your *ln* command. This modified directory file now has the same pairs of filenames and inode numbers as the original directory files. In both directory files, you can think of *memo1* in both directories pointing to the same data file (inode 636) on your disk. The result is the same as if *memo1, memo2,* and *memo3* actually existed in */usr/boss/Tom/California*—and this means you save disk space. In fact, although this is a restricted definition of inode numbers, you might find it helpful to think of them as "link numbers" in a chain that connects file with file, and directory with directory.

## Using Links to Save Time

Now that you've linked your memo files, another advantage of linking should become evident. Suppose you were to make changes to any of those three memos. You don't need to copy those changes into the *boss* directory to be certain that user has the most recent version. When "boss" accesses those files from his or her own account, the changes will be evident: The files that person will see are the actual files you changed, not some outdated duplicates.

Similarly, whenever you create a new memo, you can link it to the *boss* directory by entering the following command:

```
ln California/Memos/new_memo /usr/boss/Tom/California
```

You can use any other source directory, filename, and destination directory you choose, as long as you have access permission to place files in the destination directory. In sum, links can help you save both time and disk space.

# 5

# The *vi* Editor

In the previous chapter, you saw how useful *ed* can be when you need to create a quick note or memo. Now you'll learn about a more powerful text editor, *vi*. The *vi* editor does everything *ed* can do, and more. Unlike *ed*, *vi* displays changes to your document as you make them (hence the name "visual" editor). Using *vi*, not only can you create a document, you can immediately see the result of inserting or appending text, searching for and replacing characters, deleting text, and so on. You can display on the screen any part of your document at any time. When you can see a line of text on the screen, you can move to it and change it as much as you want.

Despite its capabilities, however, you should not think of *vi* as a word processor. It is not intended to be the equivalent of a dedicated word processing program such as Microsoft Word or The Santa Cruz Operations' Lyrix, both of which also run under SCO UNIX. For example, *vi* doesn't rearrange the lines of a paragraph for you as you insert and delete text.

When you are accustomed to working with *vi*, however, and you are comfortable with its commands and capabilities, you might use it whenever you want to create, display, or make changes to a relatively short or simple letter or memo. Furthermore, you are not restricted to working with files created within *vi*. You can use *vi* with any data file that you've saved in ASCII format—a storage option offered by many, if not most, word processing programs.

# YOUR TERMINAL AND *vi*

Because *vi* works intensively with your screen, it demands a considerable amount of control over your terminal's display. Most likely, you can use *vi* with no trouble, but occasionally users encounter difficulties because their terminals lack the screen-control capabilities required by *vi*. Without the ability to control the screen, *vi* could not function. If your terminal doesn't display *vi* properly, talk to your system administrator. If the matter can't be corrected, you'll still be able to use *ed*.

But in all probability the *vi* editor and your terminal will cooperate perfectly. The easiest way to find out whether they will is to try, so let's get started. In this chapter, we'll cover some basic cursor-movement and text-handling commands. For your future reference, they're summarized, with brief descriptions, in Appendix A.

# HOW IT WORKS

The *vi* editor has two modes: insert mode and command mode. The purpose of having these two modes becomes obvious when you consider how you use a text editor.

Sometimes all you want to do is enter text as if you were typing a document on a typewriter. When you're doing this, you want *vi* to interpret all your keystrokes as text. This is insert mode.

At other times, you want *vi* to interpret your keystrokes as commands to be carried out. This is command mode.

You are in command mode as soon as you start *vi*. To change from command mode to insert mode, use one of *vi*'s command-mode commands, such as *i* (insert). (The command-mode commands are described shortly.) To return to command mode from insert mode, press the Escape key. When you become familiar with *vi*, you will switch between modes without giving your actions more than a passing thought. If you forget whether you are in insert mode or command mode, press the Escape key. If you are already in command mode, your terminal will beep, and you will remain in command mode. If you are in insert mode, you will change to command mode.

## An Alternative to *vi*

You also can use a version of the visual editor called *vedit*. For all intents and purposes, the *vedit* editor is identical to *vi*. Its only real variation is a helpful one if you're not accustomed to an editor with modes: It distinguishes between the editor's modes by displaying the message *INSERT MODE* in the lower right portion of the display while you're in insert mode. In the following descriptions, use the alternative form simply by typing *vedit* instead of *vi*.

# STARTING *vi*

Just as *vi* can operate in either of two modes, you can start it in either of two ways: with or without the name of the file you want to work on. For example, at your shell prompt, you can start *vi* by entering the following command:

```
vi
```

Because you have not supplied the name of a data file to work on, this is the equivalent of beginning a typewritten document with a blank sheet of paper.

The alternative way to start *vi* is to use the following format:

```
vi filename
```

With this method, you're telling *vi* to begin and also to look for a file with the name you've supplied. If the file exists, *vi* loads a copy of it into memory, displays as many lines as the screen will show, and waits in command mode for your next instruction. If the file does not exist, *vi* leaves the screen blank and holds the filename in reserve, as the default name for the document you're about to create. (You'll need the pathname only if the file is or will be in a directory other than your current working directory.)

No matter whether you named a file or whether the file actually exists on disk, you are working with the file *in temporary memory only*. None of your changes, corrections, or new text are stored on disk for future use until you specifically tell *vi* to save a document. As with any other computer application, save your work on disk periodically to avoid losing it if, for some reason, the system becomes inoperative.

# USING *vi*

In Appendix A, you can see that *vi* offers you a number of basic commands for moving the cursor and editing a document. Because trying out a command is the most effective way of learning it, let's begin an editing session. We'll start by entering a short document on which you can practice.

From the Bourne shell prompt ($), enter the following command:

```
vi flier
```

You will soon see the following screen:

```
_
~
~
~
~
~
~
~
~
~
~
~
~
~
~
~
~
~
~
~
~
~
~
~
"flier" [New file]
```

From top to bottom, this is what you see:

■ The cursor (_) is at the top line of the display. Unless you specify the line of text at which you want *vi* to start, this is the beginning position of the cursor.

■ The tildes down the left side of your display mark the positions of lines on your screen. They are only indicators and are not part of the file. They never appear in your printed documents.

■ The line at the bottom of your display is the status line. This is where *vi* displays error messages, strings you are searching for, simple file information (press Ctrl-G for additional statistics), and commands that you type. At the moment, the line is displaying the filename you specified and *[New file]*, telling you that *flier* is a new file. If you had started *vi* without including a filename, the status line at the bottom of the screen would be blank.

74

Right now, *vi* is in command mode waiting for you to enter a command. You have no document, so tell *vi* you are ready to create one. You could use one of the following three basic commands:

- *i* to insert text beginning before the current cursor position. You can also use this command to insert words (or any other combination of characters) within an existing line of text.

- *a* to append text beginning after the current cursor position. With a new file, *a* has the same effect as *i*. If you use this command with existing text, the cursor moves one space to the right before the text is added. Small though it might now seem, the distinction between *i* and *a* will become both apparent and useful when you begin editing a document.

- *o* to open a new, blank line immediately below the one that contains the cursor. If you begin a document with this command, *vi* will start the text one line below the top of the screen (in other words, leaving a blank line as the first line of your document).

These commands are different in a couple of respects from SCO UNIX commands you've seen so far. When you are in command mode, *vi* interprets any key or combination of keys you press as a command. You don't need to tell *vi* to carry out the command by pressing the Enter key; *vi* carries out the command as soon as you press the key or the key combination. Also, some commands require that you press the Shift key as you press a letter key. This means that one letter key might carry out two different commands depending on whether you also press the Shift key. For example, *i* (which you issue by pressing only the I key) and *I* (which you issue by holding down the Shift key while pressing the I key) are different commands. Throughout the rest of this book, we'll simply say "use the *i* command" when we want you to press only the I key or "use the *I* command" when we want you to hold down the Shift key while pressing the I key.

Right now, use the *i* command.

Now you are in insert mode. As you enter text, when you reach a point where you want to end a line, press the Enter key to end the line and move down to the beginning of the next line. If you make a mistake, either backspace to the incorrect character and retype the line, or leave it alone for a few minutes. You'll soon learn how to move to and to correct an error.

Here is the text to type:

```
    It's that long, hot summer again.  Time for ball
games and lemonade, picnics, the Fourth of July.
Time to keep that lawn watered, too, and check for
all those pests that kill your carnations and ruin
your rutabagas.
    Need help?  Call 555-BULB.  Rhodie's Nursery--for
everything your garden needs.
```

**When you are finished, your screen should look like this:**

```
    It's that long, hot summer again.  Time for ball
games and lemonade, picnics, the Fourth of July.
Time to keep that lawn watered, too, and check for
all those pests that kill your carnations and ruin
your rutabagas.
    Need help?  Call 555-BULB.  Rhodie's Nursery--for
everything your garden needs._
~
~
~
~
~
~
~
~
~
~
~
~
~
~
~
~
"flier" [New file]
```

You've finished entering the text, so press the Escape key to return to command mode. The cursor moves back one space, highlighting the last character (.) in the last line of text that you typed.

# Ending Lines with Enter

As you've seen, *vi* is much like a typewriter in one respect: You must tell it where and when to end a line. Although it *will* wrap letters around to the next line, *vi* does not wrap by word. If *vi* finds that the next character would extend the current line beyond the right edge of the display, it will carry that character down to the next screen line, fragmenting the word. Thus, if you were typing the word *UNIX* at the end of a line, *vi* might break it into *U-NIX*, *UN-IX*, or *UNI-X*, depending on the point at which you went beyond the limit of the screen display.

Realizing this, you should keep your lines under the 80-character limit allowed by the screen width of most monitors. Although many SCO UNIX utilities such as *nroff* accept lines that have wrapped around several times, text entered in this manner usually doesn't look good.

Also, despite its appearance on the screen, if you didn't use the Enter key to end each line, your document would consist of one large block of text occupying about four screen lines rather than a tidy document composed of seven individual lines. The difference might not seem important, but bear in mind that when you edit a *vi* document, you can specify the line you want to edit. The limit for each *vi* line is 512 characters (about 6½ lines on your screen). If you exceed this line length, you'll have some problems with *vi* until you restart the program.

# MOVING ON

Now that you've created a document, you have several courses of action available. Your document resides only in temporary memory, or RAM (Random Access Memory), so you can take one of the following actions:

- Save it on disk under the filename that you used when you started, and continue working with *vi*.

- Save it on disk under the filename you used when you started, but quit working with *vi*.

- Save it on disk under a new filename.

- Abandon it.

Let's look at each of these options.

## Saving with the Same Filename

The first course of action you could take—in fact, the course of action you need to take to follow along with the examples in this chapter—is to save the file with the name *flier*.

You are in command mode. If you are not or if you are not certain, press the Escape key. Type a colon, immediately followed by *vi*'s *w* (write) command, as follows:

```
:w
```

When you used the *i* command, *vi* gave no visual indication to acknowledge that command. Here, notice that as soon as you press the Shift-colon sequence to produce the colon, the bottom line of the screen clears and then the colon appears as the first character on that line.

```
    It's that long, hot summer again.  Time for ball
games and lemonade, picnics, the Fourth of July.
Time to keep that lawn watered, too, and check for
all those pests that kill your carnations and ruin
your rutabagas.
    Need help?  Call 555-BULB.  Rhodie's Nursery--for
everything your garden needs._
~
~
~
~
~
~
~
~
~
~
~
~
~
~
~
~
:
```

Press the Enter key after typing :*w*.

The *vi* editor saves the document on disk with the filename you gave it (or the filename you last used if you had saved the document before). When the document has been saved, *vi* displays information about the file on the status line and places you back in command mode.

```
    It's that long, hot summer again.  Time for ball
games and lemonade, picnics, the Fourth of July.
Time to keep that lawn watered, too, and check for
all those pests that kill your carnations and ruin
your rutabagas.
    Need help?  Call 555-BULB.  Rhodie's Nursery--for
everything your garden needs._
~
~
~
~
~
~
~
~
~
~
~
~
~
~
~
~
~
"flier" [New file] 7 lines, 302 characters
```

If you had finished your session with *vi* but wanted to save your document on disk and, at the same time, quit the editor, you could have done so by using the following command:

`:x`

Note that a colon precedes this command as well. When you use *:x*, *vi* saves your document on disk under the filename you gave it at startup, displays a message telling you the document has been saved, and returns you to the shell from which you started. (If you had not yet specified a filename, *vi* would print the message *No current filename* on the status line at the bottom of the screen.) You can use the *:x* command with an argument to specify a new filename, save your document on disk under that filename, and also exit *vi*, by using the following form:

`:x filename`

## The colon

The colon you type in front of *w*, *x*, and certain other commands is a necessary part of their format. These commands are known as editor commands. The colon tells *vi* to evaluate and act on these commands outside the normal text-handling environment, which includes screen commands, such as the *a* and *i* commands.

Although you must type the colon, you don't have to remember which commands are editor commands and which are screen commands: If you try to type an editor command without a colon (or if you enter any other combination of keystrokes that *vi* doesn't recognize), *vi* will remind you by causing your terminal to beep—and no harm will have been done.

## Saving Under a New Filename

You could also save your document as a file with a name other than the name it had when you started working on it by using the following form:

`:w filename`

If *vi* finds that a file with that name already exists on your disk, it will tell you so. You then must decide whether you want to overwrite (and thus destroy) the existing file with the contents of the new document. If you are sure that's what you want to do, you can modify the *w* command this way:

`:w! filename`

The exclamation point, which you can use after other commands as well, tells *vi* that the command is absolute—*vi* carries it out despite the consequences. For this reason, be certain you know what will happen when you include an exclamation point in a command.

## Abandoning the Document

Finally, you could decide that you need to start over. To do that, you would use the following command:

`:q`

When you use this command, *vi* checks your document before it responds and lets you quit only if you haven't made any unsaved changes to the document. If the document is new or contains changes you haven't saved on disk, *vi* tells you so with the message *No write since last change (:quit! overrides)*—that is, you must type the absolute form of the command (*:quit!* or *:q!*) to abandon the document.

## Changing the Document

You might want to make some changes before you save your document, although from the standpoint of safeguarding your work, it's not a particularly good idea. Suppose you change your document too radically. If you haven't saved the original, you have no prior version to fall back on. Because *vi* lets you change names and overwrite outdated files so easily, you should always save the current version of a document before you make any changes to it. That way, you can always retrieve an earlier copy and start over again.

But making changes to a document is a major element of using any editing program, and now that you've saved this document, we'll look at how you can make some changes to it.

# MOVING THE CURSOR

Generally, before you can change any part of your document, you need to move the cursor to the word or character you want to change. The following sections of this chapter show you how to attain this mobility. Provided you've saved your practice document, you can try out the cursor-movement commands described here. Remember, you don't need to memorize or master each of these commands. They're summarized in Appendix A. In addition, as you work with *vi*, you'll probably find that your own work habits and preferences lead you to rely extensively on some commands but not at all on others.

To start, press the Escape key to be sure you're still in command mode.

## Moving by Line or by Character

If your terminal is an IBM PC or compatible, you can move the cursor one character or one line at a time by pressing the Left, Right, Up, and Down direction keys on your keyboard.

If your terminal is not IBM PC–compatible, the direction keys might not work for hardware-related reasons, even if you have them on your keyboard. But you can still use four keyboard characters: the lowercase *h*, *j*, *k*, and *l*. The cursor movement associated with each is shown in the following table. The command option *number* means that you can specify the number of characters or lines you want to move the cursor. The only restriction on using this option is that you cannot specify more than the number of characters remaining in a line or more than the number of lines above or below the current cursor location.

| | |
|---|---|
| *number* h | Moves the cursor left. |
| *number* l | Moves the cursor right. |
| *number* j | Moves the cursor down. |
| *number* k | Moves the cursor up. |

From command mode, you can also use the Spacebar to move the cursor to the right, and you can use the Enter key to move the cursor down the left margin. As with the direction keys and the four keyboard characters, you can also precede these with the number of characters or lines you want to move. Use these if you prefer, but be certain you are in command mode when you do so; in insert mode, using the Spacebar and the Enter key will add extra spaces and lines to your document.

## Other keys for up and down movement

Picture your display screen as a grid, like a piece of graph paper, on which blank spaces are neatly arranged in rows and columns. Each space can contain one character, and as you move the cursor, it travels from one space to another.

When you use *j* to move the cursor down, you are telling *vi* to move the cursor down one line but to keep the cursor in the same place within the line—within the same column of spaces on your graph paper. With *k*, you move the cursor up but maintain its relative position in the line it moves to.

You can also move up and down in a document. Use the + command to move down to the first character in a line, or use the − command to move up to the first character of your destination line. You can precede either + or − by a number specifying how many lines you want to move down or up.

You can also move the cursor by pressing the Enter key. Just as pressing Enter moves the cursor to the start of a new line in insert mode, pressing Enter moves the cursor to the first character of a line when you are in command mode. The difference is that in command mode *vi* interprets each press of the Enter key as a cursor-movement command rather than as the command to end one line and begin another.

# Moving to a Specified Character

As varied and flexible as the preceding commands are, you also need faster ways to move around in a document. Again, *vi* gives you many options.

One quick way to move around in a line is to move the cursor to a specific character. Suppose, for example, you've typed the following line:

```
The quick brown fox jumps over the lazy dog.
```

In command mode, you could move to a specific character within that line by using the commands in the following table:

| | |
|---|---|
| f *char* | Moves the cursor to the right, stopping at the first occurrence of the character specified by *char*. |
| F *char* | Moves the cursor to the left, stopping at the first occurrence (moving right to left) of the character specified by *char*. |
| t *char* | Moves the cursor to the right, stopping at the character immediately to the left of the first occurrence of *char*. |
| T *char* | Moves the cursor to the left, stopping at the character immediately to the right of the first occurrence (moving right to left) of *char*. |

If the cursor were at the beginning of the preceding sample line, you could easily move it to the *d* in *dog* with the command *fd*. To move it back to the *b* in *brown*, you could use the command *Fb*.

When you use these commands, remember that SCO UNIX—and *vi*—distinguish between uppercase and lowercase characters. Thus, to move the cursor right, to the first occurrence of the letter *Q* in a sentence, you would need to specify *fQ*, not *fq*.

Whether you use *f*, *F*, *t*, or *T* to move the cursor will depend on what you intend to do next. For instance, if you wanted to insert characters within a word, you would use *f* or *F* to move the cursor to the character that will immediately follow the new letters. Then you would select the *i* command, type the characters, and continue on your way.

If you want to add a new word, use *t* or *T* to place the cursor on the space between words, and then use either *a* or *i* to add the text.

If you've been practicing adding characters or words to your sample document, press the Escape key to return to command mode. (We'll stop mentioning this shortly, but don't forget. If you do, you'll inadvertently add unwanted characters to your document.)

## Expanded Cursor Controls

Now you know the basic cursor-movement commands. Others are available that expand your control over cursor movement within the document. The easiest of these are *H* and *L*, which enable you to move directly to the first or the last line on the screen, as shown in the following table:

| | |
|---|---|
| H | Moves the cursor to the top left corner of the screen. |
| L | Moves the cursor to the beginning of the last line on the screen. |

Here's an easy memory aid: *H* is High and *L* is Low.

## Moving by the Word

In *vi* you can also move across a line by the word, as well as to and from the beginning and end of the line. If you specify more words than are on the current line, *vi* will continue to look in the direction you're searching.

From command mode, the following are valid movement instructions:

| | |
|---|---|
| *number* w | Moves the cursor *number* words to the right; counts punctuation marks as words. |
| *number* W | Moves the cursor *number* words to the right; does not count punctuation marks as words. |

| | |
|---|---|
| *number* b | Moves the cursor *number* words to the left; counts punctuation marks as words. |
| *number* B | Moves the cursor *number* words to the left; does not count punctuation marks as words. |
| 0 (zero) | Moves the cursor to the beginning of the line. |
| $ | Moves the cursor to the end of the line. |

If you don't specify a number, these commands move the cursor one word.

As shown in the preceding table of commands, *vi* lets you begin the *w*, *W*, *b*, or *B* command with a number to indicate how many words you want to move the cursor. For example, if the cursor were beneath the letter *l* of the word *lemonade*, the following command would move the cursor six words forward (including punctuation) to the first character of the word *of*:

6w

## Moving to a Specific Line

You can move directly to a specific line on the screen by using the following command:

line numberG

The *line number* option is the number of the line at which you want *vi* to stop. When *vi* executes the command, it places the cursor on the first character of the specified line.

You can also use *G* by itself to tell *vi* to go to the last line in the document. (This is not necessarily the last line on the screen—remember, a document can easily contain many screenfuls of text.)

## Displaying Line Numbers

For a short document of one screenful or less, it's relatively simple to determine line numbers. In a document that is longer than a single screenful, it's not that easy. Fortunately, *vi* associates a line number with each line of text you enter. It doesn't display those numbers until you ask for them, but several ways to make them appear are available.

To display your file with its associated line numbers, enter the following command while in command mode:

:set number

When you use this command, the line numbers remain on the screen until you tell *vi* to turn them off again. To do that, enter the following command:

:set nonumber

Other variations let you display line numbers temporarily. To tell *vi* to temporarily display the current line and its line number, enter the following command:

`:nu`

To tell *vi* to temporarily display a numbered range of lines, enter this command:

`:number,numbernu`

For example, the following command would display lines 1 through 5 of your document, with line numbers added:

`:1,5nu`

You can also use the $ character, meaning "the last line of the document," and display a temporarily numbered version of your entire document by entering the following command:

`:1,$nu`

In some instances, you might find *:1,$nu* preferable to using *:set number*, followed by *:set nonumber*.

If you use either of *nu*'s temporary display forms, *vi* prompts you to press the Enter key to continue. When you press Enter, your text display reverts to its original unnumbered format.

> **NOTE:** *When you use either* setnumber *or* nu, *your lines of text might shift eight characters to the right. This is normal, and even if some characters disappear from the right edge of the screen, there's no cause for concern. Your text remains undisturbed. Also, when you use the* nu *command, you'll notice that* vi *displays the numbered line at the bottom of the screen immediately above a message telling you to press Enter to revert to unnumbered lines.*

## Moving the Contents of the Screen

Finally, four *vi* commands scroll full or partial screens of text.

| | |
|---|---|
| Ctrl-U | Scrolls up half a screen. |
| Ctrl-D | Scrolls down half a screen. |
| Ctrl-F | Scrolls forward one screen (toward the end of the document). |
| Ctrl-B | Scrolls backward one screen (toward the beginning of the document). |

For continuity, Ctrl-F and Ctrl-B actually scroll two lines less than one full screen, letting you see that amount of text from the previous screen.

## Changing Line Lengths

Adjusting the length of each line is the simplest kind of change you can make to a document, and *vi* has two commands that can help you do it: *J* and *r*. If a line is too long, move the cursor to the space immediately to the left of the character at which you want to break the line. Enter the *r* command; *vi* will make the remainder of the line a new line, and all succeeding lines in your document will shift down accordingly. For example, suppose you had the following lines:

```
Vi can take a very long line and break it into two new lines.
To them you can join a third.
```

You could place the cursor on the space between the words *into* and *two*, use the *r* command, and then press Enter. The result would look like this:

```
Vi can take a very long line and break it into
two new lines.
To them you can join a third.
```

Now let's say you want to lengthen the very short new line. Move the cursor to the end of this new line, and use the *J* command. The line below shifts up and attaches itself to the end of the short line. Notice that spaces are added to maintain the document's integrity. In the preceding example, you could use this command to join the second and third lines, as follows:

```
Vi can take a very long line and break it into
two new lines. To them you can join a third.
```

You can continue using *r* and *J* in this way to adjust the lengths of as many lines as you want.

# EDITING YOUR DOCUMENT

So far, you've entered a document, learned to move the cursor, and, perhaps, used the Backspace key to back up in a line and correct a typing error. Right now, this is what your *flier* document should look like:

```
1    It's that long, hot summer again.  Time for ball
2 games and lemonade, picnics, the Fourth of July.
3 Time to keep that lawn watered, too, and check for
4 all those pests that kill your carnations and ruin
5 your rutabagas.
6    Need help?  Call 555-BULB.  Rhodie's Nursery--for
7 everything your garden needs._
~
~
```

The line numbers are for your reference. You'll see them like this only if you've used the *:set number* command. We'll use this example in the next chapter too, so for the rest of the chapter refrain from saving your edited file on disk.

If the cursor is at any location other than the first character of the first line, be certain you are in command mode and then use the *H* command to move the cursor to our starting point.

## Deleting Characters

To begin, let's change the word *Time* in the first line to read *Ripe*. Move the cursor to the first occurrence of the letter *T* in line 1 by entering the following:

```
fT
```

With the cursor now in position, the easiest way to make the change is to delete the characters *Tim* and replace them with *Rip*. To do that, enter the following:

```
3x
```

The *x* command is a delete-character command. By prefacing it with the number 3, you've told *vi* to delete three characters, beginning at the current cursor location and moving to the right. You could accomplish the same task by using the *x* command three times—once for each character. If you did this, you would see the other characters on the line move left to fill the void left by each deleted character.

You can also delete characters to the left with the uppercase version of this command, *X*. Suppose, for example, that you had moved the cursor to the *e* in *Time*. You could enter the following command:

```
3X
```

You could also use the *X* command three times to delete *m*, *i*, and *T*.

Note one subtle difference in the characters deleted by *x* and *X*: The lowercase command includes the character at the cursor position in the deletion; the uppercase command does not include this character.

## Inserting Characters

To complete the change from *Time* to *Ripe*, you now need to insert some new letters. You are still in command mode, so use the *i* command to switch to insert mode. Next type the following:

```
Rip
```

As you do, each letter appears, and the remainder of the line moves to the right to accommodate the addition.

When you've finished typing, press the Escape key to exit from insert mode, and your substitution is complete.

# Deleting Lines and Undoing Commands

You've already saved the *flier* file in the version you'll need later, so you can now play with a few of the lines on the screen and simply not save the changes. (Remember, any changes you make will be in temporary memory only.)

First let's delete an entire line of text. Move the cursor to anywhere in a line and, from command mode, use the *d* (delete) command twice.

The line containing the cursor disappears.

But suppose you have quite a few lines to delete. Eliminating them one at a time could become tedious. Several versions of the *d* command can help you here. For example, if you wanted to remove all of the lines in your file, you could enter the following command (from command mode):

`:1,$d`

Remember your brief experience with *ed.* The following general format specifies a range of line numbers:

`number,number`

You could have indicated any starting and ending line numbers in the document, but as you found earlier with the *1,$nu* command, *vi* applies *1,$* to the first through the last lines of the file.

If you used the preceding example and deleted every line you typed, you now need to restore some text so that you can continue working with the file. Ordinarily, you would read a document into *vi* with the following command:

`:r filename`

You could also simply enter *:r* (or *:r!* if *vi* insists that you use the absolute form) because *vi* remembers the name of the current file until you supply a new one.

But there's no need to do even that much. Instead, to tell *vi* to retract the last command you issued, from command mode use the *u* (for undo) command.

Your deleted lines reappear in their entirety. Use *u* again and your lines disappear once more because you undid the *u* command. Use *u* a third time to bring the lines back yet again. (Alternatively, if you use *U, vi* will restore the current line to its original state—no matter how much editing you've done.)

## Buffering text

How did *vi* know what to restore when you told it to undo the *d* command?

Whenever you delete characters from a document, *vi* places the deleted text in a buffer—a segment of memory that can store text that's in transition. Altogether, *vi* has nine buffers for deleted material and manages them in rotation, with the first buffer containing the last (newest) deletion. When you tell *vi* to undo a deletion, it can thus go to the first buffer, retrieve whatever text it finds there, and place the text back on the screen. When you undo an undo, *vi* re-deletes the text and places it back in the first delete buffer. Because *vi* has nine buffers, it can handle up to nine separate deletions. You probably won't need to keep track of which deletion is in which buffer—at least under ordinary circumstances. Bear in mind, however, that a tenth deletion causes the first (oldest) deletion to be discarded. The following illustration might help you visualize the way in which *vi* manages its delete buffers.

**Delete Buffers**

**Deleted characters: A B C D E F G H I J**

|  | (Newest deletion) |  |  |  |  |  |  | (Oldest deletion) |  |
|---|---|---|---|---|---|---|---|---|---|
|  | 1 | 2 | 3 | 4 | 5 | 6 | 7 | 8 | 9 |
| **First deletion** | A |  |  |  |  |  |  |  |  |
| **Second deletion** | B | A |  |  |  |  |  |  |  |

. . .

| **Last (tenth) deletion** | J | I | H | G | F | E | D | C | B |
|---|---|---|---|---|---|---|---|---|---|

We'll cover buffers in more detail in the next chapter; this explanation is intended simply to help you understand how *vi* can find deleted text. As long as we're on the subject, though, let's take a quick look at inserting. As you might expect, *vi* lets you undo inserts too. It allocates delete buffers as needed, discarding text whenever the buffers become too crowded. But you can manage up to 26 additional buffers (labeled *a* through *z*) as insert buffers, into which you can place text and from which you can retrieve it. These insert buffers are independent of the delete buffers but, like delete buffers, they can hold as much text as was affected by a single command. Because *vi* considers all your keystrokes, from the time you use the *i* command until you press Escape, as being part of *one* command, you can use *u* to remove all the text you insert with any one command.

## Deleting a Relative Range of Lines

More often than not, you'll probably find that you want to remove only a portion of your document, as opposed to either one line or all of the lines. You can delete selectively by indicating a range of line numbers, as follows:

`:start,endd`

If you're composing your document as you type, you might decide you want to delete only the current line and the line above it. In a four-line file, you can easily tell what the line numbers are without resorting to the *set number* command. But in a longer document, it might not be that easy.

Rather than going through the trouble of turning on the line numbers, try the following procedure. If necessary, move the cursor so that you have at least one line of text above the line the cursor is in. Press the Escape key to enter command mode, and then enter the following command:

`:-1,.d`

This command tells *vi* to delete these two lines.

Just as when you deleted all the lines in your document, you've used a range of line numbers here too. This range is a little different from any you've used before.

The period is a shorthand method of indicating the current line ("here"—the line containing the cursor). The comma, of course, separates the two values in the range (as it did when you used *1, $*). And the *−1* is a relative line number indicating that the range to be deleted includes both the line *above* the current line and the current line.

You could have used a positive range as well. A *+1* would have deleted the current line and one line below it. If this document were long enough, you could just as easily have specified *−13* or *+9*. The limit to relative line numbers is the number of lines in the document itself—*vi* will not erase more lines than exist. When using a range, pay attention to the order in which you specify them. The line you specify first should always be the line closest to the top. For example, *:2,5d* would be acceptable, but *:5,2d* would cause the error message *First address exceeds second* to be generated.

## Deleting Words

Finally, let's delete some words. Move the cursor to the beginning of a word you want to delete. (Remember, your file is safe on disk, so you can play with the version now displayed on the screen.) In command mode, enter the following command:

`dw`

After you enter this command, *vi* deletes the word and then rearranges the line to fill the gap.

Had you used the following command, *vi* would have deleted three words (including punctuation marks) immediately to the right of the cursor:

3dw

Again, any number is valid within the command, up to the actual number of words remaining beyond the cursor's position.

## Repeating Commands

You can repeat any of the screen commands you've seen (those that are not preceded by a colon and are not echoed on *vi*'s status line at the bottom of the display) as many times as you want. To repeat the last command you used, press the period (.) key while in command mode.

Cursor-movement commands do not affect your ability to repeat a screen command. If you've just deleted a line, you can move the cursor up or down to the next candidate and press the period key. The line will be deleted in the same way as the one before. Pressing the period key to repeat a command works with *any* of the screen commands.

## MORE ABOUT *vi*

The commands you've learned in this chapter give you the foundation you'll need to start working with *vi*. In the following chapter you'll see how to use the text you create to its best advantage. If you have not saved the original version of the file *flier*, do so. You'll be using it again when we cover cutting and pasting and using boilerplate text.

# 6

# Expanding
# Your Use of *vi*

The basic cursor-movement and editing commands that you learned in Chapter 5 are all you need to create short, simple memos and other documents. But *vi* offers much more. As you'll see in this chapter, you can also use *vi* for such sophisticated tasks as cutting and pasting, creating boilerplate text, and searching for and replacing letters, words, or even whole lines of text.

First we'll take a look at alternative ways you can start *vi*—ways that not only let you begin with the cursor at a particular location in a file but also enable you to queue up a group of files to work on. As before, don't feel you must memorize these commands; they're summarized for you in Appendix A.

## OTHER WAYS TO START *vi*

Sometimes when you call up a data file, you want to start editing at the beginning. At those times, starting *vi* with the following command is all you need to do:

`vi filename`

At other times, though, you might not want to start at the first line of the file. Perhaps you want to continue writing a partially completed document. Or you might want to verify that the file you requested is, indeed, the one you wanted. You might also want to recycle an existing document after making a few appropriate changes to specific sections. With *vi*, it's easy to begin editing a file at a location other than the first line of text.

To start *vi* at a particular line, the command form is as follows:

```
vi +line_number filename
```

For example, use the following command to start *vi* with the cursor on line 3 of the file named *flier*:

```
vi +3flier
```

You can also use this startup method to continue writing a document at another time. The next time you call up the file, use the following command to start *vi* with the cursor on the last line of the file:

```
vi +$ filename
```

You can then use the *o* command both to open a new line at the end of the document and to enter insert mode.

You can also start *vi* at the beginning of the line containing the first occurrence of a particular word. To do this, the command form is as follows:

```
vi +/word filename
```

Thus, the following command would begin *vi* with the cursor on the beginning of the line containing the first occurrence of *VCR* in the file named *sales_rept*:

```
vi +/VCR sales_rept
```

This startup method offers you another way to return to your prior position in a document. Suppose, for example, you must end your *vi* session before you complete your work on *sales_rept*. To be able to pick up where you left off, insert a unique word—*StarTrek, Scheherazade*, anything you want—in the document before you save it on disk. Later you can start a new session with the following command to return to your prior location in the document:

```
vi +/StarTrek sales_rept
```

## Queuing Files

Have you ever been in the middle of a thought and found that you needed to refer to another document in order to complete it or to verify your facts and figures? With a little forethought on your part in deciding which documents you might need, *vi* lets you jump from one document to another.

Going back to our *sales_rept* example, suppose you know that in composing this document you will want to refer to the files *budget* and *sales_1-90* through *sales_6-90*.

You can start *vi* with all these files on tap by putting them into a queue, and you can do so with a single command in the following form:

```
vi filenames
```

If the files you want to see share enough common characters in their names, you can also use wildcards (* and ?) in requesting a queue. So, for example, you could queue the files in our example with the following command:

```
vi budget sales*
```

Recall that the * wildcard can represent any number of characters. Here, it will cause *vi* to queue all files beginning with *sales*. If you would like to specify a more limited list of your sales files, such as *sales_1-90*, *sales_2-90*, and *sales_3-90*, specify a range instead with the following command:

```
vi budget sales_rept sales_[1-3]-90
```

Note that you would have to request *sales_rept* separately because it would not be included in the range you specified.

If, during a session with *vi*, you happen to forget which files you've queued, you can find out quickly by typing the following command from command mode:

```
:args
```

On the status line at the bottom of the screen, *vi* shows you the list of all files with which you began the queue, displaying in square brackets the name of the current file.

## Moving about in the queue

When you queue files by using wildcards, *vi* places those files affected by the wildcards into the queue in numeric order, alphabetic order, or both numeric and alphabetic order, following the ASCII coding system. Otherwise, it uses the sequence in which you entered filenames to establish each document's position within the queue. In our example, *vi* would thus begin by displaying the file named *budget*.

Assuming that you want to work on *sales_3-90*, how would you tell *vi*? The sequence of your files in the queue would be: *budget, sales_rept* and then *sales_1-90* through *sales_3-90*. You want to jump from the beginning of the queue to the end, and *vi* gives you two ways to do so.

You could use the *n* (next) command over and over to move sequentially through the queue, or you could use *vi*'s *e* (edit) command, which moves you to the file you specify—if necessary, loading the file if it is not in the queue.

To use the *n* command, you would enter the following:

```
:n
```

When you do so, *vi* displays *sales_rept* for you. If you entered *:n* again, *vi* would move to *sales_1-90*, and so on. An easier way, however, would be to enter the following:

```
:e sales_3-90
```

This command would move you directly to the file you want. Note, however, that although you're editing another file, your position in the queue has not changed.

To move back to the beginning of the queue, you would use the following command:

```
:rew
```

That's short for *rewind*, which is a holdover term from the days of tape storage. Functionally, this command closes the current document and moves you back to the first file in the queue.

During your session with *vi*, you could also use the *:n*, *:rew*, and *:e* commands to skip about between files. If you do so, you can use the following command to return to the file you edited immediately prior to the current file:

```
:e#
```

The # symbol tells *vi* you want the previous file. Pressing the Ctrl key and the 6 key (Ctrl-6) at the same time also takes you directly to the previous file.

If you use *:n* to move to the next file, bear in mind that *vi* takes you to the file that *it* considers to be next in the queue. Thus, if you begin at file number 1, use the *:e* command to edit file number 6, and then use the *:n* command to move to the next file, *vi* displays file number 2—the next in the queue—rather than file number 7 as you might expect.

When working with queued files, you should also keep in mind that *vi* does not maintain them all in memory. Each time you move from one file to another, *vi* abandons the current file and reads in the new one. If you have made any changes to the current file and try to move to another file without saving first, *vi* reminds you that you haven't saved the new version. As in other situations, you can add an exclamation point to the command (for example, *:rew!*) to confirm your intent, but doing so could cause the loss of any revisions you have made. Whenever you want to keep the editing you've done, be certain to use the *:w* command to save changes before you use the *:rew* command or move on to the next file.

# COPYING AND MOVING TEXT

Editing a document involves more than inserting and deleting text. Perhaps you've had the experience of writing a letter, memo, or report and later thinking to yourself "This document needs reorganizing" or "This section would fit right into another document I'm working on" or "If I changed a few words here and there, I could borrow whole sections from document *xyz*."

To do any of these tasks, you can use *vi*'s memory—specifically, its delete and insert buffers.

## Using *vi*'s Buffers

Recall that *vi* has nine delete buffers, numbered 1 through 9, in which it holds information that is in transition. You can use these buffers for text that you cut out of one document, and you can reinsert that text either in the same document or in a different document by calling for the contents of the appropriate buffer.

Likewise, for text that you want to duplicate rather than delete, *vi* has 26 insert buffers that you can use as holding areas. These insert buffers are labeled *a* through *z*. To move information, you refer to the buffers by number (for deletions) or by letter (for insertions), so it's always necessary to remember which segment of text has gone to which buffer. But bear in mind that sequence is important in working with deletions: They don't stay put—they are moved successively through the buffers, with the latest one occupying buffer number 1.

The commands you use with *vi*'s buffers are as follows:

- The *d* (delete) command to move text to a delete buffer.

- The *y* (yank) command to copy text to an insert buffer.

- The *p* (put) command to move text from a delete or an insert buffer.

You were introduced to the *d* command in Chapter 5, so here we'll concentrate on *y* and *p*. First we'll look at how they're used, and then we'll move on to a practice document in which you can try out these and other commands.

### Yanking to an insert buffer

Yanking text means copying text to an insert buffer. Whenever you yank text, you must specify the insert buffer. The general format of the command is as follows:

`"buffer number_of_lines yy`

(Don't put a space between *buffer* and *number_of_lines* or between *number_of_lines* and *yy*; we show spaces here only for readability of this format.)

As an example of the *yy* command, the following command tells *vi* to yank three lines, beginning with the current line, to buffer *a*:

```
"a3yy
```

Normally, *a* would be *vi*'s command to append text. By preceding the *a* in this command with a double quotation mark, you have told *vi* to accept the character literally; it's your signal telling *vi* to open the *a* insert buffer.

When you use a lowercase buffer letter, the text you move replaces any text currently in the buffer you name. When you capitalize the letter of the buffer you'd like to append, *vi* appends the text to the current contents of the buffer rather than overwriting the existing material. You use the following form:

```
"BUFFER number_of_lines yy
```

(Again, don't put spaces between *BUFFER*, *number_of_lines*, and *yy*.)

As you use these commands, don't be concerned if you get no response from *vi*. Just as when you use the insert commands, your keystrokes are not echoed on the screen; with the *y* command neither your typing nor the loading of buffers (in most cases) will provoke any visible response from *vi*.

## Marking lines for yanking

Yanking a specified number of lines to an insert buffer works well with a relatively short range of lines. There's also another method you can use—one that does not involve knowing or even counting the number of lines you're yanking. In this method, you move the cursor to the first line of text you want to duplicate and then use the following command (with no colon or quotation mark):

```
mk
```

This command marks the current line with the letter *k*. (You can use a different letter if you want.)

Now you can jump the cursor to the last line you want to copy by using any of the cursor-movement commands. When you are at the last line, you can yank all lines from the one containing the cursor, up to and including the one you marked, by using the following command form:

```
"buffery'k
```

Note that you again use the double quotation mark to tell *vi* to interpret the buffer name literally. The *'k* part of the command tells *vi* to copy everything from the current line to the line containing the *k* marker.

### Putting text into a document

You use the *p* (put) command to move the contents of either an insert buffer or a delete buffer to the line (or lines) immediately below the current line. The *p* command takes the following form:

`"bufferp`

Using *P* (uppercase) places text in your document either above the current line or immediately before the current cursor location.

# CUTTING AND PASTING
# IN THE SAME DOCUMENT

To see how to use the delete and insert buffers, let's suppose you've written the letter in the following illustration. (The letter is based on the file *flier*, which you created and saved on disk in the preceding chapter. If you want to try cutting and pasting on your own document, start *vi* with *flier* and insert the additional text shown here.) When you're finished, your letter should look like this:

```
    It's that long, hot summer again.  Time for ball
games and lemonade, picnics, the Fourth of July.
Time to keep that lawn watered, too, and check for
all those pests that kill your carnations and ruin
your rutabagas.
    Need help?  Call 555-BULB.  Rhodie's Nursery--for
everything your garden needs.
    This month's Special Offers include mowing,
seeding, and fertilizing--two hours for the price
of one--and half-price specials on roses, petunias,
and geraniums.
    Our thanks to all our valued customers for your
continued patronage and support.
~
~
~
~
~
~
~
~
~
~
~
```

A little reorganizing might be in order. As long as you've saved this or any other document on disk, you can reorganize it as many times as you want; you can change a copy of it to your heart's content because you always have the prior version to fall back on if your editing is less than successful.

# Copying Text Within a Document

Sometimes, when you're revising a document, you might wonder whether a block of text should remain where it is or be moved and inserted somewhere else. With *vi*, you can easily "try out" potential relocations. You actually have two approaches from which to choose. One involves using the insert buffers, the other relies on *vi*'s *copy* command. Suppose you're wondering whether paragraph 4 might not be better as the opening paragraph. Duplicate it at the beginning of the document, and see where you prefer it. If you're not already there, press Esc to enter command mode, place the cursor on the line that begins *Our thanks*, and then use the following command to yank the two-line paragraph to buffer *a*:

```
"a2yy
```

Now move the cursor to the first line of the document, and enter the following command to duplicate the paragraph at the top of your letter:

```
"aP
```

If the paragraph had been longer—more than one screenful of text, for instance—you could have marked the lines to yank, as described earlier, with the commands *mk* and *"ay'k*. The means you choose for specifying the lines to yank will vary according to your own preferences and the length of the text you are working with.

An alternative method, using the *co* (copy) command to duplicate the text, involves either knowing or displaying the line numbers of your document. The format of the *co* command is as follows:

```
:first,last co destination
```

In this example, the lines you want to move are lines 12 and 13, so the copy command would be as follows:

```
:12,13 co 0
```

Using line number 0 tells *vi* to put the copied text at the beginning of the document. If you specify a destination line other than 0, *vi* places the copied text immediately below the line you specify. If you want to copy only the line you are on, the *first,last* range is not needed. If necessary, display some or all line numbers with the *:nu* command or the *:set number* command.

Let's assume that you ultimately decide that paragraph 4 is, in fact, better as your opening paragraph, and you've moved it to that position in your document. To delete it from its original location, move the cursor to the first line of the two-line paragraph you want to delete, and then use the following command to remove the current line and the one immediately following it:

```
2dd
```

You could also have used relative notation and typed the following:

```
.,+1d
```

# Moving Text Within a Document

Now suppose you decide to transpose the third and fourth paragraphs in the revised letter. You have three alternatives that you can choose from: You can use _vi_'s delete buffers, you can use the _co_ command, or you can use the _m_ (move) command.

If you want to use the delete buffer, move the cursor to the beginning of the line that starts _Need help?_ and, from command mode, enter the following command to delete the paragraph:

```
2dd
```

Because this is your most recent deletion, the text is placed in buffer number 1. To re-insert it at its new location, move the cursor to the line beginning _and geraniums_ and enter this command to finish transposing the paragraphs:

```
"1p
```

Like the _co_ command, _vi_'s _m_ command requires that you either know or display line numbers. The command's format is as follows:

```
:start,endmdestination
```

In the preceding example, you would want to move lines 8 and 9 to immediately below line 13, so the command would be as follows:

```
:8,9m13
```

The result of your reorganizing now looks like this:

```
    Our thanks to all our valued customers for your
continued patronage and support.
    It's that long, hot summer again.  Time for ball
games and lemonade, picnics, the Fourth of July.
Time to keep that lawn watered, too, and check for
all those pests that kill your carnations and ruin
your rutabagas.
    This month's Special Offers include mowing,
seeding, and fertilizing--two hours for the price
of one--and half-price specials on roses, petunias,
and geraniums.
    Need help?  Call 555-BULB.  Rhodie's Nursery--for
everything your garden needs.
~
~
~
~
~
~
~
~
~
~
~
```

# CUTTING AND PASTING BETWEEN FILES

Moving text between documents combines two techniques presented so far in this chapter: queuing files and using *vi*'s delete and insert buffers. You've completed the letter in our preceding example and saved it on disk with the *:w* command. You are about to begin a new letter you'll call *prospect*. For purposes of cutting and pasting, we'll use one of the paragraphs in *flier*. Begin by queuing the two filenames in which you're interested. Quit *vi* and then restart by using the following command:

```
vi prospect flier
```

Because you listed *prospect* first, *vi* begins with a blank screen and a message telling you that *prospect* is the new file.

Insert the following two lines of text (indenting the first line by three spaces and pressing the Enter key at the end of each line):

```
   Thank you for your recent inquiry regarding
our landscape installation and maintenance service.
```

Now you're ready to try cutting and pasting between documents. Save your new file to disk with the *:w* command. Then call up the next file in your queue by using the following command:

```
:n
```

When *vi* displays *flier*, move the cursor to the paragraph beginning *This month's Special Offers*, and copy the paragraph to an insert buffer using either of the following methods.

Specify the lines to copy with the following command:

```
"b4yy
```

Or mark the first line with this command:

```
mk
```

And then move the cursor to the last line of the paragraph and yank all text between the current line and the marked line with the following command:

```
"by'k
```

Now return to *prospect* by entering either of the following commands:

```
:e#
```

or

```
:rew
```

Finally, when *prospect* reappears on the screen, move the cursor to the last line of text and enter the following to put the contents of buffer *b* into the document below the current line:

```
"bp
```

You can now add to or edit the letter, save it, abandon it—whatever you want to do to it.

Before we move on and discover more about *vi*, let's look quickly at one other approach you could have taken to cutting and pasting between documents.

# Beginning from *vi*

If you had already begun a session with *vi* when you decided to begin your new file, your procedure would have been a little different. After saving (or abandoning) the current document, you would start the new file with the following command:

```
:e prospect
```

As in other situations, *vi* would tell you this is a new file, and you could then enter text as described in the preceding section. When you wanted to call up *flier*, you could not use the *:rew* command because you have no queue. You could, however, enter the following if *flier* were the file you had just worked with:

```
:e#
```

If it were not, you would then use the following command to specify the correct file:

```
:e flier
```

From that point, you could cut and paste between documents as described earlier.

# USING BOILERPLATE TEXT

Cutting and pasting within or between documents is closely related to another time-saving technique—using "boilerplate" text. Using boilerplate text allows you to compose different "templates" containing information that can be mixed, matched, and individualized to cover a variety of situations. Boilerplate documents don't have to be simple form letters, either. Using *vi*'s buffers, queues, insert modes, and powerful text-handling abilities, you can transform a basic, all-purpose document into one that is both personal and unique. As an example, we'll use the files *flier* and *prospect* as two elements of a form-letter system.

## Creating a Template

To practice on your system, begin from *vi* by using the following command:

```
:e form_letter
```

If you're starting from the shell, enter the following command:

```
vi form_letter
```

From either starting point, use the *i* command to switch to insert mode. As you enter the following sample text, type the greater than and less than signs and the identifying words within them, and press the Enter key to start each new line and to create blank lines where indicated. Use two blank lines between the date and salutation and between the closing and the sender's name; other blank lines are single.

Here is the sample text:

```
<date>


Dear <name>:

<news>
   In keeping with our policy of maintaining close
contact with all of our valued customers, I am happy
to enclose a copy of our new booklet, "Dusty's Guide
to Growing Roses."
<comment>
   Remember Rhodie's, and see how your garden grows!

Sincerely,


Dusty Miller
Rhodie's Landscaping and Nursery
```

When you finish, return to command mode and use *:w* to save the document on disk.

The words enclosed in <> symbols indicate places in the document where specific text will be inserted or changed as you customize your form letter. The words are unimportant beyond the scope of our example. The symbols are unnecessary; they are used here only to make the words they enclose stand out.

Let's assume you have a mailing list that includes three groups of people: one group that will be sent *flier*, another that will get *prospect*, and a third that will get only the basic letter. To create the letters, you simply assemble the components.

## Substituting Text

Let's compose a letter for a customer named Mr. Wright. You want to begin at the top of the letter, so move the cursor to the top with the following command:

```
1G
```

This first line of text contains a reminder. You want to substitute the actual date for <date>, so enter the following:

```
:s/<date>/June 25, 1990
```

The *:s* (substitute) command tells *vi* to substitute the text *June 25, 1990* for the text *<date>* that it finds in the first line of your document. You'll learn more about replacing text later in this chapter. For now, it's enough to know that the existing text must always precede the substitution text in the command. The slashes (/) separate the two.

Right now you want to make another substitution. Move the cursor to the line containing *<name>*, and enter the following to replace *<name>* with *Mr. Wright* in the salutation:

```
:s/<name>/Mr. Wright
```

Move the cursor to the first character in *<news>*, and use the *D* (delete) command, which removes all text from the cursor position to the end of the line without disturbing the position held by that line.

## Inserting Another File

With the cursor still at the first position of the now vacant line, enter the following command:

```
:r  prospect
```

The *:r* (read) command tells *vi* to read the contents of the file you specify and insert that file at the current cursor position. Thus, in response to your command here, *vi* reads *prospect* and inserts the text in that file at the line containing the cursor. The rest of your document moves down to accommodate the new material, as follows:

```
June 25, 1990


Dear Mr. Wright:

    Thank you for your recent inquiry regarding
our landscape installation and maintenance service.
    In keeping with our policy of maintaining close
contact with all of our valued customers, I am happy
to enclose a copy of our new booklet, "Dusty's Guide
to Growing Roses."
<comment>
    Remember Rhodie's, and see how your garden grows!

Sincerely,


Dusty Miller
Rhodie's Landscaping and Nursery
~
~
```

That leaves only your *<comment>* line to account for. You could maintain a set of appropriate one-line comments, but let's use an editing command instead.

## Replacing Lines of Text

Move the cursor to the *<comment>* line and, once there, enter the *cc* command, which deletes the entire line containing the cursor and retains the line's position within your document. Although *cc* might seem much like the *D* command, it differs in two important respects. First it deletes the entire line, whereas *D* deletes only from the cursor location to the end of the line. Second *cc* not only deletes but puts you into insert mode at the beginning of the line; the *D* command does not activate insert mode.

To insert your comment, press Enter, type three spaces, and type the following:

```
Please call if you would like a free estimate.
```

Press Enter and then press Escape. Your letter is finished, with only minimal effort on your part.

# SEARCHING A DOCUMENT

One short example cannot possibly show you all the ways in which you can use *vi*. For instance, you might want to replace one or more words a number of times within a long document. Or you might simply want to search for a particular word or set of words. It's not difficult to scroll through a short document to find what you're looking for, but in a long document the line-by-line approach is hardly practical.

By design, *vi* gives you several ways around such issues.

## Searching for Words

Recall that one of the ways in which you can start *vi* is by specifying a particular word at which you want to begin. From within *vi* you have a similar option.

Suppose, for example, you want to find the specific place in your document where you used the words *alternatives are* and insert additional text at that point. You can enter the following command:

```
/alternatives are
```

When you do so, *vi* searches forward from the position of the cursor (toward the end of the document), stopping on the line containing the first occurrence of *alternatives are*. If you start the search in the middle of the document, *vi* will not stop when it reaches the end—it will go back to the top of the document and continue the search until it either finds the text you specified or returns to the starting point.

The slash character (/) preceding the search words tells *vi* to search forward through the document. You can also tell *vi* to search backward by prefacing the search text with a question mark (*?alternatives are*).

In either type of search, if you want *vi* to stop when it reaches the end (or the beginning) of the document, you can tell it so with the following command:

```
:set  nowrapscan
```

To return *vi* to its normal mode, use the following command:

```
:set  wrapscan
```

If the first occurrence of your text that *vi* finds is not the one you are looking for, continue the search by using the *n* command.

## Ignoring Case

Of course, the search phrase you're looking for could appear as *Alternatives are* at the beginning of a sentence. Or it might appear in both uppercase and lowercase within your document.

If you want *vi* to ignore such variations in case, use the following command before beginning the search:

```
:set  ignorecase
```

The following command restores *vi*'s case sensitivity:

```
:set  noignorecase
```

## Searching with Wildcards

You've already seen wildcards and ranges used with filenames to broaden SCO UNIX's flexibility in matching patterns of characters. You can also use wildcards and ranges when searching for words with *vi*.

To find all uppercase characters, you can use the following command:

```
/[A-Z]
```

The command for the search for lowercase characters would be as follows:

```
/[a-z]
```

And the variations that you saw in Chapter 4 for numbers, uppercase letters, lowercase letters, and mixtures of uppercase and lowercase letters are all valid here as well.

You can also exclude certain characters from your search by including a caret (^) within the range brackets. If you wanted to find the first word beginning with a capital letter followed by the letters *at*, for instance, you would use the following command to tell *vi* you are interested in all ASCII characters *except* lowercase letters:

```
/[^a-z]at
```

This command tells *vi* to stop at *Bat*, *Cat*, *Fat*, or *Hat* but not at *bat*, *cat*, *fat*, or *hat*.

The first and last characters or words in a line are also viable candidates for search criteria. The following command would find the first line, including the current line, that started with the word *in*:

```
/^in /
```

Note that the caret symbol has an entirely different meaning when used without brackets—it restricts the search to the first word of each line (provided that word is not a space or a tab character). Note, too, that a space is included in this example to ensure that only whole words are considered, rather than any words that begin with *in*. The trailing slash tells *vi* where the characters you want to search for cease. The trailing slash is usually optional, but in this case it's needed to tell *vi* that the space character is to be included in the search.

Alternatively, you can enter the following command to search for the first line in which the last word ends in *ing*:

```
/ing$
```

To match single characters within a word, you can use the dot command:

```
/ Pi. /
```

Used as in this example, the dot command matches any single character. This command would cause *vi* to find any combination of three characters beginning with *Pi—Pit*, *Pin*, *Pip*, and so on. Note the use of blank spaces to limit the search to whole words.

## Searching for Special Characters

As you've just seen, *vi* considers some search characters special. The complete list of special characters is as follows:

```
.
*
\
[
]
~
$
^
```

One or more of these characters could be part of the text for which you're searching. (An obvious example would be a dollar amount, such as $1000.00.) In that case, you need to make *vi* understand that it must accept the character or characters literally.

You saw a similar situation in using the *y* and *p* commands to move text to and from an insert buffer. There you used a double quotation mark (") to tell *vi* to interpret the letter *a* as a name rather than as a command. In searches, you precede any special characters with a backslash (\). For example, to find the figure $1000.00, you would use the following command:

```
/\$1000\.00
```

Of course, if much of the text you're searching for contains special characters, the command line might begin to look rather ungainly with all of the backslashes. (Imagine searching for a mathematical formula.) As usual, *vi* offers relief.

The feature within *vi* that enables the editor to recognize the special characters we've been looking at is called *magic*. To turn off *vi*'s ability to recognize these characters, you can enter the following command:

```
:set  nomagic
```

To restore recognition of special characters, enter this command:

```
:set  magic
```

# SEARCHING AND REPLACING

Quite often when you search for a particular word in a document, you want to replace it with another. You did that earlier when you substituted words in the form-letter example. Then, however, replacements were made on a case-by-case basis: You selected the word and the replacement each time a change was made.

For a document in which you want to replace words that appear only once, the *:s* command works well. But for a document in which you want to find and replace the same word several times, it's far easier to be able to tell *vi* to make the change globally (throughout the entire document).

The global search-and-replace command uses the following format:

```
:g/ search_for /s// replace_with /options
```

For example, suppose you had a document in which you wanted to change all occurrences of the word *we* to *I.* To make this change everywhere, including the beginnings of sentences such as *We strongly recommend*, you would first tell *vi* to ignore all uppercase and lowercase differences with the following command:

```
:set ignorecase
```

Then you could enter the following replacement command:

```
:g/ we /s// I /g
```

The *:g* tells *vi* to look at every line of the file. The */ we /* says to search for *we*, preceded by and followed by blank spaces.

The *s/* says substitute the next element for *we*. The */ I /*, preceded by and followed by blank spaces, is the text to be substituted for *we*.

The */g* says "Do this for each occurrence on each line of text."

The blank spaces preceding and following both *we* and *I* ensure that the command works as you want it to and that the proper spacing between words is maintained. Without the spaces, *welfare* could become *Ilfare* and *stewed* could become *steId*.

Also, even though this search-and-replace command both begins and ends with the letter *g*, the final *g* is not redundant. It is the command option that tells *vi* to make the substitution more than once per line if needed.

You can use two other options in combination with the *g* option. They are *p*, which tells *vi* to display (print on the screen) a copy of every line it changes, and *c*, which lets you confirm each replacement before it is made. To use the *p* option with the preceding example, your command would take the following form:

```
:g/ we /s// I /gp
```

If you used this option, *vi* would show you all the lines it changed, and you could check them for errors. When you finished, pressing Enter would eliminate the display of changed lines.

Likewise, to use the *c* option in our example, your command would be as follows:

```
:g/ we /s// I /gc
```

This time, *vi* would show you each occurrence of *we* before the substitution was made. To accept the change, you would press the Y key only (not Shift and Y); to reject the change, you would press the Enter key.

Both *p* and *c* are valuable aids in verifying the accuracy of a global search-and-replace command. The *c* option, in particular, is a good one to get in the habit of using even though it adds a little time to the substitution process.

# ENTERING THE SHELL
# WITHOUT EXITING *vi*

Suppose you tried to save a document, and *vi* told you that a file of the same name already existed in the same directory. You would have to choose a different name or overwrite the existing file. But what if you couldn't remember what that file contained?

You could save the document under an alternate name, exit *vi*, and then use the *cat* command to look at the contents of the file that obstructed your original intention. But that's not necessary.

At any point in your work with *vi*, as long as you are in command mode, you can use the following command to enter the Bourne shell:

```
:!sh
```

To enter the C shell, the command would be *:!csh.*

In each of these instances, the exclamation point at the beginning of the command line becomes an escape command that lets you temporarily slip out of *vi* and use any valid shell command, including the command to enter the shell itself. If this concept seems elusive, try thinking of it this way: When you start *vi*, you do so from one of the shells; *vi* is active within that shell. When you use the exclamation point, you are opening a temporary doorway into the shell you request.

Actually, you can use the exclamation point to temporarily leave other parts of SCO UNIX too—the *mail* facility, for example—so the subject will crop up again, in other parts of this book.

Right now you want to look at the contents of a file. You can shorten the procedure even further by using the *cat* command (or any other command) directly from *vi*. Thus the following command will take you directly to the file because *cat* is a valid shell command and hence is as effective when used this way as it is when you enter it at the shell prompt.

```
:!cat filename
```

If you haven't saved your document before you use the exclamation point and a shell command, SCO UNIX will tell you to. But your text and *vi* are not disturbed when the command you request is carried out, so the message is more of a friendly reminder than anything else. It's a good practice to save your document before you start the shell, though. As long as your document resides only in temporary memory, the second or two it takes to type *:w* is well worth the effort.

# Returning to *vi*

If you use the exclamation point to enter either the Bourne shell or the C shell, press Ctrl-D to return to *vi*.

Ordinarily, Ctrl-D is the logout command for users of the Bourne shell. In a sense, it is the same here, but instead of taking you off the system completely, it returns you to the shell level from which you arrived—the one containing *vi* and the work you were doing. Using Ctrl-D is like backing up and closing the door you just opened.

In all cases, whether you've entered the shell or just used a shell command (such as *cat*), after the command has run its course, you'll be prompted to press the Enter key to continue with *vi*.

# SIZING UP YOUR DOCUMENT

Before we leave *vi*, we should look at one more topic: the size of a *vi* document. Because your document is carried in user memory, its size is limited by the amount of memory *vi* has available. This amount can vary from one installation to another but should remain relatively constant within any one system so that the document that fits in memory today will still fit tomorrow. As a general guideline, we recommend you never edit a file larger than 250 KB in size.

However, a document might become so large that you can no longer edit it. Or your system administrator might need to change the system for some reason and, in the process, reduce the amount of memory available. If either of these situations occurs, you have an aid in the form of *split*, an SCO UNIX utility that lets you break one long file into two shorter ones. The command format looks like this:

```
split -lines_per_file filename new_name
```

For example, suppose you had a 3000-line file named *unix_book*. You could use *split* to break it into two 1500-line files identified by the new name *unix_files* with the following command (entered at the shell prompt):

```
split -1500 unix_book unix_files
```

Here the - symbol is the usual lead character for SCO UNIX command options; *1500* is the number of lines per file; *unix_book* is the original file; and *unix_files* is the name you specify for the new files. (If you don't supply a *lines_per_file* number, *split* will use 1000 lines as the default. Your 3000-line file would become three 1000-line files.)

When SCO UNIX carries out your command, it adds a two-character suffix to the new name. The suffixes begin with *aa* and proceed through the alphabet, so the resulting two files would be as follows:

```
unix_filesaa
```

```
unix_filesab
```

The *split* command also lets you divide the file into more than two pieces if you want. To do so, specify a size that is a smaller multiple of the file's total line length. For example, if the file *unix_book* were 110 lines long and you wanted it broken into six files (five 20-line files and one 10-line file), you could enter the following command:

```
split -20 unix_book unix_files_
```

The underline character added to the end of the filename (*unix_files_*) makes the names more readable after the suffixes are added (for example, *unix_files_aa*).

# CHECKING YOUR SPELLING

SCO UNIX includes a utility called *spell* that can help you catch the spelling and typographical errors in your writing.

The *spell* utility matches patterns of characters and words in your document against the contents of a dictionary data file that contains as many as 20,000 words. All words that have no match in the dictionary are reported as errors, including legitimate words, such as your name, that are not included in the program's dictionary.

Spelling checkers do not verify context. A spelling checker would find no error in the sentence *That is fare*, when you meant *That is fair*.

SCO UNIX's *spell* program can perform functions that you would not typically find in a spelling checker. The easiest way to see how *spell* works is to use it.

Let's check a document named *sample*, into which we've deliberately introduced a number of errors. Try *spell* for yourself by using *vi* to enter the lines shown in the following illustration (a quotation from Thoreau) and then saving the file on disk:

```
    Here is a test for the SCO UNIX spelling checker.
All errors will be flagged.  What could be easier?
    "Why shoudl we be in such desperate haste
to suceed, and in such desperate enterprises?
If a man does not keep pace with his companions,
perhaps it is because he heers a different
drummer.  Let him step to teh music which he
hears, however measured or far awey."
```

Check the file you've created by entering the following command:

```
spell sample
```

In a few seconds, *spell* produces the following display:

```
$ spell sample
SCO
awey
heers
shoudl
suceed
teh
$_
```

Although *SCO* is spelled correctly, it's listed as a misspelled word because *spell* could not find it in the dictionary.

Not all of the words in *sample* are actually in the dictionary, so *spell* made certain assumptions about word construction, based on the rules it knows. You can see these assumptions by using *spell*'s *-v* option, as follows:

```
spell -v sample
```

Applied to the same file, the *-v* option of *spell* produces the list of misspelled words, but it also displays another list of words, along with the rules it used to determine whether they are spelled correctly.

```
$ spell -v sample
SCO
awey
heers
shoudl
suceed
teh
+er      checker
+s       companions
+s       does
+m+er    drummer
-y+ier   easier
+s       enterprises
+s       errors
+g+ed    flagged
+s       hears
+d       measured
+ing     spelling
$_
```

In the left column, you see *spell*'s assumptions. With *checker*, for example, it found both the word *check* and the valid suffix *er*. Putting the two together, *spell* assumed that *checker* was a valid word.

It also found the word *flag*, doubled the *g*, and added the suffix *ed*. In the same way, when it found the word *easy* and the suffix *er*, it used the spelling rule about dropping the *y* and adding an *i*.

Among *spell*'s other features is the *b* option, which checks for British spellings, such as *colour, civilise, centre*, and *travelled*.

# REDIRECTING OUTPUT

You can tell *spell* to send its output (for example, the output from the preceding demonstration of *spell*'s *-v* option) somewhere other than the screen—perhaps to a data file on disk. This technique is known as *redirecting output* and uses the greater than symbol (>) to "point to" the new destination. Thus, the following command would perform the spelling check and would save the results in a data file called *sample_errors*:

```
spell sample > sample_errors
```

This technique is identical to the one you used with *ed* when you created a memo file in Chapter 4. You can give the output file any name you want, and you can store it in any valid directory. If a file with the same name already exists in the same directory, the existing file will be overwritten by the new version. As you did with *ed*, however, you can add the new text to an existing file by using double greater than symbols, as with the following command:

```
spell sample >> sample_errors
```

(You can redirect both input and output to perform many tasks. Because redirection is such a valuable tool, we will also cover it in Chapter 8, "Advanced File Techniques.")

## Checking More Than One Document

Just as you can handle multiple documents with *vi*, you can use *spell* to check more than one document at a time. For example, if you had four files, named *doc1*, *doc2*, *doc3*, and *doc4*, the following command would instruct *spell* to check the four documents and place any errors in a file called *doc_errors*:

```
spell doc[1-4] > doc_errors
```

The resulting file would contain an alphabetized list of the errors found in all documents. (It would not, however, identify the file in which a particular misspelling occurred.)

## Refining *spell*

As you can see, *spell* can be a valuable aid in helping you find inadvertent spelling errors. Most documents, however, include a number of proper names, acronyms, and other valid words that *spell*'s dictionary does not contain. If you rely on *spell* fairly often, you might want to "educate" it so that these words are not reported as misspellings time after time. To do so, you need to create a file that contains these words (one word to a line). Then, when you run *spell*, include that filename as an option. For example, if you create a file named *mydict* containing words like *George*, *Halifax*, or *RAM*, you can use the following command form to have *spell* include these words as valid spellings:

```
spell +mydict letter
```

# WORKING IN THE BACKGROUND

If you tried any of the preceding examples, you found that checking your spelling is not quick. It can't be. Even if your document were only 10 words long, *spell* would have to check or otherwise account for each word. If you chain several long documents, you further extend the time required for the operation.

But because SCO UNIX is a multitasking operating system, you can relegate a task to the background. You tell SCO UNIX to execute a task in the background simply by ending a command line with an ampersand (&). For example, you could use the background to check the spelling of all files beginning with *doc* and redirect the output to a file named *doc_errors* with the following command:

```
spell doc* > doc_errors &
```

SCO UNIX responds to a request for background processing by placing a number on the line immediately below the command line. This number is the *process identification number*, or *PID*, for the task. Your shell prompt appears on the line below the process identification number. When the shell prompt appears, you can move on to any foreground task you want, including another request for a background task.

Here's a different example. Suppose you used *vi* to create a long document, *doc1*. You will send it to an important client, so you want to check your spelling. You have more documents to create with *vi* and cannot afford to wait while *spell* performs its check of your spelling.

To switch from *vi* to the shell, request a spelling check, redirect the output to a file on disk, and send the process into the background, you'd use the following command:

```
:!spell doc1 > errors &
```

The *vi* editor will prompt you to press Enter to continue. When you do so, you'll be back in *vi*, able to continue your work while *spell* checks your document and puts any misspelled words in a file named *errors*.

When you use foreground and background processes as in this example, remember to redirect your output to a disk file rather than let it appear on the screen. Redirection is useful in its own right, and it can become important in situations such as the preceding one.

If you did *not* redirect the output in this example, the list of misspelled words would still be printed on your screen. Just because you assign the *spell* process to the background does not mean you also reassign its output to any location other than where it normally appears.

With no redirection, *spell* will print its output on your screen, despite any foreground process you are working on. The *spell* utility doesn't care what you're doing. It knows only that it must present the results of its check to you. Needless to say, if you happen to be in the middle of another document, the appearance of a list of spelling errors on your screen will create a lot of visual confusion. (If this happens when you're in *vi*, don't be concerned. No changes will have been made to your document, and pressing Ctrl-L will redraw your screen.)

Despite their many advantages, redirecting and background processing are less efficient than working in the foreground because of the difficulty in responding to error messages. If, for some reason, the process you initiate encounters any errors, those errors will be reported in your disk file, not on the screen. You won't know about them until you look at the contents of the file. On the other hand, you can rest assured that any errors will be reported, and you will be able to try to resolve any problems later.

## Using Background Processing Effectively

You can send quite a few different types of tasks to the background. Spelling checks are one possibility. Sorting lists numerically or alphabetically is another. But should you push everything you possibly can into the background?

If you are the only user on the system, that answer might be "Yes." But if others are using the system, the answer must be "No." The more processes you push into the background, the more you burden the entire system. Eventually, the delays caused by background work can slow the foreground processes you and your coworkers are attempting.

You can't avoid that delay, but you can reduce its effect. Find out from your system administrator when the peak use of your system occurs. Background processes slow the system most when the most people are logged in. If you can limit your background work to the times when the fewest users are on the system, you will help minimize delays. In effect, your background tasks will be taking only the time that would normally be assigned to other users.

## Logging Out While Running a Background Process

Unless you're calling in on a dial-up line, a background process you've initiated on SCO UNIX will continue, even if you log out. If SCO UNIX terminates a background process when you log out, no damage will be done to your source files, but your output file will be incomplete, and you will have to restart the process when you next log in.

For that reason, it's wise to protect your background work, just as you protect unsaved editing changes while you are working with *vi*. For a background process, begin the command line with the *nohup* (no hangup) command. For example, to protect a background spelling check of the documents *sample* and *proposal*, with the results stored in a file named *errors*, you would type the following command:

```
nohup spell sample proposal > errors &
```

After you take this precaution, whether you log out or not, SCO UNIX will continue the spelling check to completion.

# PRINTING

The last phase in processing a document usually is printing it. You can print a document in one of two ways: locally (directly from your terminal) or through the system (through the SCO UNIX computer).

## Printing Locally

Many computer terminals on the market today have local printing facilities. You can attach a printer to the back of the terminal. When you press a particular key, anything that appears on your display is sent to that local printer, as well as to your screen. With these terminals, timing is important because the key to printing successfully is to activate the printer at the right time.

Some terminals, however, have their own memory and can capture several "pages" of information, so printing is easier. When you activate a local printer connected to such a terminal, you usually have the option of printing either whatever is on the screen or whatever is in the terminal's memory. Timing, on these terminals, is not critical.

Other terminals, such as the IBM 3101, are supplied with instructions—usually a keyboard sequence—that tell them to retain incoming text in a special buffer until the key sequence is given again. By giving the instruction again, you tell the terminal to print the contents of the buffer. If you're using this or a similar type of terminal with a local printer, consult the terminal manual for specific instructions.

Finally, if you're using a microcomputer with telecommunications software that places it in terminal-emulation mode, you can probably capture all text that's printed on the screen in a text file and then send it to your printer.

## Printing Through the System

If you don't have a local printer, you're probably using a printer that is connected to the SCO UNIX computer. The key to using this type of arrangement is the following command format:

```
lp filename
```

This command prints the document named *filename* to the line printer that is attached to the system.

## Spooling printed text

If you've used a single-user operating system, such as MS-DOS, you know that unless the printer is shut off or configured improperly, when you send a document to the printer, either it is printed immediately or it waits its turn in a queue.

With SCO UNIX, the opposite situation generally holds true. The reason is that SCO UNIX *spools* your printing, and the reason for spooling is that other users on the system might want to print. In fact, the printer might even be in use when you issue your print command. To handle multiple printing requests, SCO UNIX provides a directory on the hard disk called */usr/spool*. In */usr/spool* is a subdirectory called *lp* in which SCO UNIX places a copy of the file you want printed. The actual printing of the document thus occurs from */usr/spool/lp*.

Printing your file from the *lp* subdirectory serves two purposes. First it keeps you from waiting while your document is printed. Second your document is in a first come, first served queue while it's in *lp*. If the printer is busy or otherwise unavailable, your printing isn't canceled, as it would be in some other operating systems. Rather, SCO UNIX holds your document until the document reaches its turn in the print queue.

# Keeping Informed About Your Printing

If your system printer is not within sight, you won't know when your document is printed. But you can use the SCO UNIX *mail* system, which you'll meet in the next chapter, to keep yourself informed. Simply by including an *m* option in your print command, as follows, you can send your document to the printer and rest assured that you will be told when it is printed:

```
lp -m filename
```

SCO UNIX will send you mail telling you so.

# 7

# Communicating
# with Others

Until now, your activities with SCO UNIX have been strictly between you and the system. Now it's time to see how you can communicate with the other people on your system by sending them messages. If a user is not logged in when you send a message, SCO UNIX stores the message. When the recipient logs in, SCO UNIX notifies the user that a message is waiting. If the recipient is currently reading messages, SCO UNIX sends immediate notification. You can also use the system to send yourself messages about important events on your calendar.

## USING *mail*

One of the strongest features of SCO UNIX is its *mail* system. You saw some *mail* messages briefly when you first logged in. It's time for a closer look. Why not send a message to yourself?

## Composing and Sending
## *mail* Messages from the Shell Prompt

You use SCO UNIX's *mail* system either because you already have messages and want to read them or because you want to send a message to someone. You want to send a message to yourself.

To begin, enter the following command at the shell prompt:

```
mail user_name
```

Substitute your own user name for *user_name*. After a few moments, SCO UNIX's *mail* system responds:

```
Subject:
```

You don't need to include a subject with your message, but including a subject helps *mail* users to identify the content, keep track of messages, and, as you'll see later, decide which correspondence to read first.

As the subject of your message to yourself, enter the phrase:

```
Trying out the mail
```

The cursor advances to the next screen line. You now are in *mail*'s compose mode and can enter the text of the mail you want to send. Type the following, pressing Enter at the end of each line:

```
Although none of the mail sent through
SCO UNIX is ever processed by hand, it is not
delivered instantaneously. There is a
short delay between the time that it is
sent and the time it is received.
```

Press Ctrl-D on a new line to send the message and return to the shell prompt from *mail*'s compose mode.

You'll notice a delay between the time you send the message and the time you receive it. That delay varies according to what else is happening on the system. Generally, when many background processes are running, documents are printing, or several users are online, *mail* delivery is slower than when the system is quiet.

For example, suppose you're the only person online as you try the preceding example. Immediately after you press Ctrl-D, the *mail* program will deliver the message to you. On the other hand, if your system is very busy when you try this example, your *mail* message might not be delivered for a few minutes.

> **NOTE:** *SCO UNIX notifies you that you have mail messages by displaying the words* You have mail *on the line above the shell prompt when you log in. If you are currently in the* mail *program, it also notifies you that new mail has arrived.*

When you send a message to someone who is not currently logged in, the message is saved in the *mail* system, and that person is notified of the message the next time he or she logs into the system.

## Canceling a Message

To cancel a message that you started and then decide not to send, enter the following command to quit *mail*'s compose mode:

```
~q
```

You can also press the Delete key twice to cancel a message.

Your message isn't discarded. The *mail* system saves it in a file called *dead.letter* that it creates in your home directory. Your *dead.letter* file holds your last cancelled message.

## Entering the *mail* System

To return to *mail* so that you can read the message you sent to yourself, enter the following command at the shell prompt:

```
mail
```

Assuming that the original welcome message SCO UNIX sent you is still in your mailbox, you'll see something like this:

```
$ mail
SCO System V Mail (version 3.2)  Type ? for help.
"/usr/spool/mail/danh": 2 messages 1 new 2 unread
>N  2 danh@bifrost.UUCP   Mon Oct  9 13:18    13/418   Trying out the mail
 U  1 root@bifrost.UUCP   Mon Oct  3 07:54    13/381   Welcome to bifrost
? _
```

The second line of this display identifies your *mail* system and tells you that you can type a question mark if you need help. The next line is the first item of information about your own mailbox: the number of messages currently in it, the number of messages that have arrived since the last time you ran the *mail* program, and the number of messages that you haven't read yet. That line is followed by a list of your *mail* message headers, with the newest message at the top of the list. New, unread messages are marked with an *N*, and old, unread messages are marked with a *U*. Messages you've read aren't marked with either letter. A greater than sign (>) marks the current message—the message that you can read by pressing the Enter key.

Note that each message is numbered. That number is the first entry in each line. Other entries include the user name of the person who originated the message; an @ sign; the name of the machine from which the message originated; the day, date, and time the message was received; the number of lines and characters (*lines/characters*) in the message; and the subject of the message.

# Reading a *mail* Message

You can use one of four basic methods to read your messages after the *mail* system's introductory message is on your screen. The simplest is to press the Enter key. Pressing Enter displays your messages on your screen, one at a time, usually in the order in which they were received—in other words, with the oldest message first.

That's fine if all your messages have the same priority. But many times you'll want to read a message that doesn't come first in chronological order. If you press Enter to read your mail, you'll see all the low-priority messages, too, as the *mail* system goes through the list.

## Skipping with + and −

You can skip messages you don't want to read by using the + key to jump forward (toward the newest message in the list) or by using the − key to jump backward (toward the oldest message in the list). Used by itself, + is equivalent to pressing Enter. If you specify a number after the + or −, the command skips the number of messages you indicate away from the current message in the direction you indicate.

For example, if message number 11 is currently displayed and you enter +6, *mail* will display message number 17 (assuming messages 12–16 exist in the list).

Or if the current message is number 11 and you enter −6, *mail* will display message number 5.

You can also jump directly to the first or the last message in the list. To go to the first (oldest) message, enter the following command:

^

To go to the last (newest) message, enter the following command:

$

To find out which message is currently displayed, enter the following command:

=

## Accessing a message directly

You can access any message directly simply by entering its number. We'll use this method to retrieve the message you sent yourself. First, however, look at its summary header. In particular, notice that *mail* tells us our sample message contains 13 lines and 418 characters (13/418). (Because the date and your user name will vary, your sample might have a slightly different number of characters.) You can probably account for seven lines: the *To:* and *Subject:* lines and the five lines you typed. To see where the difference in line count arises, enter the message number.

```
? 2
Message  2:
From danh Mon Oct  9 13:18:37 1989
From: danh@bifrost.UUCP ()
X-Mailer: SCO System V Mail (version 3.2)
To: danh
Subject: Trying out the mail
Date: Mon, 9 Oct 89 13:18:32 PDT
Message-ID:  <8910090318.aa00365@bifrost.UUCP>
Status: RO

Although none of the mail sent through
SCO UNIX is ever processed by hand, it is not
delivered instantaneously. There is a
short delay between the time that it is
sent and the time it is received.
? _
```

You can see that *mail* has added eight header lines. (The line that reads *Message 2:* is not part of the header.)

The eight header lines are an expanded listing of the information you saw in the summary. The top header line tells you who sent the message and when it was received. The *From:* line gives the sender's full *mail* address, which includes the user name, an @ sign, the name of the machine at which the message originated, and possibly other machines that served as intermediate transmission points. The *X-Mailer:* line tells you which mailer program sent the message. You've already seen the *To:* and *Subject:* lines. The *Date:* header line shows you when the message was sent. (Note that there was a five-second delay between sending and receiving.) The *Message-ID:* header line identifies the message internally in your local *mail* system. The *Status:* line tells you additional information about the message.

## Displaying ranges of *mail* messages

The fourth method of reading your *mail* messages is much like the third, but it adds a new dimension to the way that you can display your messages. You can display the contents of several messages in a range by entering the following command:

p *start-end*

Thus, the following command displays ("prints" on the screen) the contents of messages 1 through 5:

p  1-5

(If you specify more than a full screen of messages, be prepared to press Ctrl-S to stop the scrolling—otherwise, the messages will scroll by without stopping.)

If the numbers of the messages you want to see are not sequential, you can enter the following command to display the messages identified by the numbers you supply:

```
p message_number(s)
```

For example, the following command would show you the contents of messages 1, 4, 6, and 10 while bypassing all in between:

```
p 1 4 6 10
```

The messages you specify scroll by without stopping.

You can also specify the name of a specific user with the following form:

```
p user_name
```

You must include the full name as given in the header line, including the machine name, if any is given. If you do this, *mail* will display only the messages you've received from the person you named.

In addition, you can quickly scan specified messages to find one you are seeking by telling *mail* to display only the first (top) few lines of each. Either of the following commands causes *mail* to display the first six lines of each message:

```
to start-end
```

or

```
to message_number(s)
```

As you can see, you have quite a few options. Use the ones you find most helpful.

## Reading a New *mail* Message

Whenever you press Enter in *mail*, the *mail* utility checks to see if any new messages have arrived. If one has, you'll see a message similar to this:

```
New mail has arrived.
Loaded 1 new message.
 N  3 mike@bifrost.UUCP   Mon Oct  9 13:19   10/253   Meeting
```

By itself, this message simply notifies you of the arrival of another message. The *mail* utility includes the new message's header summary in the list it displays and assigns the message a number so that you can select it. You can then read the message with any of the commands described previously.

# Replying to a *mail* Message

If you've been following our examples, your cursor is now two lines below the practice message you sent to yourself. SCO UNIX views this message as the current *mail* message and uses each command you enter (if you don't include a range) to manipulate it.

The cursor itself gives us another piece of information. When you're not composing a message and the cursor is on a line by itself, you're in *mail*'s command mode. From here, you can do anything with the messages in your mailbox: read them, remove them, print them, or reply to them. Let's assume you want to compose a reply to the current message.

If you want to reply to the person who sent the current message, you can simply enter the *r* (reply) command on the line containing the cursor. The *mail* system will respond with two header lines, as follows:

```
? 2
Message  2:
From danh Mon Oct  9 03:18:37 1989
From: danh@bifrost.UUCP ()
X-Mailer: SCO System V Mail (version 3.2)
To: danh
Subject: Trying out the mail
Date: Sun, 8 Oct 89 20:18:32 PDT
Message-ID:  <8910090318.aa00365@bifrost.UUCP>
Status: RO

Although none of the mail sent through
SCO UNIX is ever processed by hand, it is not
delivered instantaneously. There is a
short delay between the time that it is
sent and the time it is received.
? r
To: danh
Subject: Re:  Trying out the mail

—
```

The first header line indicates the user to whom your reply is being sent (in this case, yourself). The *mail* utility has taken this name from the original message's *From:* field. The second line starts with *Re:*, which means "in reference to," and then duplicates the *Subject:* field, if one exists, of the original.

When you see these header lines, you can type the reply as you would when sending someone a message.

You can also use the *r* command with a range or a list of messages and specified user names. For example, to reply to messages from users named *kenh* and *lindaz*, you would enter:

```
r kenh lindaz
```

The *mail* system would then add a subject heading from the earliest recorded message from either user. After you had composed a reply and pressed Ctrl-D, your message would be sent to both users. (Don't be concerned if you see a user listed more than once in the *To:* section of a message you're sending. Each user will receive only one copy of the message.)

If the message or messages you're replying to include more than your name in the *To:* field or if the originator sent "carbon copies" to other users (by a means you'll see shortly), you can send your reply to one and all by entering an uppercase *R* instead of a lowercase *r* before beginning your message. The uppercase version of the *r* command ensures that everyone who was sent the original message receives a copy of your response.

## Composing and Sending a Message in *mail*

In addition to replying to messages, you can compose an entirely new message while you're in *mail.* While the cursor is on a blank line waiting for a command, use the following form:

```
m user_name
```

After entering the *Subject:* line, you can begin composing a new message to the person you've specified.

To send one message to a group of people, you can use the following format:

```
m user_name user_name ... user_name
```

You can also address multiple users in this way when you use *mail* at the shell prompt.

When you finish composing a message, send it by pressing Ctrl-D on a new line. If you have at least one message in your mailbox, you'll remain in the *mail* environment.

## Quitting *mail*

To leave *mail*, press Ctrl-D again, or use the *q* command.

## Forwarding a *mail* Message

On occasion, you might need to forward a copy of the current message to another user. Simply enter the command in the following form:

f *user_name*

The original message remains in your mailbox, and the recipient receives both the forwarded message and a header showing that you are the person who sent it. For example, if *danh* forwarded the sample message to *boba*, the result would look like this:

```
From danh Mon Oct  9 15:39:05 1989
From: danh@bifrost.UUCP ()
X-Mailer: SCO System V Mail (version 3.2)
To: boba
Subject: Trying out the mail
Date: Mon, 9 Oct 89 15:39:21 PDT
Message-ID:  <8910090338.aa00423@bifrost.UUCP>
Status: R

         From danh Mon Oct  9 15:38:05 1989
         From: danh@bifrost.UUCP ()
         X-Mailer: SCO System V Mail (version 3.2)
         To: danh
         Subject: Trying out the mail
         Date: Mon, 9 Oct 89 15:37:03 PDT
         Message-ID:  <8910090337.aa00415@bifrost.UUCP>

         Although none of the mail sent through
         SCO UNIX is ever processed by hand, it is not
         delivered instantaneously. There is a
         short delay between the time that it is
         sent and the time it is received.
?  _
```

Note that the message you forward is indented one tab stop inside the new message. At times, you might not want the forwarded message indented—perhaps because the indent would cause the text of the message to go beyond the right border of the screen. You can omit the indentation by using an uppercase *F*.

For example, if *danh* were to forward the preceding message to *joannew* in this way, the result would be this:

```
Message 3:
From danh Mon Oct  9 15:39:05 1989
From: danh@bifrost.UUCP ()
X-Mailer: SCO System V Mail (version 3.2)
To: joannew
Subject: Trying out the mail
Date: Mon, 9 Oct 89 15:39:21 PDT
Message-ID:  <8910090338.aa00423@bifrost.UUCP>
Status: R

From danh Mon Oct  9 15:38:05 1989
From: danh@bifrost.UUCP ()
X-Mailer: SCO System V Mail (version 3.2)
To: danh
Subject: Trying out the mail
Date: Mon, 9 Oct 89 15:37:03 PDT
Message-ID:  <8910090337.aa00415@bifrost.UUCP>

Although none of the mail sent through
SCO UNIX is ever processed by hand, it is not
delivered instantaneously. There is a
short delay between the time that it is
sent and the time it is received.
? _
```

# Moving a *mail* Message

In a typical system, *mail* messages build up at an alarming rate, so simply allowing all your messages to accumulate is not the best approach.

SCO UNIX's data-handling ability centers on files and directories, so you have many options for storing and renaming the messages you've received. Let's look at some techniques for collecting and moving messages to places where you can best use them.

### Moving a *mail* message to *mbox*

SCO UNIX maintains a separate area for *mail* message storage in your home directory. It's called *mbox*, and you can transfer specific messages to it. From *mail*'s command mode, use the following command format to store a message:

```
mb message_number
```

If this is the first message you're placing in *mbox*, a file named *mbox* is created to accommodate it. If *mbox* exists, any messages you send there are appended to those already in it.

The *mb* command doesn't remove the message from your mailbox and transfer it to *mbox* until you quit the *mail* session.

As with other *mail* features, you can transfer lists and ranges of messages, as well as messages from specified users.

### Moving a *mail* message to another file

You can also save messages to a file other than *mbox.* If you do so from outside *mail*, at the shell prompt, every message in your mailbox moves to the file you name.

To select only the messages you want to save, use the following format:

```
s message_number filename
```

You can also use a list or a range. The *s* (save) command copies the entire message, including all six header lines, into the file you've named.

An alternative is as follows:

```
w message_number filename
```

Here, again, you can use a list or a range of messages. The *w* (write) command moves only the body of the message, without the headers, into the file you name.

In either case, if the text file you've specified does not exist, *mail* creates it. If the file does exist, the messages you've selected are appended to the end of it. Here, too, the messages remain in the mailbox until you exit the *mail* session.

## Printing a *mail* Message

If you want a printed copy of some or all of your *mail* messages, you can send the messages to the line printer attached to your system by using the following command format to print the range of messages indicated by the numbers you supply:

```
l start-end
```

You can also use a list of numbers for non-continuous messages, or you can specify a user name if you want to view only the messages from a particular person from within that list or range.

If your system has more than one printer attached to it, or if you need more specific information about when and where printouts are distributed, check with your system administrator.

## Deleting a *mail* Message

If you decide that you don't want to save a message or leave it in your mailbox, you can delete it. If the message is the current message, enter the *d* (delete) command. To delete other messages in the list, enter the command by using the following format:

```
d message_number(s)
```

You can use a range of messages or indicate only those originated by a specific user. The *mail* system doesn't display summary lines for deleted messages again during the current session, so you have no way to access them. The messages themselves, however, are not eliminated until you actually exit the *mail* system by using the *q* (quit) command or by pressing Ctrl-D.

A timesaving alternative, particularly when you are clearing out the contents of an over-full mailbox, is the *dp* command, which not only deletes the current message or the one whose number you've included but also displays the next message in the list.

## Undeleting a *mail* Message

If you haven't yet left the *mail* system and decide that you really don't want to throw away one or more of the messages you deleted, you can use the following format:

```
u message_number
```

Again, you can specify a range or list of messages that you have deleted. The *u* (undelete) command recovers any messages you specify that you've marked for deletion during the current session. Keep in mind, however, that the *u* command works only if you have not ended the current *mail* session. After you exit *mail*, deleted messages are irretrievably lost.

## Recovering a Removed *mail* Message

At any time during the current *mail* session, you can redisplay a list of the summary lines for your mail by entering the *h* (header) command to redisplay the headers for all of the undeleted messages in your mailbox.

If you've marked mail for transfer, the leftmost field will contain *M* or *.

```
? h
  N  6 mikem@bifrost.UUCP  Mon Oct  9 10:17   15/411   Printer use
 >M  5 janed@bifrost.UUCP  Mon Oct  9 10:10   13/318   Contracts
     4 kerric@bifrost.UUCP Mon Oct  9 09:40   14/351   deadlines
  U  3 susanh@bifrost.UUCP Mon Oct  9 08:22   13/323   New Offices
  U  2 terryr@bifrost.UUCP Mon Oct  9 08:12   13/308   Meeting
  U  1 root@bifrost.UUCP   Mon Oct  9 07:58   10/237   disk space
? _
```

132

If you've transferred messages to *mbox*, the leading character on the summary header will be an *M*. If you've used either the *s* command or the *w* command to transfer the message to another file, the first character in the summary will be an asterisk (*).

In any case, when you exit the *mail* system by using the *q* command or by pressing Ctrl-D, all of the marked messages will be removed from your mailbox. If you decide you really want to keep some or all of them in the mailbox, use the following command format to have *mail* hold the specified messages and not remove them:

```
ho message_number
```

You can also use a list or a range.

## Exiting the *mail* System

When you've finished using the *mail* system, you can exit it in one of three ways. If you want to return to your shell, press Ctrl-D once, enter *q* or enter *x* (exit) on the line containing the cursor.

With the *q* command or Ctrl-D, you're told which (if any) messages you've stored in *mbox*, and how many remain in the mailbox. The messages you've marked for deletion are removed from your mailbox, and you're returned to the shell.

The *x* command ignores any changes you might have specified for your mailbox and leaves all files intact. It's actually an abort request that immediately returns you to the shell, leaving the contents of your mailbox unchanged.

If you're using the Bourne shell and you finished using SCO UNIX altogether, press Ctrl-D twice on the line containing the cursor—once to signal *mail* that you've finished and the second time to log out.

# EDITING a *mail* MESSAGE

The *mail* system has no inherent editing features, but it does offer alternatives to continually deleting not-quite-right messages.

## Viewing a *mail* Message

If you're comfortable with the text of a message that you're currently composing but would like to review its entire contents before you send it, use the following command:

```
~p
```

This will display the *To:* and *Subject:* fields, followed by the text of the message.

## Tilde Escape Commands

The tilde (~) is the *mail* system's escape command. The tilde is a signal to *mail* that the next character you type is to be interpreted as a command, not as part of your text. The *mail* system includes a number of such tilde escapes, or compose escapes. They let you move out of compose mode temporarily, and they increase *mail*'s flexibility enormously. You enter a tilde escape at the beginning of a new line. You can request a summary of them by entering the following command on a new line while you're composing a message:

~?

The *mail* system displays the following help screen:

```
-------------------- ~ ESCAPES ----------------------------
~~              Quote a single tilde
~a,~A           Autograph (insert 'sign' variable)
~b users        Add users to Bcc list
~c users        Add users to Cc list
~d              Read in dead.letter file
~e              Edit the message buffer
~f messages     Read in messages, do not right-shift
~h              Prompt for To list, Subject and Cc list
~i string       Insert string into message (~a := ~i sign)
~m messages     Read in messages, right-shifted by a tab
~M messages     Read in messages, do not right-shift
~p              Print the message buffer
~q,~Q           Quit, save letter in $HOME/dead.letter
~r file         Read a file into the message buffer
~s subject      Set subject
~t users        Add users to To list
~v              Invoke display editor on message
~w file         Write message onto file
~x              Quit, do not save letter
~< file         Read a file into the message buffer
~.              End of input
~!command       Run a shell command
~!command       Pipe the message through the command
~^command       Pipe the message through the command
~:command       Execute regular mailx command
~_command       Execute regular mailx command
------------------------------------------------------------
~
```

As an example of a tilde escape command, you can include a *mail* message in a message you are sending by using the following command format on a new line:

~m *message_number*

This is useful if you want to include a message on which you are commenting. The receiving user will see a message like this:

```
? Message  5:
From danh Mon Oct  9 16:21:41 1989
From: danh@bifrost.UUCP ()
X-Mailer: SCO System V Mail (version 3.2)
To: joannew
Subject: of interest
Date: Mon, 9 Oct 89 16:21:40 PDT
Message-ID:  <8910090421.aa00590@bifrost.UUCP>
Status: R

Below is a message I sent to myself that might be of interest to you:

        From danh Mon Oct  9 15:37:05 1989
        From: danh@bifrost.UUCP ()
        X-Mailer: SCO System V Mail (version 3.2)
        To: danh
        Subject: Trying out the mail
        Date: Mon, 9 Oct 89 15:37:03 PDT
        Message-ID:  <8910090337.aa00415@bifrost.UUCP>
        Status: O


        Although none of the mail sent through
        SCO UNIX is ever processed by hand, it is not
        delivered instantaneously. There is a
        short delay between the time that it is
        sent and the time it is received.

Let me know what you think!

Dan
? _
```

Note that the included message is indented one tab stop to set it apart from the rest of the message. Using an uppercase M will avoid the indent.

As with other commands, you can use ranges, lists, and user names to forward or to include a message.

# Including Text Files in a *mail* Message

Among other possibilities, *mail* lets you use either *vi* or *ed* to write a message . You can use these editors either before or while you are composing your message. The *mail* system does not let you jump from line to line, but you can create all or part of the message in *vi* (or *ed*), save it, and then send it as all or part of your message.

For example, suppose you create a text file named *activities* and you want to send it to user *danh* for review. You could create the file in *vi* and, from the shell prompt, enter the following command:

```
mail danh < activities
```

To include a text file as part of a message, enter the *mail* system as usual and start typing. When you reach the line on which you want the insert to appear, use the following command form:

```
~r filename
```

The text contained in the file you specify will appear in the message.

### Editing the body of a message

On the other hand, at any point after you begin the body of your message (that is, after you've filled in whatever header information you want included), you can enter the following command:

```
~v
```

In this case, the *~v* loads *vi*, which reads in any text you've typed so far and assigns a temporary filename to it. (If you prefer *ed*, enter *~e*.)

While you're in the text editor, you can use all of its features. When you've finished, exit the editor and save the document with the *:x* command. You're deposited back in the *mail* system's compose mode. You'll see the message *(continue)*. Any text you've typed or changes you've made while in the editor will be included in your message, and you can go on as if you had never left *mail*.

# Editing the *Subject:* Field

Perhaps when you started your message you didn't foresee a need for an entry in the *Subject:* field. If you later change your mind or want to alter the text you did include, the following command format will do that for you:

```
~s subject
```

The text you supply as *subject* will replace the contents of an existing *Subject:* field.

# Editing the *To:* Field

After entering the name of your message's recipient in the *To:* field, you might decide that the message should be sent to other people as well. The following command format adds recipients without replacing the name you originally entered:

```
~t user_name(s)
```

## Sending Copies

Another way to send mail to several people is the carbon-copy approach. While you're in the body of your message, the following command format sends a copy of your message to the users you've indicated:

`~c user_name(s)`

When you use this command, *mail* adds a ninth field, *Cc:*, to the message's header. The field includes the names of all the people to whom copies have been sent.

You can also use the following variation to send blind carbon copies of the message:

`~b user_name(s)`

With a blind carbon copy, recipients' names are not listed in the *To:* or *Cc:* field.

## Editing Header Lines

You can edit any of the header lines in your message, whether you've supplied entries for them or not, by entering the following general-purpose command at the beginning of a new line while you're composing your message:

`~h`

The *mail* systems displays each field (*To:*, *Subject:*, *Cc:*, and *Bcc:* with its current contents, or it leaves the field blank if nothing has been entered. You can then change the fields as you see fit.

## Creating a Mailing List

So far, we've looked at sending mail to multiple recipients by stringing together a list of user names in the *To:*, *Cc:*, and *Bcc:* fields. However, if you send *mail* messages to the same group of people on a regular basis, you might find that typing the same names each time is a chore. In those circumstances, it's much better to create a mailing list.

Creating such a list is not a difficult task in *mail*. To create a mailing list, use the following command format:

`alias alias_name user_names`

In this command, *alias_name* is the name you want to assign to the group. That name is followed by the names of the people you want to include, with each separated by a space. Suppose you send regular mailings to a group of users named *barryp*, *jeffh*, *chrisk*, and *daver*. Rather than type their names each time, you can gather them into a mailing list under an alias called *teched* with the following command:

```
alias teched barryp jeffh chrisk daver
```

When you want to send a message to this group, you can simply enter the following command to reach all four of your correspondents:

```
mail teched
```

However, if you define an alias during a *mail* session, the *alias* list disappears as soon as you leave *mail*. You can make that list permanent, but to do so, you need to know something about the options that are available with *mail*.

## Creating a *mail* Options File

Like the rest of SCO UNIX, the *mail* system is flexible and can be molded to suit your needs. The *mail* system starts with certain defaults, but you can change them. To see the defaults, from within the *mail* system, enter the following command:

```
set
```

When you do, you'll see a screen full of information such as the following:

```
? set
DEAD = "/usr/danh/dead.letter"
MAILRC = "/usr/danh/.mailrc"
MBOX = "/usr/danh/mbox"
askcc
asksub
header
keep
mchron
save
? _
```

These are the options in effect during your *mail* session.

When you enter *mail*, the program looks at a file called */usr/lib/mail/mailrc*, the general options file for everyone on the system. It also checks for another file, called *.mailrc*, which is located in your home directory. These two files contain specific *mail* options—either *mail*'s default settings or those that you've requested. Your personal *.mailrc* file is the place to include all the options, such as system-wide aliases, that you would like to enjoy.

By the way, if you haven't used it, don't bother looking for *.mailrc* in your home directory. The dot in front of its name means that it's an invisible file—a file not normally displayed in directory listings. You can list invisible files with the command *ls -a* from the shell, but if you don't already know about that file it probably doesn't exist for you. And because it doesn't exist, you're using the default options in the general *mail* system file.

If you prefer other option settings, you can create your own *.mailrc* file. The command to turn on an option is *set*, and the command to turn off an option is *unset.* You can turn on or turn off several options on a single command line. To make changes to *.mailrc*, you can use *vi* to edit the file.

If you're in the *mail* system, precede the command to edit the *.mailrc* file with an exclamation point (!), which enables you to escape to the shell temporarily. From the shell, enter the following command:

```
vi .mailrc
```

When you are in the editor, you can set your own options. For example, you might include a *set* command and an *alias* command in a *.mailrc* file, as in the following:

```
alias teched barryp jeffh chrisk daver
set askcc nosave
```

Note that the alias doesn't require a leading *set* command.

Use *:x* to write the file on disk, quit *vi*, and then enter *mail.* (If you've used *vi* from within *mail*, you'll return to *mail* after you use *:x.* If you are already in *mail* when you create or make changes to *.mailrc*, however, you need to exit and then re-enter *mail* for the *.mailrc* options to take effect.)

In the preceding example, the first line you entered created an *alias* list. You can create as many as you like, provided that each list has a unique name and is entered on a separate line.

The second line sets two *mail* options. The first option, *askcc*, tells *mail* to prompt for the names of any people you want included in the *Cc:* field. After that option is set, any time you press Ctrl-D to send a message, you'll see a *Cc:* prompt asking for the names of people to whom you want to send copies of your message. You have to respond to this prompt before *mail* will send your message. Simply press Enter to leave the *Cc:* field blank. To eliminate the prompt, remove the *askcc* statement from your *.mailrc* file.

The second option in our example, *nosave*, can be a major convenience. As already mentioned, when you abort a message, *mail* saves it in a file called *dead.letter.* The *nosave* option tells the *mail* system to discard aborted messages rather than save them in the *dead.letter* file for possible future reference.

### Altering other options

As you saw in the *mail* options list, you can set quite a few other options in *mail*. For example, the *top* command is a default that shows the first six lines of the messages you specify. If you prefer to see fewer lines, you can use a command such as the following in your *.mailrc* file:

```
set toplines=3
```

Your new setting will cancel the default value.

Here's another example. If the thought of using Ctrl-D both to send messages and to log out makes you uncomfortable, you might include the following option:

```
set dot
```

After including this option, you could enter a period (.) instead of pressing Ctrl-D at the beginning of a new line to send a message.

Then, too, you could keep copies of all outgoing mail in a file of your choice, with a command like the following:

```
set record=my_mail
```

As we noted earlier, you can also use *set* to turn on or *unset* to turn off any option for the duration of your *mail* session by using the command while in command mode.

# COMMUNICATING WITH YOURSELF

As you've seen, you can send *mail* messages to yourself as a reminder of tasks you need to do. But there's a better way—especially if you have a tendency to forget to remind yourself. SCO UNIX has an excellent calendar system that can help you keep track of days, weeks, months, and years. Short of a system breakdown, SCO UNIX never forgets.

Before you see how to tie SCO UNIX into your time-critical responsibilities through *mail*, let's look at the calendar system itself.

## Accessing the Calendar

The simplest way to become acquainted with SCO UNIX's calendar is to enter the command *cal*, with the month and (optionally) year of your choice, as follows:

```
cal month year
```

You can specify the month either by number (1-12) or by typing enough letters to identify the month uniquely. (For example, enter *Jun* or *Jul* instead of *Ju*, which would be ambiguous.) If the year you want is the current year, you don't need to specify it. If the year is other than the current year, however, specify it as a four-digit number; *cal 87*, for example, would refer to the year 87, not the year 1987.

To see a calendar for the entire current year, type *cal* and the year. If you don't specify either a month or a year, SCO UNIX will show you a calendar for this month, last month, and next month. Here are a few interesting examples.

If the current year is 1992, enter the following:

```
cal dec
```

You'll see this:

```
$ cal dec
   December 1992
 S  M Tu  W Th  F  S
          1  2  3  4  5
 6  7  8  9 10 11 12
13 14 15 16 17 18 19
20 21 22 23 24 25 26
27 28 29 30 31

$ _
```

Now enter the following:

```
cal 7 1776
```

You'll find that the Fourth of July fell on a Thursday. Now enter this:

```
cal 9 1752
```

You'll find 11 days missing from the month of September. SCO UNIX's calendar is based on English chronology, and September 1752 is the year England changed from the Julian calendar to the Gregorian.

Finally, enter the following:

```
cal Jan 2000
```

You'll see that the next century will begin on a Saturday.

All of the responses to the different varieties of the *cal* command are based on information SCO UNIX obtains from your computer's clock, which actually records the current day and date. If you find that the displays are not accurate, check with your system administrator to see if the system clock needs to be reset. If the SCO UNIX computer does not have a clock, the time and date might have been entered incorrectly when the computer was last booted.

# Creating a Calendar File

Now that you know SCO UNIX has a calendar, you can create some reminders. You'll place them in a special text file named *calendar*. (The name of the file cannot be varied—it must be *calendar*.) You can create *calendar* with *vi* or *ed* or by redirecting output with the *cat* command, as we'll do here. At your shell prompt, enter the following command:

```
cat >> calendar
```

If you remember from Chapter 4, that command takes all further input from the keyboard and, in this case, directs it to the file called *calendar*. By using the double greater than symbols, you are ensuring that if such a file already exists, the input will be appended to the file rather than overwriting the information already in it. Of course, if the file doesn't exist, it will be opened to hold your input.

Let's assume that today is Saturday, December 16, 1989. Enter the following:

```
12/16 Call Sally to confirm scheduling meeting at 10:00 a.m.
December 16 Final Cost Analysis due
12/18 Pick up Tahoe tickets
12/17 Lunch with Support Group at 12:00 p.m.
```

Press Ctrl-D on a new line when you finish to close the *calendar* file.

Notice the format suggested for the file. Each reminder is on its own line, and each begins with the appropriate date. The reminders themselves need not be in chronological order, and the format for the date is flexible. As you can see, it can be in *mm/dd* or *mmm dd* format.

## Reminding yourself

With the calendar available and the *calendar* file in place, enter the following command:

```
calendar
```

Even though you have a data file named *calendar*, this command tells SCO UNIX to look for a program file with that name.

The *calendar* program is one of SCO UNIX's utilities. It refers to your *calendar* data file and, based on the information it finds there, shows you a list of all your reminders for today and tomorrow.

```
12/16 Call Sally to confirm scheduling meeting at 10:00 a.m.
December 16 Final Cost Analysis due
12/17 Lunch with Support Group at 12:00 p.m.
```

Note that the reminder for 12/18 is excluded here. It will, however, be included as of 12:00 a.m. on December 17. (SCO UNIX is also considerate of a five-day work week—on weekends, "tomorrow" extends to the following Monday.)

## Mailing a reminder

You can, as mentioned earlier, also use the *mail* system to jog your memory about upcoming events. All you need are the *calendar* data file and the discipline to update it faithfully.

Once each day, SCO UNIX scans the home directory of each user, looking for a *calendar* data file. If it finds one, it searches through the file for entries dated for that day or the following day. (SCO UNIX's search is actually an automatic version of the *calendar* command.)

If SCO UNIX finds entries for today or tomorrow (or for Saturday through Monday if it's Friday), SCO UNIX sends you a message containing the information it found. In your mailbox, you'll find that the message has been sent by *root*.

The one initial stumbling block to this automatic reminder service is that on the day you establish your *calendar* file, you might not receive any reminders, even if you've generated some for that and the following day because SCO UNIX has no way of telling whether you've created the file before or after it made its daily rounds looking for *calendar* files. If SCO UNIX has already checked your home directory, it will not send you reminders for today and tomorrow.

If this happens to you, be patient. SCO UNIX will begin to catch up on the following day, and on the day after you can count on its being reliable and up-to-date. After that, your auto-reminder should work flawlessly.

# 8

## Advanced File
## Techniques

Among its many utilities, SCO UNIX has commands that enable you to manipulate the character patterns stored in files in more ways than most operating systems offer. You've already seen some of those commands—the editing commands of *vi* and the simple file-handling commands described in Chapter 4. In this chapter, we'll look at more advanced data-manipulation and file-handling commands.

Let's start with a simple application: an electronic phone book.

## CREATING A PHONE BOOK

With SCO UNIX, your terminal, and a little bit of preparation, you can eliminate the need to resort to paper when you want to look up the phone number. You can create your own electronic phone book and let SCO UNIX help you find the phone number when you want to make a call.

To begin, use the *cat* command, as follows:

```
cat >> phonebook
```

Recall that the double greater than sign either appends information to an existing file or creates a new file if one doesn't already exist. You can thus use this command at any time to add entries to your phone book or to any other file.

Now make a few entries, such as the following ones:

```
Theresa Jugh (413) 555-5422
Fred Perez (808) 555-1233
Wil Ohmsford (617) 555-9866
Ira Fein (743) 555-3476
Deb Ziffle (808) 555-3443
```

When you've finished, press Ctrl-D on a new line to end the file.

> **NOTE:** *Be very careful when you use any form of output redirection in SCO UNIX. The double greater than sign does not overwrite a data file, but the single greater than sign does.*

Now you have some data. How do you manage it?

## Matching a Pattern

To search for a number in your phone file, you might use *cat* to display the entire contents of a file on the screen, but *cat* is not always the best command to use. With only five entries, you'd have no problem scanning the file for the number you want. But if you had a hundred entries, the first 76 would quickly scroll off the top of your screen.

You need a way to find a particular entry among all those in the file, and SCO UNIX has a command that's almost custom-made to do the job. It's the search command *grep*. The name *grep* comes from the search pattern *g/re/p*, which means "globally locate a pattern and print it." In a nutshell, *grep* searches for a particular pattern in every line of a set of files that you specify. The command takes the following form:

```
grep [-options] pattern filename(s)
```

For example, if you want the phone number for Wil Ohmsford, you can enter the following command:

```
grep Ohmsford phonebook
```

In a few seconds, *grep* replies *Wil Ohmsford (617) 555-9866*.

Because *grep* is a pattern-matching command, you supply the pattern you want it to search for (in this case, the word *Ohmsford*), and it searches through the file you've specified. If it finds a match, *grep* displays the entire line on the screen.

If you want to search for an exact match of the pattern you entered, surround it with single quotation marks and add blank spaces where appropriate. For example, if you'd like to search for occurrences of the name *Wil* but not *Will*, *William*, or other words that begin with *Wil*, you would enter the following at the shell prompt:

```
grep 'Wil ' phonebook
```

**146**

Note the initial capital letter *W* and the extra space after *l*. Given this command, *grep* would search for and display all occurrences of *Wil* followed by a blank space.

Note in the preceding example that *grep* is case sensitive. If you had typed *wil*, *grep* would not have found a match. You can make *grep* less selective by entering the command as follows:

```
grep -y wil phonebook
```

The *y* option causes *grep* to ignore case differences between the pattern and any potential matches contained in the file. With the *y* option included, you can enter the search word in any combination of uppercase and lowercase, including *wIl* or *wIL*.

## Adding variety

You can use two variations on *grep*—*egrep* and *fgrep*—for slightly different situations.

To search for more than one pattern of characters within a file, use *egrep*. For example, suppose you need to call both Fred Perez and Deb Ziffle. You can search for both numbers with the following single command:

```
egrep 'Perez¦Ziffle' phonebook
```

Notice that the pattern you're searching for is again enclosed in single quotation marks. Although not always necessary, the single quotation marks are used to avoid possible confusion and errors. However, if the pattern you're searching for consists of more than a single word, as it would if you specified *'Wil Ohmsford'*, the pattern must be enclosed in single quotation marks.

In *egrep*, the broken vertical bar (a solid vertical bar on some terminals) represents an either-or function, telling *egrep* to display any lines that contain the pattern *Perez*, the pattern *Ziffle*, or both.

The *fgrep* command searches for fixed patterns of text. We'll look at *fgrep* again in Chapter 9, but we can use *fgrep* here to match an entire line of text in our *phonebook* file. The *fgrep* command has an *x* option, which displays a match only when the entire line it finds matches the character pattern you specified. For example, if you entered the following, *fgrep* would display a match only if *Wil Ohmsford* were on a line by itself in the *phonebook* file:

```
fgrep -x 'Wil Ohmsford' phonebook
```

# CHANGING FILE ACCESS PERMISSIONS

In Chapter 3 you were introduced to the concept of file-access permissions. In any multiuser environment, controlling access to files is fundamental to maintaining order and offering privacy to individual users. Data (and program) files need protection from unauthorized change, and sensitive or confidential information needs to remain private. File-access permissions are SCO UNIX's method of controlling who can work on which files and with what degree of freedom.

For example, even though you now can have the convenience of keeping a phone book on the system, you might want to make it accessible to a larger group, such as your department. Recall that a SCO UNIX system might have three types of users (not counting the system administrator):

- You, the owner of your files and directories.

- Group users sharing a common set of files and directories. You are a member of at least one group. For example, you might be user *johnd* in the user group *accounts*.

- All other users of the system.

When your user account was created, the system administrator most likely left the various components of your account inaccessible to group and public users. To get a listing of these permissions, enter the *ls* command with the *l* (long) option at the shell prompt in the directory you'd like to check, as follows:

```
ls -l
```

As you might recall from Chapter 3, an *r* in the permissions field means a file is readable, a *w* means a file is writable, and an *x* means a file is executable.

You can alter permissions for individual files and directories with the *chmod* (change mode) command. Use the following format:

```
chmod   who permission_level   file/directory
```

The *who* option can be any of the following:

| | |
|---|---|
| a | All users. |
| g | The group. |
| o | Others, or the public. |
| u | The user or creator of the file or directory. |

The *permission_level* option can be any of the following:

| | |
|---|---|
| + | An operator that adds the specified permission. |
| − | An operator that removes the specified permission. |
| = | An operator that adds the specified permission but removes any others already in effect. |
| x | The permission to execute a file. |
| r | The permission to read a file. |
| w | The permission to write to a file. |

Now look at the permissions for your *phonebook* file by using the *l* option of the *ls* command, as follows:

```
ls -l phonebook
```

You'll see that the current permissions are *-rw-------*, meaning that you have read and write permission (*rw-*) but neither your group nor the public have any permission for access to your file.

To add the read permission to *phonebook* for both your group and the other users on the system, use the *chmod* command as follows:

```
chmod go+r phonebook
```

Read permission has now been added (*+r*) to the group and other users.

Notice the order in which the options are included. First you specify the group to which the change applies. Next you include the assignment operator that either adds or removes permissions. Finally you set the actual permission levels themselves. (Be careful not to include spaces between these three parts.)

You can set different levels for different people. If you later decide to add restricted phone numbers so that persons in your group can read and write to the phone book and anyone else on the SCO UNIX system will be denied access, use the following command line to add the new levels:

```
chmod g+w,o-r phonebook
```

Notice that you segregate the access permissions for the two sets by separating them with a comma.

# CREATING A DATABASE

Many people find that, in addition to a phone list, they often refer to lists of names and addresses. For that reason, you might want to consider creating a file called *adlist*, which contains 1000 names and addresses. A portion of it might look like this:

```
John Jonzz, 13 Waverly Pl, NYC NY 10033
Tim Brahms, 132 Amsterdam Ave, NYC NY 10143
Fred Jonzz, 16 Oxford Rd, Buffalo NY 13221
Ed Porter, 1232 Maiden Lane, NYC NY 10101
```

If you want to try these examples, enter these lines and name the file *adlist*.

To do any extensive file handling with a data file like this one, you must first give that file some structure based on how you intend to manipulate and use it. Our *adlist* file will serve as a sample database.

All databases generally have the following three elements in common:

| | |
|---|---|
| The file | Known by a descriptive title that indicates the entire contents of the database. |
| A record | A segment of the file, a record holds all of the facts associated with a single entry in the database. In *adlist*, each line is a record. |
| A field | A segment of a record. In a name and address file, one field could contain the name, another could contain the street address, another could contain the city, and so on. |

These three elements form a natural hierarchy: Fields are contained in records, which are contained in the file.

Although the distinction between a record and the file might be obvious, the exact nature of a field might not be, especially when the fields are stretched out along a single line. Under those conditions, the delimiters that you include set off one field from another.

In our example, you face two possibilities. You can choose either the spaces or the commas to show where one field of information ends and another begins. From a conceptual point of view, it might not seem to make much difference which you choose. But from a structural point of view, your choice of delimiter does make a difference. If you choose the space character, each record has eight fields, and the commas are part of the fields. If you declare that the comma is the delimiter, there are only three fields, and the spaces are contained within them.

From an operational point of view, the character you decide on will depend on how much control you want to exert over the record. Generally speaking, you have more flexibility when you break a record into more, rather than fewer, individual units of information. In our example, that would be the case if you chose the space as your delimiter. Luckily, the space also happens to be SCO UNIX's default delimiter.

## Retrieving Information

If you needed to extract from *adlist* all of the information about everyone who has a 10143 zip code, you could use the following simple *grep* command:

```
grep 10143 adlist
```

But remember, the whole of *adlist* is 1000 records long. The matches from your *grep* command, perhaps several hundred in all, could scroll off your screen. It would be better to redirect *grep*'s output to a new file with the following command:

```
grep 10143 adlist > zip10143
```

All of the output will now be sent to a file named *zip10143* for future reference.

But even though you've got the information you want, you don't need to leave the data in the new file, or even in the old one, in the same order in which it was created. Wouldn't it be more useful if the data were alphabetized?

# Sorting Information

SCO UNIX's *sort* utility can put the information in a file in alphabetic order. Perhaps you want to sort the original file by last name. If *adlist* were as short as our example, you could use the following form of the *sort* command:

```
sort adlist
```

After a few seconds, you'd see the following results:

```
$ sort adlist1
Ed Porter, 1232 Maiden Lane, NYC NY 10101
Fred Jonzz, 16 Oxford Rd, Buffalo NY 13221
John Jonzz, 13 Waverly Pl, NYC NY 10033
Tim Brahms, 132 Amsterdam Ave, NYC NY 10143
$ _
```

That isn't quite what you had in mind. The file is, indeed, sorted, but the records are sorted by *first* name. If you don't include any sorting options, the sort is made on the basis of the entire entry line, with the order determined by the first and following characters in each line. Some of the *sort* options that make this utility more flexible are as follows:

| | |
|---|---|
| b | Ignores leading blanks in field comparisons. |
| d | Sorts in dictionary order. Only letters, digits, and blanks are significant; punctuation marks and special symbols are not. |
| f | Interprets lowercase letters as uppercase. |
| i | Considers only the ASCII characters in the decimal range 32 through 126 in non-numeric comparisons. (This includes every visible character on standard English keyboards but excludes various foreign language, graphics, and control characters.) |
| n | Sorts numbers according to their arithmetic value not the ASCII value of each of their components. (This implies the *b* option.) |
| o | Precedes the name of the output file in which the sorted data are to be stored. This file can have the same name as one of the files being used for input. |
| r | Reverses the order of the sort (high to low). |
| t*character* | Recognizes *character* as the new delimiter. (Use this, for example, to change the delimiter from a space to a comma.) |
| c | Checks to determine if the file is already sorted according to any other options included in the command. |

151

+*number*–*number*    Begins the sort on the field number you specify. Fields are numbered from 0 (at the extreme left edge of the record). If the
–*number* option is included, the sort examines only the field between the + and – numbers; if a –*number* option is not included,
the sort examines the record to the end of the line.

Even though all those *sort* options might look bewildering, you have the tools you
need to sort a file with the results you want. For example, you can see that you need to
specify the field (with the + option) if you want to sort the records by the last names,
as follows:

```
sort +1 adlist
```

This command produces the following screen display:

```
$ sort +1 adlist
Tim Brahms, 132 Amsterdam Ave, NYC NY 10143
John Jonzz, 13 Waverly Pl, NYC NY 10033
Fred Jonzz, 16 Oxford Rd, Buffalo NY 13221
Ed Porter, 1232 Maiden Lane, NYC NY 10101
$ _
```

That's better, but it's still not correct. The last names were nicely alphabetized, but
*sort* didn't sort the entries for the Jonzz brothers in the order we want.

The first sorting field (the only one you specified) is called the key field. But SCO
UNIX also permits you to specify at least a secondary field to act as a "tiebreaker." You
want *sort* to examine first names so that the Jonzz brothers entries are correctly alphabetized, so try the following command:

```
sort +1 +0 adlist
```

Notice how the field-selection options work. The specification *+1* is actually the second
field, not the first, and *+0* is actually the first field. Remember that in specifying sort
fields you must begin counting from 0, not 1. Also notice that these field numbers are
separated by a blank space.

This time, you've told *sort* to begin by judging the contents of each line at the first
character in field one. When that's done, you've told it to resolve duplicate records by
using field 0 as the second criterion. The result looks like this:

```
$ sort +1 adlist
Tim Brahms, 132 Amsterdam Ave, NYC NY 10143
John Jonzz, 13 Waverly Pl, NYC NY 10033
Fred Jonzz, 16 Oxford Rd, Buffalo NY 13221
Ed Porter, 1232 Maiden Lane, NYC NY 10101
$ _
```

Even with the addition of the second field criterion, the sort is still incorrect. Why?

**152**

When you specified field 1, you gave *sort* the starting position within the record. You didn't restrict it to that field, so it used the entire line, beginning at the first character of field 1, as the basis for its initial sort. So the sort on field 1 was done on the following line fragments:

```
Jonzz, 13 Waverly Pl, NYC NY 10033
Jonzz, 16 Oxford Rd, Buffalo NY 13221
```

Notice that the lines are not identical. When *sort* compared the first *3* in John Jonzz's record and the *6* in Fred Jonzz's record, John Jonzz's took precedence. The *sort* command found no duplicate records, so the secondary field you specified became immaterial.

To narrow *sort*'s focus, change the line one more time to read as follows:

```
sort +1 -2 +0 adlist
```

This time, your addition of −2 tells *sort* to end its first sort at field 2—in other words, you've restricted the first sort only to field 1. This time, you'll see the correct display, with the names in proper order.

```
$ sort +1 -2 +0 adlist
Tim Brahms, 132 Amsterdam Ave, NYC NY 10143
Fred Jonzz, 16 Oxford Rd, Buffalo NY 13221
John Jonzz, 13 Waverly Pl, NYC NY 10033
Ed Porter, 1232 Maiden Lane, NYC NY 10101
$ _
```

Here's one more example. Suppose you wanted to sort on the zip code field, with secondary and tertiary sorts on the last names and the first names, respectively. The field numbers are as follows:

```
                   Fields

0     1      2       3      4    5  6     7
|     |      |       |      |    |  |     |
┌─┐ ┌─┐  ┌─┐ ┌──────┐ ┌──┐ ┌─┐┌─┐┌─┐ ┌───┐
Tim Brahms, 132 Amsterdam Ave, NYC NY 10143
```

The command would be as follows:

```
sort +7n +1 -2 +0 adlist
```

In more familiar words, the first option means "Sort on field 7, which is numeric." Notice that you can include a letter option in a field assignment. No limiting field is needed because this is at the end of the line. The rest of the options mean "Within identical groups of zip codes, sort again on field 1. If field 1 contains identical information as well, sort again starting on field 2 and continuing to the end of the line."

## Detailing Similarities Between Two Files

One problem with mailing lists is the possibility that you will include an entry in more than one file. For example, suppose you have two files, called *mlist1* and *mlist2*. The contents of the file *mlist1* look like this:

```
Ed Porter, 1236 Maiden Lane, NYC NY 10101
Frank Jeffries, 1717 Third Avenue, NYC NY 10101
Frank Jonzz, 26 Oxford Rd, Buffalo NY 13221
Fred Jonzz, 16 Oxford Rd, Buffalo NY 13221
Jim Jonzz, 13 Waverly Pl, NYC NY 10033
John Jonzz, 18 Waverly Pl, NYC NY 10033
Sam Winters, 1712 Third Avenue, NYC NY 10101
Ted Porter, 1232 Maiden Lane, NYC NY 10101
Tim Brahms, 132 Broadway, Albany NY 12143
Tom Brahms, 152 Broadway, Albany NY 12143
```

The contents of file *mlist2* look like this:

```
Ed Porter, 1232 Maiden Lane, NYC NY 10101
Frank Jeffries, 1717 Third Avenue, NYC NY 10101
Sam Winters, 1712 Third Avenue, NYC NY 10101
Ted Porter, 1232 Maiden Lane, NYC NY 10101
```

We're using small files as examples, so the similarities are obvious. SCO UNIX sorts large files rapidly too, and you will find that this command is very useful when you work with them.

To determine the names that are duplicated in these two files, you can use SCO UNIX's *comm* utility, which tells you the lines that are common to both files.

Unless you specify otherwise, *comm* displays three columns of information about the two files you specify. The first column displays all the lines that occur only in the first file, the second column displays all the lines that occur only in the second file, and the third column displays all the lines that are common to both files.

The lines in our sample files are long, however, so this three-column output is not very easy to read. The *comm* utility has three options—the numbers *1*, *2*, and *3*. If you include one or two of these numbers as arguments in your command, *comm* will suppress the corresponding column of output. You wouldn't want to include all three numbers—that would amount to suppressing all lines of output.

Before you use *comm*, however, you might need to do some preparatory work. The *comm* utility can't compare the lines in any files if the lines aren't sorted (beginning with the first field) in ASCII order, according to the first character in each line. Although *mlist1* and *mlist2* are already arranged in this order, to perform such a sort with another set of files, you would use the following commands:

```
sort -o mlist1 mlist1
```

and

```
sort -o mlist2 mlist2
```

The *o* option tells *sort* to send its output to the specified filename. Essentially you are telling *sort* to send its output back to the input file.

Note, however, that you face a potential danger. Using this form of the *sort* command will overwrite the original file. Overwrite your source file only if you're sure that what replaces it is correct. Other commands don't offer this option, and attempting to write the output of another command to the input file—with the redirection operators, for instance—will generally cause trouble.

After the two files are sorted correctly, enter the following command:

```
comm -12 mlist1 mlist2
```

You'll see the following response:

```
Frank Jeffries, 1717 Third Avenue, NYC NY 10101
Sam Winters, 1712 Third Avenue, NYC NY 10101
Ted Porter, 1232 Maiden Lane, NYC NY 10101
```

The option *-12* suppresses the display of lines that appear exclusively in either file. Only the lines that are common to both appear on the screen. If you wanted to redirect the output to a disk file named *mlistcomm*, you would use the following command:

```
comm -12 mlist1 mlist2 > mlistcomm
```

You might wonder at first why the record for Ed Porter in our example was not included in the list of common lines. If you check the lines, you'll see a difference in the last digit of the street number. So *comm* didn't display that line.

## Removing Duplicate Entries from a File

Now that you know which lines are in both files, you probably want to extract the duplicates. If you want to keep both lists separate and simply cull entries from one file or the other, you can use the output of the *comm* command as a reference while you edit the two files with *vi*.

The approach we'll look at now, however, is to remove all duplicate entries from one of the original two lists. To do this, use a SCO UNIX utility called *uniq*. (Like *comm*, *uniq* requires a certain amount of preprocessing.)

Let's assume the same starting point, the files *mlist1* and *mlist2*.

In order for *uniq* to work, duplicate lines must occur in the same file, and they must be adjacent to each other. To prepare such a file, you'll need to merge the source files and then sort the result.

To accomplish the merging and sorting (by last name) in one step, use the following command:

```
sort +1 -2 +0 -o mlistmerge mlist1 mlist2
```

You've produced the single output file *mlistmerge*. Use the *cat* command to view its contents. You'll see the following:

```
Tim Brahms, 132 Broadway, Albany NY 12143
Tom Brahms, 152 Broadway, Albany NY 12143
Frank Jeffries, 1717 Third Avenue, NYC NY 10101
Frank Jeffries, 1717 Third Avenue, NYC NY 10101
Frank Jonzz, 26 Oxford Rd, Buffalo NY 13221
Fred Jonzz, 16 Oxford Rd, Buffalo NY 13221
Jim Jonzz, 13 Waverly Pl, NYC NY 10033
John Jonzz, 18 Waverly Pl, NYC NY 10033
Ed Porter, 1232 Maiden Lane, NYC NY 10101
Ed Porter, 1236 Maiden Lane, NYC NY 10101
Ted Porter, 1232 Maiden Lane, NYC NY 10101
Ted Porter, 1232 Maiden Lane, NYC NY 10101
Sam Winters, 1712 Third Avenue, NYC NY 10101
Sam Winters, 1712 Third Avenue, NYC NY 10101
```

You're ready to use *uniq* to extract the records that are duplicated.

The *uniq* command has three options. They are as follows:

| | |
|---|---|
| u | Omits all occurrences of duplicated lines in the output (only the lines that are not repeated are printed). |
| d | Includes one copy of each duplicated line in the output (disregards all other lines). |
| c | Includes one copy of each line in the source file, preceding the line with a number showing how many times it is repeated in the file. |

Used without any options, *uniq* blends the *u* and *d* options: Its output includes all unique lines in the file plus one copy of any duplicated lines. The remaining duplicates are discarded.

Applied to *mlistmerge*, *uniq* without any options would produce a list containing the unique records from both *mlist1* and *mlist2*. The *c* option is purely statistical in value. What you really want is a file that contains only unique lines—only one copy of each line. For that you need to use *uniq* without any options, as in the following command:

```
uniq mlistmerge mlistuniq
```

This command processes the lines in *mlistmerge* and places the results in the file *mlistuniq*. Note that you do not need a greater than symbol to redirect the output from the screen to the disk file *mlistuniq* because *uniq* assumes redirection if you include a file name for the output.

Indeed, if you were to display the contents of *mlistuniq*, you would now see the desired results. Any lines that appeared more than once in the input file would be gone. You've successfully used the commands *comm* and *uniq* to create the file *mlistuniq* which forms a complete mailing list with no duplicate entries.

## Testing for unique fields

You can use the following two additional options with *uniq*:

| | |
|---|---|
| −*number* | Skips the first *number* fields in each line and begins the comparison at field *number*+1. |
| +*number* | Skips the first *number* characters at the beginning of the line or at the beginning of a field, if one is specified. |

In any of our mailing-list files, you could use these options to exclude more than one person with the same first or last name or from the same street address, city, state, or zip code. It also points out one problem that can arise in the absence of careful planning.

Look at the first and last lines of *mlistmerge*:

```
Tim Brahms, 132 Broadway, Albany NY 12143
Sam Winters, 1712 Third Avenue, NYC NY 10101
```

If you count the fields in each line, you'll notice that one contains seven, and the other contains eight. In Tim Brahms's entry, the street address occupies only two fields; in Sam Winters's, it occupies three.

Because of this inconsistency, you could not make a meaningful comparison of the information on the lines beyond the fourth field position unless you used the *sort* command with the *t* option to redefine the field separator. In that case, specifying the comma as the separator would let you process the file on the basis of lines containing three fields.

You have two other possible solutions. The first is to plan ahead or edit your file to be certain that all lines have the same number of fields. The second is to combine fields.

For example, *Third Avenue* could be rewritten as *Third_Avenue* to standardize the lines at seven fields.

With the latter alternative, of course, you would want to remove the underline when it came time to print mailing labels. Actually, you would want to do more than that, so let's move on to see about readjusting the output file.

# EDITING A FILE WITH *sed*

As mentioned earlier, one of the reasons to extract information of this kind is to create a mailing list for printing labels. Unfortunately, mailing addresses, when printed, are vertically oriented, not horizontally oriented as the addresses in the mailing list are.

To convert the result of a *grep* or a *sort* routine from horizontal to vertical orientation, you need to adjust the shape of the file. You need to strip out all of the commas and separate each of the three fields by putting it on its own line. Furthermore, a standard one-inch-high label is six printed lines tall. The label file contains only three fields, so you need to pad it with three additional lines. But first, let's look at the editing you'd need to do.

If you had 100 records to edit (not to mention the original 1000 for *adlist*), you would be faced with a substantial editing session. You would have to replace each occurrence of a comma and a space with one carriage return (called a *newline* character in UNIX terminology), and you would have to replace the end of each line with a newline character.

You could choose either *vi* or *ed* and use its global find-and-replace commands. But inserting a carriage return with *vi* or *ed* is not as easy as replacing *abc* with *xyz* because both editors interpret a carriage return to mean "Do what I just typed on this line."

You have another alternative, though. It's called *sed*, the SCO UNIX stream editor. Generally, you can use *sed* to perform editing functions on data files that are too large to fit into memory with *vi* or *ed*. But *sed* has some excellent features that you can use with a file of any size.

## Creating a Script

In the next chapter, you'll be introduced to a special type of text file called a *shell script*, which contains a series of commands that you can use in place of keyboard input to control various aspects of SCO UNIX's operation. (If you're familiar with macros or batch files, you'll find that scripts are similar in function.)

Scripts are not confined solely to shell operations, though. At the lowest level, scripts are simply lines of text. Instead of recording dialogue in a play, however, scripts in SCO UNIX record actions and responses, and instead of being interpreted by actors, these scripts are interpreted by SCO UNIX.

Let's create a script based on the editing commands we need to convert *adlist* into a usable mailing list.

Use the following command to start *vi* and have it accept the name *label* for the script file you'll create:

```
vi label
```

When *vi* is on the screen, you can begin to insert the contents of the script. Let's examine the procedure for adjusting *adlist* one step at a time.

First, for all lines in the file you're processing, you want a carriage return to replace every occurrence of a comma followed by a space. That replacement requires a global command. Use the *i* command to enter insert mode, and type the following without pressing Enter:

```
1,$s
```

Earlier in this book, you learned that *1,$* is a shorthand means of indicating the range of all lines in a file. The starting line is 1, and the wildcard $ refers to the last line, no matter what its number. The *s* you typed stands for substitute.

Substituting requires two parameters, the text you want to replace and the text you want in its place. The general format is as follows:

```
ranges/look_for/replace_with/global_parameter
```

Note the slashes denoting the beginning and end of each parameter. Continue your *vi* line, then, by adding the text you want to replace. The line looks like this:

```
1,$s/, /
```

But how do you indicate a carriage return? A carriage return is a special character, and entering one would only move the cursor down to the next line in the file.

To include a special character in a line, you must precede it with the escape character, the backslash (\). Add the escape character to your current line, and then press Enter. Fill in the new line that you're on so that both lines look like this:

```
1,$s/, /\
/g
```

You've just done what you set out to do. When *sed* reads this script, it will accept the first three characters as a range command. It will also understand that the comma and space between the first and second slashes are the values you want replaced. When *sed* comes to the escape character, the backslash will tell SCO UNIX to interpret the next character, the carriage return, literally. Because the carriage return is followed by the third slash, *sed* will accept the carriage return as the character to be substituted for the comma and space. The *g* ending the line makes the command global, so the command will affect every occurrence of comma and space on each line, not only the first.

Because this is a script that the operating system reads, you have literally, with a one-line command, finessed a change that would be awkward if attempted manually from within the editor.

All that remains now is to space the label entries vertically on the printed copy. Because a standard one-inch-high label has six lines, but each entry has only three lines, you need to add three lines to each entry. If you put all three lines at the end of each entry, the text would be printed at the top of each standard label, and all the blank lines would be at the bottom. We can move the text towards the center by putting one line at the start of each entry and two lines at the end. The question is how to tell *sed* where the beginning and the end of a line are.

Fortunately, two characters have special meaning in the *look_for* section of the command: the caret (∧) and the dollar sign ($). The caret matches the beginning of a line, and the dollar sign matches the end of a line. To finish the script, we need to find the beginning of each entry and insert a newline, and then we need to match the end of each entry and insert two newlines. The finished script looks like this:

```
1,$s/, /\
/g
1,$s/^/\
/
1,$s/$/\
\
/
```

You don't need to include the *g* for a global search at the end of the commands that look for the beginning or the end of a line because each line has only one beginning and one ending. The caret and dollar sign have special meaning only in the *look_for* section. In the *replace_with* section, they are not special characters; they stand for themselves. If the caret and dollar sign have special meanings in the *look_for* section, how then do you look for caret or dollar sign characters? The answer is that you precede them with the escape character (\). To look for a caret character (rather than the start of a line), you type \∧. To look for a dollar sign (rather than the end of a line), you use \$.

Now that you've finished the script, press the Escape key to exit insert mode, and then use *:x* to write the file on disk and quit *vi.*

For your future reference, note that the script commands used here were taken directly from the commands available with *ed.* Although we haven't covered that line editor in much detail, refer to Chapter 4 and your *SCO UNIX User's Reference* manual for more information.

# Using *sed* to Create a Script

The *sed* editing utility has the following three options:

n   Suppresses output. This option can be used to test an editing script without sending the results to the screen or to a file.

e   Precedes script instructions that are written into the command line instead of read from a separate file.

f   Precedes the name of the file from which *sed* should read its script (editing commands).

Now that the entire cast is assembled, you can start the production. Use the following command to tell *sed* to read the script file called *label*, use it to process the data file called *adlist*, and redirect the output to a file called *labels*:

```
sed -f label adlist > labels
```

If you look at *labels* with *vi*, the results should be in this form:

```
John Jonzz
13 Waverly Pl
NYC NY 10033




Tim Brahms
132 Amsterdam Ave
NYC NY 10143




Fred Jonzz
16 Oxford Rd
Buffalo NY 13221




Ed Porter
1232 Maiden Lane
NYC NY 10101
```

As your script directed, each group of three lines has one blank line before the start of each original line and two blank lines after the end of each original line. All you'd need to do now is to set up your line printer with label stock and use the *lp* command to send the file off for printing. Knowing the procedure, you could now include instructions in your script that would substitute a space for any underline characters you've used to even out the number of fields in your records.

Finally, one of the nicest features of *sed* is its ability to process several files at the same time. If, for example, you had extracted lists for different zip codes (or for some other criterion), you could use a command such as the following to process all of the files and send the output into the file called *labels*:

```
sed -f label file1 file2 file3 > labels
```

# PREVIEWING PRINTED OUTPUT

At the end of Chapter 7, we discussed printing a document locally. This is an ideal solution for printing labels because you don't need to halt other printing within your SCO UNIX system, change the paper to label forms, and then change back again after your labels are printed.

For printing locally, you can use a simple *cat* command to preview a document before printing. But *cat* doesn't have to be the only way you print a document to the screen. The SCO UNIX *pr* utility and a host of related options can emulate paper printing on the screen. The *pr* command line format is as follows:

```
pr [-options] filenames
```

Some of the *pr* options appear by function in the following table:

| Page-setup options | |
|---|---|
| w*number* | Sets the line width to *number* characters when the document contains multicolumn output. (The default is 72.) |
| o*number* | Sets the page offset to *number* character positions. (The default is 0.) |
| l*number* (lowercase L) | Sets the page length to *number* lines. (The default is 66.) |

| Output-formatting options | |
|---|---|
| +*number* | Starts printing at page *number*. (The default is 1.) |
| d | Double-spaces printing. |
| p | Pauses and beeps before displaying the next page and waits for a carriage return before continuing. |
| f | Uses a form feed instead of a series of line feeds to advance to the next page and pauses before beginning the first page. This feature is handy if you're using a terminal with paper output instead of a video screen or if you are printing locally. |

*(continued)*

*continued*

### Output-formatting options

| | |
|---|---|
| h | Uses the next argument as the output page header. The defaults are the date, filename, and page number. |
| n | Prints each line in the file with an accompanying line number. This feature is used to its best advantage when you are printing programming source code. |

### Multiple-column printing options

| | |
|---|---|
| *number* | Formats printing into *number* columns. (See the *Command Reference* manual's descriptions of options *e* and *i*, as well.) |
| a | Prints multicolumn output across the page. This option is not the same as *–number*, it prints line 1 to the left, line 2 to the right, line 3 to the left, and so on. It's not suitable for all output. |
| m | Merges and prints all files, one per column. Use of this option negates the effects of the *–number* and *–a* options. |
| t | Suppresses the default five-line header and five-line footer for the top and bottom of each output page. |

Applying this information to the *labels* file you created with *sed*, you can preview the output on the screen with the following command line:

```
pr -2 -124 -tp labels
```

The *pr* command prints the contents of the file in two-column format on a 24-line page (the length of your screen) with no header or footer and a pause between pages. Because you've included a pause, *pr* causes your terminal to beep and wait for you to press Enter before each page, including the first, is printed. The output will look like this:

```
$ pr -2 -124 -tp labels


John Jonzz            Fred Jonzz
13 Waverly Pl         16 Oxford Rd
NYC NY 10033          Buffalo NY 13221



Tim Brahms            Ed Porter
132 Amsterdam Ave     1232 Maiden Lane
NYC NY 10143          NYC NY 10101

$ _
```

After you've previewed the printing on the screen for accuracy, you can make any necessary changes (in page length, for example) to suit your label paper. If you have a label sheet that is more than two columns wide, you can increase the column value.

Finally, you can use whatever procedures are required in order to send the file to your local printer.

# DEALING WITH MS-DOS FILES

If you are moving to SCO UNIX from an MS-DOS environment, you'll probably want to move some of your data files with you. You can move only text (unformatted, or ASCII) files. That restriction isn't as great as it might seem, however. Many programs, including Microsoft Multiplan and Microsoft Word, can produce text output.

You can use any of eight commands to look at, modify, and transfer MS-DOS files to SCO UNIX. But before we discuss the commands, let's cover three important facts.

## Accessing MS-DOS Disks

First and foremost, if you want to handle files on MS-DOS disks, you must have an MS-DOS disk mounted in one of your SCO UNIX computer's floppy disk drives. SCO UNIX also allows you to access the hard disk's MS-DOS partition (if you have one) from SCO UNIX. Only one person at a time can access an MS-DOS disk. If more try, only one will succeed and the others will see a message from SCO UNIX similar to this:

```
$ dosls a:/admin
dosls: can't open /dev/fd148ds9
$ _
```

## Accessing MS-DOS Disk Drives

During the initial phase of your transition from MS-DOS to SCO UNIX, you'll probably remain more familiar with MS-DOS drive names than with their SCO UNIX counterparts. To assist you, SCO UNIX allows you to address an MS-DOS disk with MS-DOS drive names. You can enter the drive names in uppercase or lowercase.

If your system has only a single floppy disk drive, either A: or X: is the drive name. In dual floppy disk drive systems, the leftmost or top drive usually has the A: or X: designation, and the rightmost or bottom drive has the B: or Y: designation.

If your hard disk has an MS-DOS partition in addition to the SCO UNIX partition, you can access it by giving the name *C:* to the partition. If your SCO UNIX system has another disk drive, you can access the MS-DOS partition of that device by giving the name *D:* to the drive. You will find that accessing these partitions from SCO UNIX is useful, especially if you are the only user on your SCO UNIX system. For information on installing an MS-DOS partition, see Chapter 13.

## Converting MS-DOS Files

Typically, MS-DOS uses a combination of a carriage return and a line feed as its end-of-line character. SCO UNIX uses only a line feed. When you use the *doscat* and *doscp* commands (which we'll cover in a moment) to transfer files, the conversion from one sequence for line endings to the other occurs automatically. To suppress the removal of the carriage-return character (or to suppress its addition if the conversion is from SCO UNIX to MS-DOS), include the *r* option in the two file-transfer commands.

## The MS-DOS Commands

The following eight SCO UNIX commands handle MS-DOS text files:

| | |
|---|---|
| doscat -r *drive_name:filename* | Prints the contents of an MS-DOS file to the screen. It's similar to the MS-DOS *type* command. |
| doscp -r *drive_name:filename UNIXfilename* | Copies the specified file from an MS-DOS disk onto an SCO UNIX disk, giving the file the specified UNIX filename. |
| doscp -r *drive_name:filename UNIXdirectory* | Copies the specified file from an MS-DOS disk onto an SCO UNIX disk and into the directory that is specified. |
| dosdir *drive_name:MS-DOSdirectory* | Lists the contents of an MS-DOS disk's directory in standard MS-DOS format. The argument can be a specific subdirectory on the disk or only the drive name. |
| dosls *drive_name:MS-DOSdirectory* | Lists the contents of an MS-DOS disk's directory in SCO UNIX format, with the filenames and no detail. The argument can be a specific subdirectory on the MS-DOS disk or it can be only the drive name. |
| dosmkdir *drive_name:MS-DOSdirectory* | Creates an MS-DOS directory on the specified MS-DOS disk. |
| dosrmdir *drive_name:MS-DOSdirectory* | Removes the specified MS-DOS directory from an MS-DOS disk. |
| dosrm *drive_name:filename* | Removes the specified MS-DOS file from an MS-DOS disk. |

For example, if you want to copy a file named *dbase10.txt* from an MS-DOS disk in the first drive of your computer, use the following command:

```
doscp x:dbase10.txt dbase10.txt
```

This command copies the file into your current working directory with the same name it had on the MS-DOS disk.

You can also redirect the screen output from *doscat*, *dosdir*, and *dosls* commands into an SCO UNIX disk file just as you could from any SCO UNIX command, but it's preferable simply to copy the text files you want into your SCO UNIX directory and use the MS-DOS disk for as short a time as possible.

# 9

# The Bourne Shell

As mentioned in Chapter 2, SCO UNIX's shells are command interpreters. They take input, examine it, and then determine how it should be handled and where it belongs.

Because the Bourne shell is the role model for the C shell, the concepts and descriptions in this chapter are valid for the C shell as well. The chapter on the C shell (Chapter 10) won't repeat any of the information here, so regardless of which shell you are assigned, this chapter is the place to begin.

We'll set out by looking at some preliminary information.

## COMPOUNDING SIMPLE SHELL COMMANDS

Whenever you sit down at the keyboard and enter a command, you initiate a process. A simple example is using the *who* command to discover which users are currently on the system. When you use this command, SCO UNIX returns a list of users presently logged in. You can then look through the list to find out whether a certain user is logged in.

Altogether, those actions result in the following series of processes:

■ One shell process—*who*.

■ Followed by a user process—scanning the list of users.

But you can turn some of your actions over to the shell and let it decide whether the person you're looking for is logged in, saving time and effort.

## Using What You Know

You already know how to have SCO UNIX look for the person you want to find. Suppose you're looking for the user named *danh*. You could enter the following two SCO UNIX commands:

```
who > loglist
grep danh loglist
```

If you want to try this yourself, substitute your user name for *danh*.

The first command line takes the output of the *who* command and redirects it into a file named *loglist*. Then the *grep* command takes the value *danh* and scans through the file you specified (*loglist*). If *grep* finds the value for which it's searching, it displays the corresponding line of text from *loglist* on your screen. Although this procedure relieves you of the need to scan the screen list yourself, SCO UNIX offers a shorter way to accomplish the same result—without creating an unnecessary disk file that, because you have no more use for it, would be a waste of the system's storage space.

## Laying a Pipeline

The redirection you used in the first of the preceding two commands actually points to a shorter method. In the first command, you redirected the output from one device (the screen) to another (the disk file). In the second command, you told *grep* to scan the redirected output for the value *danh*. The procedure works, but it's roundabout. Instead, you can skip the disk-file stage and redirect the output of the *who* command directly to the *grep* command.

The word "redirect" describes what happens, but SCO UNIX has another term for rerouting output and input: piping. Because you control the flow of a process, your piping creates a pipeline.

In the preceding example, you piped output to the hard disk by using the greater than symbol (>). When you practiced with the *mail* system in Chapter 7, you used another form of redirection, the less than sign (<), to take input *from* a file.

To pipe the output of one process directly as the input to another, you use either a solid vertical bar (|) or a broken vertical bar (¦). Which symbol you use depends on the terminal you are working from; either version is interpreted by the shell as the symbol for piping.

By way of example, let's create a compound command by using a pipeline to send the output of one command (*who*) as input to the other (*grep*). Enter the following command, substituting your own user name:

```
who ¦ grep user_name
```

Normally, two parameters follow a *grep* command. The first (your user name in this example) is the pattern to be matched. The second, which you've omitted here, is the file where you want SCO UNIX to search for the pattern. This is where the pipeline enters the picture.

By using the vertical bar in your command, you pipe the output from *who* into *grep*'s missing second parameter instead of to the screen. As a result, you see only the line from the list that refers to the user you specified instead of seeing the list of all users currently logged in. (If the person is not currently logged in, you see no response at all.)

# Piping to the Printer

In Chapter 8, you saw how to turn a mailing list into labels. To create the final output for the labels from the mailing list, you needed to complete the following steps:

1. Sort the list.
2. Find the duplicate entries.
3. Merge and sort the files.
4. Eliminate the duplicate entries.
5. Transform single-line list entries into multiple-line label entries.
6. Transform the single-column list of addresses into a multiple-column list of label entries.
7. Print the labels.

At every step, you had to create a new file. Each file was the output from the previous command and became the input for the next command. That sounds like a perfect candidate for a pipeline. Let's take a look at this pipeline.

First you need to gather all the mailing lists into one file by using the *cat* command as follows:

```
cat mlist1 mlist2 > output_file
```

Then you need to sort all the entries in the output file. To sort the entries, replace the redirection symbol with the pipe character and add the *sort* command as follows:

```
cat mlist1 mlist2 | sort +1 -2 +0 > output_file
```

This sorts the entries and puts duplicate entries together.

Continue replacing the redirection symbol and *output_file* with the pipe symbol for each step in the process of converting the mailing list to labels. When you complete the process, your command will look like this:

```
cat mlist1 mlist2 | sort +1 -2 +0 | uniq -u | sed -f label | pr -2 -t | lp -c
```

In this command line, the *pr* command prints the labels in two columns with no header or footer on the page. (Replace the *-2* option with the number of columns that is appropriate for your sheets of labels. If you want to see the results on your terminal, use the command *pr -2 -l24 -tp* and omit ¦ *lp -c.*) The *-c* option makes a copy of the temporary file that the pipe command creates. Without the *-c* option, the pipe command would erase the temporary file, leaving you without a copy.

This command line might be too long to appear on one line on your screen. However, the Bourne shell lets you continue a single command on more than one line by typing the escape character (\) and pressing Enter when you reach the edge of the screen. When you do, the Bourne shell displays its secondary prompt, the greater than sign (>), on the next line. This prompt symbol indicates that you are continuing a command, and your screen looks like this:

```
$ cat mlist1 mlist2 ¦ sort +1 -2 +0 ¦ uniq -u ¦ \
> sed -f label ¦ pr -2 -t ¦ lp -c
```

A bigger problem is the possibility of making a typing error every time you need to type the command. You can avoid this problem by creating a shell script.

# CREATING A SHELL SCRIPT

As you saw in the preceding chapter, SCO UNIX offers a way around the task of retyping commands every time you need to use them: executable text files called shell scripts.

To create a shell script to carry out the commands in our example, start by entering the following at the $ shell prompt:

```
vi mailmergepr
```

This command starts *vi* and reserves *mailmergepr* as the filename. Use the *i* command to enter insert mode and then enter these lines into the file:

```
cat mlist1 mlist2 ¦ sort +1 -2 +0 ¦ uniq -u ¦ \
sed -f label ¦ pr -2 -t ¦ lp -c
```

After you press Enter, press Escape to exit the edit mode. Enter *:x* to write the file on disk and to quit *vi.*

Simply typing the file's name, as you would to start an SCO UNIX utility program, would produce the following somewhat misleading response:

```
$ mailmergepr
mailmergepr: execute permission denied
$ _
```

The shell is telling you that it found a file called *mailmergepr* but that the file's permissions were not set to make it executable. Even though you intend *mailmergepr* to be a shell script, SCO UNIX doesn't know that's what you intend. At present, *mailmergepr* doesn't have the correct permissions to tell the shell to execute it.

One way to make your intentions clear to SCO UNIX is to invoke an SCO UNIX subshell with the command *sh* followed by the name of the text file, as follows:

```
sh mailmergepr
```

When you do this, the shell assumes that you specified a text file containing executable commands, and it responds by spawning another version—a subshell—of itself. This subshell is a process, just as *who* and *ls* are processes, and the subshell's job is to read the lines in the specified file and execute them to their completion. When all the commands (and additional processes) the subshell has created are complete, the subshell itself will terminate.

# Using Options with the Shell Command

Several options are available to the shell that alter the way it reacts. For example, to test the shell procedure you just developed without actually executing the shell instructions, you could use the following command:

```
sh -nv mailmergepr
```

The *n* (no execute) option causes the shell to check each line in the process for syntax errors without actually executing any of the commands. That's possible because the shell reads and interprets the entire script before it begins to act on the individual lines.

The *v* (verbose) option in the command causes each line of your script to be displayed on the screen as it's evaluated. Without the *v* option, any error would appear only as a line number and a terse explanation of the mistake. With the *v* option in effect, both the line and a fuller explanation appear on the screen (if you've also selected the *n* option).

Using the *v* option also lets you double-check your work for typographical errors in messages you want echoed to the screen as the shell processes the file.

An additional option you can use is the *x* option. When you include this option, each script command and its arguments is displayed on the screen, preceded by a + symbol, as it is executed. In our example, the results would look like this:

```
$ sh -x mailmergepr
+ cat mlist1 mlist2
+ sort +1 -2 +0
+ uniq -u
+ sed -f label
+ pr -2 -t
+ lp  -c
$ _
```

You can also insert these options *within* the script with the following format:

```
set -options
```

Place this command on its own line anywhere in the script that you want it to take effect. When you enter the following command, the script process is based on the options you've included from the point in the file at which you included them.

```
sh script_name
```

If at some point you'd like an option turned off, use the following format on a new line in the script:

```
set +option
```

# CREATING AN EXECUTABLE SHELL SCRIPT

Using the *sh* command is fine for files, such as our sample, that you will use sporadically, and it's ideal when you're testing a new script. But if you create shell scripts that you'll use every day, you can alter the script files themselves to make their execution even simpler than entering the *sh* command.

To make this change, let's first find out what is preventing *mailmergepr* from being an executable file. Request a long directory listing of *mailmergepr* by using the following command:

```
ls -l mailmergepr
```

Unless they've been changed, the file's permissions fields will look like this:

```
-rw-------
```

The permissions indicated are read (*r*) and write (*w*) for yourself and no access for everyone else. But the *x* that would indicate that this file is executable isn't present. As you saw in the previous chapter, you can easily change this situation. Enter the following command:

```
chmod u+x mailmergepr
```

Look at the file's permissions field again. This time, it appears as follows:

```
-rwx------
```

As simply as that, you have made a text file executable. When you want to run the file, enter its name or the appropriate path and name if you're in a different directory.

# SHELL SCRIPT ARGUMENTS

The sample shell script is easy to run, but it's still not very useful because it lets you merge, sort, and make labels from only two files: *mlist1* and *mlist2*. You might want to combine several mailing lists to create labels for mailing to a variety of target groups. The shell gives you a simple way to use different files.

Most commands in a shell script can accept an argument specified as one of two types: literal or variable. A literal argument is the name of something that actually exists. The filename *mlist1*, for example, is a literal argument because it refers to *mlist1* by its literal name. A variable, on the other hand, might be a word such as *filename*, which stands for any one of a set of actual filenames. A variable represents something real but is not a real entity. Let's examine how assigning literal values to variables works.

The shell maintains a list of all the arguments on the command line. This built-in argument list is also available to shell scripts. Each argument in the list has a number that corresponds to its position on the command line. The first argument following the command is number 1, as you might expect. You specify it in the shell script as *$1*. In this case, the dollar sign indicates a variable. You specify the second argument as *$2*, the third argument as *$3*, and so on.

To specify as many as nine variable arguments for the sample shell script, you would use the following command:

```
cat $1 $2 $3 $4 $5 $6 $7 $8 $9 : sort +1 -2 +0 : uniq -u : \
```

Now you can enter the following command on the command line:

```
mailmergepr mlist1 mlist2 mlist3 mlist4 mlist5 mlist6 mlist7 mlist8 mlist9
```

If you have fewer than nine files, the shell assigns no value to the variables that don't have corresponding filenames, and it doesn't create labels for them. This format can handle as many as nine files, but it doesn't work with 10 files because the shell interprets *$10* as *$1* followed by a *0*. To represent 10 or more files, you need to use a variable similar to the wildcards that you used in Chapter 3 to list every file in a directory. The variable *$\** stands for all the arguments. When the shell encounters *$\**, it replaces the variable with all the arguments it finds on the command line.

To represent 10 or more files in the sample script, you'd enter the following command:

```
cat $* : sort +1 -2 +0 : uniq -u : \
```

With this change, you can type as many arguments on the command line as you want, including the indefinite number of arguments created by using filenames with wildcards, such as *mlist\**.

# LOOPING BY USING VARIABLES

You've learned to create shell scripts for automatic command execution, but you can do still more. So far, you've simply waited while the script merged, sorted, edited, and printed or displayed the labels. But while you're waiting, you might be wondering whether the shell script is really doing anything or whether an error in its organization has sent it off into some computer limbo somewhere. You can remedy that uncertainty by having the shell script report on its progress.

Imagine that each day you must create labels for separate projects from a number of different mailing lists without merging the lists. The names of the files you use to create the lists change each day, but you always have more than one file. This type of task is repetitive—not so much because you need to do it frequently, but because you must repeat the procedure to complete the task.

If you were a programmer, you might create a routine called a *for* loop to accomplish this task. The general format in the Bourne shell is as follows:

*for* every element in a list
    *do*
          -select the next item
          -process the list item as specified
  *done*

To use such a *for...next* loop in your list of files to be printed, you must move the file-names sequentially from the list into the command. These names are the arguments for the command.

In the previous shell script, you saw the variables that the shell creates and maintains. Those variables (*$1, $2, $3,* and so on) and the variable that represents all the arguments (*$\**) are useful when you need to process all the arguments at one time, as when you merged several files into one and then processed the combined file. But the variables aren't useful when a shell script repeatedly needs to process a single file at a time. In this case, you want to be able to use one variable in all the commands in your shell script but change the variable's value from one argument to the next as the shell script repeats the commands in the *for* loop. The shell allows you to choose a variable name. In the *for* loop, the shell repeatedly sets the value of the variable to the next argument on the command line.

To create a shell script for our example, enter the following command at the $ shell prompt to start *vi*:

```
vi maillistpr
```

Use the *i* command to enter insert mode, and then enter the following lines into the file:

```
for filename
    do echo "Now processing $filename"
    sort +1 -2 +0 $filename : sed -f label : pr -2 -t : lp -c
done
```

When you've entered the last line, press Escape to exit the edit mode. Use the *:x* command to write the file and to quit *vi*. Now use the following command to change *maillistpr* into an executable shell script:

```
chmod u+x maillistpr
```

As you can see, the Bourne shell's version of a *for* loop consists of three keywords: *for*, *do*, and *done*.

The *for* keyword sets up the list of arguments—in this case, represented by the variable *filename*. (The construction *for variable* is a shorthand notation for *for variable in $\**. In other words, the shell looks at all the arguments on the command line in turn.) The *do* keyword begins the list of commands that you want applied while you're cycling through the loop. Our example has the following two *do* commands:

- The words *echo "Now processing $filename"* echo on the screen the name of the file that's being processed. The $ sign preceding *filename* tells the *echo* command that *filename* is a variable and should not be printed literally. The *echo* line isn't essential. It's included simply to keep you informed as each file is formatted and then printed.

- The command *sort +1 -2 +0 $filename : sed -f label : pr -2 -t : lp -c* sorts and edits the file and pipes the output to the line printer without first creating an intermediate file.

The *done* keyword ends the loop, but not until the commands in the *for* loop have processed the last item in your list. Between the *sort* command and *done*, the shell knows it must go back (loop) to the top of the list and look for another item.

Where does the list come from? It comes from you. You enter it as a series of arguments when you run the shell script. Let's assume you need to process the files *mlist1*, *mlist2*, and *mlist3*. After you create an executable script, you can use the following command:

```
maillistpr mlist1 mlist2 mlist3
```

The text of the actual script looks like this:

```
for  filename
    do echo "Now processing $filename"
    sort +1 -2 +0 $filename: sed -f label : pr -2 -t : lp -c
done
```

The first time through the loop, the shell "sees" it as follows:

```
for mlist1 mlist2 mlist3
     do echo "Now processing mlist1 "
     sort +1 -2 +0 mlist1 : sed -f label : pr -2 -t : lp -c
     (mlist2 and mlist3 remaining)
done
```

Changes are italicized for emphasis. The second time, your script becomes this:

```
for mlist1 mlist2 mlist3
     do echo "Now processing mlist2 "
     sort +1 -2 +0 mlist2 : sed -f label : pr -2 -t : lp -c
     (mlist3 remaining)
done
```

And finally, on the third pass, it becomes this:

```
for mlist1 mlist2 mlist3
     do echo "Now processing mlist3 "
     sort +1 -2 +0 mlist3 : sed -f label : pr -2 -t : lp -c
     (no more files remaining)
done
```

After the third pass, the process ends.

The shell counted the number of arguments you entered (three filenames) and processed the loop an equal number of times, substituting each successive filename in the argument list for the variable.

## Creating Filenames from Variables

You might have a number of different mailing lists targeted for specific purposes, but in some cases, you might want to construct a new mailing list to target specific geographic areas. The zip codes contain the geographic information, but you need to extract the entries and then combine them in a separate file.

To extract the entries for one zip code from a number of lists and combine the entries into one file, use *vi ziplist* to create the following script:

```
zip=$1
shift
for filename
     do echo "Now extracting $zip addresses from $filename"
     grep $zip $filename >> zips.$zip
done
```

After you have created the script, you can make it executable by using the *chmod* command.

**176**

When you run this script, you enter a command line similar to this:

```
ziplist zipcode mailinglist1 mailinglist2 mailinglist3 ...
```

The order of the arguments is important. The first argument after the script name must be the zip code that you want to extract. The shell script uses this argument both as an argument for the *grep* command and as a part of the output filename for these zip codes. The remaining arguments are filenames from which you want to extract addresses with the specified zip code.

The first line of the script sets the variable *zip* to the value of the first argument on the command line. If the first argument were *10101*, *$zip* would have the value *10101*. The next line, *shift*, shifts the arguments one position to the left in the list: 9 becomes 8, 8 becomes 7, and so on. What happens to argument 1? It disappears from the list. After the *shift* command, the argument list has the same entries as if you had typed the following:

```
ziplist mailinglist1 mailinglist2 mailinglist3 ...
```

The *for* loop then uses that list to substitute for the value of the variable *$filename* as it processes the loop.

When you execute the shell script, the script first displays a message on your screen telling you which zip code entries it is extracting and which file those zip code entries are coming from. Then the *grep* command takes the value of the variable *$zip* as its search parameter and searches for matching entries in each file in turn.

The double greater than signs (>>) tell the script to *append* each matching entry to the following file. Remember from Chapter 8 that the double greater than signs append entries to the file you specify if a file with that name exists; otherwise, SCO UNIX creates one with that name before appending entries to it. The filename that this shell script uses is a combination of the literal text *zips* and the value of the variable *$zip*. In this example, the shell script would create a file named *zips.10101* if it didn't exist, and then the shell script would put the entries in that file. If *zips.10101* did exist, the shell script would simply add the entries to the end of the file.

After you create the zip code list, you could then sort it and create labels using the shell scripts you previously created.

# Controlling a Script

The only reservation you might have about this last script is that you have no control over it. After you press Enter, the script goes off and does everything it's meant to do until it's finished or until you press the Delete key to interrupt the process. Rather than have only the ability to terminate a process, it's far better to be able to monitor and direct the process. SCO UNIX gives you that type of control with three conditional clauses and two commands.

### Specifying the condition for execution with *if*

The first conditional clause, called *if*, uses the following general syntax:

> *if* a specified condition exists
>> *then* execute a command or command list
>> [*elif* else if another condition exists
>> *then* execute another command or command list]
>> [*else* execute another command or command list]
>
> *fi*

As with the *for...next* loop described earlier, only the keywords in italic type should be included in your script literally. The explanatory phrases are shown as guidelines.

In SCO UNIX, as in everyday English, *if* is part of a compound clause that is often used in one of three variations. The first is an *if...then* statement, in which you add a command that is executed only if the result of the conditional is true. (This is equivalent to, "If the sun shines, then I'll go to the beach.") You *must* include *then* to indicate that this command is a continuation of the *if* statement. The *fi* command (*if* spelled backward) ends the entire conditional statement. The second variation is an *if...then...else* statement, in which you add a second alternative always to be executed if the conditional is false. (This is equivalent to, "If the sun shines, then I'll go to the beach, else I'll go to the library.") A third variation is *if...then...else if...then...else* statement. This form lets you put one or more conditional alternatives after the first *if* conditional and before the *else* alternative.

You must include the *if*, *then*, and *fi* portions of this conditional clause. The *elif* and *else* portions are optional, which is indicated by the square brackets ([]). You can include as many *elif* portions as you need, but you can include only one *else* portion. You can include only one *else* portion because it is performed unconditionally if all other conditions are false.

### Specifying the duration of a condition with *while*

The second conditional clause, called *while*, uses the following general syntax:

> *while* a specified condition exists
>> *do* a command or command list
>> -check to see if the condition has changed
>> -if it has not changed, redo the command or command list
>> -if it has changed, end
>> *done*

When you use a *while* clause, you specify a condition that exists (for example, while a list contains the names of files to be printed). As long as the condition remains unchanged, your command is repeated. When the condition changes (for example, when the list becomes empty), the process is complete. You'll do something practical with *while* in a moment.

### Matching a pattern with *case*

The third conditional is *case*, which is a little more involved than *while*. The syntax for *case* is as follows:

```
case "of this text occurring" in
    "this pattern of text" ) perform this command or list of commands;;
    "this pattern of text" ) perform this command or list of commands;;
    ⋮
    "this pattern of text" ) perform this command or list of commands
esac
```

Here you tell the shell that for each case in which the text you specify appears within another pattern of text you specify, the command or list of commands following the second pattern are to be carried out. If no match is found, the shell continues on to the next command in the script (if one exists).

Because *case* lets you include more than one pattern to match, you can match a line of text against several patterns and execute different commands for each match. Note that you must use double semicolons (;;) to end each line of possible commands except the last.

Note too that you must include a right parenthesis between the pattern you're examining for a match and the command list you want to execute if a match is found. Finally, keep in mind that the shell's cue to exit a *case* clause is *esac* (*case* spelled backward).

# Starting and Stopping a Loop

The *for...next*, *if*, *while*, and *case* conditionals enable you to control the manner in which commands are processed in a script. Two other commands also are essential, and they are actually your means of controlling the process itself. These commands are *break* and *continue*, and they're used inside *while* and *for...next* loops. The *break* command terminates execution of the loop level at the point at which the *break* command occurs, and *continue* restarts the loop when the *continue* command occurs. But rather than try to explain these commands abstractly, let's use them.

# Creating an Interactive Script

We'll use the same general example we've used before: You need to search your mailing lists and extract entries that have a given zip code. This time, though, let's assume you want to enter each filename individually and to be able to stop the process at any time.

> **NOTE:** *As we mentioned earlier, the lines in this script were given a structured look by indenting them (here, with the Tab key). The alignment isn't needed to make the script run correctly, but it's useful. When you review this script (or one of your own) at a later date, these "nested" indents can help you see immediately where the different levels begin and end. The shell considers the tab character as a delimiter, so for all practical purposes, such indents are ignored when used as they are here.*

To create the script, start *vi* with the name of a text file called *interact*. When *vi* opens, use the *i* command to enter the insert mode, and enter the following series of lines:

```
echo "Enter the zip code: \c"
read zip
while true
do echo "Enter the file's name: \c"
    read answer
    case "$answer" in
    "end")    break
              ;;
    "")       break
              ;;
    *)        if ls | fgrep -x $answer
                  then ziplist $zip $answer
                  echo "$0: $answer processed and added to zip.FP"
                  else echo "$0: No such file..."
              fi
    esac
done
```

After you enter the last line, press Escape to leave insert mode, and use *:x* to write the text on disk and to quit *vi*. Now let's step through the script and see what you've accomplished.

The first line displays the prompt *Enter the zip code:* on the screen. You'll notice that the *echo* command has the characters \c at the end of the string of characters to be echoed. These characters prevent *echo* from printing a newline when it displays the string of characters on the screen, so the cursor remains on the prompt line that you are responding to. The *read* command in the second line causes the shell to wait for an answer and then to capture your response. It reads every character that you type until you press the Enter key and assigns your response to the variable *zip.*

The third line is the key to the whole procedure. The phrase *while true,* with no additional condition specified, is a command to repeat the entire process forever. The SCO UNIX command *true* always returns the condition *true.* Although forever might seem like a long time, this is really the way you want to construct this script. Bear in mind that you won't always format the same number of files. One day perhaps you'll work on only two or three, and the next day you might have 10 or 12 to do. Because your script is ready to go on forever, it's flexible enough to accommodate any number of files. Besides (as you'll see in a moment), you've built in a way to stop whenever you want.

Next the script displays the prompt *Enter the file's name:* on the screen. The shell waits for an answer and then captures your response with the *read* command, assigning your reply to the variable *answer.*

Now the *case* comparisons begin. You've told the shell to compare the answer it received to three values: *end, " ",* and *.*

If you have finished your formatting session and have typed the reply *end,* your reply matches the comparison pattern *end,* and the shell carries out the following command, *break.* As a result, you break out of the process, and the session is over. If your reply does not match *end,* the shell moves on to the next comparison.

The double quotation marks here indicate a *null* (empty) string of text, as would be transmitted if you pressed the Enter key without typing any characters. This line, then, tells the shell that in addition to the word *end,* pressing the Enter key signals the end of the session, and the *break* command is to be carried out. If your reply was not a null string, the shell goes on to the next comparison.

Here you see the familiar asterisk (*) wildcard. As you know, it matches *any* string of text. Essentially, its use here tells the shell, "No matter what is typed, perform the next command."

The entire *if* statement is that next command. You're using *fgrep* to verify that the filename you typed is included among the list of files in your directory. This variation of the *grep* command is the only one that allows the *x* option, which tells *fgrep* to search only for complete lines that exactly match the variable *$answer.*

In essence, the *if* clause causes the shell to search your file for entries with the given zip code if the file is found, or it prints the message *No such file...* if the filename you typed doesn't exist in your working directory. In either case, you then return to the beginning *while* statement.

You see from this example that you can use your executable shell scripts—in this case, *ziplist* —as you would any other command in SCO UNIX. The shell makes no distinctions among them. In the *echo* command, you also see that the shell script uses the variable *$0*. You used *$1* in the *ziplist* shell script. But what does *$0* refer to? It refers to the executable shell script itself—it's the *zeroth* position on the command line. This convention is useful when shell scripts execute other nested shell scripts. If your shell scripts include informational messages or especially error messages, you need to know which shell script displayed the message. For this reason, you should return to the *ziplist* shell script and include *$0* in its *echo* commands.

You might also wonder why the *if* clause and *fgrep* were included in the script. After all, you don't really need to use them. If the filename you supplied didn't match one of the files in your directory, the shell would display an error message on the screen. Your script would simply cycle back to the beginning and start over, so why bother with extra command lines? The answer is that your procedure would not be as precise as it could be if you left them out. By letting the shell handle the error, you relinquish a small amount of control over the process. And the more control you keep for yourself, the less room you leave for unexpected and potentially frustrating errors to occur.

## Testing Conditions

Your script, as it stands, is complete and ready to use. Now let's broaden our viewpoint a bit. You've stepped through the commands in this script, so you know how it works and why. But what about the other people on your system who might want or need to use it?

They can if they specify the complete pathname to the script and if you've set the permissions properly. Actually, though, from their point of view, the result of the *fgrep* command could be distracting. If *fgrep* finds the filename you typed in response to the *Enter the file's name:* prompt, it displays that name on the screen. The sudden appearance of the filename on the screen might not confuse you, but a stray response of that sort might confuse someone who doesn't know how the script works. And, as we mentioned earlier, if you're going to take the time to control a process, do so as completely as you can.

A new command that you can use in place of *fgrep* is called *test*. And as a side benefit, *test* is actually processed faster than *fgrep*. The *test* command also maintains the conditional nature of the *if* statement. If *test* finds the file you've named, the statement is evaluated as *true*. Otherwise it's *false*, as in the case of *fgrep*.

The first line of the *if* statement is as follows:

```
*)        if ls ¦ fgrep -x $answer
```

Now change it to look like this:

```
*)        if test -s $answer
```

The *s* option causes *test* to return a value of *true* only if it finds the file *and* and that file has a size greater than zero. This characteristic is another advantage of *test*. At one time, you might have created a blank (empty) file in your directory and given it the same name you've supplied in response to the script's prompt for a filename. As far as the shell is concerned, a blank file is as valid as a nonblank file. Being empty, however, the file contains nothing for *ziplist* to find. With *fgrep*, *ziplist* will try anyway, and the net result could be another blank file. With *test* and the *s* option, a blank file will not be processed.

Like most other SCO UNIX commands, *test* has many other options. In the case of *test*, the options provide true/false responses to conditions ranging from single bits of information on the disk to variables you supply. You will find details in the SCO UNIX User's Reference manual and in Appendix A, but three options in particular deserve mention here: =, *eq*, and *!*.

To the shell, the = sign symbolizes equivalence. When used with *test*, however, the = sign is non-numeric. It tells the shell to check two character patterns, rather than two numbers, for equality. For example, the command *test dog=cat* would be true if *dog* and *cat* were variables describing two identical character strings.

For numeric expressions, you would compare variables with the *eq* option, as in the command *test number1 eq number2*.

The functional opposite of = in the *test* command is the *!* symbol. Elsewhere in this book, you've seen the exclamation point used as an escape key to temporarily exit the shell. Here it is used in combination with the = sign to test whether character strings are not identical. For example, the command *test dog != cat* yields the true result when *dog* is not identical to *cat*.

# SHELL VARIABLES

So far, you've been dealing with variables that *you've* created. But the shell has its own set of variables too. It uses them to keep and transmit information about you when you log in. In fact, you saw one in Chapter 3—HOME, the variable that defines your home directory. (You might recall that you type it as *$HOME*, indicating that it's a variable.) Others are as follows:

IFS    With *vi* or any other procedure that lets you access several text files sequentially, you leave a blank space as a delimiter between the names in the list. The other delimiters recognized by the shell are the tab and the carriage return. IFS (Internal Field Separators) can be used to add new delimiters to that list.

| | |
|---|---|
| *MAIL* | Your mailbox is a file that's given the same name as your login name and is kept in the subdirectory */usr/spool/mail.* The *MAIL* variable can be used to change the names of that directory and file. |
| *PATH* | A quick listing of your home directory will show that none of the SCO UNIX utility programs can be found there. Yet whenever you type a valid command or program name, SCO UNIX accurately finds what you're asking for. These programs are stored in the directory */usr/bin,* although your home directory is */usr/[user name].* How does SCO UNIX know to look in *bin?* It uses the *PATH* variable, which contains the names of all the valid directories that should be searched and the order in which they should be searched whenever you issue a command. |
| *TERM* | When you see the message *Terminal type is* on your screen, SCO UNIX has used the *TERM* variable to extract the name of the particular terminal type following that message. |
| *TERMCAP* | The actual definition of your terminal type must be found somewhere. *TERMCAP* supplies the pathname to the data file that contains that definition. |
| *PS1* | For the Bourne and C shells, this variable contains the characters used as the shell prompt. The default value is either the $ sign (for the Bourne shell) or the % symbol (for the C shell) and a space character. |
| *PS2* | This variable contains the secondary shell prompt that you see when the shell expects more input than you've supplied—for example, when a command line extends onto a second line, as it did earlier in this chapter. |

Armed with this information, let's set out to explore how some of those variables are used.

## Reading Your *.profile* File

When your user account was created on the system, SCO UNIX generated a file called *.profile.* It's pronounced "dot profile," and it holds some login parameters that SCO UNIX associates with you. (The file has a different name and slightly different parameters in the C shell.)

You can look in your directory, but you won't necessarily find your *.profile* file. The period (.) used as the first character in its name makes the file invisible to the normal *ls* or *lc* command. If you want to see it listed, add *a* as an option to either of those commands. This option makes any invisible files in your directory appear in the listing.

Your *.profile* doesn't incorporate all of the shell variables, but it does use quite a few. If you're curious, you can display its contents to the screen from the shell prompt by entering the following command:

```
cat .profile
```

In response, you'll see the following:

```
:
#
#       .profile-- Commands executed by a login Bourne shell
#
#       @(#) profile 1.1 89/02/15
#
# Copyright (c) 1985-89, The Santa Cruz Operation, Inc.
# All rights reserved.
#
# This Module contains Proprietary Information of the Santa Cruz
# Operation, Inc., and should be treated as Confidential.
#

PATH=/bin:/usr/bin:$HOME/bin:.          # set command search path
MAIL=/usr/spool/mail/'logname'          # mailbox location
export PATH MAIL

umask 077                               # set file creation mask

eval 'tset -m ansi:ansi -m $TERM:\?${TERM:-ansi} -r -s -Q'
```

You can see the ways SCO UNIX uses the shell variables. Most of them should be recognizable from the table in the preceding section. The comments on the right side of the screen should help you interpret what they mean.

Notice that some SCO UNIX commands are also contained in the file. The *tset* command is one of them. As the comment field indicates, *tset* is used to set the terminal initializations. The *r* parameter causes the terminal type to be displayed on the screen during the login opening message.

The *umask* command is another SCO UNIX command. It is used to further restrict the system-defined default permissions level for files you create. The three numbers that follow the *umask* command are octal (base 8) rather than decimal (base 10) numbers. Technically, they compose what is called a *mask*, whose values SCO UNIX combines with any system-wide default values (using a binary "subtract" technique, the details of which are beyond the scope of this book). The result of this operation is three individual masks: for the owner, for the group, and for the public.

The current *umask* settings provide read and write permission for you as the file's owner (the 0 mask), no permission for the group (the first 7 mask), and no permission for the public (the last 7 mask). You could reset this default to include read and write permission for the group and public by changing the mask to 000 (or any combination of digits from 0 through 7 for any combination of permissions).

Changing *umask* sets new default permissions for any new files you create, but you might find that the *chmod* command described in Chapter 8 is easier to use. Then, too, because you know how to write a shell script, you could create one that uses *chmod* to change the permissions for several files at the same time. Combining the *while*, *case*, and *read* commands, you could even create a script that would prompt for a choice of permissions.

In the last line of the file is one more SCO UNIX command, *export*. It's used to send the values contained in the shell variables out to the system, where they are put into effect either until the current session ends or until you change them.

The only question remaining is "How can you modify *.profile* and your login characteristics?" As you have done many times, begin by starting *vi*.

# Changing *.profile* Defaults

At some time in your work with SCO UNIX, you might need to use a terminal of a different type from the one assigned to you, especially if you're a dial-up user. Such a need could arise from any situation, from equipment failure to simply being at a different site with a different terminal.

Ordinarily, you'd need to ask your system administrator to redefine the terminal type for you. But if the change is only temporary, another redefinition will be needed when you return to your original equipment. In such circumstances, you can redefine the terminal yourself.

## Changing your terminal type

To change your terminal type, you will need to place a new definition for the TERM variable in *.profile*. You can find a list of the most common terminal names in the file */etc/termcap* and some additional descriptions in Chapter 13. If you have difficulty finding the correct terminal type, check with your system administrator.

For a onetime change, effective only for your current session with SCO UNIX, you can change the TERM variable directly from the keyboard. Immediately after logging in, use the following command format:

```
TERM=terminal_name;export TERM
```

For a change that lasts longer than one session with SCO UNIX, use *vi* to change the contents of *.profile*. To do this, load the *.profile* file and move the cursor to the line containing the *tset* command. Next use the O command both to open a new line above the current one and to move into insert mode. Now enter the *TERM* command as described earlier, and press the Escape key to leave insert mode. Use *:x* to write the new file on disk and to exit *vi*.

From now on, the new terminal type you've set will be what is defined for your terminal. When you need to change the terminal type again, follow the same procedure, using the new terminal name.

# Expanding Your Directory Path

As your ability to create and use shell scripts increases, you might find them beginning to clutter your home directory. You might store them in a subdirectory called *Scripts*, which you've created for that purpose. The only drawback to this approach is in accessing *Scripts* from some other directory. From your home directory, you would enter the pathname in the following form:

```
Scripts/script_name
```

But suppose you want to access one of your script files while you're in a general data directory called *Data*, and it's on the same level as *Scripts*. Then the pathname to *Scripts* would take the following form:

```
../Scripts/script_name
```

As directory levels expand and you move among them, keeping track of where you are in relation to *Scripts* and to other directories can become more complex. However, SCO UNIX offers a solution.

## Examining the *PATH* variable

Recall that SCO UNIX has a shell variable called *PATH*. When you displayed your *.profile* on the screen, you saw a *PATH* variable that looked something like this:

```
PATH=/bin:/usr/bin:$HOME/bin:.
```

The *PATH* variable in this particular example describes four paths that SCO UNIX takes to find any program, command, or executable file. They are */bin*, */usr/bin*, *$HOME/bin*, and the current directory (.).

The first three paths are obvious—their names are used. In contrast, the pathname of the current directory, which is any directory you happen to be in at the time, is an implicit instruction created by the final colon (a delimiter) and the dot (.) in the list. SCO UNIX always interprets that construction as the current directory.

The order in which SCO UNIX searches for any command contained in a request you initiate is implied in sequence of the pathnames in the *PATH* variable. In this case, the search begins in */bin*. If the command is not there, SCO UNIX searches */usr/bin*, then *$HOME/bin* and, finally, the current directory.

It's a simple matter to modify *PATH*, either to include one or more additional directory paths or to alter the search order of those that are currently included.

To add a directory path, simply include it at the point you feel is most appropriate. For example, if you often use script files in a directory named *Scripts* and you want SCO UNIX to search that directory after it has searched the other paths indicated in the *PATH* variable, add the path *:$HOME/Scripts* to the end of the current *PATH* statement. (You might also want to delete some of the space between the *PATH* statement and the comment, which has now spilled over the right margin.) Your *PATH* assignment would now look like this:

```
PATH=/bin:/usr/bin:$HOME/bin:.:$HOME/Scripts
```

You can also change the order in which the paths are listed. For example, to move the current directory (.) to the beginning of the search on the *PATH* statement we just created, change the line to read as follows:

```
PATH=.:/bin:/usr/bin:$HOME/bin:$HOME/Scripts
```

After you've made the changes to *.profile*, the most reliable way to implement them is to log out and then log in again. In the short time it takes to do that, you'll have reset the shell variables you've changed.

# A FEW USEFUL SUGGESTIONS

Although we haven't stepped through all the procedures, you now have the knowledge to add any of the shell variables, even program names, to your *.profile* file. If you maintain a list of reminders on SCO UNIX, you might, for example, want to add *calendar* to your *.profile* file. Doing so will produce a current reminder list each time you log in.

Another helpful use for a script file is including its name as the last line in your *.profile* file. The next time you log in, the script will be run as soon as SCO UNIX's introductory messages have finished. (You'll need to have made the script executable with the *chmod* command and included the appropriate pathname in the *PATH* variable if the script is in a directory other than your home directory.) With some imagination, you'll be able to create scripts that save you both time and trouble, and you will have greater control over your electronic environment.

# 10

# The C Shell

The C shell (*csh* for short) was created at the University of California at Berkeley to provide a command interpreter with a command structure similar to the C language. You can execute some of the procedures you learned in the last chapter in *csh*, but the C shell also has its own commands and variables. As a general rule, however, a command that works in the Bourne shell also works in the C shell. Let's take a look at the *csh* environment for a user named *mikeh*.

## ENTERING THE C SHELL

You can enter the C shell in either of two ways: by logging in directly if your system administrator set up your account to use the C shell or by using the *csh* command from another shell. If you log in directly, your prompt appears as a percent symbol (%) preceded by a number. If you enter from another shell, your prompt is a percent symbol without an accompanying number. However, quite a bit happens before the prompt appears on your screen.

When you enter the C shell, *csh* checks your home directory for a file called *.cshrc*. If it finds this file, *csh* carries out the commands contained in the file. Next, if you're logging in rather than entering from another shell, *csh* reads a second file named *.login*.

After the shell prompt appears on your screen, the C shell is ready. From this point on, every command you type is handled in the following three-step sequence:

1. The shell reads your command line and breaks it into units called words (usually delimited by blank spaces or tab characters).

2. The shell saves lines of these words for future reference in a list called the history list. Lines of words are called events.

3. The shell carries out the commands on the line itself.

# BUILT-IN VARIABLES

Like the Bourne shell, the C shell contains a number of built-in variables. To see some, let's take a look at your *.cshrc* file. Enter the following command at the C shell prompt:

```
cat .cshrc
```

In response, you'll see a display like the following:

```
#
# .cshrc     -- Commands executed by the C-shell each time it runs
#
#    @(#) cshrc 3.1 89/06/02
#
# Copyright (c) 1985-1989, The Santa Cruz Operation, Inc.
# All rights reserved.
#
# This Module contains Proprietary Information of the Santa Cruz
# Operation, Inc., and should be treated as Confidential.
#

set noclobber              # don't allow '>' to overwrite
set history=20             # save last 20 commands
if ($?prompt) then
     set prompt=\!%\        # set prompt string
# some BSD lookalikes that maintain a directory stack
     if (! $?_d) set _d = ()
     alias    popd     'cd $_d[1]; echo ${_d[1]}:; shift _d'
     alias    pushd    'set _d = ('pwd' $_d); cd \!*'
     alias    swapd    'set _d = ($_d[2] $_d[1] $_d[3-])'
     alias    flipd    'pushd .; swapd ; popd'
endif
alias print 'pr -n \!:* ! lp'        # print command alias
```

Although they're used somewhat differently here, some commands, such as *alias*, should be familiar from preceding chapters.

# Setting Shell Variables

You've already used the *set* command with *vi* to turn line numbering on and off with the *number* and *nonumber* options. The C shell puts the variables into effect when the shell executes the commands in this file, and the *set* command initializes these variables. The variables themselves are defined as follows:

- The *noclobber* variable protects files from being overwritten through accidental use of output redirection commands and ensures that the >> redirection symbol will not overwrite an existing file.

- The *history* variable, when assigned a numeric value, sets the number of previously executed shell commands that will be saved in the history list. In the default *.cshrc* file, the last 20 commands are saved.

- The *prompt* variable sets the prompt character—in this case, the percent symbol. The exclamation point indicates that the prompt is to be preceded by a number indicating the current event (line). The second backslash (\) is an escape character used to include the following space character in the prompt. This character separates what you type from the prompt characters on the command line and makes the command line easier to read.

When you start the C shell, the system checks the *if ($?prompt) then* line to see if the C shell will display its output on the screen and if a prompt (the variable *$prompt*) is associated with this shell. If a prompt is called for, the system executes the lines following the *then* phrase. One line assigns a value to the prompt, as we have already seen.

The *.login* file also sets some variables if you are logging in to the C shell. To look at your *.login* file, enter the following command at the C shell prompt:

```
cat .login
```

Unless you or your system administrator has modified the file, you'll see a display like the following:

```
#
# .login      -- Commands executed only by a login C-shell
#
#    @(#) login 3.1 89/06/02
#
# Copyright (c) 1985-89, The Santa Cruz Operation, Inc.
# All rights reserved.
#
# This Module contains Proprietary Information of the Santa Cruz
# Operation, Inc., and should be treated as Confidential.
#

setenv SHELL /bin/csh

set ignoreeof                        # don't let control-d logout
set path = (/bin /usr/bin $home/bin .)  # execution search path

set noglob
set term = ('tset -m ansi:ansi -m :\?ansi -r -S -Q')
if ( $status == 0 ) then
     setenv TERM "$term"
endif
unset term noglob
```

In this file, the *set* command initializes the following other variables:

- The *ignoreeof* variable prevents you from logging out with Ctrl-D. You must use the command *logout* instead. Using this variable prevents you from inadvertently logging out when you merely want to stop a command from running but you inadvertently press Ctrl-D more than once.

- The *path* variable sets the list of directories SCO UNIX will search to find the command that you've typed on the command line. The search begins in the system directories */bin* and */usr/bin* and then proceeds to any directory that begins with your home directory (the variable *$home*) and is followed by */bin*. If you are *mikeh*, with a home directory (*$home*) of */usr/mikeh*, SCO UNIX will search */usr/mikeh/bin*. If SCO UNIX doesn't find the command in any of the previous directories, it will search the current directory (.), also called dot.

The *.login* file also sets your terminal type so that the output is displayed correctly for the type that you are using.

As you can see, the *set* command is used to activate all these variables. To remove the effect of a variable that you've set, use the *unset* command. (Deactivating a variable in this way is similar to using *set* in *vi*, where, for example, you turn off line numbering with the command *set nonumber*.)

You can set variables from within *.cshrc* (or *.login*) by loading the file into *vi* and making changes to it there. You can also set variables from the shell prompt.

## Setting Your Own Variables

As mentioned earlier, if you enter the C shell from another shell, your prompt character is the percent symbol (without an accompanying event number). You have escaped from your home shell into a subshell. As a result, even though *csh* searched your home directory, it found no *.cshrc* file. Therefore, it hasn't been told to set any variables indicating either that it should keep a history or that it should number events.

If you want to set features such as numbered events, you can use a simple solution: Create your own *.cshrc* file. You can use the lines shown in the previous example.

If you already have a variable set (such as *PATH* in your *.profile* file) and you are satisfied with it, you don't need to add it to the *.cshrc* file. Also, keep in mind that if you include the *set ignoreeof* line, Ctrl-D will no longer let you leave the subshell. You will have to use the command *exit* to return to your own shell.

After you enter the subshell, you can also set only those variables that you want to set from the keyboard. (This holds true for all of the shell commands and works whether or not you have a *.cshrc* file.) For example, enter the following two commands to put only those variables into effect until you log out:

```
set history=20
set prompt=\!%\
```

In the second command, put a space after the second \.

# CHANGING YOUR HOME DIRECTORY

As you learned in Chapter 3, SCO UNIX returns you to your home directory whenever you use the *cd* command without an argument. One of the C shell variables, *home*, sets the path to your home directory. Initially, *home* has the same value as the Bourne shell's *HOME* variable. Thus, for a user named *mikeh*, *home* would be */usr/mikeh*. You can also use the *$home* variable within a pathname, just as you can use *$HOME* from the Bourne shell. Note the difference in capitalization. Also note that a $ sign precedes the *home* variable when it should be expanded to the path it represents.

In addition, you can use a metacharacter in the C shell in place of the *$home* variable: the tilde (~), which you can incorporate into a directory path. For example, suppose you have a subdirectory called *Temp* immediately below your home directory. The following pathnames are all functionally equivalent:

```
/usr/mikeh/Temp
$HOME/Temp
$home/Temp
~/Temp
```

Likewise, if you generally work from a directory named */usr/mikeh/Scripts*, you can change the value of *$home* to reflect that directory path with the following command:

```
set home=(/usr/mikeh/Scripts)
```

Now you can use */usr/mikeh/Scripts* as your home directory no matter where you are in your directory system.

To return to your original home directory, */usr/mikeh*, simply enter the following command:

```
cd $HOME
```

As you'll see later in this chapter, *$HOME* is distinct from *$home*.

Also, if you change these variables and forget which assignments you've made, use the following command to display their current values:

```
echo $home $HOME
```

# SETTING THE ENVIRONMENT

If you refer back to our sample *.login* file, you'll notice that one instruction helped to set up the environment. But what is the environment? Isn't it the C shell in which you are working, and isn't that environment already set up for use? Yes, it is—for you. These instructions, however, refer to the environment relative to the C shell itself. That environment is the Bourne shell, from which the C shell originates. That's why *set* commands use C shell variables and *setenv* commands use Bourne shell variables.

In particular, you use the *setenv* command to establish the shell that you want to use for scripts that do not begin with the pound symbol (*setenv SHELL /bin/csh*).

You could also use *vi* to add the following other environment variables:

■ The database of terminal types and of terminal capabilities (*setenv TERMCAP /etc/termcap*).

■ The destination for *mail* messages that do not originate from the C shell (*setenv MAIL /usr/spool/mail/$LOGNAME*). You'll probably want to keep all your *mail* messages together, so both the Bourne shell's *MAIL* and the C shell's *mail* variables are defined as the same location.

If you find it necessary to modify your terminal type, you can do so by using *setenv*. The command syntax is as follows:

```
setenv TERM terminal_code
```

You substitute the correct terminal code for *terminal_code*. (For a list of terminals and their codes, check the file */etc/termcap*, which is described in Chapter 14.)

Also, as you did for the *home* variable, you can use *setenv* to change the value of *HOME* (the directory in which you're placed when you log in). However, you can't substitute a metacharacter for *$HOME* as you can substitute a tilde for *$home*.

# GAINING ACCESS TO *history*

Earlier in this chapter, you learned about the *history* variable, which saves the last 20 commands you used. To produce a list of these command lines and their event numbers, enter *history*. You'll see a display something like the following:

```
20% history
     1   mail
     2   lc
     3   cd Scripts
     4   ls -l
     5   vi accounts
     6   cp accounts
     7   history
     8   mail danh
     9   cd
    10   show /usr/Scripts/accounts
    11   pwd
    12   mail
    13   who
    14   mail susang
    15   cd Scripts
    16   ls -l
    17   cd $HOME
    18   mkdir Pastdue
    19   cd Pastdue
    20   history
21% _
```

You might wonder what good this list does for you. How can you access any of the last 20 commands that you used, and when would you want to? Try the command *cat file_name* using the name of one of your own files. Then enter the following command:

```
cat !$
```

The *cat* command is repeated.

As it does in the *prompt* variable, the exclamation point starts the *history* mechanism. You've included the dollar sign in the command to indicate the argument you used for the command in the last line. In effect, *cat !$* tells the C shell to execute the *cat* command by using the file on the preceding line as its argument. To simply repeat the last line in the C shell, enter *!!* at the % prompt.

You could also use the following command to indicate the relative command (or event number) that is one less than the current command number:

```
!-1
```

Or you could enter the following absolute command:

```
!event_number
```

For *event_number*, you use the number of the line the *cat* command is on—the number preceding the shell prompt (%). Recall that if the *history* variable in your *.cshrc* file is set to 20, you'll only be able to reference commands as far back as 20 event numbers.

The following command carries out the last command that began with a *c*:

```
!c
```

In this example, the last and only command was *cat*, so the single letter *c* is enough to specify it. In other situations, you can provide longer partial lines, such as *!ca* or *!cat*, if you need to refine the specification further.

If you're unsure of the exact command that SCO UNIX will carry out, you can add *:p* to your request. So, for example, the following command would display the last command that began with a *c*, but it would not execute that command:

```
!c:p
```

The *:p* lets you verify that the command is actually the one you want to execute, without actually executing it.

## Editing Commands

You can use your access to historical events to correct typing errors. The following command line is an attempt to list the files contained in the directory *Marketing/Accounts*:

```
la Marketing/Accounts
```

But the typing error caused by hitting the *a* key instead of *s* as in *ls* results in the error message *la : Command not found.*

. You could retype the entire command, correctly substituting *s* for *a* to produce the result you want. Or you could simply enter the following command to substitute the letters *ls* for *la*:

```
^la^ls
```

You've already seen this type of substitution with *vi* and in the *sed* script in Chapter 8. In each case, you used the following command format to perform the operation:

```
s/find/substitute
```

In C shell history substitutions, you use the caret (^) instead of the slash. The C shell makes substitution to the command line immediately preceding the current one. Note that the exclamation point is unnecessary, and the *s* (substitute) is assumed. You could also have simply used the following command:

```
^a^s
```

The first occurrence of the letter *a* would have been changed in the last command line. The degree of substitution that you use depends on the possible variations in the pattern that you're trying to match.

# ANALYZING ALIASES

As you learned in Chapter 7, you can use aliases in the *mail* system to shorten command lines and make them easier to remember. In *mail*, you saw how to compress a list of user names into a single alias. In the C shell, an alias becomes a miniature shell script.

The *.cshrc* file mentioned at the beginning of this chapter contains four useful aliases that you can use as commands to simplify your work: *pushd*, *popd*, *swapd*, and *flipd*. The lines following the *then* phrase set up these aliases, which you can use instead of *cd* to change directories.

When you enter the *pushd* command (followed by a directory name), the command stores the current directory in a list, or a stack (the variable $_d), and then it changes to the directory name that you typed. Notice that the two commands in the alias *pushd* are separated by a semicolon (;). You can separate any number of commands on one line in SCO UNIX by semicolons.

When you enter the *popd* command, SCO UNIX finds the first directory on the stack created by *pushd*, changes to that directory, and removes that directory name from the stack.

The *swapd* command switches the order of the first two directories in the list.

The *flipd* command changes to the first directory on the stack and stores the current directory on the stack.

These aliases let you easily change from one long directory name to another and back again without worrying about typing mistakes. They also let you switch from one directory to another with one command. For example, you can change from the directory */usr/mikeh/Admin/Memos/May* to the directory */usr/mikeh/Accounts/January* with the following command:

```
pushd /usr/mikeh/Accounts/January
```

Now the directory */usr/mikeh/Admin/Memos/May* is on the top of the stack. If you enter the following command, you return to the */usr/mikeh/Admin/Memos/May* directory and leave nothing on the stack:

```
popd
```

If, on the other hand, you enter the following command, you also return to the directory */usr/mikeh/Admin/Memos/May* but the directory */usr/mikeh/Accounts/January* is on the top of the stack instead:

```
flipd
```

## Creating Your Own Aliases

You can design your own aliases in the C shell. In fact, you can write one that can help MS-DOS users make the transition to SCO UNIX.

To request a directory listing in MS-DOS, you enter *dir*, which is roughly equivalent to the SCO UNIX *ls* command with the *l* option. Simply by inserting the following line into *.cshrc*, you can ensure that whenever you (or someone else) slip and enter *dir* instead of *ls -l*, SCO UNIX doesn't display the error message *dir : Command not found*:

```
alias dir ls -l
```

This alias tells SCO UNIX to execute an *ls -l* command either on the current directory or on the directory that was named after the *dir* part of the command.

You can also expand your alias both to make the C shell friendlier yet and to eliminate a potential problem. The command *ls -l* produces a significant amount of information about a list of files, but in a directory containing 20 or more files, some of that information can scroll off the top of the screen. You can, of course, use the Ctrl-S combination to start and stop the scrolling, or you can use your alias to make the procedure more useful. Try the following line (type *l24* as a lowercase L and the number 24):

```
alias dir '\ls -l \!:* | pr -ptl24'
```

Thereafter, whenever you enter the command *dir*, SCO UNIX will tell your terminal to beep. When you press the Enter key, SCO UNIX will display one screenful (24 lines) of a long listing of the current or named directory by using *pr*, the print-to-screen command. If you press the Enter key again, the next 24 lines of the listing will appear, and so on, until all of the files have been displayed. (Note the *t* option we used with the *pr* utility. This option suppresses the default five-line header and footer usually included.)

You can add other simple aliases to your *.cshrc* file using *vi*. For example, adding *alias v vi* lets you start *vi* simply by entering *v*, adding *alias h history* lets you use the history buffer simply by entering *h*, and adding *alias print 'pr \!:* ¦ lpr'* lets you print simply by entering *print*.

The third alias is an exercise in using pipelines. Essentially, this alias compresses two procedures into a single command. You enter *print* in the following form:

```
print filename
```

The *pr* command processes the file you specify for printing to the screen. Then the output of the *pr* command puts the default header—the current date, the filename, and the page number—on each page of the printed copy. The output of the *pr* command is piped into the *lp* utility, which sends the file to the printer. If you include several filenames after *print*, each file will begin on a new page.

Of course, as with the *history* and *prompt* variables mentioned earlier, you can make the alias temporary (but immediate) by entering the alias only at the shell prompt and not including it in the *.cshrc* file. The C shell remembers the alias only for the duration of the current session. Aliases that you add or change in *.cshrc* do not take effect until the next time you log in.

# CREATING A C SHELL SCRIPT

When you request a directory listing by using the *dir* alias, you hear a beep. Because you devised the alias, you know what that signal means. But would anyone else know? Quite conceivably, someone who is unfamiliar with your alias could sit staring at the terminal waiting for something to happen. And, of course, nothing would. The simple solution is to expand the alias into a shell script that also includes a prompt.

If you have created the *dir* alias, you first need to "uncreate" it by using the following command:

```
unalias dir
```

Likewise, if you ever want to remove all of the aliases that are in effect, use the asterisk wildcard as follows:

```
unalias *
```

To find out which aliases are in effect, you can print a list of all current aliases by typing *alias* with no arguments.

Now, to create your script, start by redirecting all keyboard input to a disk file called *dir* with the following command:

```
cat > dir
```

Then enter the following three lines:

```
#This script file prints the contents of various directory elements.
echo 'Press Enter when you hear the tone...'
ls -l $argv ! pr -ptl24
```

Press Ctrl-D to close the file. Next add execute permission to the file as follows:

```
chmod +x dir
```

This command gives you an executable shell script that does several tasks.

Suppose someone types *dir /usr*. First, the script echoes the prompt *Press Enter when you hear the tone…* on the screen. Then it uses a C shell variable called *argv*, which designates the arguments from the shell's command line. If you enter only one argument in your command, the first script command line that contains *argv* extracts that single argument. (As you'll see shortly, if you enter more than one argument, *$argv* extracts successive arguments for use in successive script command lines.)

In this script, however, the *$argv* in the third line extracts the only argument you entered (*/usr*) and uses it in an *ls -l* command to produce a long directory listing. Then the output from this listing is piped into the *pr* utility, which causes a beep to sound. SCO UNIX then prints the listing to the screen (*p*), with a "page" length of 24 lines (*l24*) and no five-line default header and footer (*t*).

You can use this new *dir* script as *dir directory_name*, *dir filename*, or simply the command *dir*. In any case, the script will assign to *argv* the name of either the specified directory or file or the contents of the current directory. As a result, SCO UNIX will display a directory list that includes as many lines of information as will fit on the screen. The script then causes the terminal to beep, pauses until you press Enter, displays another screenful of information, and pauses again. The script will repeat the display of the listing until it runs out of directory entries.

The line *#This script file prints the contents of various directory elements* represents a C shell comment. C shell comments are denoted by the pound sign at their start. The beginning of the *.cshrc* file contains another example of this type of line.

The pound sign has two meanings to SCO UNIX. First the pound sign tells the C shell to interpret the following characters on the line as comments. Second, because the pound sign is at the beginning of the file, SCO UNIX should use the C shell as an interpreter when you type the script's filename. If your login shell is not the C shell and you omit the pound sign, you'll have some problems when you type *dir*, because SCO UNIX uses the Bourne shell as the general default command processor.

# A CLOSER LOOK AT C SHELL SCRIPTS

Using the *ls* command, you can specify more than one file or directory. Knowing this, you could, for example, use the *dir* script file you created to display the long listing for the subdirectory *Scripts*, for the subdirectory *New_York*, and for the data file *fred*, one after another, by entering the following at the shell prompt:

```
dir Scripts New_York fred
```

Now you can modify the script to tell you which of the arguments that you entered are directories and which are files. You can also change it to give the option of seeing a directory's long listing, of viewing a file's contents, or of moving on to the next argument you entered. Designing such a script is no problem in the C shell. Before we get to the specifics, though, let's take a look at two of the fundamental C shell structures we'll need to carry out the task: the *foreach* loop and the *if...then...else* conditional.

## Looping with *foreach*

The basic format for a *foreach* loop is as follows:

> *foreach* variable (variable_list)
>> -Carry out the command list
>> -Get the next variable from variable_list
>> -If no more variables exist in variable_list then end the loop
>
> *end*

The equivalent of this structure in the Bourne shell is the *for...next* loop. Just as *for...next* does, the *foreach* loop repeats a series of commands (called the command list) specified between the initial *foreach* statement and the concluding *end* statement. Each time the loop is executed, a new variable is taken from *variable_list* (the old variable is discarded) and is made available for use in the body of the loop. This process ends when all arguments specified in *variable_list* are used.

You can also change the *dir* script to include a *foreach* loop that takes as its variable list the names of each file or directory that you enter on the command line. Such a script would look like this:

```
#This script file lists the contents of various directory elements.
echo 'Press Enter when you hear the tone  .  .  . '
foreach dirname ($argv )
    ls -l $dirname : pr -ptl24
end
```

The variable *argv* in the variable list section of line three is a special C shell parameter that's used to send variable information from the shell to the script. (Recall that we used this in the first *dir* script.) Each time the loop is executed, *argv* brings in a variable until every argument specified on the command line in the shell is sent.

After it's in the script, the variable information is transferred from the *argv* parameter to the script variable *dirname*. From here, *dirname* is used throughout the body of the *foreach* loop as needed. As in the first *dir* script file, a dollar sign signifies that a variable should be transformed from a variable name to the information the variable actually represents. When the script is executed, the variables are transformed into any specified directory names.

Our new *dir* script pauses and produces a beep before displaying the file or directory's long listing. This script gives us quite a bit of flexibility in manipulating the information passed into the loop. We'll be using this flexibility in a moment, but first let's look at another C shell structure, the *if...then...else* conditional.

## Using *if...then...else*

The format of the C shell's *if* statement differs from the Bourne shell version you saw in the last chapter. The format is as follows:

```
if ([conditional  – 1]) then
    [command list]
else if ([conditional  – 2]) then
    [command list]
⋮
else [command list]
endif
```

Note that *if* and *else if* must appear on the same lines as their related *then* statements. Also notice that you can include any number of *else if...then* pairs. Using *else* with only a command list is optional. The *else* statement used in this way can be included only if it is the last *else* statement in the conditional.

The basic operation of the *if...then...else* conditional is this: If *conditional _1* is true, then the commands following the *then* statement are executed, and the loop terminates. If *conditional _1* is not true, then the direction of the loop is guided to the *else if* statement, which evaluates *conditional_2*. This process continues until either a command list has been executed or all the conditionals have been evaluated as false.

## Writing a Conditional Script

Now let's use some of the elements of the *dir* script file we created earlier to write a script that pulls together the preceding concepts. The *dir* script is fine for listing the contents of directories, but suppose we would also like to view the contents of files and, when appropriate, be notified if one of the arguments does not represent a file or a directory. The C shell gives us access to the specific file information we'll need, and the *if...then...else* conditional gives us a way to compare and evaluate that information.

Start by redirecting your input to a new script file named *show* by entering the following at the shell prompt:

```
cat > show
```

We're ready to enter the script. Indent lines by pressing the Spacebar a few times, but don't press Enter until you reach the end of each line. The script is as follows:

```
#This script file identifies and displays files and directories.
foreach file ($argv )
   echo ''
   if (-d $file) then
      echo $file 'is a directory.'
      echo 'When you hear the tone, press Enter to list it or Del to continue.'
      ls -l $file : pr -ptl2 1
   else if (-f $file) then
      echo $file 'is a file.'
      echo 'When you hear the tone, press Enter to view it or Del to continue.'
      cat $file : pr -ptl21
   else echo $file 'is not a file or directory.'
      echo 'When you hear the tone, press Del to continue.'
      cat errormessage : pr -pt
   endif
end
```

Notice that the number of lines displayed at a time by *pr* has been changed from 24 to 21. This change was made to accommodate three extra lines of text *show* will display.

When you've finished, press Ctrl-D on a new line to close the file, and then make the file executable by entering the following at the shell prompt:

```
chmod +x show
```

Next redirect your input to another file named *errormessage* by entering the following at the shell prompt:

```
cat > errormessage
```

Add the contents of this one-line text file by entering the following:

```
That file or directory does not exist!
```

Press Ctrl-D on a new line to close the file.

Let's run *show* to see what it does and, in the process, find out what the C shell variables and structures are doing. In our example, we'll use the directories */bin* and */usr/mikeh/Scripts* and the files */usr/mikeh/fred* and */usr/mikeh/accounts*. Substitute your own directories and files. For clarity, we'll also specify an absolute path to each directory and file. You can use relative referencing if you prefer.

At the shell prompt, enter your equivalent of the following:

```
show /bin /usr/mikeh/accounts
```

SCO UNIX responds with a display like this:

```
37% show /bin /usr/mikeh/accounts

/bin is a directory.
When you hear the tone, press Enter to list it or Del to continue.
─
```

You included two arguments when you started the *show* script. The first, the */bin* directory, is being processed now. If you refer to the *show* script itself and compare it with the revised *dir* script we created, you can see that the second line in *show* is essentially the same as the third line of *dir* : *foreach file ($argv )*.

This line signifies the beginning of the *foreach* loop and marks the place at which files and directories are passed from the shell into *show*, through the *argv* parameter. Now, however, the command list of the *foreach* loop is many lines long, rather than one line, as it was in the *dir* script.

As you can see on the screen, the first command executed in the *foreach* loop's command list is the *echo* command. Followed by two single quotation marks and no specified text, *echo* will display a blank line on the screen each time the loop is executed. This helps separate *show*'s responses to the arguments and makes the display easier to read.

The next command in the loop is the *if...then...else* conditional. We are taking advantage of some information the C shell can give us about each file's structure.

**204**

The *if* ... *then* ... *else* conditional lets you search for the following file attributes:

| | |
|---|---|
| r | Read access |
| w | Write access |
| x | Execute access |
| e | Existence |
| o | Ownership |
| z | Zero size |
| f | Ordinary file |
| d | Directory |

You want to know if the argument passed from the C shell represents a directory, an ordinary file, or neither. The initial *if* conditional on line 4 checks whether the file is a directory. If the current argument (*$file*) is a directory, then the directory name is displayed with the message *is a directory*.

Next, the line *When you hear the tone, press Enter to list it or Del to continue* is displayed on the screen and the long listing of the directory is piped to the *pr* utility. If you press the Enter key, you'll see the long listing of the directory (*/bin* in our example) displayed one screen at a time. (Remember, with the *p* option, *pr* waits for you to press the Enter key.) You can also press the Delete (Del) key, instead of Enter, if you want to continue on to the next file or directory you entered. The Delete key is SCO UNIX's break key, which lets you escape from the loop you're currently in. In this case, the Delete key terminates the current command list and moves you back up to the top of the *foreach* statement. If no more new arguments are in the variable list, the shell script is terminated.

But if the file is not a directory, the flow of the *if* ... *then* ... *else* conditional moves to the first *else* statement, which reads *else if (-f $file) then*.

As did the first conditional, this conditional also checks *$file*'s structure. If the file is an ordinary file, an appropriate message is printed, and you can either press Enter to view the file or press the Delete key to continue to the next argument. This time, *$file* is first processed by the *cat* command, which then pipes its output to the *pr* utility.

SCO UNIX is still waiting for you either to list the */bin* directory or to continue. Press the Delete key to continue. SCO UNIX next displays a prompt like this:

```
/usr/mikeh/accounts is a file.
When you hear the tone, press Enter to view it or Del to continue.
```

Recall that our second argument was a filename. The *show* script is telling you so. After the beep, you could press Enter to view the contents of that file. In our example, the results would look like this:

```
/usr/mikeh/accounts is a file.
When you hear the tone, press Enter to view it or Del to continue.
```

```
Assets            June 1988      June 1989      June 1990
- - - - - - - - - - - - - - - - - - - - - - - - - - - - - - - - - -

Cash            $  18,790      $  20,007      $  24,886

Securities         12,503         31,777         46,000

Inventory         234,578        222,687        267,232

Prepaid expenses    4,200          3,799         12,557

Accounts receivable 21,505        29,125         28,430


- - - - - - - - - - - - - - - - - - - - - - - - - - - - - - - - - -

Total assets    $ 291,576      $ 307,395      $ 379,105

38% _
```

We didn't specify any more directory names or filenames when we ran *show*, so the script has completed its conditionals and loops and has terminated at this point.

Let's try one more example. This time, we'll run *show* with the following arguments:

```
show /usr/mikeh/fred /usr/mihek /usr/mikeh/Scripts
```

Note the misspelling of the current directory in the second argument. As you would expect, the first message tells us that */usr/mikeh/fred* is a file and we can either view it or continue on to the next argument. If you press the Delete key to move on, the next response looks like this:

```
40% show /usr/mikeh/fred /usr/mihek /usr/mikeh/Scripts

/usr/mikeh/fred is a file.
When you hear the tone, press Enter to view it or Del to continue.

/usr/mihek is not a file or a directory.
When you hear the tone, press Del to continue.

_
```

The *show* script is telling you that the argument */usr/mihek* is not a file or a directory and is prompting you to press the Delete key to continue.

To see exactly why the script found this spelling error and told you the word wasn't a file or a directory, let's take another look at the *show* script itself.

If the *$file* argument is neither a directory nor an ordinary file, then the flow of the *if...then...else* conditional moves to the final *else* statement. Recall that these read as follows:

```
else echo $file 'is not a file or directory.'
   echo 'When you hear the tone, press Del to continue.'
   cat errormessage ! pr -pt
endif
```

Notice that this script doesn't have a conditional. That means all the remaining commands in the command list will be executed.

We could have simply used a single *echo* statement to display the appropriate message, but doing so would have made our script inconsistent. As you design scripts, be sure to create an environment, however small, that processes each request in the same manner. Therefore, we've used the *cat* command and the *pr* utility to provide users with a consistent "interface" within the script. Although we have no intention of displaying anything on the screen, we used *pr* to pause and beep for us. Perhaps one of humanity's most predictable traits is curiosity, and for that reason we've created and included the *errormessage* file. Script users aren't advised to press Enter, but if they do, they see the message *That file or directory does not exist!* and are moved on to the next file or directory. (It is assumed that the *errormessage* file exists in your current directory. If this situation is not practical for you, include an absolute path to the *errormessage* file.)

Also note that the change in options for the final *pr* command in the script. The *errormessage* file is only one line long, and we don't expect that it will ever be more than a few lines long, so we've removed the *-l21* option that displays more than one screenful of text. As a rule, it's always a good idea to clean up loose ends like this immediately. You might even want to include a comment or two (preceded by a pound sign) to help refresh your memory the next time you work on the script.

You now have a script that lets you view a file or lets you request the long listing of any file or directory you specify. More importantly, you've stepped through the design and implementation of a C shell script. You've begun to develop a new and useful talent.

# 11

# Open Desktop

When you turn your computer on and log into SCO UNIX, the screen provides no clue
to what you must do to accomplish a task, such as reading your *mail* messages or writing
a memo in *vi*. All you see is the opening screen, ending with the $ character of the
Bourne shell or the *1%* characters of the C shell and the blinking cursor. To carry out a
task, you need to know how to enter commands, and you need to know the commands
to enter.

SCO's Open Desktop alleviates this obscurity. Open Desktop is a complete graphical environment in which SCO UNIX System V Release 3.2 is embedded. Open Desktop
displays files, directories, and programs as graphical representations called icons. In
addition, you can have more than one program running at a time, with each program
displayed in its own window — a separate portion of the screen framed by borders. The
program can receive its input and display its output within its window. By opening
more than one window, you can monitor more than one program at a time on the
screen, and you can respond to each in turn as it requires your attention. You can move
information directly from one window to another. You can also run multiple programs
in SCO UNIX either by using the & command to put programs in the background or by
using SCO's Multiscreens. In contrast to Open Desktop, however, one program takes the
entire screen for its display in SCO UNIX.

Open Desktop is much more than simply a graphical environment. Open Desktop
also provides standard networking protocols, database management capabilities, and
access to the MS-DOS operating system. The combination of these different features
in one package provides a rich and powerful environment in which to work. Open

Desktop assumes that your computer is connected to a network and provides the basic tools for communicating on the network and for requesting services from other computers on the network. And because access to structured data can increase your efficiency, Open Desktop provides a networked relational database management system.

With SCO UNIX installed on your computer, you can run UNIX or you can run MS-DOS, but you can't run both at the same time. With Open Desktop installed, you have an integrated environment in which you can run MS-DOS applications and the multiuser, multitasking SCO UNIX operating system simultaneously. You can create an MS-DOS operating system environment, or you can access MS-DOS commands directly from an SCO UNIX window. Open Desktop integrates the filesystem for MS-DOS and SCO UNIX, giving you complete and transparent access to all files for both operating systems. Because of this integration, your hard drive doesn't need a separate MS-DOS partition. You can use MS-DOS commands through SCO UNIX shell scripts, you can redirect the input and output of MS-DOS programs and SCO UNIX programs, you can simultaneously run several MS-DOS programs in MS-DOS environments, or you can simultaneously run multiple MS-DOS and SCO UNIX processes.

Rather than serving as the operating system for a central computer with a number of attached terminals (as SCO UNIX does), the basic Open Desktop system turns each computer into a graphical workstation, allowing each user access to services on a networked system of computers. You can also add components from SCO to provide Open Desktop services to attached terminals or to create Open Desktop servers for use by other workstations on the network.

> **NOTE:** *To try out the examples in this chapter, you must have Open Desktop installed on your computer, and you must have a valid Open Desktop user account. If your system uses Open Desktop but you don't have a valid Open Desktop account, have your system administrator create one for you. If you are the system administrator, create a user account for yourself.*

This chapter is intended as an introduction to Open Desktop, not as an in-depth exploration. However, it should give you the flavor of what Open Desktop offers by presenting its major features. Should you want more information, talk to your system administrator or consult the manuals.

# THE COMPONENTS OF OPEN DESKTOP

The two major components of Open Desktop are the operating system and the display system. Let's look briefly at each component so that you'll have an overview of Open Desktop before you begin using it.

## The Operating System

As was mentioned earlier, SCO UNIX System V Release 3.2 is the operating system of Open Desktop. The version of SCO UNIX that is part of Open Desktop is virtually the same as the SCO UNIX described throughout the rest of this book except that it is limited to two users. In addition, the screens and prompts probably won't appear as they are described elsewhere in this book because Open Desktop is usually installed so that the windowing system appears when you log in. If you need to use SCO UNIX commands, you can start a UNIX shell in its own window. The commands that you type appear in that window, and the output is confined to the window.

## The Display System

The system for screen display has three basic components: the X Window System, the Motif Window Manager, and the Desktop Manager.

The X Window System was originally developed at the Massachusetts Institute of Technology. The X Window System Version 11 that is part of Open Desktop consists of servers, which display images, and clients, which are programs that create and transmit images to servers for display. This system of servers and clients provides the ability to display several independent windows on a server's screen. Each window serves a separate client program, and these programs can be on the local computer or on any other computer that runs the X Window System and that is connected to the network.

The Motif Window Manager, originally developed by the Open Software Foundation, creates the graphical borders around each window on the display, displays the graphical representations of the controls for each window, and interprets your input by moving, resizing, or hiding windows.

The Desktop Manager, an application for managing Open Desktop's graphical representations, is an X Window client that attaches icons to files and programs and that defines the actions that result when you manipulate them.

These three components work together to display and manipulate information on your screen.

# USING OPEN DESKTOP

Because Open Desktop is so transparent, the best way to become familiar with it is to use it. Unlike a character-based environment, Open Desktop's graphical environment encourages exploration. So let's start Open Desktop and begin our exploration.

## Starting Open Desktop

With Open Desktop installed, when you start your computer, the screen displays the following message followed by the login prompt:

```
scosysv

Welcome to SCO System V/386

scosysv!login: _
```

Just as you can start SCO UNIX as a C shell user or as a Bourne shell user, depending on your user account definition, you can use the C shell, the Bourne shell, or Open Desktop on a computer running Open Desktop. To start Open Desktop, type your user name and press Enter. When the password prompt appears, type your password and press Enter. The opening screen for Open Desktop appears on your display as follows:

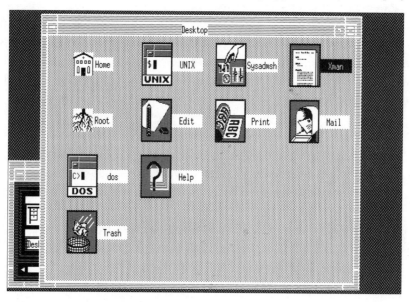

## Using the Mouse

After you start Open Desktop, much of your interaction with it requires you to use the mouse. In case you're unfamiliar with using the mouse, let's quickly look at the basics.

When you move the mouse across your desk, the mouse pointer moves a corresponding distance on your display. You use the mouse buttons in three basic mouse actions: clicking, double-clicking, and dragging.

Clicking simply means pressing and immediately releasing the left mouse button once. When you click with the mouse pointer on an object on the display, you cause some event, such as the appearance of a menu or the selection of a menu item.

Double-clicking means pressing and immediately releasing the left mouse button twice in rapid succession. When you double-click with the pointer on an object on the display, the results are different from those caused by clicking.

Dragging means positioning the pointer on an object, pressing the left mouse button, and holding the mouse button down while you move the mouse. When you drag an object, you move it from one location to another.

## The Desktop Window

The principal window displayed on the opening screen is the *Desktop* window. The *Desktop* window contains the following elements:

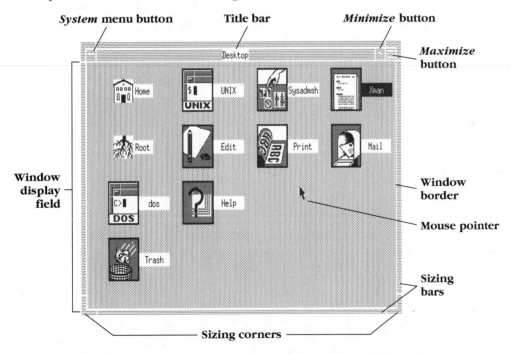

From the *Desktop* window, you can access all the features of Open Desktop.

The window display field is the area under control of the X Window System. In the *Desktop* window, the window display field contains icons.

The window border contains all the controls for manipulating the window. The border is under control of the Window Manager.

The sizing bars and sizing corners in the window border let you use the mouse to change the size of the window. The sizing bars on each side of the window let you expand or contract the window on that side. The sizing corners let you expand or contract the window both horizontally and vertically.

The *System* menu button is at the upper left corner of the window. Clicking this button once displays the *System* menu for the window. Double-clicking it closes the *Desktop* window.

The title bar at the top of the window contains the name of the file, program, or directory that the window represents.

The *Minimize* and *Maximize* buttons are in the upper right corner of the window. The *Minimize* button is on the left; the *Maximize* button is on the right. Clicking the *Minimize* button reduces the window to an icon. Clicking the *Maximize* button expands the window to cover the entire display.

As was mentioned earlier, the pointer is the graphic symbol on the window that moves in response to mouse movements. The position of the pointer in the window determines which element of the window responds when you use the mouse buttons. On most areas of the window, the pointer is an arrow, but the pointer changes shape in certain areas. The pointer moves independently of any text cursor (a block or an underline) that appears in a window. You use the keyboard to control the movement of text cursors, but in some applications you can position the pointer and then click a mouse button to move the text cursor to a new location.

## Opening a Window

A window opens when you double-click a file icon or a directory icon or when you start up a program by double-clicking the program's icon.

To see how a window opens, open the *Root* directory window by moving the pointer in the *Desktop* window to the *Root* directory icon and double-clicking the left button on the mouse.

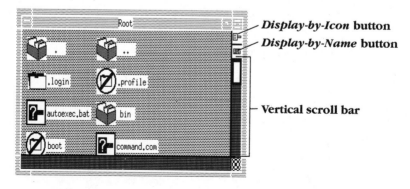

*Display-by-Icon* **button**

*Display-by-Name* **button**

**Vertical scroll bar**

The *Root* directory window is now the active window, the window that accepts input from the keyboard or mouse. The active window is distinguished from other windows by its colored border on a color display or by its white border on a monochrome display. Inactive windows have gray borders. To make an inactive window active, move the pointer onto it and click the left mouse button.

A directory window, such as the *Root* directory window, has controls on the window border for changing the display within the window. Two buttons are located on the right border, immediately below the *Maximize* button: the *Display-by-Icon* button, which contains a miniature icon, and the *Display-by-Name* button, which contains the word *FILE*. Double-clicking either of these buttons changes the window display to the corresponding type of listing.

The *Root* directory window contains icons for various data files and programs. The root directory contains more data files and programs than the ones represented by the icons you can see right now. To see the icons representing the additional files and programs, you need to scroll the window down. On the right edge of the window is the vertical scroll bar, which contains a white box immediately below the *Display-by-Name* button. To see the rest of the directory contents, drag the white box down the scroll bar to scroll the window. Doing so brings the other icons into the display field. The length of the white box indicates how much of the total directory you are currently viewing; the position of the box indicates where in the directory you currently are. You can also click above or below the white box of the bar to scroll by one windowful.

## Changing the Size of a Window

Sometimes, rather than scrolling a window, you'll find it more convenient to enlarge the window. To make the *Root* directory window larger, move the pointer into a sizing corner in the border of the window, and drag the corner diagonally away from the center of the window. Only an outline of the window moves while you hold down the mouse button. When you release the mouse button, the window becomes its new size. To make the window smaller, drag the sizing corner diagonally toward the center of the window.

You can also change the size of the window by using the *Maximize* and *Minimize* buttons. These buttons are next to each other on the right side of the title bar. Click the *Maximize* button on the *Root* directory window to expand the window to take up your entire display. Click the *Maximize* button again to restore the window to its previous size. Click the *Minimize* button to change the window to an icon in the *Icons* box behind the other windows on your display. Move your pointer to the lower left corner of the screen, and click the bit of window that's showing behind the *Desktop* window to bring the *Icons* box into view.

The icons in the *Icons* box represent open files, directories, and programs, whether they are expanded to windows or minimized to icons. The icons for expanded windows have dark borders; the icons for minimized windows have white borders. If a number of windows are open, you can minimize them and store them in the *Icons* box to reduce the clutter on your screen.

The *Desktop* window is partially hidden behind the *Icons* box. To make *Desktop* the active window, move the pointer into it and click. Click anywhere in the *Icons* box to move it to the top again. Double-click the *Root* directory icon in the *Icons* box to expand it to a window and make it active.

## Moving a Window

You now have two windows open on your display: the *Desktop* window and the *Root* directory window. The *Root* directory window is the active window, and it overlaps the *Desktop* window. Let's move the *Root* directory window out of the way to get at another icon—the *Edit* icon, which is in the *Desktop* window, behind the *Root* directory window. The *Edit* icon is in the second row of the second column of icons in the *Desktop* window. To move the *Root* directory window, position the pointer in its title bar, and drag the window out of the way.

## Running a Program

The *Edit* icon—the icon that looks like a pencil—represents an executable program, the *vi* editor. To start *vi*, double-click the *Edit* icon. (If you wanted to start *vi* and load a file, you could drag the file icon onto the *Edit* icon.)

The *Edit* window, containing the *vi* editor, appears. The white border (or colored border on a color monitor) shows that the *Edit* window is active and that it is now ready to accept input for *vi*. All the commands and techniques described in Chapters 6 and 7 work under Open Desktop.

Before we leave *vi*, let's create a small test file that we can use a little later when we work with files.

Use the *i* command, and then enter the following text (or any other sample text that you want to use):

```
This is a sample file.
```

Press the Escape key to return to command mode. Save the file on disk in your home directory, and give it the name *test* by using the following command:

```
:w test
```

For the time being, we'll keep *vi* running in the *Edit* window.

## Closing a Window and Stopping a Program

You can close a window by choosing the *Close* command from the *System* menu. To do so, first move the pointer to the *System* menu button in the upper left corner of the *Desktop* window, and click the left mouse button. The *System* menu appears.

The *System* menu contains the following commands:

| | |
|---|---|
| *Restore* | Restores a minimized window to its previous size. |
| *Move* | Moves the window. The pointer becomes a four-headed arrow. Moving the pointer moves the window, and clicking any mouse button redraws the window at the new location. |
| *Size* | Resizes the edge of the window to which you move the cursor. |
| *Minimize* | Reduces the window to an icon. |
| *Maximize* | Enlarges the window to fill the display. |
| *Lower* | Moves the window to the bottom of the stack of windows. The window remains active. |
| *Close* | Closes the window and stops any program running in it. |

To close the window, move the pointer to the *Close* command and click the left mouse button.

You can also display the *System* menu by moving the mouse cursor anywhere onto the outer edge of the window border and then pressing and holding down the right mouse button. The *System* menu appears at the pointer location. Move down the menu until the pointer is on the command you want, and then release the mouse button. If you decide that you don't want to choose a command, move the pointer off the menu before you release the button. You can use this method when the *System* menu button for the window is not visible.

You can use the *System* menu for a number of the tasks you've already done with the mouse, such as minimizing or moving a window. You can also close a window by double-clicking the *System* menu box. Doing so has the same effect as displaying the

*System* menu and then choosing *Close*. Closing a window also stops any program running in that window.

Double-click the *System* menu box on the *Edit* window to close it and to stop *vi*.

## Manipulating a File by Using Its Icon

If you look at the *Desktop* window, you see a number of different icons. These icons represent files with special meaning. The *Home* icon represents your home directory. Similarly, the *Root* icon represents the root directory of the filesystem. Several of the other icons represent programs that you can run. For example, the *Xman* icon represents the program that displays the online reference manual pages in Open Desktop, the *Mail* icon represents the *mail* program, and the *Sysadmsh* icon represents the system administration shell.

To explore how to use icons, let's first open a window to display your home directory. To open this window, move the pointer onto the *Home* icon and double-click.

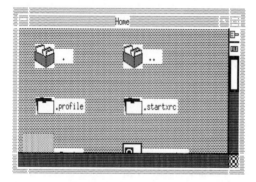

The *Home* directory window contains a number of files that were created when your account was created. The names of most of these files begin with a dot (.) character, which in the UNIX file-naming conventions usually signifies a configuration or information file that a program uses when it starts. The graphical representation for these icons is one of the general icon types. A general icon type represents a data file or text file. One file in the *Home* directory window should be familiar to you: the *.profile* file that the Bourne shell uses when it starts.

## Creating a Directory

Let's create a new subdirectory in your home directory and move some copies of the *test* file we created earlier into it. To create a new subdirectory, move the mouse into the display field of the *Home* directory window away from any of the icons. Press and hold down one of the mouse buttons to display the *Directory* menu.

The *Directory* menu contains the following commands:

| | |
|---|---|
| *Alphabetic* | Displays the directory contents in alphabetic order. |
| *By Time* | Displays the directory contents in order of creation or last modification, with the most recent first. |
| *By Class* | Displays directory files first, followed by text files, followed by executable files. |
| *By Size* | Displays directory contents by file size, with the smallest first. |
| *Select All* | Selects all the icons in the directory. |
| *Icon Info* | Displays information about the files represented by the selected icons. |
| *Duplicate File* | Copies the file represented by the selected icon. |
| *New Directory* | Creates a subdirectory in the current directory. |
| *New Empty File* | Creates a new empty file. |
| *Close* | Closes the directory window. |

Without releasing the mouse button, move the pointer over the command name *New Directory*, and then release the mouse button. A message box requesting the name of the new directory appears. Type *Icontest* as the name of the new directory, and press Enter. A new directory icon with the label *Icontest* appears in your *Home* directory window at the location of the message box. The graphical representation used in this icon is another of the general icon types — it represents a directory. Your *Home* directory window contains two other icons of this type — dot (.), representing the Home directory, and dot-dot (..), representing the directory immediately above your home directory in the filesystem's directory structure.

## Duplicating a File

To make a copy of a file, you must first select that file. To select the *test* file, move the pointer over the *test* icon, and click the left mouse button. You have selected the icon, and you can see that it is now highlighted. Be sure to put the pointer over the icon rather than over the name, and be sure you click the left mouse button rather than the right button. If you move the pointer over the name of the icon and you click the right mouse button, Open Desktop displays a message box for renaming the icon. If you position the pointer on the icon but you click the right mouse button, you deselect the icon.

Move the mouse pointer away from any icons in the *Home* directory window display field, and hold down any mouse button to display the *Directory* menu. Move the pointer to the *Duplicate File* command on the menu, and release the mouse button to display the message box for a duplicate file. (It looks identical to the message box for a new directory.) Type *first.test* as the name for the new, duplicate file in the box, and press Enter. Now duplicate *test* again, and call the second copy *second.test*. The two icons for the duplicate files appear in your *Home* directory window. Using this operation produces the same result as using the *cp* command in SCO UNIX.

## Moving a File

Next we want to move both copies of the *test* file to the *Icontest* directory. Let's open the window for the *Icontest* directory. Move the pointer onto the *Icontest* icon and double-click the left mouse button. The *Icontest* window appears, empty except for the . and .. directory icons. If necessary, size or move the *Icontest* window so that you can see the icons for the copies of the *test* file in the *Home* directory window. You might also need to size or move the *Home* directory window as well. We'll move both files by selecting them and then dragging them out of the *Home* directory window and into the *Icontest* window. To select both icons, use the right mouse button. Move the pointer over the first icon and click with the right mouse button to select it. Then move the pointer over the second icon and click with the right mouse button again. Both icons are now selected.

To drag them to the *Icontest* window, move the pointer over one of the icons, press and hold down the right mouse button, and move the pointer into the *Icontest* window. Outlines of the icons move with the pointer into the *Icontest* window. When you release the mouse button, the icons disappear from the *Home* directory window and reappear in the *Icontest* directory window. You have moved the files represented by the icons from your home directory to the . directory. Doing so is the equivalent of using the *mv* command in SCO UNIX.

## Deleting a File by Using the *Trash* Icon

We really don't want to keep both copies of the *test* file, so let's get rid of one copy, the *second.test* file. If necessary, rearrange your windows so that you can see both the *Trash* icon in your *Home* directory window and the *second.test* file icon. You might need to size or move the *Home* and *Icontest* windows and perhaps reduce other windows on your desktop to icons in the *Icons* box. When you can see the *Trash* icon and the *second.test* icon on your screen, drag the *second.test* icon from the *Icontest* window onto the *Trash* icon. Release the mouse button to throw away that file. If you want to think of what you've done in terms of SCO UNIX, you've removed a file as if you had used the *rm* command. Moving an icon to the *Trash* icon is different from removing an SCO UNIX file, however. If you want to retrieve a file from the *Trash* icon, double-click the *Trash* icon with the left mouse button, and drag the icon that you want to retrieve away from the *Trash* icon. On the other hand, if you're certain that you don't want any of the files you've moved to the *Trash* icon, and you want to recover the disk space that they are taking up, double-click the *Trash* icon with the right mouse button.

If, for some reason, you can't rearrange the windows to see the *Trash* icon and the icon for a file you want to remove, you can drag the file icon in two steps. First drag the icon into the *Desktop* window. When the icon is in the *Desktop* window, its name changes to */Icontest/second.profile* to indicate its original location. You then can use one of three methods to display your *Home* window. If any portion of the *Home* window is visible, click that portion of the window. If the *Icons* box is visible, click the *Home* window icon in the *Icons* box. If neither the *Home* window nor the *Icons* box is visible, display the *Root* menu by moving the pointer into the background field, holding down any mouse button, and then selecting the *Shuffle Up* command repeatedly to shuffle windows in the stack until your *Home* window is on top. When your *Home* window is on top of the stack, drag the file icon from the background onto the *Trash* icon.

## Printing a File

Because the print spooler is simply another program, you can send a text file to the print spooler by dragging an icon onto the *Print* icon. To print the *test* file, for example, drag the file icon onto the *Print* icon in the *Desktop* window.

## Getting Help from Open Desktop

If you need help while you're running Open Desktop, you have two ways to get information from the system itself: through the online help program (*Help*) or through the online reference manual pages (*Xman*). The online help program tells you about the Open Desktop windowing system. The online reference manual pages tell you about the programs available under Open Desktop.

The online help program is represented in the *Desktop* window by the *Help* icon, a question mark over the Open Desktop logo. To start the online help program, double-click on the *Help* icon. The *Help* window appears.

The top line in the window is the *Help* menu, which lists the commands in the *Help* program. To move from one command to the next, use the cursor-movement keys on the keyboard; the mouse has no effect inside the *Help* program. However, as in any other window, you can use the mouse in the window border to size, move, or close the window. Immediately below the *Help* menu is a description of the currently highlighted command. When you press Enter, the *Help* program executes the highlighted command. The next line displays the name of the topic for which information appears in the rest of the window. To find out how the *Help* program works, press the H key at any time to display *Help on Help*. To return to the main *Help* window from *Help on Help*, press the Escape key. When you finish with the *Help* program, choose the *Quit* command from the menu, and press Enter both to end the program and to close the window.

Alternatively, you can minimize the window so that you can reactivate *Help* quickly by merely clicking on the *Help* window icon in the *Icons* box.

The program for displaying the online manual reference pages is represented by the *Xman* icon in the *Desktop* window.

To start *Xman*, double-click on the icon to display its *topBox* window.

The three buttons in the *topBox* window let you look at a manual page, get information about how to use *Xman*, and quit *Xman*.

**NOTE:** *The* Xman *program expects a three-button mouse. If you have a two-button mouse, when the instructions request you to press the middle mouse button, hold down the Shift key and press the left mouse button.*

To begin viewing manual pages, click the Manual Page button. The manual page for *Xman* appears.

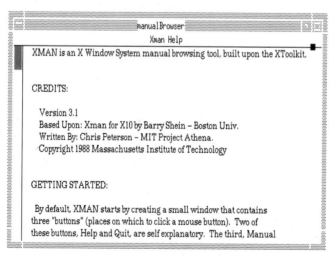

Move the pointer onto the manual page, and press the left mouse button to scroll down. Press the right mouse button to scroll up.

Suppose, however, that you're not interested in *Xman* but that you need to look at the manual page for *vi*. To find the manual page for *vi*, move the pointer onto the manual page title bar, labeled *Xman Help*, and click the left mouse button. The *Xman Options* menu appears.

Move the pointer to the *Change Section* command, and click the left mouse button. Doing so displays the list of command sections for which *Xman* can display manual pages. (These correspond roughly to the manual sections for SCO UNIX described in Chapter 2 of this book.) Choose *Commands* from this menu. The *Xman* program fills the window with columnar lists of commands. Scroll down in the window, if necessary, until the entry for *vi* is displayed on the screen. Move the pointer over that entry, and click the left mouse button to display the manual page for *vi*.

After you choose a command section, you can return from a manual page to the list of commands by pressing the middle button of a three-button mouse. If you have a two-button mouse, press the Shift key and the left button.

When you finish using *Xman*, click the *Quit* button in the *topBox* window to stop the program and to close the window.

# Using Other Open Desktop Menus

Open Desktop uses two other menus for certain tasks. In some cases, the choices duplicate tasks that you can perform with the mouse or the keyboard. Which method you choose depends on the task and the context; sometimes the mouse is more convenient, sometimes the menu.

## The *Desktop* menu

To display the *Desktop* menu, move the pointer into the field of the *Desktop* window away from any icon, and then press and hold down any mouse button. The *Desktop* menu appears. Continue to hold down the mouse button while you move the pointer to the command you want, and then release the mouse button to choose the command.

The *Desktop* menu contains the following commands:

| | |
|---|---|
| *Align* | Lines up the icons in the window. |
| *Reorganize* | Rearranges all the icons in the window in rows at the top of the window. |
| *Select All* | Selects all the icons in the window. |
| *Put back* | Returns the selected icons to their original directories. |
| *Icon Info* | Displays information about the selected icons and lets you change the permissions for the associated file. |
| *Shell Window* | Opens a *UNIX* window. |
| *Stop Desktop* | Quits Open Desktop. |

## The Root menu

To display the *Root* menu, move the pointer into the background field (the pointer becomes an X), and then press and hold down either mouse button. The *Root* menu appears. Continue holding down the mouse button until the pointer is on the command you want, and then release the mouse button.

The *Root* menu contains the following commands:

| | |
|---|---|
| *Clients* | Displays a menu with more client windows, including a clock window and a calculator window. |
| *xterm* | Starts an *xterm* client window. |
| *Shuffle Up* | Brings the bottom window to the top of the stack. |
| *Shuffle Down* | Moves the top window to the bottom of the stack. |
| *Refresh* | Redraws the entire display. |
| *Restart* | Restarts the Window Manager. |

# Stopping Open Desktop

To stop Open Desktop, display the *Desktop* menu, and then choose *Stop Desktop* from the menu. Open Desktop stops, and your computer displays its login prompt. Alternatively, you can double-click the *System* menu button in the upper left corner of the *Desktop* window to stop Open Desktop.

> **NOTE:** *If programs are running when you stop, Open Desktop does not remind you that the programs are running and that you might need to take action to save your work. Before stopping Open Desktop, be sure that you have saved any work that you have completed.*

# RUNNING SCO UNIX UNDER OPEN DESKTOP

Open Desktop lets you access all the SCO UNIX commands described throughout the rest of this book. To do so, you open a window for an SCO UNIX shell as a client in one of the following three ways:

■ Double-click on the *UNIX* icon in the *Desktop* window.

■ Choose the *Shell Window* command from the *Desktop* menu.

■ Choose the *xterm* command from the *Root* menu.

The default shell in a *UNIX* window is the Bourne shell. In the window, the shell prompt is followed by the cursor, waiting for you to type commands. All the output from commands given in the window appears in the window.

You can manipulate the window for the SCO UNIX shell in the same way you manipulate any other Open Desktop window, with one exception: The scroll bar for the *UNIX* window is on the left window border. To scroll up in the window, move the pointer into the scroll bar, and click the left mouse button. To scroll down in the window, move the pointer into the scroll bar, and click the right mouse button. The distance of the pointer from the top of the scroll bar determines the distance the window scrolls.

But why would you want to scroll the window? Unlike standard SCO UNIX, a *UNIX* window in Open Desktop can retain what appears in it. You can scroll up and down in the window to look at the commands and subsequent output. You can also use the mouse to mark commands that you have given, copy them to the command prompt, and execute them again. You can even copy commands from one *UNIX* window to another. Let's look more closely at this feature.

Open a *UNIX* window by double-clicking the *UNIX* icon in the *Desktop* window. Notice that in the *UNIX* window, the pointer becomes an I-beam, and a text cursor appears after the prompt in the window. The prompt consists of your machine name, two exclamation points, and your login name, all enclosed in brackets, as follows:

```
[bifrost!!mikeh]
```

Let's list the contents of the current directory by using the *ls* command. Enter the following at the prompt:

```
ls
```

The *UNIX* window displays a list of the contents of the current directory. Nothing extraordinary in that. But suppose you want to repeat the command. To repeat the command, move the I-beam pointer in front of the *l* in *ls* at the previous prompt, hold down the Shift key, and then move the I-beam pointer over the command and to the right until the entire line is highlighted. Still holding down the Shift key, move the I-beam pointer to the position of the text cursor after the current prompt, and release the Shift key. The command appears there and is executed. Highlighting the line all the way to the end copies the carriage-return keystroke as well, which causes the shell to execute the command.

The ability to copy commands is particularly useful when you have mistyped a long command. For example, let's say you want to create a backup file on a floppy disk drive, but you accidentally type the following:

```
find . -depth -print ! cpio -o -O /rfd1135ds18
```

The operating system replies with the following:

```
cpio: ERROR: Cannot open </rfd1135ds18> for output.
        Permission denied
```

You meant to type the following:

```
find . -depth -print ¦ cpio -o -O /dev/rfd1135ds18
```

After SCO UNIX reports your error, you can copy the correct portion of that command to the current prompt without executing it and then correct the error without retyping the entire command. Move the I-beam pointer to the position immediately before the *f* at the start of the command, hold down the left mouse button, and drag across the command to the slash so that you highlight the part of the command that you want to copy. Release the mouse button, move the I-beam pointer to the current prompt, and then press and hold down the Shift key while you click the left mouse button. The portion of the command that you copied appears at the prompt with the text cursor at the end of the line. You can now type the rest of the command, and press the Enter key to run the command. (If you don't have a floppy disk in the drive or your system doesn't have a second 1.44-MB floppy disk drive, the system will merely report an error; no harm is done.)

If you open two *UNIX* client windows by double-clicking the *UNIX* icon two different times, you can copy a command from one window to another in exactly the same fashion.

To exit the SCO UNIX shell when you're done, double-click the *System* menu button in the upper left corner of the window, or type *exit* at the prompt and press Enter. Both methods stop the SCO UNIX shell and close the window.

# RUNNING MS-DOS UNDER OPEN DESKTOP

You can use the facilities of MS-DOS in Open Desktop in either of two ways.

You can start an MS-DOS environment, which creates a separate window while MS-DOS is running. You interact with the MS-DOS environment in the window exactly as you would interact with an MS-DOS computer. In fact, Open Desktop creates what is known as a virtual MS-DOS machine on your computer. The only difference between this virtual machine and an independent MS-DOS computer is that the virtual machine is contained in and under the control of Open Desktop—that is, it is a client program of your machine's X Window server.

You can also run MS-DOS commands directly from a *UNIX* window. Open Desktop has an integrated filesystem, which allows both SCO UNIX and MS-DOS files and programs to reside in it. When you type a command in an SCO UNIX shell, the shell interprets the commands according to the file type and takes the appropriate action: The SCO UNIX shell runs SCO UNIX commands in the SCO UNIX operating system, and it temporarily sets up an MS-DOS virtual machine to run MS-DOS commands.

# Entering an MS-DOS Environment

When you enter an MS-DOS environment under Open Desktop by opening an MS-DOS window, the window acts as if it were an MS-DOS computer only as long as you remain in the MS-DOS environment. The display in the window looks much as it would look on any computer running only MS-DOS. You can enter the MS-DOS environment from Open Desktop in one of the following three ways:

- Double-click the *DOS* icon in the *Desktop* window.

- Type the command *dos* at the prompt in a *UNIX* window, and press Enter.

- Double-click on the icon for any executable MS-DOS program.

In the first two instances, the MS-DOS environment creates a window, and the MS-DOS command prompt appears in the window. In the third case, the MS-DOS environment takes over the screen. If the program is interactive and windowed, as Microsoft Word is, the window for that program appears on the screen.

Your initial directory in an MS-DOS environment is your SCO UNIX home directory, prefixed by the *C:* drive designator. For example, if your SCO UNIX home directory is */u/mikeh*, your initial directory after starting an MS-DOS environment would be *C:\U\MIKEH*.

# Running a Program in an MS-DOS Environment

To run an MS-DOS program in an MS-DOS environment, simply type the program name (preceded by the pathname if the program is not in a directory on your search path).

You will notice some differences between working in a standard MS-DOS environment and working in an MS-DOS environment under Open Desktop because you are executing programs in a multiuser, multitasking operating system. One difference is that the UNIX filesystem appears in your MS-DOS environment as drive C. Also, if you have a physical MS-DOS partition on your hard disk that is separate from the integrated filesystem under Open Desktop, the MS-DOS partition appears as drive E in an Open Desktop MS-DOS environment. More than one MS-DOS process can read from the MS-DOS partition at any one time, but only one MS-DOS process can write to the MS-DOS partition or to a floppy disk drive at any one time. If one process tries to write to the MS-DOS partition (drive E) or to a floppy disk drive while another process is writing to the same partition or drive, the system responds with a general failure error message for that device. Use of the serial ports is even more restricted: Only one MS-DOS process can use a serial port at one time.

You can print from the MS-DOS environment by using printer ports LPT1, LPT2, LPT3, and PRN as you can from MS-DOS. You can use the MS-DOS Copy command to copy files to the printer ports, the MS-DOS Print command to print files, the printing functions in MS-DOS programs, and the MS-DOS Shift-PrtSc key combination to print the current screen. The MS-DOS environment sends the printed output to the SCO UNIX printer *doslp* and on to the SCO UNIX print spooler. You can also press the Ctrl-Shift-PrtSc key combination to save screens in a temporary file.

Memory specifications in the MS-DOS environment also differ from standard MS-DOS. When you start up the MS-DOS environment, you can request that the environment provide any amount of expanded memory (as defined by the Lotus/Intel/Microsoft Expanded Memory Specification, or LIM EMS) from 512 KB to 8 MB. You don't need to have an expanded memory card in your computer or to have the actual physical memory requested. The MS-DOS environment simulates expanded memory by using SCO UNIX virtual memory. To specify 4 MB of expanded memory when you start the MS-DOS environment at the SCO UNIX prompt, enter the following command:

```
dos +aems4
```

If you need to use the COM ports in the MS-DOS environment, you also need to specify this need when you start the MS-DOS environment.

To use COM1, you would use the following command:

```
dos +acom1
```

If one MS-DOS environment tries to access COM1 while another MS-DOS environment is using COM1, the operating system will report an error.

You can specify more than one requirement on the command line when you start MS-DOS. To specify that you need both 4 MB of memory and the use of COM1, give both requirements on the command line, as follows:

```
dos +aems4 +acom1
```

If you regularly use certain resources, you can specify them in the *dosenv.def* file, as described in the following section titled "Setting Up the Open Desktop MS-DOS Environment." Note that although you can have as much virtual memory as you want for every user working in an MS-DOS environment, you can't provide virtual communication ports. Communication ports either exist or don't exist, and only one MS-DOS user at a time can access them.

The mouse poses a potential conflict in an MS-DOS environment: Open Desktop uses the mouse, as do many MS-DOS programs. Which part of the system controls the mouse? To resolve this potential conflict, move the mouse pointer into the MS-DOS window. When you do so, the pointer turns into an I-beam. Press Alt-D to display the *dos* menu. Choose the focus command. Now, within the *DOS* window, the mouse is under the control of the MS-DOS program. When you no longer want to use the mouse with the MS-DOS program within that window (for example, if you want to copy text to another Open Desktop window), press Alt-D again to display the *dos* menu, and choose the *unfocus* command.

The *zoom* command, the only other command on the *dos* menu, causes the MS-DOS environment to take over the entire screen. The window borders disappear, and the screen looks as though you had started your computer directly from MS-DOS. (Using the *zoom* command is different from using the *Maximize* button, which expands the window, borders and all, to fill the entire screen.)

To return to the *DOS* window, press Alt-D again. Doing so does not display a menu but returns you to the Open Desktop display containing the *DOS* window.

Another difference between standard MS-DOS and an MS-DOS environment is a result of how the multiuser operating system and the integrated filesystem in Open Desktop work. Although the directories on drive C (the UNIX partition) look exactly like the directories under standard MS-DOS, they aren't—Open Desktop maintains a record of directory ownerships and permissions. You might not be able to change to some directories, to run programs in some directories, or to edit (or even read) files in some directories. The access rights depend on the way in which permission modes are set in your SCO UNIX operating system. Open Desktop does not maintain these records for directories on a physical MS-DOS partition (drive E, if one exists), and all files are accessible for all operations for all users.

## Stopping an MS-DOS Program

If you enter an MS-DOS command, such as *tree /f*, which displays the contents of every directory and subdirectory on the current drive, and you want to stop the command before it wastes too much of your time, press either Ctrl-C or Ctrl-Break. If you enter a command that neither of these key combinations can stop, press Ctrl-Alt-Del, or press Ctrl-Esc followed by Ctrl-K. In Open Desktop, these commands cause the running program to abort, and they also cause the current MS-DOS environment to abort. The computer does not reboot, however; it returns you to an Open Desktop screen.

## Leaving an MS-DOS Environment

When you want to leave an MS-DOS environment, enter the following command at the MS-DOS prompt:

```
quit
```

You return to an Open Desktop screen.

If you started an MS-DOS environment by double-clicking an icon to start an MS-DOS program, exit the program to return to an Open Desktop screen.

Alternatively, you can double-click the System menu button in the upper left corner of the *DOS* window. Doing so is similar to pressing Ctrl-Alt-Del, however. Whatever is running in the *DOS* window is stopped, and the window is closed whether you've saved your work or not.

## Setting Up the Open Desktop MS-DOS Environment

When you start an MS-DOS environment, Open Desktop sets it up much as your computer would if the computer booted under standard MS-DOS. The computer looks for a file named *dosenv.def*, either in the */etc* directory or in your home directory. You can modify this file with the *dosopt* command in a SCO UNIX shell window to customize the options that Open Desktop should use when creating an MS-DOS environment.

With the default *dosenv.def* file, Open Desktop runs the files CONFIG.SYS and AUTOEXEC.BAT but in a slightly different way than does standard MS-DOS. Open Desktop first runs the CONFIG.SYS and AUTOEXEC.BAT files that it finds in the filesystem's root directory (/ in the UNIX representation or *C:\* in the MS-DOS representation). Then if it finds CONFIG.SYS and AUTOEXEC.BAT in your home directory, it runs them, too. As a result, you can have a default MS-DOS environment for all users of Open Desktop, and you can have custom MS-DOS environments for any users who want to create one. If neither the CONFIG.SYS file nor the AUTOEXEC.BAT file specifies a search path with the Path command, Open Desktop sets the MS-DOS search path to be identical to the SCO UNIX search path. This path includes the directories \usr\dbin (with standard MS-DOS commands) and \usr\ldbin (with MS-DOS applications).

In an MS-DOS environment under Open Desktop, the MS-DOS virtual machine runs any MS-DOS application program, including MS-DOS programs that are known as "ill behaved" (they directly access the computer's hardware). Because each virtual MS-DOS machine runs in a specific segment of memory and is under the control of Open Desktop, the virtual machine can't alter memory outside of its segment and can't affect other MS-DOS virtual machines or SCO UNIX processes. When you start an MS-DOS environment, Open Desktop examines *dosenv.def* and determines from the *+a* parameter how much LIM EMS memory to make available.

Open Desktop recognizes files that you create while you are using MS-DOS and lets you access them with MS-DOS commands. You can also access text files created under SCO UNIX for use with MS-DOS commands. Because SCO UNIX and MS-DOS text file formats are different, you need a utility program that converts files from the SCO UNIX text file format to the MS-DOS format and vice versa. Because the underlying

SCO UNIX operating system keeps track of file ownership and permissions for its files, Open Desktop overlays the SCO UNIX file permissions on any MS-DOS files that you create. When you create an MS-DOS file on the filesystem, the operating system specifies you as the owner of the file and gives you permissions for the file. Unless you explicitly change the permissions on the file, other Open Desktop users on your computer can't access the file.

Permissions have another effect on using the filesystem under MS-DOS. The entire filesystem is considered to be drive C in an MS-DOS environment under Open Desktop, and the root directory is named *C:\*. When you start up an MS-DOS environment under Open Desktop, your current working directory is the same as the directory that you were in when you started MS-DOS. This startup procedure is not the same as the startup procedure for standard MS-DOS, where the startup directory is the root directory (\). If you start MS-DOS immediately after logging into Open Desktop, your current working directory is your home directory. Also in contrast to using standard MS-DOS, you might not be able to access all the directories on drive C because some directories belong to the superuser (*root*) or to other users with accounts on your computer. The permissions on those directories might permit access only to their owners.

You can maintain a separate MS-DOS partition if you want. When you do, Open Desktop displays the physical MS-DOS partition as drive E when you start up an MS-DOS environment. You can read and write files on drive E, transfer files between drives C and E, and run programs stored on drive E.

# RUNNING MS-DOS COMMANDS FROM AN SCO UNIX WINDOW

In addition to running MS-DOS commands from an MS-DOS environment under Open Desktop, you can run MS-DOS commands directly from the prompt in an SCO UNIX shell in a *UNIX* window. You can use many MS-DOS commands without specifying anything on the command line other than the command name. You can also run multiple MS-DOS commands or multiple MS-DOS and SCO UNIX commands simultaneously by having them execute in the background, exactly as you can run SCO UNIX commands alone. If you need to specify special characteristics to run an MS-DOS command, you can enter the command *dos*, the special requirements (such as expanded memory), and then the particular MS-DOS command, all on the same line. You also use the *dos* command to distinguish between commands that have identical names in MS-DOS and SCO UNIX but that have different functions, results, or operations.

For example, to run the MS-DOS Sort command instead of the SCO UNIX *sort* command, enter the following at the shell prompt:

```
dos sort < names > names.srt
```

If you don't precede the command with *dos*, SCO UNIX will run its own version of the command.

You can also specify the full pathname with a command to ensure that SCO UNIX runs the version you want.

Let's look at some of the ways you can mix the two command sets. Let's start with a simple directory command that illustrates one facet of the integration. Enter the following at the SCO UNIX shell prompt:

```
dir /usr/dbin
```

The command, *dir*, is an MS-DOS command, but the path separators are the SCO UNIX slashes (/) instead of the backslashes (\) that MS-DOS uses. Nonetheless, this hybrid produces an MS-DOS listing for the */usr/dbin* directory.

If you want a short MS-DOS listing, add the switch *-w* to the end of the command, as follows:

```
dir /usr/dbin -w
```

Unlike standard MS-DOS, the command uses the hyphen (-) character as a switch, but, unlike most SCO UNIX commands, the switch falls at the end of the command rather than before the arguments.

The order of the command elements—the command syntax—follows the MS-DOS rules. The interpretation of characters at the SCO UNIX prompt follows SCO UNIX rules. MS-DOS commands must be in lowercase letters—*dir* works; *DIR* fails. You must use the SCO UNIX path separators and the SCO UNIX switch characters with MS-DOS commands at the SCO UNIX prompt. Be aware that the following characters are interpreted according to SCO UNIX rules:

| | |
|---|---|
| < | " |
| > | ' |
| * | ' |
| ? | ^ |
| ! | ( |
| & | ) |
| $ | [ |
| ; | ] |
| \ | # |

Sometimes it seems as if a command takes forever to complete its task. In standard MS-DOS, after you start a command you can do nothing more until the command is completed. When you run a time-consuming MS-DOS program from an SCO UNIX shell in Open Desktop, however, you can put the task in the background, let it continue running, and proceed to other tasks while you wait for it to finish. If you have the Microsoft C compiler installed, you could compile and link the *hist.c* file with this command:

```
cl hist.c &
```

As was mentioned earlier, the ampersand (&) tells the operating system to execute the command in the background. After starting the command, the operating system immediately displays the command prompt and waits for another command.

. You can also combine MS-DOS and SCO UNIX commands on one command line by using pipes and redirection. For example, to find all the files with *report* in their directory entries, you can run the following command:

```
dir ¦ grep report
```

In this command, *dir* is an MS-DOS command, and *grep* is an SCO UNIX command. In Open Desktop's integrated filesystem, the commands work well together. Similarly, script files can contain a mixture of MS-DOS and SCO UNIX commands.

You can also use some hybrid commands created especially for Open Desktop. One such command is *udir*, which displays a directory listing for a directory in the SCO UNIX partition. The resulting directory listing is a hybrid between a directory listing that entering *dir* in MS-DOS would produce and a directory listing that entering *ls -l* in SCO UNIX would produce. To see the result, enter the following command from the SCO UNIX prompt in an SCO UNIX shell:

```
udir /u/mikeh
```

The following command entered at the MS-DOS prompt in an MS-DOS environment produces a similar result:

```
udir c:\u\mikeh
```

Both commands produce a listing similar to the following:

```
Volume in drive C is bifrost
 Directory of c:/u/mikeh

.                .               mikeh    drwx------   <DIR>         3-04-90   6:25p
..               ..              root     drwxrwxrwx   <DIR>         3-04-90   2:19a
Trash            TRASH'H         mikeh    drwx------   <DIR>         3-04-90   5:24p
xdtinitial.xde   XDTIN'CD.XDE    mikeh    -rw-------          424    3-04-90   6:25p
autoexec.bak     AUTOEXEC.BAK    mikeh    -rw-------          327    3-04-90   1:18p
tmp              TMP             mikeh    drwx------   <DIR>         3-04-90  12:34p
word5            WORD5           mikeh    drwx------   <DIR>         3-04-90  10:56p
mw.ini           MW.INI          mikeh    -rw-------          225    3-04-90  12:38p
config.bak       CONFIG.BAK      mikeh    -rw-------          282    3-04-90   1:19p
dosenv.def       DOSENV.DEF      mikeh    -rw-------          105    3-04-90   1:11p
core             CORE            mikeh    -rw-------         8300    3-04-90   6:25p
test             TEST            mikeh    -rw-------         1064    3-04-90   5:09p
config.sys       CONFIG.SYS      mikeh    -rw-------          283    3-04-90   1:21p
autoexec.bat     AUTOEXEC.BAT    mikeh    -rw-------          335    3-04-90   1:20p
Icontest         ICONT'B5        mikeh    drwx------   <DIR>         3-04-90   5:24p
     15 File(s)          74395648 bytes free
```

Notice that the integrated filesystem reconciles the different naming conventions in the two operating systems. The left side of the listing consists of SCO UNIX names for the files. The right side consists of the MS-DOS names for the same files. When an SCO UNIX name has a form that is illegal in MS-DOS, the SCO UNIX name is mapped onto an MS-DOS name. Each mapped MS-DOS name has a single quotation mark, followed by an index, which uniquely identifies the file. SCO UNIX filenames with uppercase letters are mapped in this way: *Mail* is mapped onto *MAIL'FPE*. SCO UNIX filenames that are longer than MS-DOS filenames are also mapped, as follows: *messagetoall* is mapped onto *MESS'BAQ*. SCO UNIX filenames with more than three characters after a period are mapped as follows: *message.tobob* is mapped onto *MESS'BBF.BOB*. This system never needs to map MS-DOS filenames onto SCO UNIX filenames because all MS-DOS names are allowable under the SCO UNIX naming conventions.

The listing from *udir* displays the file permissions for the files in the shared filesystem in the fourth column. You can change the permissions on any files in the integrated filesystem by using the *chmod* command, as follows:

```
chmod a=rx filename
```

This command gives all users permission to read and to execute *filename*. Unless you are the superuser, you can change the permissions only on files that you own.

# RUNNING SCO UNIX COMMANDS FROM AN MS-DOS ENVIRONMENT

Just as you can run MS-DOS commands in an SCO UNIX shell in Open Desktop, you can also run the following useful SCO UNIX commands from an MS-DOS environment:

| | | | |
|---|---|---|---|
| *cat* | *diff* | *grep* | *pr* |
| *chmod* | *dosopt* | *ln* | *spell* |
| *cmp* | *du* | *lp* | *tail* |
| *cp* | *egrep* | *ls* | *wc* |
| *df* | *fgrep* | *mv* | |

# NETWORKING AND FILESHARING

The philosophy behind Open Desktop recognizes that networks are a basic feature of computer installations in most organizations. For this reason, Open Desktop includes a standard suite of protocols, called TCP/IP, and related applications for communication, file transfer, and terminal emulation among other tasks. TCP/IP allows connections with many other devices on both local and remote networks and provides the transport layer of services for other networking software in Open Desktop, including the X Window system and the database management system. Open Desktop can share files residing on a remote computer by using the Network File System (NFS) protocol to become a client of a remote NFS server. Open Desktop can also access remote disk drives or remote printers with the Server Message Based (SMB) protocols in its LAN Manager/X client. (For an overview of network features, see Chapter 15.) Operating through the windowed display and running simultaneously with local programs, these network services extend the computing power of your computer to encompass all the resources available on your network.

# THE DATABASE MANAGEMENT SYSTEM

The database management system contained in Open Desktop is based on the INGRES system developed by Relational Technology Incorporated. With this database management system, you can access data on databases on your computer or on databases on other computers connected to your network. Open Desktop's windowing system lets you open as many database management windows as you choose in order to access multiple databases. You can use Open Desktop's facilities—copy and paste operations with the mouse, for example—to move information from a database in one window to a database in another window.

In the database management system, you can use either of two methods for accessing data: Query-by-Forms (QBF) and the Structured Query Language (SQL). The QBF method uses a series of menus and forms with which you can view and update data or display and print reports. QBF provides step-by-step guidance for common database tasks. SQL is a more versatile tool for accessing database information. It is essentially a database programming language, with built-in abilities to use functions, make calculations, define sets, and so on. You can use SQL to create tables in the database, add data, extract data, examine data, and create reports.

# SECTION

# II

# FOR THE
# SYSTEM
# ADMINISTRATOR

# 12

# Installing
# SCO UNIX

If you are the system administrator for your SCO UNIX system, your first task is to set up a viable SCO UNIX environment. You do so by installing SCO UNIX. If your system configuration is simple, you can install SCO UNIX easily by using the Automatic Installation option. If you use the Automatic option, you need to know your time zone and the language used on your keyboard, and you should allow yourself three to four hours to install the system completely. If your system configuration is complex or if you have special requirements for the layout of your hard disk, you can install SCO UNIX by using the Fully Configurable Installation option. However, in this chapter, we'll consider only the Automatic Installation option.

You don't need to know anything about SCO UNIX to use the Automatic Installation option. But a little background information will make some parts of the installation more comprehensible.

## INSIDE YOUR HARD DISK

In the process of installing SCO UNIX on your hard disk, you might encounter terms that are new to you, so let's take a quick and simplified look at the way your hard disk is constructed.

Unlike a floppy disk, which you can see and hold, a hard disk is tucked away from view (and dust, smoke, and air currents) inside a rigid case. The disk itself consists of two or more polished metal platters mounted on a spindle. Information is read from and written to each side of each platter by a read-write head that moves horizontally over the surface in much the same way the tone arm on a phonograph turntable moves across the surface of a record. Unlike the tone arm of a phonograph, the read-write head never actually touches the surface of a platter, and data is recorded on the hard disk in a series of concentric circles rather than in one continuous spiral, as it is on a phonograph record.

The read-write heads, one for each side of each platter, are arranged one above the other on a vertical assembly, as shown in Figure 12-1. When the hard disk is in operation, the read-write heads move in unison, each reading from or writing to the same relative location on its own platter.

Information on a hard disk is stored magnetically, as it is on a floppy disk. Likewise, the data on each platter is recorded in concentric rings, or tracks, that are "drawn" on the disk by the operating system and are numbered consecutively, beginning with 0 on the outer rim.

Unlike a floppy disk, however, a hard disk has depth, in the form of several platters. Because the platters are stacked one above the other, a track on one platter is matched by corresponding tracks on each of the other platters. These matching sets of tracks are called cylinders, after the geometric shape they would form if you were able to peer downward at them through the different platters in the disk. Cylinders are numbered according to the track location they represent. Thus, cylinder 51 refers to track location 51 on all disk platters. Sequential data is recorded vertically, in cylinders, rather than horizontally (filling one platter before moving to the next and the next).

Even though a hard disk actually consists of several platters and a series of separate disk surfaces, operating systems and people alike treat these surfaces as if they were all together on a single large platter. Thus, we refer to the hard disk's surface, not surfaces, and storage space on this surface is considered to be contiguous (uninterrupted) even if it is not physically located on a single platter.

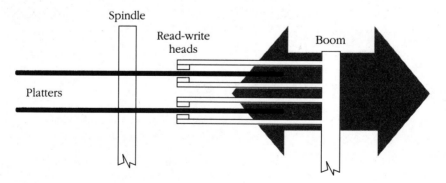

**Figure 12-1.** *Typical hard disk construction.*

# Dealing with Partitions

On your hard disk, a partition is a portion of available disk space that is set aside for a specific purpose. An analogy would be the rooms in your house: The kitchen is a partition used for cooking; the bedroom is a partition used for sleeping. If you intend to install SCO UNIX on a computer that currently runs the single-user, MS-DOS operating system, at least one partition on your hard disk has already been dedicated to MS-DOS and the files and programs you've used with it.

To run, SCO UNIX requires its own, separate partition. The installation procedure allocates the space for that partition on your hard disk and prepares the hard disk for use with SCO UNIX. SCO UNIX requires at least 40 contiguous megabytes of space on your hard disk for its partition; a 50-MB (megabyte) hard disk is the minimum size recommended on which to install both MS-DOS and SCO UNIX systems. Part of this partition is used for SCO UNIX filesystems, which are the storage areas for the operating system, application programs, data files, utilities, and user-created files. The installation program always creates a root filesystem, named /, for the operating system and utilities. It might also create a filesystem named /u for user files if your disk is large enough.

In addition to the filesystems, the SCO UNIX installation program also creates a swap space on the SCO UNIX partition. The swap space is not a filesystem accessible to users but is essentially an extension of the hardware memory. The memory image of an inactive program is transferred from memory to the swap space on disk ("swapped out") while it waits for input or access to devices. SCO UNIX might swap out several inactive programs, and the programs would be stored on disk for input or access to a device. This approach lets the programs that can use the central processor continue work without waiting for the inactive programs. Because an exact memory image (including the current state of the program) is moved back and forth, the transfer is very fast. Unless the load on your system becomes heavy, normally you won't even be aware that SCO UNIX has swapped a program to the disk's swap space. The Automatic Installation option creates a swap space that takes up about 20 percent of an SCO UNIX partition of up to about 50 MB. For partitions from 51 through 139 MB, the Automatic Installation option creates a 10-MB swap space. For partitions larger than 139 MB, it creates a swap space that is 10 MB plus 10 percent of the size over 140 MB up to 64 MB.

# KNOWING YOUR OPTIONS

The two options you're given when you install SCO UNIX—Automatic Installation and Fully Configurable Installation—both create partitions for SCO UNIX on your hard disk. We'll concentrate on installing the SCO UNIX system by using the Automatic

SECTION II: FOR THE SYSTEM ADMINISTRATOR

Installation option. If you've previously installed MS-DOS and partitioned your hard disk, the Automatic Installation option leaves the first existing MS-DOS partition on the hard disk and takes the rest of the hard disk for the SCO UNIX operating system.

## A Look at Your System

Before moving on to the actual installation procedures you must follow, we'll look at the three possible directions from which you might approach SCO UNIX.

First you might plan to devote your entire system to SCO UNIX and SCO UNIX–based application programs such as Microsoft Word and Microsoft Multiplan. This type of installation is discussed later, in the section titled "The Installation Procedure."

Second you might plan to replace an existing MS-DOS system entirely with SCO UNIX. In this case, you must back up all the MS-DOS files that you want to save for use on the SCO UNIX system. After backing up the files, you must then use the MS-DOS utility Fdisk to remove the existing MS-DOS partition. (See your MS-DOS documentation on using Fdisk.) If you don't remove the partition, the Automatic Installation option will preserve the MS-DOS partition. You could instead use the Fully Configurable Installation option and have that option use the whole disk for its SCO UNIX partition. In most cases, however, choosing the Fully Configurable Installation option means answering more questions to achieve the same result as would the Automatic Installation option.

Finally you might plan to use both MS-DOS and SCO UNIX on the same hard disk. If this is so, your hard disk might already contain MS-DOS data files and directories. Before you install SCO UNIX, back up all of your important MS-DOS files. Although the installation of SCO UNIX does not alter the first MS-DOS partition in any way, backing up your MS-DOS files is prudent because of the small chance that you might inadvertently damage the files or make them inaccessible.

## Planning Ahead

If MS-DOS is installed on your system, you can use Fdisk to create, modify, and delete MS-DOS partitions and view information about partitions that you have already created. Fdisk can divide your hard disk into one full-disk partition or several partial-disk partitions.

Before you install SCO UNIX, you do some initial planning. As mentioned earlier, SCO UNIX requires 40 MB of uninterrupted disk space. If you have already created one or more functional MS-DOS partitions, be sure the first MS-DOS partition is smaller than 32 MB, and check to see how much space is available in addition to the first MS-DOS partition. Use the MS-DOS Ver command to ensure that your MS-DOS version is 3.3 or later. If the first MS-DOS partition is larger than 32 MB or if the remaining space is smaller than 40 MB, back up all your important files and then use Fdisk to reinstall a single MS-DOS partition of 32 MB or less. When you use the Automatic Installation option, SCO UNIX retains the first MS-DOS partition but removes any subsequent MS-DOS partitions. (SCO UNIX considers OS/2 partitions to be MS-DOS partitions.) If you don't back up files from subsequent partitions, the files will be lost. In addition, if your version of MS-DOS is earlier than version 3.3, you need to install version 3.3 or later. To install a later version of MS-DOS on your hard disk, you first need to use the Fdisk program to create a functional MS-DOS partition, and then you need to install the later version of MS-DOS on that partition.

> **NOTE:** *If you plan to use OS/2 with SCO UNIX, you must use the Fully Configurable Installation option. If you plan to use both MS-DOS and OS/2, you must use the MS-DOS Fdisk command to install the MS-DOS partition first. Then install SCO UNIX, followed by OS/2. Check the documentation for your hardware to ensure that your system can run OS/2 with MS-DOS and SCO UNIX.*

## Backing Up Your Files

You can use one of several methods to transfer files you want to save from the hard disk. The slowest is the MS-DOS Copy command. Copy transfers files one by one, and you must determine whether the destination medium has enough room to hold each file before you attempt to copy it.

You can also use backup software or an archival storage command, such as Store or Backup.

Some backup programs perform a rapid file-by-file transfer of information to either floppy disks or tape cartridges. The program determines when a new disk or cartridge is needed during the procedure and prompts you to insert one at the appropriate time. Essentially, this method duplicates the features of the Copy command—but at a much faster rate—and requires a minimum of participation from you. This file-by-file method is the one you should use if you plan to create partitions or alter the sizes of existing partitions.

Other backup programs transfer files from your hard disk by using a streaming system that creates a mirror image of the hard disk on disks or tape cartridges. Streaming is one of the fastest transfer methods, but it is not advisable if you're planning to restore files to new or modified partitions on the hard disk. A streaming system recreates the disk contents exactly, so any changes you make to the disk after backup are ignored and overwritten.

## Managing partitions

If you're backing up files and changing partition sizes, the quantity of material you take off the hard disk might not fit when you try to return it to a new, smaller partition.

For example, suppose that you have a 64-MB hard disk, which is currently divided into two 32-MB MS-DOS partitions. You will need a minimum of 40 MB for SCO UNIX, which leaves approximately 24 MB available for MS-DOS. Simple arithmetic is enough to show that you will have to allocate and manage those 24 MB much more carefully than you managed 64 MB—perhaps archiving on storage media more often or trimming extraneous program and data files that you seldom, if ever, use.

# Using MS-DOS and SCO UNIX

If you plan to install both SCO UNIX and MS-DOS on the same computer, bear in mind that you will be working with two distinct operating systems. They cannot run simultaneously. Nor can MS-DOS run from any attached terminals. You must access MS-DOS from the SCO UNIX computer, so while you're using the MS-DOS system, your SCO UNIX system is effectively shut off to anyone who might want to use it.

As you'll see later, you can easily move back and forth between the SCO UNIX and MS-DOS partitions, but the point here is simply to remind you of the importance of planning ahead and, if possible, scheduling convenient hours of operation for both operating systems. Also, if the hard disk in your system is relatively small (in the 50-MB range), you might want to consider using SCO UNIX alone, rather than both SCO UNIX and MS-DOS.

# Disk Compatibility

If you run both SCO UNIX and MS-DOS, remember that they use different floppy disk formats. SCO UNIX provides eight commands for reading and working with MS-DOS disks, but you cannot, for example, use the MS-DOS Dir command to view the contents of the SCO UNIX installation or program disks. If you try, you'll see a partially scrambled list.

> **NOTE:** *If you are already familiar with MS-DOS, you might know that you can handle some disk problems with the MS-DOS Chkdsk (Checkdisk) command. However, Chkdsk doesn't work with SCO UNIX disks. An SCO UNIX disk is not readable under MS-DOS (nor should it be). In fact, using Chkdsk, especially with its /F option, can destroy the information on an SCO UNIX disk. SCO UNIX provides no disk utilities compatible with OS/2.*

# THE INSTALLATION PROCEDURE

Now that we've covered the most likely approaches to a new SCO UNIX system, let's move on to the installation itself. Your first step is to make certain your hard disk is formatted. Most likely, your hard disk was formatted for you when you bought it. If it was not, check your hardware manual. If you cannot tell whether the hard disk is formatted, try to use it. If the hard disk isn't formatted, SCO UNIX will generate error messages telling you that it isn't able to use the hard disk.

After you check your hard disk, locate the SCO UNIX disk labeled *SCO UNIX System V/386 Operating System (Installation) Volume: N1 BOOT.* The SCO UNIX Automatic Installation option asks one or two multiple-choice questions, but otherwise it requires almost no intervention from you. Even if you make a mistake answering the questions, the programs SCO UNIX uses to accomplish the installation know that the operating system is to be installed on a hard disk. The programs will not damage your installation disk. At most, you might need to correct an answer.

# BEGINNING THE INSTALLATION

Whether your system is currently turned off or on, begin by inserting the installation disk in the high-density floppy disk drive. If your system has only one floppy disk drive, place the installation disk in it. If your system has more than one floppy disk drive, place the installation disk in the "boot" drive. (The boot drive is usually on the left or on the top.) For SCO UNIX System V/386 (version 3.2) you must have a high-density disk drive to accept the high-density SCO UNIX installation disk.

Now, if your system is off, turn it on. If you made a mistake in selecting the boot drive, note which drive light comes on first, wait until the startup process goes as far as it can, place the installation disk in the appropriate drive, and reboot the system by pressing the Ctrl-Alt-Del key combination. If the computer is already on, reboot the system by pressing Ctrl-Alt-Del. If you're reinstalling UNIX and UNIX is currently running, turn your computer off and then turn it on again. For the protection of its multiuser environment, SCO UNIX disables the Ctrl-Alt-Del key combination.

The computer will check the installation disk, check the hard disk, and then come back to the installation disk to begin reading it. After some introductory memory statistics, a message like the following will appear on your screen:

```
SCO System V/386

Boot
: _
```

The display on your screen might vary somewhat from this sample display. This illustration, like the rest in this book, shows what you see with SCO UNIX version 3.2 (sometimes called SCO UNIX System V/386). If you're installing another version of SCO UNIX, the messages might be slightly different. Such differences are acceptable.

On the other hand, if you see an error message, such as *Unable to load operating system from disk*, you might have a faulty installation disk. Likewise, if your system ignores the installation disk and boots directly from the hard disk, you might have an inoperative or incompatible floppy disk drive. For example, as already mentioned, SCO UNIX for 386–based PCs is supplied on high-density floppy disks. If you have a PC equipped with low-density (360-KB or 720-KB) drives, you cannot install SCO UNIX unless you purchase and install a high-density floppy disk drive.

Assuming that your system is ready for the installation procedure, note that SCO UNIX is now waiting for your input at the colon (sometimes called the program prompt because it appears on a line by itself whenever SCO UNIX expects you to enter the name of a program). Because you're booting from the floppy disk drive, the installation program assumes you want to run SCO UNIX from the floppy disk, and expects you to press Enter to begin the installation program.

## Running the Installation Program

After you press Enter to start the installation, the following data appears on your display:

```
SCO System V/386

Boot
:
fd (64)unix root=fd(64) swap=ram(0) pipe=ram(1) swplo=0 nswap=16 ronly

loading .text
.....................................................................................
.....................................................................................
.....................................................................................
...............................................................
loading .data
.................................................................
loading .bss
```

When the program is successfully loaded, you see the following message:

```
Insert N2 (Filesystem) floppy and press <Return>_
```

Find the distribution disk labeled *SCO UNIX System V/386 Operating System (Installation) Volume: N2*, remove disk *N1* from the floppy disk drive, insert *N2*, and press

Enter. The next display gives you some information about the SCO UNIX copyright, your version of SCO UNIX, and the computer on which you're installing it.

SCO UNIX then displays the message *Setting installation display environment...* and changes to the appropriate display characteristics for your monitor. It assumes that you have an ANSI-compatible terminal—one that uses screen-control codes defined by the American National Standards Institute. This is a safe assumption because most 386-based computers are ANSI-compatible.

The installation program then asks you to select your keyboard type from this list:

```
Keyboard Selection
        1. American
        2. British
        3. French
        4. German
        5. Italian
        6. Spanish
Use the Numeric Keypad if present, using <Num Lock> if
necessary, to select one of the above options: _
```

If necessary, press the Num Lock key to activate the numbers on the numeric keypad of your computer. Then press the number corresponding to your keyboard type on your numeric keypad. If you don't have a numeric keypad, press the appropriate number key on the keyboard.

# INITIALIZING THE HARD DISK

The installation program is ready to begin one of its most important functions: initializing the primary hard disk on your system. You'll now see information about the configuration choices, and you'll be asked to select one of the choices, as follows:

```
        System V Hard Disk Initialization

The primary hard disk in the system will now be initialized.
This will create a UNIX partition on the disk and divide it
into filesystem(s) and a swap space.

You can choose a fully configurable disk initialization,
which requires you to set the disk parameters, specify the
size of the UNIX partition, and control the layout of
filesystems and swap area.  You will be presented with
defaults at each selection.
```

*(continued)*

*continued*

```
You can also choose an automatic disk initialization
that creates a complete disk layout and configuration using
system default values.

Choose one of the following:
1. Fully Configurable Installation
2. Automatic Installation (use system defaults)
3. Exit Installation

Enter your choice: _
```

You were introduced to these options early in this chapter. If you haven't already done so, you now must decide which option you want to use. As was mentioned earlier, we'll use option 2 for Automatic Installation. The SCO UNIX installation program tells you what it intends to do and asks you to confirm your choice with the following display:

```
Verify Automatic Disk Initialization

You have chosen to initialize the primary hard disk
automatically using the system defaults.

This option requires that your system was set up to recognize
the hard disk at the factory, or that you have run the proper
setup floppy disk prior to System V Operating System installation.

The hard disk initialization will preserve any pre-existing
DOS partition, but will overwrite any non-DOS partitions.
A single, active UNIX partition will be created and divided
into a root filesystem, a swap area, and if the UNIX partition
is 140 megabytes or larger, a user (/u) filesystem.

Setting up the hard disk may take as long as one minute per megabyte
of space on the disk.

Are you sure you wish to do this (y or n): _
```

Type *y* and press Enter.

The installation program begins initializing the hard disk. As it works, it displays a series of messages similar to these:

```
%disk    0x1F0-0x1F7   16      -        type=W0 unit=0 cyls=1024 hds=9 secs=17
Creating UNIX partition...
Scanning disk...



Dividing UNIX partition into filesystem and swap divisions...

Making filesystems

Setting up hard disk root filesystem...
```

When it has completed the initialization of the hard disk, the installation program displays these messages:

```
Initialization of the hard disk is now complete.

AFTER you see the message    **     Safe to Power Off     **
                                        -or-
                             ** Press Any Key to Reboot **

remove the N2 (Filesystem) floppy from the floppy drive and
insert the N1 (Boot) floppy. (The floppy light will stay on.)
Close the floppy door, then press any key.

The screen will clear and you will see the boot message:

        Boot
        :

Press <Return> to reboot the system and continue the installation.



**     Safe to Power Off     **
            -or-
** Press Any Key to Reboot **
—
```

Note that the light on the boot floppy disk drive stays on. Remove the *N2* disk anyway, insert the *N1 BOOT* disk, and press Enter to continue the installation process.

The installation program loads again, resulting in a display something like this:

```
SCO System V/386
Boot
:
fd(64)unix root=hd(40) swap=hd(41) pipe=hd(40)

loading .text
..........................................................................
..........................................................................
..........................................................................
...........................................................
loading .data
................................................................
loading .bss
```

The installation program then displays copyright information and information about the computer that you are using. The installation program might also display the message ** *Invalid Serial Number* **, which you can safely ignore. It next sets up SCO UNIX for the type of monitor that you are using. Finally, the installation program prompts you to verify that the *N1 BOOT* disk is in the boot drive by using a display looking something like this:

```
                        ** Invalid Serial Number **
Setting Installation display environment...

Verify that the N1 (Boot) floppy is in the drive and the
floppy door is closed and press <Return>: _
```

Press Enter to continue with the installation.

# INSTALLING THE BASE OPERATING SYSTEM

After you have completed the hard disk portion of the installation, the installation program begins installing a minimal set of programs necessary to run the SCO UNIX operating system. With this base operating system, you can run most application programs, such as Microsoft Word or Microsoft Multiplan. After you have completed the installation of the base operating system, you can later add any other portions of the operating system that you want. At this point, your display looks like this:

```
Insert Operating System (Base Utilities) volume B1
and press <Return> or enter q to quit:_
```

Insert the Base Utilities disk *B1* in the drive and press Enter. The installation program first creates a list of the files that it needs to install. It then copies the first of those files from disk *B1*.

Chapter 12: Installing SCO UNIX

When it has copied files from the first disk, it prompts you for the next disk. The resulting display looks like this:

```
Installing custom data files ...
Creating file lists ...
Extracting files ...

Insert Operating System (Base Utilities) volume B2
and press <Return> or enter q to quit:_
```

Insert the requested disk in the boot drive and press Enter. This process is repeated for all the Base Utilities disks. When the installation program has copied the files from the last of the Base Utilities disks, it prompts you for the *N* disks again. Your display will look like this:

```
Insert Operating System (Installation) volume N1
and press <Return> or enter q to quit:_
```

After you insert *N1* and press Enter, the installation program copies parts of the operating system from the *N* series of disks. After completing this portion of the installation, the system displays a copyright message followed by a prompt for the serial number of your copy of the software as follows:

```
Operating System Serialization

Enter your serial number or enter q to quit: _
```

The serial number appears on the pink card labeled "Activation Key" that is packed with the Release Notes for your software. Type the serial number and press Enter. The installation program then prompts you as follows for the activation key for your copy of the software:

```
Enter your activation key or enter q to quit: _
```

The activation key also is on the pink card. Type the activation key and press Enter.

The final portion of the installation initializes the correct time zone for your system. This part of the initialization, among other functions, lets your system maintain its *cal* program correctly over the course of the year. You see this question on the display:

```
Time zone initialization

Are you in North America? (y/n) _
```

If you are in North America, type *y* and press Enter. If you are not in North America, type *n*, press Enter, and follow the resulting instructions. If you press *y*, you now see this request on your display:

```
1. NST - Newfoundland Standard Time
2. AST - Atlantic Standard Time
3. EST - Eastern Standard Time
4. CST - Central Standard Time
5. MST - Mountain Standard Time
6. PST - Pacific Standard Time
7. YST - Yukon Standard Time
8. HST - Hawaiian/Alaskan Standard Time
9. NST - Nome Standard Time
Enter the number that represents your time zone or enter q to
quit: _
```

Choose the entry for your location, type the number, and then press Enter. The program then displays the following question about daylight savings time:

```
Does daylight saving time (summer time) apply at your location? (y/n)_
```

Enter the appropriate response for your location and press Enter.

The installation program next sets up the *terminfo* database containing information for the terminals that it has detected. Programs such as *vi* use the *terminfo* database to display information correctly on attached terminals. Finally the installation program requests you to install disk *N5* by displaying the following message:

```
Insert Operating System (Installation) volume N5
and press <Return> or enter q to quit:_
```

Insert disk *N5* and press Enter. After the installation program copies more files from the disk, it checks the file permissions for all the files in the base operating system to ensure that all users who need to access them can and that all users who shouldn't be able to access them can't. The installation program displays this message when it is finished:

```
Checking file permissions ...

You have now installed the SCO System V minimum Run Time System.
The Run Time System will support most application programs,
so you may choose to stop the installation now and preserve
the maximum available disk space for user files.

The remainder of the SCO System V product (including
Operating System and Development System sets) are
installable in small packages. You may either
install each set entirely or selectively choose
which packages of the set to install.
```

*(continued)*

252

*continued*

```
                Current Disk Usage
-----------------------------------------------------------------
Mount Dir  Filesystem      blocks      used     free   %used
/          root            72074      27968    44106    38%
-----------------------------------------------------------------


       1. Finish installation
       2. Install additional software now

Enter an option: _
```

The current disk usage table shows how much of your disk is allocated to the root filesystem and how much is taken up by the base operating system. The figures are given in blocks of 512 bytes. In this case, the root filesystem takes up about 36 MB, and the base operating system takes up about 14 MB of that. This leaves about 22 MB free for you to use for applications and data files, or for other packages of the operating system if you choose to install them. In addition, the installation creates a swap space, which takes up about 20 percent of the size of the entire SCO UNIX partition. The swap space in the preceding installation is about 10 MB. (The entire SCO UNIX partition in this case is about 46 MB: approximately 36 MB for the root filesystem and 10 MB for the swap space.) If your hard disk is larger than 140 MB, you will see another filesystem (*/u*), which was created by the Automatic Installation option. This is the filesystem for all the users' home directories and user-created files.

At this point, you can either install other software packages or complete the basic installation.

In the installation program, if you choose *2. Install additional software now*, the installation program runs the custom software installation program, *custom*. You make your choices in exactly the same way that you make choices to install SCO UNIX. After you install the optional software packages, exit from *custom* by choosing the menu option *Quit→Yes*. Choosing this option ensures that the basic installation program sets up a password for the system administrator, as described in the following section.

# COMPLETING THE BASIC INSTALLATION

To complete the basic installation, you need to set up a password for the account used by the system administrator. SCO UNIX gives this account the user name *root*. The system administrator is also known as the superuser. As the name implies, the superuser password is the key that unlocks the door to the entire SCO UNIX system. As the system administrator, you will need access to all of the SCO UNIX maintenance and account-creation utilities. Like any other key, the superuser password must be used wisely and protected adequately. Without the password, you cannot use the SCO UNIX utilities. If you've forgotten the password, the only way to assign a new superuser password is to reinstall SCO UNIX. (You can change the password after you're logged into the system, but without it you can't even log in.) Conversely, if your password is common knowledge or available to everyone, the door to the SCO UNIX system, like an unlocked door to your house, is wide open to whoever wants to enter.

The basic rule of thumb is to keep the superuser password simple enough to remember easily, yet not so simple that anyone might guess it. Because SCO UNIX differentiates between uppercase and lowercase characters, one easy method of rendering your superuser password both easy to remember and difficult to guess is to use a combination of uppercase and lowercase letters. For example, *JONes* or *jonES* would be much more secure than *jones* or *JONES*. Likewise, adding a few random letters or punctuation marks to a simple password—for example, *g&jonesxl* or *RE%JONESN*—makes it significantly more difficult to guess while keeping it easy to commit to memory. SCO UNIX rejects any password with fewer than six characters; it accepts passwords with as many as 80 characters.

SCO UNIX now displays the following:

```
1. Finish installation
2. Install additional software now
```

```
Enter an option: _
```

If you respond with *1*, SCO UNIX starts *passwd*, the program used to change passwords, and presents this display:

```
Please assign a password for the super-user account, "root".
Last successful password change for root: NEVER
Last unsuccessful password change for root: NEVER


                Choose password

You can choose whether you pick your own password,
or have the system create one for you.

        1. Pick your own password
        2. Pronounceable password will be generated for you

Enter choice (default is 1): _
```

A password that you choose will be much easier to remember than a password that SCO UNIX generates for you, and in the case of the superuser password, it is doubly important: If you forget, it is impossible to administer the system. So type *1* and press Enter. The password program prompts you for your choice of password with this message:

```
New password:_
```

Type your password and press Enter.

As a security precaution, SCO UNIX does not echo the letters to the screen as you type them. The same is true whenever you enter your password. This approach prevents anyone who might be walking by from seeing the password as you type it.

When you press Enter after you type your password, SCO UNIX prompts you to retype the password to ensure that you typed the password correctly the first time. If for some reason the password you type the second time is not identical to the one you originally entered, SCO UNIX will respond with the following message:

```
They don't match; try again.
```

After you have successfully typed the password again, the installation program reminds you that you should keep the password in a safe place.

After you assign a password to the system administrator's account, installation of the base operating system is complete, and the installation program displays the following message:

```
Installation and configuration of the System V Operating System
is now complete.

AFTER you see the message    **    Safe to Power Off    **
                                       -or-
                             ** Press Any Key to Reboot **


reboot the system by opening the floppy door and pressing any key.

The screen will clear and you will see the boot message:


        Boot
        :


Press <Return> to reboot the newly installed system.



**    Safe to Power Off    **
              -or-
** Press Any Key to Reboot **
```

Press any key to reboot the system. When the boot prompt (:) appears, press Enter to start the system.

# DIFFERENCES IN SUPERUSER MODES

When SCO UNIX starts, it can run in either of two modes: single user (system maintenance) mode or multiuser mode. After rebooting, the system displays copyright messages, information about the computer, and then this message:

```
INIT: SINGLE USER MODE

Type CONTROL-d to proceed with normal startup,
(or give root password for system maintenance): _
```

As this display indicates, you can simply enter the superuser (root) password to enter system maintenance mode. While you are in the system maintenance mode, you can reconfigure SCO UNIX, install any system packages you have not already installed, and generally do whatever is needed to maintain the system.

While the system is in single user mode, you cannot install accounts for other users—a vital part of your responsibilities as system administrator—nor can other users log in to the system. To perform other tasks besides system maintenance, you need to initiate a normal startup by pressing Ctrl-D. When you do this, SCO UNIX displays the new level of use and prompts for the current system time and date as follows:

```
INIT: New run level: 2

Current System Time is Mon Nov 27 15:29:00 PST 1989
Enter new time ([yymmdd]hhmm): _
```

If the displayed date and time are correct, simply press Enter to continue. If you need to change the date and time, note that you use a 24-hour clock and you don't separate the digits by any characters at all. That is, 4:40 P.M. is represented as *1640*.

Next SCO UNIX displays a *login:* request that looks something like this:

```
The system is coming up.  Please wait.
System auditing is not enabled.
! *** cron started ***    pid = 155 Mon Nov 27 15:30:10 1989

The system is ready.

scosysv

Welcome to SCO System V/386

scosysv!login: _
```

**256**

When this happens, enter the following as the login name:

root

Then enter the superuser password you created. (Although any valid login name and password would work, you have only the superuser password right now if you've followed our sample installation.)

# PREPARING THE SYSTEM FOR USE

After completing the basic installation, you should take some additional steps to ready the SCO UNIX system for general use. Instead of dedicating your SCO UNIX system to running specific application packages, you might want to install some or all of the following packages from the installation disks:

- The shell utility for administering the system
- The utilities used to back up files on the system
- The print spooler
- The MS-DOS file-manipulation tools
- The full set of *mail* utilities
- Additional SCO UNIX tools
- The *ex* and *vi* editors
- The C shell
- The online reference pages

Besides these packages, the installation disks contain other software packages. You can install all the packages on the installation disks, any package or combination of packages, or any file or files from a package.

## SCO UNIX security features

If your system is required to be a trusted system—that is, a system that complies with the requirements of the C2 level of trust as defined by the *Trusted Computer System Evaluation Criteria* (also known as the Orange Book), published by the U.S. Department of Defense—you must not install any part of the UUCP package distributed with SCO UNIX that the *Release Notes* lists as compromising security. UUCP, the *uucp* utilities for copying files from one UNIX system to another, compromises the C2 level of trust because it allows unauthorized users access to your system, thereby compromising system security. Not installing *uucp*, however, might mean that your system won't have *mail* connections or file transfer connections with remote systems unless you install another, secure communications package.

# Installing Additional Packages

If you completed your basic installation earlier by choosing a superuser password, exiting the installation program, and rebooting your system, you need to log in as the superuser. You then can install additional software packages by running the *custom* program. The *custom* program customizes your SCO UNIX installation by letting you install only those programs that are necessary for your use of your system.

If you choose option 2, *Install additional software now*, when you run the basic installation program, the basic installation program runs *custom*. You choose options in exactly the same way that you choose basic installation options. After you install the optional software packages, you must exit *custom* by choosing the menu options *Quit→Yes*. Doing this ensures that the basic installation program sets up a password for the superuser. Otherwise, you won't be able to log in, and you will need to reinstall the SCO UNIX software.

At this point, you should make some decisions about the packages necessary to your system. The types of users and the types of intended uses for the system should dictate the packages that you choose. *Release Notes* lists all the packages available for installation. If your system is going to support only dedicated applications, such as databases, the only software package you will probably want to add is the one with backup utilities so that you and other users will be able to back up files on a regular and organized basis. You might have many experienced UNIX users, who will want to use the C shell and who will want to edit text files with *vi*. If this is the case, you need to install the CSH package and the EX package. If maintaining the C2 level of security is not important and you need to communicate with other UNIX systems, you might want to install the UUCP package. Any packages that you install take up space on your hard disk, however, and you will quickly find that no hard disk is ever big enough. You don't want to start operations on your system by taking up space for programs that no one on your system will ever use. The *custom* program will help you decide by listing the approximate size in 512-byte blocks for each package that you can install.

After you have decided which packages are appropriate for your system, begin *custom* by entering the following command:

```
custom
```

You will see this display on your screen:

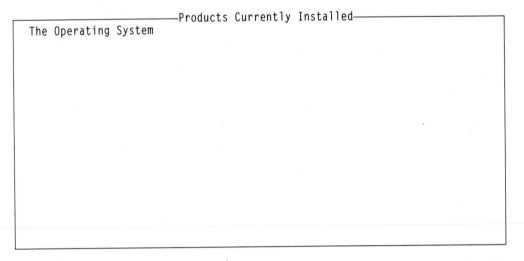

```
                                                              Custom

Install Remove List Quit
Install software_
                                          Thursday June 14, 1990 10:30

┌─────────────────────Products Currently Installed─────────────┐
│   The Operating System                                       │
│                                                              │
│                                                              │
│                                                              │
│                                                              │
│                                                              │
│                                                              │
│                                                              │
│                                                              │
│                                                              │
│                                                              │
└──────────────────────────────────────────────────────────────┘
```

The name *Custom* appears in the upper right corner of the display in reverse video. The second line of the display lists the choices that you can make in a horizontal menu. On the first display in the *custom* program, the menu choices are *Install*, *Remove*, *List*, and *Quit*. The default choice, *Install*, is also highlighted in reverse video. You can select the default menu item by simply pressing Enter. To make another choice, you can move the highlight with the direction keys, or you can press the first letter of your choice. Pressing L selects the *List* menu item. On this menu, the following selections result in the action indicated:

| | |
|---|---|
| *Install* | Installs all or part of a software package. |
| *Remove* | Removes all or part of a software package. |
| *List* | Lists the installed packages or files in a package. |
| *Quit* | Exits from the *custom* program. |

When you select a menu item, the help line immediately below the horizontal menu tells you briefly what you can accomplish by choosing that menu item (for example, the *Install software* item for the *Install* selection). Immediately below the help line is a highlighted line with status information. This status line indicates the current directory, which is the root directory (/), and the current date and time. The *custom* program initially shows a window labeled *Products Currently Installed* and in that window a list of products that you have installed on your system. Because you have installed parts of the operating system, that product is listed in the window.

If you want to abort the installation of a package or the selection of a form at any time in *custom*, press the Escape key. Depending on where you are in the process, you will return either to the *Custom* form or to the immediately preceding window.

Now that you understand what the display is telling you, it's time to install the packages that you have chosen.

For our purposes, we'll install the C shell, the backup utilities, the *ex* and *vi* editors, and the printer spooler. To begin the installation, select *Install* by pressing Enter. The *custom* program displays this form for you to fill in:

```
                                                            Install

Select a product to install and press <Return>
Press <ESC> to cancel, movement keys are active

                                          Thursday June 14, 1990 10:30

   ┌─────────────────────────────Install─────────────────────────────┐
   │                                                                  │
   │          Select a product   : [                      ]           │
   │                                                                  │
   │     Choose an option   : [Entire Product]     Packages     Files │
   │                                                                  │
   │                                                                  │
   │                                                                  │
   │                                                                  │
   │                                                                  │
   │                                          ┌───────────────────────┤
   │                                          │ * A New Product       │
   │                                          │ The Operating System  │
   └──────────────────────────────────────────┤                       │
                                              └───────────────────────┘
```

The first highlighted field in the form is for the product of your choice. In the lower right corner of the display is a second window with possible products listed in it. The choice for *A New Product* is highlighted. Because you want to install only the operating system, press the Down direction key to move the highlight to *The Operating System* and press Enter. The window that lists the products disappears, *The Operating System* appears in the form following *Select a product*, and the highlight moves to the *Entire Product* field on the next line of the form. On this line, you can choose to install

all the packages of the selected product, selected packages from the product, or individual files from a selected package. Press the Right direction key to move the highlight to *Packages* and then press Enter. The menu line displays *Install functional groupings of files*, which refers to the contents of a package. (You can also simply press *p*.) After you make your selection, the menu line displays *Updating package data...* as *custom* gathers information about the files in the package. It then displays a list of the packages in the Operating System product in a window on the form, as follows:

```
                                                              Install

Select packages to install and press <Return>
Press <ESC> to cancel, movement keys are active
                                          Thursday June 14, 1990 10:30

┌──────────────────────────Install──────────────────────────┐
│                                                            │
│     Select a product   :  [The Operating System       ]    │
│                                                            │
│     Choose an option   :  Entire Product   [Packages]   Files │
│                    ─────────The Operating System─────────  +│
│     Name    Inst   Size    Description                      │
│   * ALL     Part   52160   Entire Operating System set      │
│     PERM    Yes    152     UNIX contents and permissions lists│
│     RTS     Part   24376   UNIX run time system             │
│     BACKUP  No     314     System backup and recovery tools │
│     BASE    Yes    2162    Basic extended utility set       │
│     CSH     Part   144     The C-shell                      │
│     DOS     No     504     DOS utilities                    │
│     EX      No     494     The ex and vi editors            │
│     FILE    Part   1122    File manipulation tools         v│
│                                                            │
└────────────────────────────────────────────────────────────┘
```

In this list, the current package that you can choose is highlighted. You can move the highlight with the direction keys, or you can use the PgUp and PgDn keys to see the entire list. Along the right margin of the list, *custom* indicates that the list extends beyond the bottom of the window by putting a *v* at the bottom of the vertical margin. Near the top of the vertical margin is a plus sign (+), which indicates the approximate position of the highlight in the entire list. If you move the highlight down the list by using the direction keys, the plus sign moves down the margin as well.

You can select several packages to install at one time. To select the first package, the backup utilities, move the highlight down to *BACKUP* and press the Spacebar. The highlight moves to the next entry, and an asterisk (*) appears beside *BACKUP*. The asterisk marks *BACKUP* as the name of one of the packages you've selected. Next move the highlight to *CSH* by using the direction keys, and press the Spacebar. Again the highlight moves to the next selection but leaves an asterisk beside your choice. Select *EX* and *LPR* in the same way. At this point, your four choices should all have asterisks next to them. To proceed with the installation, press Enter. Remember that you can cancel the installation by pressing the Escape key.

The menu line briefly displays the message *Creating file lists...* as it determines which files it needs to extract to install the packages that you have chosen. The window then requests you to insert one of the installation disks as follows:

```
                                                                            Install
Insert the requested volume and press <Return> to continue the installation _

                                                           Friday June 15, 1990 10:30

┌───────────────────────Products Currently Installed───────────────────────┐
│                                                                            │
│    Insert:  Operating System (Extended Utilities)                          │
│    Volume:  X8                                                             │
│                                                                            │
│    Continue              Quit                                              │
│                                                                            │
│                                                                            │
│                                                                            │
│                                                                            │
│                                                                            │
│                                                                            │
│                                                                            │
│                                                                            │
│                                                                            │
└────────────────────────────────────────────────────────────────────────────┘
```

**NOTE:** *The installation program might not request the disks in the exact order shown here. The order depends on the packages that you chose and the arrangement of packages on your installation disks.*

After you insert the requested disk and press Enter, the *custom* program begins copying files from the installation disks. While it is extracting files, it displays the message *Extracting files...* on the menu line. If the files for the package you requested are on more than one disk, *custom* will ask you to insert the next disk and press Enter again to continue with the installation.

When *custom* has installed all the files required for the packages that you chose, it returns to the initial window that it displayed. To quit *custom*, move the highlight to *Quit*, or press *q* and then select *Yes*. If you started *custom* from the basic installation program, you now continue with the installation by selecting a password for the superuser. If you ran *custom* after completing the initial installation, you return to the SCO UNIX prompt.

# Installing the Complete *mail* Package

You might want to install the complete *mail* package so that you and the users can send messages to remote machines as well as to other users on your system. If you do, the *custom* program will run the Operating System Init Script. This script initializes variables and names in various files that your installation of SCO UNIX will use, ensuring that all the programs have the information that they need to access all the remaining parts of the system. In the Operating System Init Script, the following message asks you to give your machine a name:

```
Executing The Operating System Init Script


Your system name is set to scosysv.  Do you wish the mail system to use a
  different name? (y/n) _
```

The name that you give your system now is the one that will appear with all the login prompts and will appear as the name of the sending system on *mail* messages sent from your system. You shouldn't leave the default name *scosysv* because that probably won't distinguish your system from others. The name that you choose will be presented to the world, so choose carefully. If you type *y* and press Enter, you will be asked to enter the name of your choice, as follows:

```
Executing The Operating System Init Script


Your system name is set to scosysv.  Do you wish
the mail system to use a different name? (y/n)


Input your machine's name, or enter q to quit: _
```

Type the name that you want, and press Enter. After you press Enter, the following screen message appears:

```
Executing The Operating System Init Script


Your system name is set to scosysv. Do you wish
the mail system to use a different name? (y/n)
```

*(continued)*

*continued*

```
Input your machine's name, or enter q to quit: your_machine
The system name will be your_machine.UUCP.  If you want to
change this, please edit the file /usr/mmdf/mmdftailor, and
any files in the directory /usr/mmdf/table that contain the
old name, and then run /usr/mmdf/table/dbmbuild.
```

```
Press any key to continue_
```

Press any key to continue with the software installation program.

# SWITCHING BETWEEN SCO UNIX AND MS-DOS

If you retained your MS-DOS partition on your hard disk, you will want to be able to switch back and forth between MS-DOS and SCO UNIX and to be able to boot either MS-DOS or SCO UNIX from the hard disk. The procedure to switch from one to the other is simple.

> **NOTE:** *Remember, SCO UNIX and MS-DOS do not run simultaneously. If other SCO UNIX users are on your system, protect their work by making certain everyone has logged out before you boot MS-DOS.*

Both SCO UNIX and MS-DOS are bootable from the hard disk. When SCO UNIX starts, it displays its boot prompt, as follows:

```
SCO System V/386

Boot
: _
```

To select the MS-DOS partition, enter the following at the boot prompt (:):

```
dos
```

SCO UNIX is always the boot system and always prompts for an SCO UNIX hard disk boot, but it also gives you the option of booting MS-DOS if you choose. If you don't type anything within one minute after this prompt appears, the system automatically boots SCO UNIX.

**264**

If you want to return to SCO UNIX from MS-DOS, be sure you don't have a disk in the floppy disk drive, and then press the Ctrl-Alt-Del key combination to reboot your computer. Soon after, you'll see the SCO UNIX boot message.

If you want to boot MS-DOS directly, prepare a bootable floppy disk that holds a CONFIG.SYS or an AUTOEXEC.BAT file modified to point to the correct disk and sub-directories. Put this bootable disk in drive A and reboot your computer.

# 13

# Managing
# the System

Now that SCO UNIX is installed on your hard disk, you are ready to open up the system—install user accounts and tell SCO UNIX the types and locations of the terminals you'll connect to it. If your hard disk partition was large enough for the installation program to create a separate user filesystem (/u), you also need to prepare that filesystem for general use.

Because the SCO UNIX computer is at the heart of your system, we'll work outward from there, beginning with a fundamental rule of system management: As system administrator, you must control access to the SCO UNIX computer; if you must relinquish to others the authority to undertake administrative functions that could compromise your system's security, you should do so only with great care.

## USING THE SCO UNIX COMPUTER

While SCO UNIX is in operation, a great deal of behind-the-scenes activity goes on. You've been introduced to some of this activity in the form of foreground and background processing, the *mail* system, and so on. But much more happens that you never see or directly influence. One such process is the automatic generation of temporary files in which SCO UNIX maintains work in progress while the system is running. When the system shuts down properly, SCO UNIX neatly closes these temporary files and puts them away. SCO UNIX also systematically terminates all current activities and appropriately saves or updates any needed files.

But if you or anyone else turns off the SCO UNIX computer without going through the shutdown procedure, SCO UNIX abandons its temporary files, and the files become inaccessible for the next session. At the very least, the next time you start up, SCO UNIX will request permission to do housekeeping, which includes closing and deleting the temporary files that were left open when the system was improperly shut down. In some instances, you will be able to recover the contents of these abandoned files, but generally speaking the housekeeping functions exist to correct the shutdown error and restore the system's integrity rather than to retrieve the contents of abandoned files.

More serious than this is when the system is shut down incorrectly while other users are on line at their terminals: Any of the work they have not yet saved on disk is irretrievably lost.

Keep in mind that the most capable of people can fall victim to habit. Someone accustomed to shutting off the terminal after logging out might reflexively reach for the on/off switch on the SCO UNIX computer. Given these possible consequences, the easiest and safest means of protecting your SCO UNIX system and all work being done on it is simply to restrict physical access to the SCO UNIX computer.

# INSTALLING TERMINALS

When you connect a terminal and the SCO UNIX computer, you must provide the two with a means of communicating. In local-access situations, the most visible link between the computer and a terminal is the cable that connects them. The cable might run across the floor, or it might run through the walls, but in every instance it is the physical connection between the two machines. In remote-access situations, the connection is somewhat more elaborate because both the terminal and the computer require modems that act as intermediaries, translating information into a form that can be sent and received through the telephone system. Nonetheless, as in local-access setups, machines in remote-access situations are joined by hardware of some sort.

In addition to modems and cables, both the terminal and the computer need outlets, through which information can be transmitted. For each, that outlet is a serial port—a type of channel that sends and receives a well-defined stream of data bits in the form of high and low electrical voltages representing the binary numerals 1 and 0.

The serial port is another piece of hardware. On the outside of each machine, the port looks somewhat like an electrical outlet into which you can plug the end of a cable. If you look inside the machine, however, you will notice that a serial port is part of a printed circuit board which is plugged into a network of processing hardware. In a personal computer, the board fits into one of several expansion slots inside the case.

If you are using a ready-made terminal, you don't need to concern yourself with serial ports. The port you need is built-in and properly set up to receive a cable.

In the case of an SCO UNIX computer, however, you might find that your machine does not have enough serial ports to handle the number of terminals and other devices you want to attach to the system. Each terminal requires a different port, so if you have six terminals, you need six serial ports. You have a number of choices, but all of them boil down to adding more ports to the system. Where and how you add the ports depends on your preferences and the advice of your hardware dealer. You can buy serial ports with or without extra memory and built-in parallel ports and clocks. You can also purchase serial ports that are multiplexers, which expand one serial port into many.

## How Many Terminals?

As you review the following procedures, you might wonder whether to install all the terminals you think you might need at one time or to install some now and the rest in the future. As efficient as installing all the terminals at one time sounds, it actually might not be your best choice.

As a multiuser operating system, one of SCO UNIX's many tasks is to keep track of what is happening on each of the terminals attached to the system. It must know when commands are issued and at which terminals. To monitor such activity, SCO UNIX polls (checks) each of the serial ports to which it has been told that a terminal is connected. That polling process requires a portion of the system's overall response time.

On machines with high-speed chips (in the range 20 to 33 MHz and greater) as their central processing units, the serial-port polling interruptions for several terminals are hardly noticeable. On slower systems, those same interruptions can slow the system's response time and become annoying to users.

Furthermore, after a port is activated, SCO UNIX polls it to find out if a terminal is turned on or even physically connected to it. Polling is part of what SCO UNIX has been designed to do, but it is a waste of time if SCO UNIX is polling ports that are not currently or never will be in use.

Now, with these preliminaries out of the way, let's get to work.

# LOGGING IN AS SUPERUSER

As was mentioned in Chapter 12, as superuser you can log in after booting SCO UNIX in either of two ways.

First you can enter the superuser (root) password when SCO UNIX prompts as follows:

```
INIT: SINGLE USER MODE

Type CONTROL-d to proceed with normal startup,
(or give root password for system maintenance): _
```

The other way is to log in as the superuser at the normal *machine_name!login:* prompt.

If SCO UNIX is not currently running on the host computer, turn the computer on or reboot it. When the boot prompt (:) appears, press Enter to run the SCO UNIX boot program from the hard disk.

Although you can activate serial ports from system maintenance mode, you can both activate serial ports and add user accounts only when you're logged into the system as the superuser. When SCO UNIX prompts you, press Ctrl-D, and at the *machine_name!login:* prompt, enter the login name *root*, followed by the system password that you chose.

If you're already logged in, you might be in system maintenance mode. Visually, you can't easily tell whether you are or not—the system prompt for either situation is the pound sign (#). If a terminal is close by, you can easily check by trying to log in on it. In system maintenance mode, SCO UNIX turns the host computer into a single-user system, so any attached terminal will not respond to your login attempt.

If you are in system maintenance mode or you suspect you might be, you can also press Ctrl-D to log off the system and then log back in again as described earlier.

## Determining Current Serial-Port Configuration

Before you attach new terminals to the system, you must know how SCO UNIX currently "sees" your serial ports and any terminals attached to them. The information in three data files governs whether SCO UNIX considers a serial port to be active, what characteristics it gives to the port and the terminal attached to that port, and whether it recognizes the specific terminal type that might be attached to that port. These files are called *inittab*, *gettydefs* and *ttytype*. You'll find them in the */etc* directory.

Let's first use *vi* to look at *inittab*, which contains information about all the devices that the system monitors for activity. Enter the following command to display the contents of the *inittab* file:

```
vi /etc/inittab
```

SCO UNIX shows you that it contains the following:

```
#      @(#) init.base 1.15 89/06/22
#
#           UNIX is a registered trademark of AT&T
#           Portions Copyright 1976-1989 AT&T
#      Portions Copyright 1980-1989 Microsoft Corporation
#      Portions Copyright 1983-1989 The Santa Cruz Operation, Inc
#                 All Rights Reserved
#
#ident      "@(#)master:master.d/init.base      1.3.1.4"

# /etc/inittab on 286/386 processors is built by Installable
# Drivers (ID) each time the kernel is rebuilt. /etc/inittab is replaced
# by /etc/conf/cf.d/init.base appended with the component files in
# the /etc/conf/init.d directory by the /etc/conf/bin/idmkinit command.
bchk::sysinit:/etc/bcheckrc </dev/console >/dev/console 2>&1
ck:234:bootwait:/etc/asktimerc </dev/console >/dev/console 2>&1
brc::bootwait:/etc/brc 1> /dev/console 2>&1
mt:23:bootwait:/etc/brc </dev/console >/dev/console 2>&1
is:S:initdefault:
r0:056:wait:/etc/rc0  1> /dev/console 2>&1 </dev/console
r1:1:wait:/etc/rc1  1> /dev/console 2>&1 </dev/console
r2:2:wait:/etc/rc2 1> /dev/console 2>&1 </dev/console
r3:3:wait:/etc/rc3  1> /dev/console 2>&1 </dev/console
sd:0:wait:/etc/uadmin 2 0 >/dev/console 2>&1 </dev/console
"/etc/inittab" 50 lines, 1969 characters
```

The lines of interest to us are at the end of this file, so press Ctrl-F repeatedly until you see lines that begin with *t* and are followed by either *1* or *2* and then a letter from *a* through *m* or *A* through *M*. The next to last entry in the line lists the serial-port device name, such as *tty1a*, as follows:

```
t1a:2:off:/etc/getty tty1a m
t1A:2:off:/etc/getty tty1A m
t2a:2:off:/etc/getty tty2a m
t2A:2:off:/etc/getty tty2A m
~
~
~
~
```

The configuration for your system depends on what you are connecting to it. If your computer doesn't have additional serial cards, the *inittab* file will probably have only those four serial ports. Each device corresponds to an entry in the */dev* directory, which lists all the devices that your operating system is aware of. The entry beginning *t1a* refers to the device known to the operating system as */dev/tty1a*. The numbers *1* and *2* correspond to the two serial ports on IBM-compatible computers running MS-DOS. These two serial ports are named COM1 and COM2. The list shows four devices: two serial interrupts and two serial ports. SCO UNIX can access each port in one of two ways, depending on your requirements: with modem control or without modem control. Lowercase letters indicate that SCO UNIX doesn't provide modem control for that device, and uppercase letters indicate that it does provide modem control.

> **NOTE:** *Although IBM-compatible computers have only two serial interrupts, some serial cards can manage more serial ports by multiplexing. If you have installed such a card, you might see devices with letters* a *through* m *and* A *through* M.

SCO UNIX displays six parameters for each device in *inittab*. The first is the device identifier:

*t1a*                    Identifies the device

The second parameter displays a number indicating the run-level at which that device is active. The run-level parameter, most often a number from 0 through 6, indicates the states of operation (such as multiuser or single-user) that the operating system can take. The *2* in our example indicates a multiuser state; a 1 would indicate single-user.

The third parameter is the action SCO UNIX will take for the program (or process) specified in the fourth parameter:

*off*                    Means "Take no action."
*respawn*            Means "Restart the process continually."
*boot*                 Means "Start the process only when the system boots."
*wait*                 Means "Start the process and wait for its termination."

These are only the most common actions; if you scroll up in the *inittab* file, you might see other parameters for other devices.

The fourth parameter is the process associated with the device:

*/etc/getty*        Sets the device characteristics, such as speed, and gets initial input from the device.

The fifth parameter is the name of the device that represents that port, and that *getty* will access when it runs. In the example display, you see four such device names:

*tty1a*               Identifies the primary serial port, equivalent to *COM1:* for MS-DOS without modem control.

*tty1A*              Identifies the primary serial port, equivalent to *COM1:* for MS-DOS with modem control.

| | |
|---|---|
| *tty2a* | Identifies the secondary serial port, equivalent to *COM2:* for MS-DOS without modem control. |
| *tty2A* | Identifies the secondary serial port, equivalent to *COM2:* for MS-DOS with modem control. |

If you scroll up in the file using Ctrl-B, you will find other display devices, such as the console (*co*), other screens that you can access on the console (*c02* through *c12*), and pseudo-terminals, (*p0* through *p7*), which you can access from serial terminals.

The sixth parameter in the entry tells */etc/getty* what line discipline to use for this device:

| | |
|---|---|
| *m* | Means "Use entry *m* in the file */etc/gettydefs.*" |

The entries in */etc/gettydefs* have different settings for a number of different types of device usage. The *m* entry specifies a device running at 9600 baud with certain display options for the terminal. To look at */etc/gettydefs*, type the following *vi* command:

```
:e /etc/gettydefs
```

You see this screen:

```
#     @(#) gettydefs 1.6 89/04/10
#
#           UNIX is a registered trademark of AT&T
#         Portions Copyright 1985-1989 AT&T
#     Portions Copyright 1985-1989 Microsoft Corporation
#     Portions Copyright 1985-1989 The Santa Cruz Operation, Inc
#                 All Rights Reserved
#
19200# B19200 OPOST ONLCR TAB3 BRKINT IGNPAR IXON IXANY PARENB ISTRIP ECHO
ECHOE ECHOK ICANON ISIG CS7 CREAD # B19200 OPOST ONLCR TAB3 BRKINT IGNPAR IXON
IXANY PARENB ISTRIP ECHO ECHOE ECHOK ICANON ISIG CS7 CREAD #login: #9600

9600# B9600 OPOST ONLCR TAB3 BRKINT IGNPAR IXON IXANY PARENB ISTRIP ECHO ECHOE
ECHOK ICANON ISIG CS7 CREAD # B9600 OPOST ONLCR TAB3 BRKINT IGNPAR IXON IXANY
PARENB ISTRIP ECHO ECHOE ECHOK ICANON ISIG CS7 CREAD #login: #4800

4800# B4800 OPOST ONLCR TAB3 BRKINT IGNPAR IXON IXANY PARENB ISTRIP ECHO ECHOE
ECHOK ICANON ISIG CS7 CREAD # B4800 OPOST ONLCR TAB3 BRKINT IGNPAR IXON IXANY
PARENB ISTRIP ECHO ECHOE ECHOK ICANON ISIG CS7 CREAD #login: #2400

2400# B2400 OPOST ONLCR TAB3 BRKINT IGNPAR IXON IXANY PARENB ISTRIP ECHO ECHOE
ECHOK ICANON ISIG CS7 CREAD # B2400 OPOST ONLCR TAB3 BRKINT IGNPAR IXON IXANY
PARENB ISTRIP ECHO ECHOE ECHOK ICANON ISIG CS7 CREAD #login: #1200

"/etc/gettydefs" 107 lines, 5386 characters
```

SECTION II: FOR THE SYSTEM ADMINISTRATOR

Scroll down in the file using Ctrl-F until you find the entry beginning with lowercase *m*. Your display will look something like this:

```
d # B134 CSTOPB HUPCL #
    B134 CSTOPB CS8 SANE HUPCL TAB3 IXANY #\r\n@!login: # d

e # B150   HUPCL # B150   CS8 SANE HUPCL TAB3 IXANY #\r\n@!login: # e

f # B200   HUPCL # B200   CS8 SANE HUPCL TAB3 IXANY #\r\n@!login: # f

g # B300   HUPCL # B300   CS8 SANE HUPCL TAB3 IXANY #\r\n@!login: # g

h # B600   HUPCL # B600   CS8 SANE HUPCL TAB3 IXANY #\r\n@!login: # h

i # B1200 HUPCL # B1200 CS8 SANE HUPCL TAB3 ECHOE IXANY #\r\n@!login: # i

j # B1800 HUPCL # B1800 CS8 SANE HUPCL TAB3 ECHOE IXANY #\r\n@!login: # j

k # B2400 HUPCL # B2400 CS8 SANE HUPCL TAB3 ECHOE IXANY #\r\n@!login: # k

l # B4800 HUPCL # B4800 CS8 SANE HUPCL TAB3 ECHOE IXANY #\r\n@!login: # l

m # B9600 HUPCL # B9600 CS8 SANE HUPCL TAB3 ECHOE IXANY #\r\n@!login: # m

n # B19200   HUPCL # B19200   CS8 SANE HUPCL TAB3 IXANY #\r\n@!login: # n
```

These entries tell *getty* how to treat the device that it is accessing. Each entry in the file has five fields, separated by pound signs (#). The first entry is the label for that entry:

  *m*        Entry label

This entry corresponds to the last parameter from the *inittab* entry.

The second field contains the settings that *getty* uses in its initial access:

  *B9600*        Sets the device to 9600 baud.
  *HUPCL*        Hangs up when the last process on the device terminates.

The next field, between the second and third pound signs, contains the final settings for the attached terminal:

  *B9600*        Sets the device to 9600 baud.
  *CS8*          Sets the bit length of characters transmitted.
  *SANE*         Sets all the terminal characteristics to reasonable values.
  *HUPCL*        Means "Hang up when the last process on the device terminates."
  *TAB3*         Sets the treatment of vertical tabs.
  *IXANY*        Allows any character to resume output.

For a complete description of all the settings in *gettydefs,* see the *stty(C)* entry in the *User's Reference* manual, and the *gettydefs(F)* and *termio(M)* entries in the *System Administrator's Reference* manual.

The third field specifies the login prompt that *getty* displays before running the *login* program:

\r\n@!login:          Means "Output a new line, and then display the name found in /etc/systemid, followed by the *!login:* argument."

The next field indicates the entry in the *gettydefs* file that *getty* should try if it doesn't successfully connect using this entry. You can use this field to have *getty* cycle among several baud rates if you are using a dial-in modem that can operate at more than one baud rate. If you scroll up in the file to the entry labeled *1*, you will see a series of entries that use this feature to switch among 300, 1200, and 2400 baud.

```
#
# 1-2-3: 300 - 1200 - 2400 baud cycle   (dialin modems)
#

1 # B300   HUPCL OPOST CR1 NL1 #
    B300 CS8 SANE HUPCL TAB3 IXANY #\r\n@!login: # 2

2 # B1200 HUPCL OPOST CR1 ECHOE NL1 #
    B1200 CS8 SANE HUPCL TAB3 ECHOE IXANY #\r\n@!login: # 3

3 # B2400  HUPCL OPOST CR1 ECHOE NL1 #
    B2400 CS8 SANE HUPCL TAB3 ECHOE IXANY #\r\n@!login: # 1
```

If entry *1* doesn't work and the user presses the Break key (usually the Del key), *getty* tries the settings at the entry with label *2*. If *2* doesn't work, it goes on to *3* and so on through the cycle.

The entries in your *inittab* and *gettydefs* might differ from the entries shown in these examples. For purposes of illustration, we'll configure the two ports shown as if we were connecting a terminal to *tty1a* and a modem to *tty2A*. Unless you want to use the example values in the following section, simply read through the instructions, or if you are comfortable with editing files, try out the commands without saving the modified file on disk.

## Setting the Serial Ports

To set up these ports to work correctly, you must change their descriptions in the *inittab* file. Let's assume you want to activate *tty1a* and you want to tell SCO UNIX that the attached terminal will communicate at 9600 baud. Although this is a standard speed, it might not be correct for the terminal you're installing. If you don't know your terminal's operating speed, check its operations manual. To enable the port, use the *enable* command. If you are still in *vi*, exit by using the following command:

```
:q
```

Then enable the port with this command:

```
enable /dev/tty1a
```

The *enable* command responds with messages such as the following:

```
/etc/inittab updated
/etc/conf/init.d/sio updated
```

You can enable the parameters of *tty2A* in the same way. As was mentioned earlier, we are assuming that the port is to be used for remote access by means of a modem. For this reason, we will choose the device that the operating system provides for modem control. SCO UNIX treats a port set up for local access the same as a port set up for remote access. To SCO UNIX, a terminal is a terminal. Provided that it can communicate properly with the terminal, the hardware can be located anywhere. In fact, you can attach a terminal instead of a modem to your remote-access port as long as you choose the correct device type (without modem control) and the terminal operates at the speed for which the port is configured. You enable the device with the *enable* command, as you did the other port, by using the following command:

```
enable /dev/tty2A
```

If your terminal runs at a speed other than 9600 baud, you need to load the *inittab* file into *vi* and change the label used for baud rate to the entry for baud rate in *gettydefs*. In the previous example, *tty1a* indicates *m* in *gettydefs* for a 9600 baud terminal. If your terminal operates at a different rate, choose the appropriate label in the *gettydefs* file. If your terminal operates at 19200 baud, for example, replace *m* as the last parameter on the *t1a* entry with *n*. To change the value, move the cursor from the upper left corner down (by using Ctrl-F) until the entry for *t1a* appears. Then move the cursor to the *m* in the *t1a* line by pressing a Right direction key or the L key. Now press the R key (to replace a single character), and then press the N key.

Next select the baud rate that the modem connected to *tty2A* uses, and change the entry labeled *t2A* in *inittab* to the correct label in the *gettydefs* file. Your system might have a private, or dedicated, telephone line, which is more expensive than a normal telephone line but much less prone to random static and line noise. Communication speed through a dedicated line can be higher than 1200 or 2400 baud, depending on the operating speed of the modem you're using. You need to set up the port for the correct speed. If the modem on your secondary serial port runs at 2400 baud, choose label *k* from the *gettydefs* file, and replace the parameter *m* with *k* in the *t2A* entry of *inittab*.

If you've followed our example, your *inittab* file should now look like this:

```
t1a:2:respawn:/etc/getty ttyla n
t1A:2:off:/etc/getty ttylA m
t2a:2:off:/etc/getty tty2a m
t2A:2:respawn:/etc/getty tty2A k
~
~
~
~
```

After you change the contents of *inittab* to match your system, save the modified file as */etc/inittab*. You can do so with *vi*'s *x* (exit) command, which saves the current buffer contents on disk and, at the same time, exits *vi*. From command mode, enter the following command:

```
:x
```

Your updating process is now complete.

> **NOTE:** *If you want your changes to the file* /etc/inittab *to become a permanent part of the system configuration, you must also make the same changes to the file* /etc/conf/cf.d/init.base. *If you relink the kernel of your operating system — perhaps after adding a new device driver — the system will rebuild* /etc/inittab *from the information in* /etc/conf/cf.d/init.base.

# FINDING TERMINAL TYPES

After you activate the ports that you'll be using, you next need to tell SCO UNIX what types of terminals will access those ports. These definitions are contained in the file called *ttytype*. Again, you can use *vi* to work with the contents of the file. As before, look at the contents of the file to see what it contains, and decide what choices must be made. At the system prompt (#), enter the following:

```
cat /etc/ttytype
```

SCO UNIX displays something like the following:

```
ansi console
ansi tty01
ansi tty02
ansi tty03
ansi tty04
ansi tty05
```

*(continued)*

```
continued
ansi tty06
ansi tty07
ansi tty08
ansi tty09
ansi tty10
ansi tty11
ansi tty12
unknown    tty1a
unknown    tty2a
dialup     ttyp0
dialup     ttyp1
dialup     ttyp2
dialup     ttyp3
dialup     ttyp4
dialup     ttyp5
dialup     ttyp6
dialup     ttyp7

~
```

The first part of each line describes the terminal type, and the second part names the port to which the terminal is attached. If your file differs from what you see here, don't be concerned. More likely than not, you'll be changing it.

## Distinguishing One Terminal from Another

In the preceding example, the console device is defined as an ANSI terminal. As was mentioned before, the ANSI designation means that character placement and removal on the screen follow a standard set of rules described by the American National Standards Institute. ANSI is widely known and accepted, so this designation almost certainly applies to your host computer. If, for some reason, it does not, check with your dealer or manufacturer for details.

The default values for *tty1a* and *tty2a*, however, as shown in our example, indicate that the terminals connected to these devices have the type *unknown*. (The designation *unknown* does not mean that SCO UNIX doesn't know anything about the terminal; it means that the terminal has very limited capabilities.) But many types of terminals exist. Yours may or may not match these descriptions.

The feature that distinguishes between two brands of terminal might be the way in which special control characters and commands are used to control their screens. Some terminals follow the ANSI rules, but at present, no overriding standard exists in this area of hardware manufacturing.

Because SCO UNIX must know what type of terminal is attached to a particular port, it contains a special data file, called *termcap*, in the */etc* subdirectory. The *termcap* file contains the information SCO UNIX needs to work with any of a wide selection of terminal makes and models. The file is quite long, but you can determine whether your terminal type is included by using a single SCO UNIX command, *grep*.

# Finding a Terminal Type

We'll use the *grep* utility, which was explained in detail in Chapter 8, to match patterns. Given the manufacturer's name (ADDS, Zenith, Hazeltine, DEC, IBM, TeleVideo, and so on), you can use *grep* to search the file */etc/termcap* to find out if that name is contained in the file. For example, suppose you use DEC as the search criterion. Your command line would read as follows:

```
grep y DEC /etc/termcap
```

Notice that we included the *y* option to search for both uppercase and lowercase occurrences of DEC. SCO UNIX would respond with the following list of DEC terminal types contained in *termcap*:

```
# grep -y DEC /etc/termcap
# Submitted by Ampex Dec 22, 1987
dv:vt52:dec vt52:\
dV:vt52so:dec vt52 with brackets added for standout use:\
dl:vt100:vt-100:pt100:pt-100:dec vt100:\
dn:vt100nam:vt100-nam:pt100nam:pt-100nam:DEC VT100 without automargins:\
ds:vt100s:vt-100s:pt100s:pt-100s:dec vt100 132 cols 14 lines:\
dt:vt100w:vt-100w:pt100w:pt-100w:dec vt100 132 cols:\
Vl:vt102:dec vt102:\
dz:vt131:vt-131:dec vt131:\
de:vt220:DEC VT220 in vt100 emulation mode:dec vt220 generic:\
#    This terminal is essentially identical to the DEC VT100 (ANSI mode).
vW:v55:visual55:Visual 55 emulation of DEC VT52 (called V55):\
vV:v50:visual50:Visual 50 emulation of DEC VT52:\
dI:dw1:decwriter I:\
dw:dw2:dw3:dw4:decwriter II:\
d4:gt40:dec gt40:\
d2:gt42:dec gt42:\
d5:vt50:dec vt50:\
dh:vt50h:dec vt50h:\
```

Each line of text *grep* reported contains the pattern *dec*. The first two characters of each line represent the terminal-definition code that SCO UNIX understands. The remainder of each line is a description of the terminal to which the code refers.

> **NOTE:** *If you were to look at the contents of* termcap, *you would see that each DEC entry actually is much more than* grep *reported. Each terminal code and description is followed by a list of parameters that SCO UNIX requires to operate the particular terminal. Right now, however, in terms of the* /etc/ttytype *file, SCO UNIX needs only the two-character terminal code itself.*

If you were using a DEC terminal, you would scan the list of *termcap* entries for your terminal model. A standard DEC VT-100 terminal, for instance, has the code *d1*. Note that you cannot simply use the first code that matches your terminal type. Codes *do*, *dn*, *ds*, and *dt* also refer to the VT-100 but with different parameters. The code *do* is for a VT-100 on which no initialization is performed; *dn* is for a VT-100 without the automargin feature; *ds* is for a VT-100 in 132-column, 14-line mode; and *dt* is for a VT-100 in 132-column mode.

## Changing a Terminal Type

Let's assume that the terminal you want to attach to *tty1a* is a DEC VT-100 with the code *d1*. To change the definition in */etc/ttytype*, you could start *vi* and specify the file by entering the following:

```
vi /etc/ttytype
```

To move down to the *tty1a* definition in line 14 of the text, enter the repeat number *13* for *vi*. After the cursor moves down 13 lines, use the *dw* command to delete the word *unknown*. Next you use the *i* command to enter insert mode.

Then type *d1* and press the Spacebar. Press the Escape key to leave insert mode, and save the new version on disk by using the *:x* command.

Remember, the description *unknown tty1a* is from our example. If different information is displayed for *tty1a* in the *ttytype* file contained on your SCO UNIX system, use that information instead.

## If *grep* Does Not Find Your Terminal

If the terminal manufacturer for which you tell *grep* to search is not represented in *termcap,* *grep* will not be able to return any lines from the file. Instead, the system prompt will reappear. But that outcome doesn't necessarily mean that *termcap* does not contain a definition of your terminal.

Your terminal or its manufacturer might be too new to be listed in the SCO UNIX file. If you suspect that this is so, check the terminal's manual to see whether the terminal is compatible with one that is listed in *termcap.*

Then, too, remember that *grep* is not intelligent—it matches patterns of characters. You might not have entered the name of your terminal as it exists in the *termcap* file. For example, you can find the Radio Shack Model 100 if you use either *radio* or *shack* as the search pattern, but you won't find it by using *tandy*. Conversely, you can find the definition for a TRS-80 model 16, an SCO UNIX-compatible computer, by using *trs*, the abbreviation for Tandy/Radio Shack.

In any case, you might simply want to print the contents of */etc/termcap* by using the command *lp /etc/termcap* and scanning the list.

## Adding an Undefined Terminal

If you cannot find in *termcap* a definition, either actual or compatible, for your terminal, you can use the terminal definition *unknown* or the definition *dumb*. (The code is *su* if the terminal is not listed in *termcap*, but *y1* if it is a Teleray terminal, model 3700).

The definition *dumb*, however, cannot let you use SCO UNIX to its fullest capacity. The control codes used by *dumb* are based on the codes used to describe Teletype equipment—terminals that print on paper rather than on a screen. Such a terminal is also called a "glass tty" and has the most limited display characteristics: A *dumb* terminal has an 80-column line with auto-wrap margins and can move its cursor only to the next line. For most of the operations you want to perform in the Bourne and C shells, these codes are fine. But they offer few alternatives in those instances in which SCO UNIX needs a considerable amount of control over the screen.

For example, *vi* controls the screen more than most other SCO UNIX programs do, and users will not get a full-screen display when trying to use *vi* with a terminal defined to SCO UNIX as *dumb* or *tty* (Teletype-like machine). If you choose *dumb* or *tty*, *vi* will run in its "open mode," which means it operates exactly like the line editor *ex*. The system administration shell, *sysadmsh*, which you might need to use from a terminal other than the console, will not run on a *dumb* terminal because it also uses a full-screen rather than line-by-line display.

## Adding Dial-up Terminal Types

After a terminal is hardwired to a system, overseeing its use or replacement is relatively straightforward. In a dial-up situation, however, you encounter a set of "what if" situations with any number of answers. Given the system's telephone number, a login name, and a password, a SCO UNIX user can plug any handy terminal into a modem and try to access the system. In addition, a number of dial-up users, each with a different type of terminal, can also require access through the same port or ports. Your solution to this situation will depend on how your system is used and by whom.

If your dial-up users access SCO UNIX from the Bourne or the C shell and use it primarily for *mail* messages and other straightforward tasks, the simplest recourse is to define the device attached to the dial-up port as *dumb*. This definition permits any dial-up terminal to communicate with SCO UNIX. The user will have no screen control, and that circumstance involves the restrictions to *vi* that we've already mentioned.

A more effective alternative, especially if you want to offer the full range of SCO UNIX's capabilities to your dial-up users, is to modify the information in each user's *.profile* file. SCO UNIX keeps a separate *.profile* file (or equivalent) for each user account on the system. These *.profile* files maintain information about each person. Additional information about each user's terminal type can be placed in it as well, as you'll see later in the chapter, after you've installed one or two user accounts.

Finally, if you cannot predict what type of terminal will be used to access SCO UNIX—for example, if you have outside salespeople who access the system from whatever terminals are available—you can have each user set the terminal type after logging in. This procedure will work well because SCO UNIX makes no screen-control demands immediately following login.

If your dial-up users can set the terminal type, you need to provide them with a list of valid terminal types for the system (as listed in */etc/termcap*) and instruct them to enter their terminal information in the following format after logging in:

```
TERM=terminal_code; export TERM
```

They substitute the correct terminal code in place of *terminal_code*. The word *TERM* in this command is an SCO UNIX variable that holds the terminal-definition code; it must be typed in uppercase. After a user enters this line, SCO UNIX is able to deal with the terminal by using the related parameters that it finds in */etc/termcap*. The result for the user (although it lasts only until logout) is no different from having the terminal defined in */etc/ttytype* or in the *.profile* file.

# Using Computers as Terminals

As was mentioned early in this book, a computer, as well as a terminal, can be used to access SCO UNIX. The computer must be equipped with a telecommunications program that enables it to emulate a terminal that SCO UNIX will recognize. Although SCO UNIX will make no distinction between a computer that attempts to communicate with it and a terminal that acts the same way, you will need to exercise some special care when you tell SCO UNIX what type of terminal the telecommunications software is attempting to have the attached computer emulate.

Almost every telecommunications software package has an option that makes your computer ANSI-compatible as part of its terminal-emulation function. In terms of emulating a terminal for use with either the Bourne shell or the C shell, this level of ANSI-compatibility is usually sufficient. Neither shell makes many demands on total compatibility with the terminal type you've assigned, and most telecommunications terminal-emulation software works well under these conditions.

For a real terminal, however, ANSI-compatibility is usually a subset of all the control instructions the manufacturer built into the device. If you experience problems, you can supply /etc/ttytype with the definition *dumb* and have the computer treated as if it were a Teletype machine with no screen-control mechanism. However, the definition *dumb* might cause problems if the person wants to use *vi*.

Also, although exceptions exist for computers that both run SCO UNIX and are used as terminals on SCO UNIX systems, be sure to remind users that present versions of SCO UNIX cannot usually interact with the filesystem of the computer being used as a terminal. For example, an IBM PC XT, used as a terminal is simply a keyboard and video display as far as SCO UNIX is concerned.

You can easily hook up terminals and provide people with access to SCO UNIX. Because SCO UNIX was designed to be both flexible and powerful, you not only have a variety of options from which to choose, you also have effective commands, such as *grep*, with which to probe the information. You'll find additional information about manipulating terminal-communication characteristics in the System Administration section of your SCO UNIX documentation.

# ADDING A PRINTER

You could, in theory, run an SCO UNIX system efficiently without ever printing a document on paper, but you almost certainly want one or more printers for system users to share. The process of adding printers is not difficult, and you can install a printer quickly by using the system administrator's shell, *sysadmsh*. We'll begin with a few definitions and then use *sysadmsh* to install a Hewlett-Packard LaserJet printer on a sample system.

Printers are always installed individually, with names of their own. You assign each printer a name of up to 14 characters (any combination of letters, numbers, and underlines). You can install each printer either as a "freestanding" printer or as part of a class, or group, of printers. In operation, a printer defined as one of a class will be used by SCO UNIX to print any document sent to that class of printers. For example, if you install two laser printers named *laser1* and *laser2*, both of which belong to the class you've defined as *hplaser*, SCO UNIX will print a request sent to *hplaser* on either *laser1* or *laser2*, depending on which is available when the system receives the request.

The actual printing request is managed by a program called *lpsched*, or the print scheduler, which you also begin with *sysadmsh*. The *lpsched* program starts up whenever you start or restart the system and as it receives them, routes requests through an intermediary called a printer interface program and then to the appropriate printer.

# Printer Interface Programs

Printer interface programs handle a number of important tasks that ensure correct print operation and that safeguard the print requests that are routed through them. Among these tasks are the following:

- Providing appropriate communication and parameters for the printer.

- Examining a system file named */etc/default/lpd* to determine whether one or more "banner" pages should be printed at the beginning of each job.

- Sending a numeric exit code to *lpsched* that indicates whether a printing job was successfully completed.

- Disabling printers when necessary (as when a paper jam occurs) and maintaining a record of print requests not yet completed.

An appropriate printer interface program must exist for each printer on your system. One general interface program already exists in SCO UNIX, in a script file named */usr/spool/lp/model/dumb*. This program assumes a basic form-feed printer with no special codes or requirements. You can install the *dumb* printer using *sysadmsh*. Doing so creates a copy of the file in the subdirectory */usr/spool/lp/admins/lp/interfaces*. You can then use *vi* to modify this copy of the file whenever you need to add specific codes for print enhancements, top-of-page commands, automatic linefeeds, and so on. (See your printer manual for this kind of printer-specific information.) Another general interface program that you can use is */usr/spool/lp/model/standard*.

As written, */usr/spool/lp/model/dumb* performs the tasks outlined earlier and also manages the following information:

- The name of the printer and the identification number SCO UNIX assigns to the file forwarded to the printer.

- The comment field of the user who is making the print request.

- The current day, date, and time.

- The number of copies to be printed.

- Any suitable print options, such as small (12-pitch) or condensed (132 characters per line) type, that are requested and that the printer can handle.

- The pathname of the file to be printed.

# Making the Connections

Physically connecting your printer to the system is easy, but you need to remember a few points as you do so. (Check your printer manual for specific instructions.) SCO

UNIX can handle both serial and parallel printers. You need to determine which type your printer is and plan accordingly. If you have a choice, you'll want to use parallel connections so that you can use the serial lines (which are often in short supply) for adding more terminals. The IBM-compatible personal computers come equipped with one parallel port but can support two. If you have two and you are connecting a parallel printer, decide which port to use, make note of it, and then make the hardware connections.

You'll be asked during the installation to which port you have attached your printer. You must respond with the correct device name. Depending on your hardware configuration, your choice could be among the following:

| | |
|---|---|
| */dev/lp0* | The primary parallel port, configured as interrupt vector 7 (IRQ7). |
| */dev/lp2* | The secondary serial port, configured as interrupt vector 5 (IRQ5). |
| */dev/lp1* | The parallel port on a monochrome display adapter, configured as interrupt vector 7 (IRQ7). |
| */dev/tty[1-2][a-m]* | A serial port without modem control. |

The interrupt vector is the code that a device (in this case, a parallel port) sends to interrupt the central processor. The interrupt requests that the central processor temporarily stop other processing, take input from the device, and then return to other processing. When you initially configure your computer, you can specify the interrupt vectors for the primary and secondary parallel ports by using the computer's setup command. Note that you cannot have printers connected to both the primary parallel port and the parallel port on a monochrome adapter at the same time. The operating system uses the same interrupt vector for both ports, and two different physical ports cannot be configured with the same interrupt vector at the same time.

Finally, you need to set the appropriate DIP switches for your printer. To do so, check your printer's manual for switch settings for your type of installation. In some cases, the settings for the DIP switches are contained in the files in */usr/spool/lp/model*. This directory includes interface files for a number of printers: AT&T 5310/20 matrix printers, Tandy DMP 1.0 printer, Hewlett-Packard 2631a line printer, Hewlett-Packard LaserJet printer, Hewlett-Packard ThinkJet printer, Hewlett-Packard QuietJet printer, the Autologic APS-5 Phototypesetter printer, Qume Sprint 1155 printer, and Texas Instruments 855 printer, among others. Setting up printers not included in */usr/spool/lp/model* will take a little work if you want to use every special feature your printer has to offer. If you don't, use the printer interface program */usr/spool/lp/model/dumb*.

# Using *sysadmsh* to Install a Printer

As was mentioned earlier, to install a new printer on an SCO UNIX system, use the *sysadmsh* command. To do so, log in as the superuser, and enter the following command:

```
sysadmsh
```

After you do so, you see the following, the first of a series of forms:

```
                                                          SysAdmSh
System Backups Accounts Printers Media Jobs Dirs/Files Filesystems Quit
Administer and configure system resources and report system status_
/                                          Friday June 15, 1990  13:16
```

Starting from this form, select the following options in turn by moving the highlight to the desired option and then pressing Enter:

```
Printers→Configure→Add
```

Alternatively, you can type the first letter of the desired option, as follows:

```
p

c

a
```

You see the following form for adding printers on your screen:

```
                                                               Add
Enter the name of the new printer

/                                        Friday June 15, 1990 13:25
```

```
┌──────────────────────────Adding a Printer──────────────────────────┐
│    Printer name           [_              ]                         │
│                                                                     │
│    Comment                [                              ]          │
│                                                                     │
│    Class name             [              ]                          │
│                                                                     │
│    Use printer interface  [Existing]  Copy   New                   │
│    Name of interface      [                              ]          │
│                                                                     │
│    Connection             [Direct]   Call-up                       │
│       Device name         [            ]                           │
│       Dial-up information                                           │
│    Device                 [Hardwired]   Login                       │
│                                                                     │
│    Require banner         Yes  [No]                                 │
└─────────────────────────────────────────────────────────────────────┘
```

The cursor is in the field *Printer name*. You can type whatever printer name you want, using up to 14 letters, numbers, and underscore characters. You cannot use hyphens because the print spooler forms print request identifiers by taking the printer name and appending a hyphen followed by a number. In our example we'll name the printer *hplaser1*. After typing that name in the *Printer name* field, press Enter.

After you name the printer, the cursor moves to the *Comment* field. Here you can type any descriptive information that will help you remember which printer it is and what its characteristics are. You could type *HP LaserJet II on /dev/lp0,* for instance, to indicate the type of printer and the device it's attached to. Press Enter to move to the next field, the *Class name* field. If you want the printer to belong to a class and to accept requests for that class of printer, type a class name. (Until you have defined classes by typing in a class name, you cannot choose from the list by pressing the F3 key as indicated by the prompt in the help line.) If you don't want to define classes, simply press Enter to move to the next field.

The options following *Use printer interface* are choices that you select rather than fields in which you type. You can select an option either by typing the first letter of the option or by moving the highlight to the desired option with the direction keys and pressing Enter. Each option selects one of the following types of interface program:

| | |
|---|---|
| *Existing* | Selects an existing interface from /usr/spool/lp/model. |
| *Copy* | Selects an installed interface from /usr/spool/lp/admins/lp/interfaces. |
| *New* | Lets you type the name of a file containing a new interface. |

For this installation example, press Enter to select *Existing*. The cursor moves to the *Name of interface* field. Here you can press the F3 key to have *sysadmsh* display the existing interfaces. The following window pops up in the lower right corner of the form:

```
* 1640          +
  5310
  TandyDMP
  crlnmap
  dqp10
  dumb
  emulator
  f450
  hp
  hpjet         v
```

This window lists all the printer interfaces in */usr/spool/lp/model.* You can use the direction keys to move up and down in the window. The plus sign (+) in the right margin of the window indicates the approximate position of the highlight in the complete list. The *v* at the bottom of the right margin indicates that more entries are below the last entry you can see. If you move the highlight down, a caret (^) appears at the top of the right margin to show you that more entries are available above the highlighted entry. The asterisk (*) marks the interface that you've chosen. Use the direction keys to move the highlight to *hpjet*, and press Enter to select it and display it in the *Name of interface* field.

In the *Connection* field, select the *Direct* option because the printer is directly connected to the computer, not by means of a modem or network. In the *Device name* field, type the name of the SCO UNIX operating system device that is connected to the printer. If it is connected to the primary parallel port, enter */dev/lp0*. (If you selected *Call-up*, you'll see a field following *Dial-up information* for a modem phone number or a network address.) In the *Device* field, select the option *Hardwired* to indicate that the device is dedicated to the printer and that it is not used as a terminal. In the *Require banner* field, select the default option, *No*, and press Enter. The *Require banner* field lets the user choose whether to print a "banner" page—an identifying cover sheet for the print job.

The *sysadmsh* then runs the programs necessary to install the printer as you have requested.

When *sysadmsh* completes this portion of the installation, the program might display this message:

```
UX:lpadmin: WARNING: "/dev/lp0" is accessible by others
            TO FIX: If other users can access it you may get
                    unwanted output. If this is not what you
                    want change the owner to "lp" and change
                    the mode to 0600
                    Processing continues.
```

If you change the owner designation to *lp* and the mode to *0600*, only the person designated *lp* will be able to send files directly to that device by means of the print spooler. The person identified as *lp*, in a sense, "owns" the print spooler that is sending the files. To change the ownership to *lp* after you exit the system administration shell, use the following command:

```
chown lp /dev/lp0
```

To change the mode to *0600*, use the following command:

```
chmod 0600 /dev/lp0
```

Press any key to resume the *sysadmsh* program and complete the printer installation, or press the Escape key twice to return to the top-level form of *sysadmsh*. Next you need to begin the print scheduler, enable the printer you have chosen, and have the printer accept print requests. To begin the print scheduler, select the following options from the menu at the top of the screen:

Printers→Schedule→Begin

You will see this form:

```
                                                                    Begin

Start the scheduler_

/                                              Friday June 15, 1990   13:29
                    ┌──────Start the Print Scheduler──────┐
                    │       Proceed        Cancel         │
                    │                                     │
                    └─────────────────────────────────────┘
```

Press Enter to select the default option, *Proceed.* When you do so, the system administration program runs the necessary programs to begin the print scheduler. When the print scheduler has begun, the system administration program displays the message *Print services started* indicating that the print scheduler can take print requests from users and spool the requests for a printer. As yet, however, the print scheduler doesn't have a printer to send the requests to. Your next tasks are to enable a printer and to let the printer accept jobs that are directed to it by users.

Press Enter to return to the menu at the top of the *Schedule* form, and then select *Enable.* You see the following form, with fields for the names of the printers that you want to enable:

```
                                                                   Enable

Press F3 to choose from a list of Destinations

/                                              Friday June 15, 1990   13:25

┌─────────────────────────Enable Printers─────────────────────────────┐
│                                                                      │
│         Destinations  [_          ] [              ]                 │
│                       [           ] [              ]                 │
│                       [           ] [              ]                 │
│                                                                      │
│                                                                      │
│                                                                      │
│                                                                      │
└──────────────────────────────────────────────────────────────────────┘
```

Press F3 to see the list of possible destinations. A window with a list of destinations pops up in the lower right corner of the form, as follows:

```
* hplaser1
```

The list for our example installation it has only one entry, *hplaser1*, so press Enter to put that entry in the field. Then move the cursor through the rest of the empty fields by pressing Enter. After the cursor leaves the last field, *sysadmsh* runs the programs necessary to enable the printer. After it does so, *sysadmsh* displays the message *printer "hplaser1" now enabled.*

Press Enter to return to the menu at the top of the form, and select the option *Accept*. A form similar to the form for the *Begin* option appears. Select the list of printers by pressing F3. A window pops up in the lower right corner of the form. Select *hplaser1* by pressing Enter, and then continue pressing Enter until the cursor leaves the last field. At that point, *sysadmsh* runs the programs that let the printer accept requests directed to it by users. When the programs end, you see the message *destination "hplaser1" now accepting requests.* Press any key to return to the menu at the top of the form.

Before you leave the printer installation portion of the program, you should specify the default printer for your system. When you specify a default printer, users don't need to know the names of all the printers on the system or the method for choosing a specific printer (using the correct arguments to the *lp* command). Users can simply use *lp* with one or more filenames and be assured that the files named will print on the default printer. (Even if you specify a default printer, users can send their files to other printers by using arguments following the *lp* command.) To specify a default printer, starting from the *Schedule* form, press the Escape key to return to the *Printers* form. Then select the following option:

Configure→Default

You see this form on your display:

```
                                                                Default
Press <F3> to choose from a list of destinations

/                                            Friday June 15, 1990  13:28
                           ┌─Change System Default Destination─────────┐
                           │                                           │
                           │                                           │
                           │                                           │
                           │     Destinations  [_            ]         │
                           │                                           │
                           │                                           │
                           │                                           │
                           │                                           │
                           │                                           │
                           └───────────────────────────────────────────┘
```

If you press F3, the following window pops up in the lower right corner of the form:

```
┌─────────────────────┐
│ * hplaser1          │
│                     │
│                     │
│                     │
└─────────────────────┘
```

Press Enter to select *hplaser1*. When *hplaser1* appears in the *Destination* field, press Enter. The system administration shell then runs the program that sets up the default printer for your system. When the program finishes running, you see the message *Press any key to continue*. Press any key to return to the menu.

You've now completed the basic printer installation. To exit from the system administration shell, press the Escape key until you return to the *SysAdmSh* form. Select *Quit→Yes* to exit from the shell and return to the superuser prompt (*#*).

## Managing Printers

After you install the printer or printers you want, SCO UNIX offers options in *sysadmsh* and some additional commands to help you manage this aspect of your system. Using these options and commands, you can stop and start print activities, create classes of printers, enable and disable particular printers, and transfer print requests from one destination to another.

## Stopping and starting the scheduler

As was mentioned earlier, all print requests for your system are handled by the print scheduler, which runs automatically whenever you start SCO UNIX. The system administration shell stops and restarts the print scheduler when you add a printer, but when administering printer operations, you need to be able to stop and start the scheduler on your own. To begin, you can find out whether the scheduler is currently running by entering the following command:

```
lpstat -r
```

If the scheduler is running and you want to stop it, enter the following command:

```
sysadmsh
```

When *sysadmsh* is running, choose the options *Printers→Schedule→Stop*. The following options window pops up:

```
┌──────Stop the Print Scheduler──────┐
│                                    │
│      Proceed       Cancel          │
│                                    │
│                                    │
└────────────────────────────────────┘
```

Press Enter to stop the scheduler and all current printing operations. When the prompt to continue appears, press Enter. Exit from *sysadmsh* by pressing the Escape key until the form *SysAdmSh* appears, and then select *Quit→Yes*. To restart the scheduler, start the system administration shell again with this command:

```
sysadmsh
```

Select *Printers→Schedule→Begin*. From the pop-up window, select *Proceed*, and press Enter when the prompt to continue appears. You can then exit from the system administration shell. At this point, you can verify that *lpsched* is running by entering the following command:

```
lpstat -r
```

## Handling print requests

On occasion, you will want to be able to shuffle print requests and printers. Perhaps you'll need to take a printer off the system for repair, or perhaps you'll need to move a print request from a busy printer to one that can do the job immediately. For this type of administration, you can use the following commands:

- The *lpmove* command moves a print request from one installed printer to another. For example, the following command moves print request *laser1-123* from *laser1* to *laser2*:

  ```
  /usr/lib/lpmove laser1-123 laser2
  ```

- The *accept* command enables a printer or printer class to accept print requests submitted with the *lp* command. For example, the following command enables the class *hplaser1* to accept print requests:

```
/accept hplaser1
```

- The *reject* command, the converse of *accept*, tells the system that the specified printer or printer class cannot receive print requests. If you include the command's *-r* option and an explanatory comment enclosed in double quotation marks, a user requesting the printer will receive a message stating that the printer cannot be used, along with your message stating the reason. For example, the following command takes *laser2* out of use and informs users of the malfunction:

```
reject -r "malfunctioning printer" laser2
```

- The *enable* command enables the specified printer to actually print the files routed to it. For example, the following command causes *laser2* not only to accept print requests (by means of the *accept* command) but to print the documents as well:

```
enable laser2
```

You must do this each time you start up the SCO UNIX system.

- The *disable* command is the opposite of *enable*. Like the *reject* command, it can be used with the *-r* option and an explanatory comment. For example, the following command disables *laser1* whether or not it is set up to accept print requests:

```
disable -r "uneven printing" laser1
```

As jobs are submitted to the printer, they are stored in a print queue. To see the jobs waiting in the order in which they arrived, enter the following command:

```
lpstat
```

You can cancel a job by using the following command format:

```
cancel request-id
```

For example, to cancel the printing of the job *hplaser1-18* you would enter the following command:

```
cancel hplaser1-18
```

# The *sysadmsh* Printer Options

The system administration shell includes all the functions necessary to administer the printers on your system. You can add or delete printers, restrict users from certain printers, set up forms on printers, move print requests from one printer to another, and perform many other tasks. The system administration shell brings all these functions together under the *Printers* option on the top form, *SysAdmSh*. Underlying all these options, however, are SCO UNIX programs that *sysadmsh* runs when you fill out a form. In some cases, using *sysadmsh* is the easiest way to accomplish some tasks, especially those tasks that you need to undertake infrequently. The system administration shell presents you with all the necessary fields to fill in, prompt you with lists of alternatives, and gives you warning information or information about fixing a result that it deems questionable. For example, you'll probably find that using *sysadmsh* to inform the spooler that you have mounted a requested print form is easier than trying to remember all the correct arguments that go with the following *lpadmin* command format:

```
/usr/lib/lpadmin -p printername -M -f formname -a -o filebreak
```

On the other hand, some tasks are much easier with a simple command. To cancel a print request for a document, it is easier to use the *cancel* command. To cancel the print request *hplaser1-3757*, you merely enter the following at the shell prompt:

```
cancel hplaser1-3757
```

To accomplish the same task with the system administration shell, you would first need to start the shell with the following command:

```
sysadmsh
```

Then you would need to select *Printers→Request→Cancel*. From the form that appears, you would then need to select the option *Request IDs*. When the field for the print request identification appears, you would enter the following command:

```
hplaser1-3757
```

Similarly, if you needed to stop requests from being spooled for an inoperative printer, you'd probably find it easier to enter the following commands than to use the options in *sysadmsh*:

```
disable hplaser1
```

```
reject hplaser1
```

With that in mind, let's take a quick tour through the choices under the *Printers* option. For each choice, we also show the alternative command. A command listed in many places undoubtedly has a long and complicated list of arguments. For example, it takes the manual 12 pages to describe the *lpadmin* command, its uses, and its multiple arguments. These commands are difficult to enter correctly from the keyboard, so you'll benefit from using the system administration shell to accomplish the same tasks.

Most of the commands listed at the end of each description are in the subdirectory */usr/lib*. If a command is not in that subdirectory, the complete pathname is listed.

## Printer configuration options

If you select *Configure* from the *Printers* form, you will see the following options:

| | |
|---|---|
| *Add* | Adds a printer to the system (*lpadmin*). |
| *Modify* | Modifies a printer configuration (*lpadmin*). |
| *Remove* | Removes a printer destination from the LP print service (*lpadmin*). |
| *Default* | Changes the system default destination printer (*lpadmin*). |
| *Parameters* | Modifies printer controls and parameters (*lpadmin*). |
| *Errors* | Sets error warning notification and recovery modes (*lpadmin*). |
| *Contents* | Specifies the type of contents which can be printed on a printer (*lpadmin*). |
| *Users* | Specifies who can (or cannot) use a printer (*lpadmin*). |

## Printer scheduling options

If you select *Schedule* from the *Printers* form, you will see the following options:

| | |
|---|---|
| *Begin* | Starts the LP print service (*lpsched*). |
| *Stop* | Shuts down the LP print service (*lpshut*). |
| *Accept* | Allows requests for destination (*accept*). |
| *Reject* | Rejects requests for destination (*reject*). |
| *Enable* | Enables line printers (*/usr/bin/enable*). |
| *Disable* | Disables line printers (*/usr/bin/disable*). |

## Printer request options

If you select *Requests* from the *Printers* form, you will see the following options:

| | |
|---|---|
| *Move* | Moves requests between destinations (*lpmove*). |
| *Cancel* | Cancels requests made to the print service (*/usr/bin/cancel*). |

## Printer auxiliary options

Using the printer auxiliary options, you can administer print-wheels, filters that convert data to output acceptable to printers, and the use of preprinted forms.

You see the following options:

| | |
|---|---|
| *Alert* | Sets or list an alert for a print wheel (*lpadmin*). |
| *Filter* | Administers filters used with the LP print service (*lpfilter*). |
| *PPforms* | Administers preprinted forms used with the LP print service (*lpadmin, lpforms*). |

## Printer priority options

The printer priority options set the priorities assigned to users' print requests when they go into the spooler. The priorities range from 0 through 39, with 0 having the highest priority. Requests with higher priority go into the print queue ahead of jobs with lower priority and print first. The default priority, unless otherwise set for a user or users on your system, is 20. On the printer priority form, you will see the following options:

| | |
|---|---|
| *Default* | Sets the systemwide priority default (*lpusers*). |
| *Highest* | Sets the default highest priority level for users (*lpusers*). |
| *Remove* | Removes users from any explicit priority level (*lpusers*). |
| *List* | Lists the default priority level and priority limits assigned to users (*lpusers*). |

# ADDING USER ACCOUNTS

Now that we've covered the main features of activating ports, assigning access devices, and installing printers, we can move on to adding user accounts.

> **NOTE:** *If you are the system administrator on a new SCO UNIX system with no current users other than you, you can try an endless variety of commands and sample situations in learning to add and modify user accounts. If one or more of your experiments go wrong, you can start over by deleting the accounts and, as a last resort, by reinstalling SCO UNIX. If you are a new administrator on an established SCO UNIX system, you might want to create a few "dummy" accounts on which you can try out modifications. You must be logged in as the superuser (root) to create user accounts. You should start the multiuser mode. If your hard disk is large enough to create an additional filesystem, SCO UNIX creates the users' home directories in that filesystem. That filesystem is not made available to the operating system.*

In SCO UNIX, you use the system administration shell to create user accounts, but you must be in a single user (maintenance) mode. If the user account needs only standard features, you can enter all the information necessary to create the account and set up the initial password on one form and a subsequent screen. To add a new user to the system, you begin by entering the following command:

```
sysadmsh
```

SCO UNIX responds with the top-level form, *SysAdmSh*. From this form, select the options *Accounts→User→Create*. You will see the following *Create* form for creating new user accounts:

```
                                                              Create
Name of new user (once set, this cannot be changed)
/                                         Saturday, June 16,-1990-10:24
 ┌─────────────────────────Make a new user account────────────────────┐
 │                                                                      │
 │   Username      : [_     ]                                           │
 │                                                                    ] │
 │   Comment       : [                                                   │
 │                                                                      │
 │   Modify defaults?   Yes    [  No  ]                                 │
 │                                                                      │
 └──────────────────────────────────────────────────────────────────┘
```

If you want to stop creating an account or filling in a form at any time in *sysadmsh*, press the Escape key. Depending on where you are in the creation process, you will return to either the *Create* form or the immediately preceding window.

## Assigning the Login Name

As you can see, this form is fairly straightforward. As with all the other forms in *sysadmsh*, as you move the cursor from field to field, this form displays a help line describing the current field or option near the top of the screen.

Try to assign a login name that is simple. The login name you choose becomes the name of the user's home directory. The login name you choose can consist of any combination of lowercase letters and numbers and can be as short as three characters and as long as eight characters. Typically, system administrators use some form of the user's name. For example, a user named Susan Gray might have a login name of *susang* or *susangr*. In general, try to use elements of both the user's first and last names. Login names formed only from the person's first name or from a word that might be a first name can cause problems when you attempt to install another user account for someone else with the same first name. Throughout this book we've used user names that comprise a first name and a last initial. You'll find this method adequate most of the time. Some administrators create task-oriented or department-oriented login names too. An example would be a login name such as *finance*, which one or more people working in the Finance department could use. (This is not the same as assigning a user to a group, as will be discussed next.)

After you enter the name, the cursor moves to the *Comments* field. This field is for information describing the user. The help line indicates the sort of information that you might include: *Full name, office location, extension, home phone.*

After filling in the *Comments* field, you are prompted to choose between retaining or modifying the defaults used to set up user accounts on your system. In most cases, for most users, the default choices serve perfectly well. The most important default choices are the shell, the home directory, and the group assigned to the user. Unless you modify these choices for your whole system, users are assigned the following defaults:

| | |
|---|---|
| Shell | Bourne shell |
| Home directory | */usr/user_name* |
| Group | *group* |

Remember from our earlier discussion that file permissions were set for owner, group, and others. Thus, if you are in group *group* and set the group file permissions to *rwx*, you are permitting all the members of your group to read, write, and execute those files.

**NOTE:** *If your hard disk is large enough to allow other filesystems, users can have home directories in subdirectories other than* /usr. *Users might, for instance, have home directories in* /u.

If you don't choose to modify the defaults for user account creation and you select the option *No*, *sysadmsh* will display the following pop-up window that asks you to confirm the account that you're creating:

```
┌──────────────────────Confirm change──────────────────────┐
│         You are creating user :  susang                   │
│                                                           │
│    Are you sure you wish to create this new user account? │
│                                                           │
│  Please choose one of: Re-examine        Yes       No     │
│                                                           │
└───────────────────────────────────────────────────────────┘
```

The highlighted choice, *Re-examine*, returns you to the preceding form, where you can make changes to any of the fields. If you are satisfied with the choices that you made, select *Yes*. The system administration shell runs the programs necessary to create the user account that you specified. As it completes the tasks for account creation, the shell displays messages about its actions. When the shell has created the user account, you will see messages similar to the following on a second screen of the *Create* form:

```
Created home directory: /usr/susang
Created sh file: /usr/susang/.profile
Greetings mail sent to user: susang

Press <RETURN> to continue: _
```

# Assigning the Password

As was explained in Chapter 2, passwords help you maintain the security of your system. You're now ready to assign one. After you respond to the message at the bottom of the *Create* form by pressing Enter, *sysadmsh* displays the following pop-up window, which prompts you to create the new user's initial password:

```
─────────────────Assign initial password────────────────
 Do you wish to assign an initial password to user :  susang

         Yes            No         Re-examine

 No-one may login into the account until a password is assigned.
```

You should choose the highlighted option, *Yes*, and immediately assign the user a password. The user will then be able to log in to the account without any further administrative tasks. When you select *Yes*, *sysadmsh* runs the *passwd* program, which maintains the password file with encrypted passwords.

Among the enhancements to achieve the C2 level of trust mentioned earlier in this chapter is a new treatment of the password file, */etc/passwd*, which was expanded into an adjunct Protected Password database. Many UNIX and XENIX systems let the superuser edit the *passwd* file using a text editor such as *vi*. SCO UNIX does not allow anyone to make modifications to a user's *passwd* file with *vi*. Instead, the superuser must use the system administration shell utility, *sysadmsh*, to create, modify, or remove user accounts. If the superuser tries to edit */etc/passwd* directly with a text editor, the system might display error messages and even prevent further logins.

First *sysadmsh* asks you to choose the method for selecting a password with the following message:

```
Last successful password change for susang: Sat Jun 16 10:24:52 1990
Last unsuccessful password change for susang: NEVER

        Choose password

You can choose whether you pick your own password,
or have the system create one for you.

1. Pick your own password
2. Pronouncable password will be generated for you

Enter choice (default is 1): _
```

In this case, you are choosing a password for *susang*. Passwords can be any combination of characters other than the carriage-return character and the linefeed character. Just as when you created the superuser password, you should make a user's password individual enough so that others cannot easily guess it but not so complex that its owner must write it down to remember it. Before assigning a password, it's advisable to talk to the user and decide on one that is mutually agreeable.

Pick whichever method that is the most comfortable for you. If you choose the default method, *passwd* prompts you for the password as follows:

```
New password:_
```

Enter the password. You can enter a maximum of 10 characters (80 if you change the default). The characters that you type are not displayed on the screen for security reasons. To ensure that you didn't make any typing mistakes the first time, you are prompted to enter the password again as follows:

```
New password:
Re-enter new password:_
```

If the entries don't match, *passwd* informs you and prompts again for the new password. If you type the password the same way both times, *passwd* accepts your choice, as follows:

```
New password:
Re-enter new password:

Press <RETURN> to continue: _
```

> **NOTE:** *Unless you modify the default choices for the system or for the user, users must keep any given password for a minimum of 14 days. After that time, users can change their passwords as often as every two weeks, and they must change their passwords at least every six weeks. If more than 365 days elapse between the last time that a user changed the password and the next login attempt, the password expires, and the account is locked until the system administrator unlocks it. This prevents old — and possibly overlooked — accounts from being reactivated. You can change any of these default values if you want.*

# Modifying the Default Values When Creating a User Account

You might decide to use the default values for creating accounts on your system because those values best serve the majority of your users. In some cases, though, you might need to modify the accounts for special cases. For instance, you might retain the Bourne shell as the default shell for most of your users but assign the C shell to others. The following are the most common default values that you might want to change:

■ Login group

■ Login shell

■ Home directory

In some relatively rare cases, you might also want to change the default values for the following:

■ User ID number

■ CPU priority

■ Type of user

■ User responsible for this account (nonindividual accounts only)

You can change any of these values in the *Create* form while you are creating a new user account. If you choose *Yes* after the *Modify defaults?* message, *sysadmsh* displays this pop-up window:

```
┌────────────────────────New user account parameters────────────────────────┐
│                                                                             │
│   Login group     :  Specify  Default  of  group                           │
│                      Value, <F3> for list :                                 │
│   Groups          :  [...            ]                                      │
│                                                                             │
│   Login shell     :  Specify  [Default] of  sh                             │
│                      Value, <F3> for list :                                 │
│   Home directory  :  Specify  [Default] of  /usr/susang                    │
│                      Value, <F3> for list :                                 │
│                                                                             │
│   User Id number  :  Specify  [Default] of  202      value:                │
│   CPU priority    :  Specify  [Default] of  0        value:                │
│                                                                             │
│   Type of user    :  Specify  [Default] of  individual                     │
│                      Value, <F3> for list :                                 │
│   Account that may su(C) to this user   :                                   │
└─────────────────────────────────────────────────────────────────────────────┘
```

From this pop-up window, you can choose to change any, all, or none of the default values. You can move directly to the field that you want to change by using the direction keys. Or you can cycle through all of the choices. When you reach the last field in the window, press Enter to have your choices take effect. The system administration shell will display a window that asks you to confirm, reexamine, or reject your choices. If you confirm your choices by selecting *Yes*, the system administration shell creates a new user account with the values that you have chosen.

## Modifying the login group

The login group is the group (or groups) associated with the user when she or he logs in. The primary reason for including someone in a login group is to give that person access to files created by others in that group (and vice versa). This access can range from the ability to read, write, or execute files to the ability to take all three actions with files shared by the group's members. (Read, write, and execute access is discussed in Chapter 4; modifications to these privileges are controlled by the *chmod* command discussed in Chapter 8.) To specify a group other than the default group (*group*), select *Specify*. The cursor moves to the field following the colon. Press F3 to see a list of other, predefined groups on your system, such as the following:

```
 ┌──Existing-groups─┐
 │* adm            +│
 │  asg             │
 │  audit           │
 │  auth            │
 │  backup          │
 │  bin             │
 │  cron            │
 │  daemon          │
 │  group           │
 │  lp              │
 │  mail            │
 │  mem             │
 │  mmdf            │
 │  network        v│
 └──────────────────┘
```

You can select a group by moving the highlight with the direction keys and pressing the Enter key. You can select additional groups by moving the cursor to the field following the colon on the second line and pressing F3. This window disappears, and the window with your choices pops up on the display as follows:

```
┌─────────────────┐
│backup           │
│group_           │
│                 │
│                 │
└─────────────────┘
```

In this window, the user is in the group associated with making system backups as well as the default group. Press the Enter key or the Down direction key until the cursor exits from the bottom of the window. The window disappears, and the name of the last group you chose appears to the right of the colon.

### Creating a new group

When the cursor moves into the *Groups* field, instead of pressing *F3* for a list of pre-defined groups, you can create a new group. An SCO UNIX group is simply a group of people who have some aspect of work in common. For example, all of the people in the word-processing department might be in a group called *words*; all accountants could be in one called *accounts*.

You begin creating a group by typing the new group name (*accounts*, for instance) and then pressing the Enter key. You will see the following pop-up window:

```
┌──────────────────────Create Group──────────────────────┐
│                                                         │
│ Group does not exist :  accounts                        │
│                                                         │
│ Do you wish to create it? :   Yes        No             │
│                                                         │
│ Group ID :  Specify   Default  of  100   Value :        │
│                                                         │
└─────────────────────────────────────────────────────────┘
```

The message in the window asks you to confirm that you want to create a new group in case you simply made a typing error. Select *Yes* to create the group. You are then asked to choose an option from the *Group ID* field. You will almost certainly want to choose *Default*. After your selection, you will see a pop-up window with your newly created group, such as the following:

```
┌───────────────────┐
│ accounts          │
│                   │
│                   │
└───────────────────┘
```

If you want to add another group, you can simply press the Enter key and type the name. You can also press the Enter key or the Down direction key until the cursor exits from the window and the window disappears. You can then move the cursor to the *Groups* field again and specify another group with any of these methods.

### Modifying the default shell

You can choose one of four shells for each user on your system:

- The standard (Bourne) shell
- The C shell
- The restricted shell
- The UNIX to UNIX Communications (UUCP) shell

The Bourne and C shells are described in detail in Chapters 9 and 10, so we'll discuss them only briefly here. The UUCP shell isn't discussed here.

The Bourne shell is perhaps the most frequently assigned shell. It closely resembles the one from which you are currently operating, although you are given a different environment when you are in system maintenance mode or are logged in as the superuser. To use the Bourne shell comfortably, a user should have an adequate grasp of SCO UNIX commands or have a reference guide such as the one in Appendix A.

The C shell was originally designed for C programmers but is well suited to anyone who is reasonably proficient at SCO UNIX. In the C shell, users have a wide range of opportunities to customize their working environment.

The third shell is used to set up restricted access to the system for certain types of users. In most respects, it is identical to the Bourne shell. In most cases, after the user logs in, the *.profile* file for this user changes the working directory to some directory other than the home directory. Because one of the restrictions on this shell is that it prevents the user from executing the *cd* command, the user can't access the *.profile* file and change the actions when he or she logs in. (For other limitations on the restricted shell see the SCO UNIX *User's Reference* manual.)

As with the password, your decision about which shell you assign should be based on discussions with the user. Although users can change from the standard Bourne shell to the C shell at any time, first impressions are significant, and a new user's introduction to SCO UNIX (or any operating system) will set the tone for the rest of that person's work with it.

In the *Login shell* field, choose *Specify* to specify a login shell. The cursor moves to the field following the colon. You can then either enter the shell command name (*sh, csh, rsh,* or UUPC) or press F3 to see the following list of the shells:

```
                        ┌─────Login shells──────────────────────────┐
                        │ C Shell                                    │
    * csh               │                                            │
      rsh               │ Restricted Bourne shell                    │
      sh                │ Standard (Bourne) shell                    │
      UUPC              │ UNIX to UNIX Communications                │
                        └────────────────────────────────────────────┘
```

You can select any one of the shells by moving the highlight to your choice with the direction keys and then pressing Enter.

## Modifying the default home directory

As was mentioned earlier, if you have a large hard disk on your system, the SCO UNIX installation process might have created a second filesystem. This second filesystem, called */u,* is an alternative location for users' home directories. In most cases, you will want to put most individual users on the second filesystem. This simplifies the regular backup procedures that you will need to initiate for your system. On larger SCO UNIX systems, with multiple disk drives, you might have installed a number of filesystems. In this case as well, you will want to assign different types of users to different filesystems to simplify your backup procedures.

To modify the default home directory, select the *Specify* option from the *Home directory* field. The cursor moves into the field following the value. When you press F3, you will see a list similar to this:

```
 * /usr      :Commonly used SCO System V/386 home directory location
   /u        :Alternative SCO System V/386 home directory location
```

Your system might show only the */usr* directory if the SCO UNIX partition on your hard disk is less than 140 MB. Choose from the list by moving the highlight with the direction keys and pressing Enter. The system administration shell will append the user's name to the chosen filesystem and display that combination as the user's home directory.

> **NOTE:** *If you have created multiple filesystems by adding multiple hard disks, you can use the system administration shell to add these filesystems to the list of choices. Choose* System→Configure→ Defaults→Home *from the SysAdmSh form. You then edit the entries in the file* /usr/lib/mkuser/homepaths *according to the instructions in the file.*

## Security and Authorizations

As was mentioned earlier, SCO UNIX has security features that comply with the C2 level of trust as defined by the Department of Defense. These security features have implications for system administration.

In many UNIX and XENIX systems, the superuser is the only user who can access and change all aspects of the system. In such systems, several users might be responsible for various administrative aspects of the systems, such as making system backups or administering system printers, print spoolers, and printer queues. All of these users need access to the superuser password to complete their administrative duties. However, having access to the superuser password, they also can gain access to areas of the system that are outside their direct administrative authority, and they can alter the system in those areas.

Unlike other UNIX and XENIX systems, SCO UNIX can divide the authority for different aspects of system administration among different users without giving each of them access to the superuser password. These users can be granted authority only in certain areas. When you set up a user account, you can give the appropriate authority to each user. For instance, you can grant a user the authority to handle all matters related to printers by granting that user *lp* authority when you set up the account.

To give a user specific authority on your system, you first create the user account. Then, in the system administration shell, you select *Accounts→User→Examine*. The form prompts you to pick a user. You can either type a user name or press F3 to select from the list of users on your system. On the *Examine* form, you can change the following features associated with a user's account:

| | |
|---|---|
| *Audit* | Audited events |
| *Expiration* | Password life and death |
| *Identity* | Groups, login shell, comment, and CPU priority |
| *Logins* | Login history and locks |
| *Password* | Password selection |
| *Privileges* | Authorizations |

To give a user specific authorizations, select *Privileges*. The system administration shell displays a pop-up window containing the fields *Kernel* and *Subsystem*. Kernel authorizations are associated with processes (programs) and give users the power to execute specific operating system services. The ability to change the ownership of a file is governed by the *chown* kernel authorization, for example. Only the superuser has *chown* kernel authorization by default. Subsystem authorizations are associated with a user and let the user execute trusted utilities. For example, a user needs the *lp* authorization to administer the printer spooler subsystem. A given administrative task might require authorizations of both types. An administrator for the printer spooler needs the kernel authorization *chown* as well as the subsystem authorization *lp*.

To give a user the authorizations to be the printer spooler administrator, for instance, select the *Specify* option in the *Kernel* field. A blank pop-up window appears. If you know which authorizations you want to give, you can type them in the window. Otherwise, press F3 to see the following pop-up window:

```
┌────────Kernel authorizations────────┐
│ * suspendaudit                       │
│   configaudit                        │
│   writeaudit                         │
│   execsuid        (system default)   │
│   nopromain       (system default)   │
│   label_terminal                     │
│   chmodsugid                         │
│   chown           (system default)   │
└──────────────────────────────────────┘
```

Move the highlight to the authorizations that you want to give, and press the Spacebar to mark them. When you have selected all the authorizations, press Enter. In this case, select *chown*, and press Enter. A pop-up window with the chosen authorizations appears. Press Enter again to accept the choices.

Next select the *Specify* option in the *Subsystems* field, and press F3 see this pop-up window:

```
 ┌──Subsystem authorizations──┐
 │* audit                     │
 │  auth                      │
 │  backup                    │
 │  cron                      │
 │  lp                        │
 │  mem                       │
 │  sysadmin                  │
 │  terminal                  │
 │  uucp                      │
 │  su                        │
 │  queryspace  (system default)│
 │  printqueue  (system default)│
 │  printerstat (system default)│
 └────────────────────────────┘
```

Move the highlight to the authorizations that you want to give, and press the Spacebar to mark them. When you have selected all the authorizations, press Enter. In this case, select *lp*, and press Enter. A pop-up window with the chosen authorizations appears. Press Enter again to accept the choices.

After you make your choices, press Enter to exit from the *Privileges* form. The system administration shell prompts you to confirm, reexamine, or reject your modifications to the user's account. Select *Yes* to complete the process of giving that user the authority to administer the printer spooler on your system.

Access to the SCO UNIX system by users who do not have administrative responsibilities also has security implications. The system allows a limited number of unsuccessful login attempts by an individual user or on a specific terminal. The system also requires a minimum amount of time between attempts to log in. Under the C2 level of security, the maximum number of unsuccessful tries is five, and the minimum wait between tries is two seconds. After the fifth unsuccessful try, a terminal is locked by the SCO UNIX system and must be unlocked from the system administration shell. These requirements make breaking into the system more difficult and time-consuming.

Because of these security measures, a user might no longer be able to log in after mistyping his or her user name or password more than five times in a row. If this happens, you will probably need to unlock the terminal. From the *SysAdmSh* form, select *Accounts→Terminals→Unlock*, and press F3 to view the list of terminals. You can then select the one to unlock.

You can use the system administration shell to change the default values used for system security. However, make your decisions about changes to system security according to the sensitivity of the information on your system; the type of use you envision for your system; the level of knowledge of the users; the degree of trust in the users; and the threat of abuse, misuse, or penetration of the system by the users or outsiders.

# The *.profile* File

Even though they might not be aware that such files exist, all Bourne shell users have a personal *.profile* file in their home directories. The dot (.) in front of the name keeps the file hidden whenever an *ls* command is used. (C-shell users have two files that form the equivalent of the *.profile* file — *.login* and *.cshrc*, which are discussed in Chapter 10.)

You can list hidden files by using the command *ls -a*. To see what type of information a *.profile* file contains, let's take a quick look inside the *.profile* file for the user whose account was created for our preceding examples. Enter the following command:

```
cat /usr/susang/.profile
```

SCO UNIX reveals the following:

```
:
#
# .profile     -- Commands executed by a login Bourne shell
#
#     @(#) profile 1.1 89/02/15

#
# Copyright (c) 1985-89, The Santa Cruz Operation, Inc.
# All rights reserved.
#
# This Module contains Proprietary Information of the Santa Cruz
# Operation, Inc., and should be treated as Confidential.
#

PATH=/bin:/usr/bin:$HOME/bin:.          # set command search path
MAIL=/usr/spool/mail/'logname'          # mailbox location
export PATH MAIL

umask 077                               # set file creation mask

eval 'tset -m ansi:ansi -m $TERM:\?${TERM:-ansi} -r -s -Q'
```

The lines and line fragments that begin with pound signs (#) are comment lines that SCO UNIX does not evaluate. The remaining lines are instructions that contain startup information—mailbox locations, command search paths, and so on.

In *susang's* *.profile* file, the PATH variable sets the list of directories through which the SCO UNIX operating system will search for a command when *susang* enters it on the command line. In *susang's* case, the operating system searches in */bin*, */usr/bin*, and in the directory formed when the $HOME variable for *susang* is replaced by its value. For *susang*, that value would be */usr/susang*. The MAIL variable is set to */usr/spool/mail/logname*, which corresponds to */usr/spool/mail/susang* when SCO UNIX adds the value generated by the *logname* command. The use of a command name between single open quotation marks tells SCO UNIX to replace that construction with the output of the command. The *tset* command attempts to evaluate the type of terminal that *susang* is using to log in. If it can't do so, it prompts *susang* to type the terminal designation when logging in.

# Changing a Password

As system administrator, you might be called on now and then to change a user's password. To make the change, log in as the superuser, and use the following command format:

passwd *login_name*

Essentially, this is the same command you used to create the root password. SCO UNIX takes you through the same double-entry procedure.

## Replacing passwords periodically

SCO UNIX users should change their passwords periodically to protect them from accidental discovery. If someone who is not authorized to use the account discovers a password, you should immediately change the password to reduce the amount of time the account is accessible. Also, you can have SCO UNIX regularly remind users to change their passwords.

## Changing the default password characteristics

You can use *sysadmsh* to change the password security features either for all the users on your system or for specific users. To change the default values for all the users, select *Accounts→Defaults→Password* from the *SysAdmSh* form. You will see this pop-up window:

```
┌─────────────Password selection─────────────┐
│                                             │
│ Minimum days between changes : [14 ]        │
│ Expiration time (days)       : [42    ]     │
│ Lifetime (days)              : [365   ]     │
│                                             │
│ Maximum password length      : [10]         │
│                                             │
│ User can run generator       : [ Yes ]    No│
│ User can choose own          : [ Yes ]    No│
│ Checked for obviousness      :   Yes    [ No ]│
│                                             │
│ Single user password required : [ Yes ]   No│
└─────────────────────────────────────────────┘
```

The choices on this form have these meanings:

| | |
|---|---|
| *Minimum days between changes* | The minimum time that must elapse before a user can run the *passwd* program. |
| *Expiration time* | The maximum time that can elapse before a user must run the *passwd* program. |
| *Lifetime* | The maximum time allowed between the last password change and the next login. |
| *Maximum password length* | The maximum length of a password. The range is between 8 and 80. |
| *User can run generator* | Users are permitted to run the *passwd* program. |
| *User can choose own* | Users can choose their own passwords rather than accepting one generated by the *passwd* program. |
| *Checked for obviousness* | The password is checked for certain obvious characteristics. |
| *Single user password required* | A password is required for users to enter the single-user, maintenance mode. |

After you have made your selections and set the values, move the cursor to the last field on the form if it isn't already there, and press Enter. You are asked to confirm your choices.

**NOTE:** *To maintain the C2 level of trust, users must let the* passwd *program generate passwords for them. To avoid obvious choices, they must not be allowed to choose their own passwords — the user's automobile license plate number, for instance — that could allow outsiders to breach the system security.*

To change the password characteristics for a single user, from the *SysAdmSh* form, select *Accounts→User→Examine:Password.* You see an abbreviated version of the preceding window. In this window, you can choose to set a different password length, let the user run the password generator or not, let the user choose a password, and check the password for obviousness. The dates for password changes are systemwide and cannot be set for an individual user.

# Removing a User

No system ever remains static, so at one time or another you will need to remove old user accounts. To do so, log in as the superuser and start the system administration shell as follows:

```
sysadmsh
```

Select *Accounts→User→Retire*. You see the *Retire* form with its window labeled *Remove a user*. Either enter a user name in the field, or press F3 for the list of all users on your system, select the user you want to remove, and press Enter. The system administration shell asks you to confirm that you want to remove the user. If you've chosen the correct user, select *Yes*.

# 14

# Disk
# Management

In this chapter, we'll cover the main points of managing your disks and disk drives effectively. We'll begin by looking at the way SCO UNIX treats the disk drives—both hard disk and floppy disk drives—that you might have connected to your computer. This information will be especially valuable if you're moving to SCO UNIX from MS-DOS. In terms of disks and disk drives, you'll find a considerable difference between the two operating systems.

## TYPES OF DEVICES

SCO UNIX "knows" about the types of devices it will encounter on your system because it comes to you with a built-in directory, called *dev*, that contains a number of files describing various types of devices. The devices themselves are categorized for SCO UNIX in several ways, the broadest being by type.

To see a list showing device types, log in as the superuser and, when your prompt appears, enter the following command:

```
ls -l /dev ¦ more
```

The command fills a screen with data and then waits for you to press the Spacebar to fill another screen. The response looks like this:

```
# ls -l /dev ¦ more
total 4
cr--r-----   1 audit    audit     21,  0 Jun 25 17:29 auditr
crw-rw----   1 audit    audit     21,  1 Dec  8 20:21 auditw
crw-rw-rw-   3 bin      bin       52,  2 Jun 25 17:29 cga
crw-r--r--   1 sysinfo  sysinfo    8,  0 Dec  8 20:20 clock
crw-r--r--   1 sysinfo  sysinfo    7,  0 Jun 25 17:29 cmos
crw-rw-rw-   3 bin      bin       52,  2 Jun 25 17:29 color
crw-rw-rw-   3 bin      bin       52,  2 Jun 25 17:29 colour
crw-------   3 root     terminal   3,  1 Dec  8 20:20 console
brw-r-----   1 10       network    1, 47 Jun 25 16:20 d1057all
drwxr-xr-x   2 root     backup        544 Jun 25 17:29 dsk
crw-rw-rw-   1 bin      bin       52,  4 Jun 25 17:29 ega
cr--r--r--   1 sysinfo  sysinfo   32,  0 Jun 24 21:52 error
brw-rw-rw-   2 bin      bin        2, 60 Jun 24 21:52 fd0
brw-rw-rw-   2 bin      bin        2, 60 Jun 25 17:29 fd0135ds18
brw-rw-rw-   1 bin      bin        2, 36 Jun 25 17:29 fd0135ds9
brw-rw-rw-   3 bin      bin        2,  4 Jun 25 17:29 fd048
brw-rw-rw-   2 bin      bin        2, 12 Jun 25 17:29 fd048ds8
brw-rw-rw-   3 bin      bin        2,  4 Jun 25 17:29 fd048ds9
brw-rw-rw-   2 bin      bin        2,  8 Jun 25 17:29 fd048ss8
brw-rw-rw-   2 bin      bin        2,  0 Jun 25 17:29 fd048ss9
brw-rw-rw-   5 bin      bin        2, 52 Jun 24 21:52 fd096
brw-rw-rw-   5 bin      bin        2, 52 Jun 24 21:52 fd096ds15
--More--_
```

Later we'll cover the names you see. Right now we're concerned with the file types that you can see indicated at the leftmost edge of the display.

The first 10 characters of each line represent the file-permissions block, and the first of these 10 characters represents the file type. Until now we've seen only two file types: directory files (denoted by a *d*) and ordinary files (denoted by a hyphen). You can see two new types of files in the *dev* directory: *c* and *b*.

Both *c* and *b* are device file types that refer to physical devices (such as hard disk drives, floppy disk drives, tape drives, printers, and terminals) that are attached to the system. Type *c* files refer to character devices, and type *b* files refer to block devices. Character devices are generally terminals, printers, or other such devices that SCO UNIX can read from or write to one character at a time. Block devices are generally disk drives (or cartridge tape drives), which SCO UNIX can read from or write to in blocks of data. Typical block sizes are 512 bytes or 1024 bytes (or characters).

# Understanding Device Files

Bearing in mind that devices can manage data either by character or by block, let's move on to another way SCO UNIX differentiates one device from the other. We'll concentrate on disk drives and again start with a directory listing. Here, however, use the following *lc* command to produce a listing in columnar format:

```
lc /dev | more
```

SCO UNIX responds with:

```
# lc /dev | more
auditr        fd1135ds9    mono         ptyp5       rfd148ss9    tty03
auditw        fd148        monochrome   ptyp6       rfd196       tty04
cga           fd148ds8     null         ptyp7       rfd196ds15   tty05
clock         fd148ds9     prf          ram00       rfd196ds18   tty06
cmos          fd148ss8     ptmx         rd1057all   rfd196ds9    tty07
color         fd148ss9     pts000       rdsk        rhd00        tty08
colour        fd196        pts001       recover     rhd01        tty09
console       fd196ds15    pts002       rfd0        rhd02        tty10
d1057all      fd196ds18    pts003       rfd0135ds18 rhd03        tty11
dsk           fd196ds9     pts004       rfd0135ds9  rhd04        tty12
ega           hd00         pts005       rfd048      rhd0a        tty1A
error         hd01         pts006       rfd048ds8   rhd0d        tty1a
fd0           hd02         pts007       rfd048ds9   rinstall     tty2A
fd0135ds18    hd03         pts008       rfd048ss8   rinstall1    tty2a
fd0135ds9     hd04         pts009       rfd048ss9   root         ttyp0
fd048         hd0a         pts010       rfd096      ropipe       ttyp1
fd048ds8      hd0d         pts011       rfd096ds15  rrecover     ttyp2
fd048ds9      install      pts012       rfd096ds18  rroot        ttyp3
fd048ss8      install1     pts013       rfd096ds9   rswap        ttyp4
fd048ss9      kmem         pts014       rfd1        rtc          ttyp5
fd096         log          pts015       rfd1135ds18 swap         ttyp6
fd096ds15     lp           ptyp0        rfd1135ds9  syscon       ttyp7
fd096ds18     lp0          ptyp1        rfd148      systty       vga
--More--_
```

Many of the filenames that appear on your screen begin with the letters *fd*, *rfd*, *hd*, or *rhd*. These are the names of the disk drive files: *fd* and *rfd* refer to floppy disk drives; *hd* and *rhd* refer to hard disk drives.

## Hard disk drives

Two types of device files refer to your system's primary hard disk: *hd* and *root*.

The *hd* type refers to the entire hard disk installed on your system. If your hard disk is the primary hard disk, the third character in the filename is 0; if your hard disk is a secondary disk, the third character is 1. As with the floppy disk device files we'll discuss next, the *hd* files are tailored to the requirements of the hard disk most commonly associated with the computer you are using. The function of the fourth character in the filename varies from one brand of UNIX to another. In SCO UNIX, it refers to the hard disk's partitions.

Note that the *hd* filenames appear twice in the listing: once in the form *hdxx* and once in the form *rhdxx*. The *r* prefixing the second group of hard disk filenames indicates that these files manage data on a character-by-character basis.

The *root* file is the device file that refers to the partition of the hard disk that, when mounted at system boot time, become the root (/) directory. For most hard disk operations, use *root* rather than *hd0* to guide SCO UNIX to the appropriate part of the disk surface. If your SCO UNIX partition was large enough for the installation procedure to create a user partition, you might also see a *usr* file. (These names are not, by the way, the same as the directory name for root (/) or for the user partition (/u; they are data files in the *dev* directory and refer to the disk itself—not the data on it.)

## Floppy disk drives

Looking at the *fd* and *rfd* filenames, you can see that they, like the names for the hard disk drives, fall into four groups: *fd0*, *fd1*, *rfd0*, and *rfd1*. Here the *0* indicates the boot floppy disk drive; the *1* indicates the secondary floppy disk drive if one is attached to the system.

The remaining characters of these filenames specify the format of the floppy disk with which the drive is used. Again, you don't need to remember which filename refers to the floppy disk drive or drives on your system, but if you want to feel more at home with these names, you can study the following two tables, which show the disk format (in tracks per inch) each refers to:

| | |
|---|---|
| 48 | 48-track drives |
| 48ss8 | 48-track drives, single sided, 8 sectors per track |
| 48ds8 | 48-track drives, double sided, 8 sectors per track |
| 48ss9 | 48-track drives, single sided, 9 sectors per track |
| 48ds9 | 48-track drives, double sided, 9 sectors per track |
| 96 | 96-track drives |
| 96ds15 | 96-track drives, double sided, 15 sectors per track |
| 135ds9 | 135-track drives, double sided, 9 sectors per track |
| 135ds18 | 135-track drives, double sided, 18 sectors per track |

In order of appearance, the following are the IBM PC and the IBM PC-compatible computers and floppy disk drives for which these files were created:

| | |
|---|---|
| 48ss8 | IBM PC with 160-KB drives |
| 48ds8 | IBM PC with double-sided, 320-KB drives |
| 48ds9 | IBM PC and PC XT with 360-KB drives, running MS-DOS versions 2.0 and later |
| 96ds15 | IBM PC/AT with 1.2-MB floppy disk drives |
| 135ds9 | IBM convertible and PS/2 Model 25 and 30 with 720-KB drives |
| 135ds18 | IBM PS/2 with 1.44-MB floppy disk drives |

As in hard disk filenames, an *r* at the beginning indicates that the device file works on a character basis rather than on a block basis. If, for example, you were to change to the */dev* directory and look at a long listing for *fd0* and *rfd0*, you would see this:

```
# cd /dev
# ls -l fd0 rfd0
brw-rw-rw-   2 bin       bin        2, 60 Jun 24 21:52 fd0
crw-rw-rw-   2 bin       bin        2, 60 Jun 24 21:52 rfd0
# _
```

Note that *fd0* is a block device file, whereas *rfd0* is a character device file. The reason for this difference is that some SCO UNIX commands require use of the "raw," or character, device name, but others require the use of the "buffered," or block, device name.

# FORMATTING A FLOPPY DISK

Even though SCO UNIX and all your system's working files might be stored on the hard disk, you shouldn't rely on it as your sole storage place. Especially in a multiuser system, valuable files might be inadvertently deleted or overwritten. Then, too, a system failure, sudden power loss, or even accidental damage or destruction can occur to the hard disk itself. Among many other features of SCO UNIX's system administration shell is a set of utilities that back up and restore files to and from floppy disks. These utilities can help you archive important data and thus safeguard the information on your system.

> **NOTE:** *High-capacity 5.25-inch (1.2-MB) drives have the capability of reading low-density disks formatted on the older systems, but they cannot reliably write information for drives of the lower densities. Formatting is the most critical write operation of all.*
>
> *You can write data files to a disk that is formatted with a lower-capacity device file. But be warned: There's no guarantee that the operation will be successful 100 percent of the time. Reading from any of the lower-capacity disks should prove no problem as long as you use the correct device filename.*

The first step in managing your files is to format blank disks. To do this, place an appropriate floppy disk in your system's boot drive.

To format the disk, enter the following command:

```
format  /dev/rfd0
```

You must include the *dev* portion of the pathname. If you can do so with your disk drive, you can specify a different device file in place of */dev/rfd0*.

To abort the format, press the Delete key. Depending on which device file you specified, the formatting itself can take from 30 seconds to about two minutes.

> **NOTE:** *Anyone can use the* format *command at the console computer. If you want to restrict access to this command, change the executable permission for the format command so that it is usable only by the root. Enter the following command:*
>
> ```
> chmod u=rwx /bin/format
> ```
>
> *You can do the same for any other SCO UNIX commands found in the* /bin *directory and thus control and protect your operating environment.*

The single, short *format* command is all you need to format a disk, but a vast difference exists between the amount of data even a high-capacity disk can hold and the amount that your hard disk can store. As you'll see, one of the options of the system administration shell automatically copies your files onto as many disks as are required. This option prompts you to insert new, formatted disks as it needs them. If you do not have enough disks on hand, you'll need to stop, format some more, and then start over. To avoid delays, always have a supply of formatted disks handy.

Regardless of how you decide on the number of disks to format, you can use SCO UNIX to help streamline the task.

# PLANNING BACKUP STRATEGIES

As the system administrator, you are responsible for ensuring the integrity of your own SCO UNIX system. You need to develop a backup strategy early. Keep notes about the growth of the filesystem during the first few weeks. If disk usage doesn't level off after everyone has had a chance to settle in, check each user directory to determine where the log jams will form, and try to anticipate problems.

You can provide adequate file protection in either of two ways. One way is to back up files on a systemwide basis, keeping copies of every file on the hard disk. The other way is a file-specific method in which you use your own criteria, perhaps based on the needs of a special user account or activity, to determine which files should be backed up and when.

NOTE: *The backup procedures described in this section use files from the SCO UNIX BACKUP package. If you have not installed the BACKUP package from the distribution disks, you must use the* custom *installation program to install it before you can use these procedures.*

Let's look at the systemwide backup method first because it is the simpler of the two procedures.

# Clearing Users from the System

Try to do systemwide backups when no users are on the system so that you don't catch users in the middle of modifying their files. You can use the *shutdown* command to inform all the users that the system is going to be shut down and to give them time to complete their work.

You can inform users and program a timed shutdown of the entire SCO UNIX system starting in 15 minutes with the following command:

```
shutdown -g15
```

SCO UNIX responds with a message similar to the following:

```
Shutdown started.    Thu Jun 14 21:22:16 PDT 1990
```

```
Broadcast Message from root (tty01) on bifrost Thu Jun 14 21:22:18...
The system will be shut down in 0 hours and 15 minutes.
Please log off now.
```

You can enter other times in the format *-g[hh]mm* to give your users sufficient time to wind up their current tasks. All the users on the system see the following message:

```
Broadcast Message from root (tty01) on bifrost Thu Jun 14 21:22:18...
The system will be shut down in 0 hours and 15 minutes.
Please log off now.
```

If the time interval that you specified is longer than 15 minutes, *shutdown* displays its broadcast message every 15 minutes. If the time interval is less than 15 minutes, it displays the message every minute; if the interval is longer than an hour, it displays the message every hour. Just before the shutdown time, users see this message:

```
Broadcast Message from root (tty01) on bifrost Thu Jun 14 21:37:18...
THE SYSTEM IS BEING SHUT DOWN NOW ! ! !
Log off now or risk your files being damaged.
```

The *shutdown* program gives users another 60-second grace period, and then on your console, it displays this prompt:

```
Do you want to continue? (y or n) _
```

Respond with *y* to continue the shutdown procedure.

When you start the system again, enter maintenance mode so that no other users can access the system while you're doing backups.

## Using *sysadmsh* for Backups

With the preliminaries over, you can now begin your systemwide backup. SCO UNIX sets up a default schedule for backing up your system on a regular basis and begins the backup schedule by backing up all the files on your entire system. This backup is level 0. SCO UNIX recommends that you keep this level 0 backup for a year. (The level 0 backup might take an hour or more if you are using floppy disks; the time depends on the size of the SCO UNIX partition on your hard disk.) You can restore the entire system from the level 0 backup if that should become necessary. After the initial backup, SCO UNIX adheres to the following four-week, weekday schedule:

- On the third Monday after the initial level 0 backup, SCO UNIX backs up any files that have changed since the level 0 backup. SCO recommends saving this backup for four months.

- Every other Monday, SCO UNIX backs up any files that have changed since the last level 0 backup. SCO recommends saving this backup for three weeks.

- Every other day SCO UNIX backs up the files that have changed since the last backup. SCO recommends saving this backup for one week.

You might want to color code your backup disks, as the backup procedure suggests, so that you can readily identify the type of backup that's stored on each set of disks. This backup schedule gives you the opportunity to recover files from various time periods in the history of the system.

Even if you don't adopt the SCO UNIX default schedule, it's a good idea to keep a schedule similar to this one so that you can restore the files in case your site suffers a power failure that corrupts open files, in case your hard disk fails, or in case a user accidentally deletes a file and doesn't discover the loss until the next month. If you back up your system only once a month and you reuse your set of backup disks, you will find that that file has disappeared.

## Modifying the backup schedule

If the default backup schedule doesn't serve the needs of your system, you can easily alter it. To alter the regular backup schedule, start the system administration shell with this command:

```
sysadmsh
```

Select *Backups→Schedule*. The system administration shell starts the *vi* editor and loads the */usr/lib/sysadmin/schedule*, which appears as follows:

```
#    @(#) schedule.src 1.4 89/08/03
#
#    Copyright (C) The Santa Cruz Operation, 1988, 1989.
#    This Module contains Proprietary Information of
#    The Santa Cruz Operation, and should be treated as Confidential.
#


#
# SYSTEM BACKUP SCHEDULE
   site mymachine

# Media Entries
#
# 48 tpi 360K floppy 0
# media /dev/rfd048ds9 k 360 format /dev/rfd048ds9

# 48 tpi 360K floppy 1
# media /dev/rfd148ds9 k 360 format /dev/rfd148ds9

# 96 tpi 720K floppy 0
# media /dev/rfd096ds9 k 720 format /dev/rfd096ds9

# 96 tpi 720K floppy 1
```

On line 10, the file lists the name of the machine that it is backing up. You can change the name *mymachine* following the word *site* to the name that you have chosen for your machine. The entries that follow list all the possible choices for backup devices. If you scroll down in the file by using Ctrl-F, you will find one entry not preceded by a pound sign (#). That entry is for the high-density floppy disk drive that you used to install SCO UNIX and looks like this on a system with a 5.25-inch drive:

```
# 96 tpi 1.2 MB floppy 0
media /dev/rfd096ds15 k 1200 format /dev/rfd096ds15
```

If you want to use some other device for your regularly scheduled backups, you need to make two changes to this file. First you need to add a pound sign at the start of this entry. (The pound sign changes the entry into a comment in the file.) Second you need to find the entry corresponding to your new device and remove the pound sign from the beginning of that line.

Scroll down to the bottom of the file to find the following section, which refers to the schedule:

```
# Backup Descriptor Table
#
# Backup Vol.    Save for    Vitality       Label
# level  size    how long    (importance)   marker
0        -       "1 year"    critical       "a red sticker"
1        -       "4 months"  necessary      "a yellow sticker"
8        -       "3 weeks"   useful         "a blue sticker"
9        -       "1 week"    precautionary  none

# Schedule Table
#
#              1 2 3 4 5  6 7 8 9 0  1 2 3 4 5  6 7 8 9 0
#Filesystem    M T W T F  M T W T F  M T W T F  M T W T F   Method
/dev/rroot     0 x 9 x 9  8 x 9 x 9  1 x 9 x 9  8 x 9 x 9   cpio
```

The last line in the file contains the schedule for backups for the device */dev/rroot*. The line follows the description of the entries for the default schedule: *0* is a level 0 backup; *1* is a level 1 backup, and so on. Each level backs up files changed since a previous backup with the same or smaller level number. In other words, level 1 backs up files altered since any previous level 1 or level 0 backup. A level 9 backup, the highest level, backs up files altered only after the immediately preceding backup, no matter what level it was. An *x* indicates no backup on that day. If you want to change the dates or types of the backups, you can change the digits to a different level number, or you can change the *x*'s to a digit to include a backup on that day.

If you add another hard disk (and consequently another filesystem) to your system, you will want ensure that your backup schedule includes a satisfactory schedule for the new filesystem. The schedule should include another line with exactly the same types of entries following the line for */dev/rroot*.

You need to adjust the time periods in this backup schedule to match the activity on your system. The default schedule is designed primarily for a system with moderately heavy use. For a heavily used system on which users generate critical information every day, you should back up daily. For a lightly used system on which critical work is limited to a few areas, such as accounting, you might be able to back up only every second or third day. Your backup schedule will depend on your feel for the system.

If you decide that your backups need not be as closely spaced as those we've described here, try to err on the side of caution in working out your own schedule. If you start on the lenient side, you might find you have nothing to fall back on. You'll be safer if you begin strong and use the daily backups as a gauge. If you find that you back up only a small amount of data each day, you can allow more time between backups. However, try not to go beyond three days. At that point, you stand to lose more than you gain in terms of time saved versus work lost.

## Creating a backup

Let's assume this is your first backup of the *root* filesystem and that your floppy disk drive is 5.25-inch and 1.2 MB. As was previously mentioned, the first backup in the default schedule is a level 0 backup of the entire *root* filesystem. Each disk used for backup files holds only 1.2 MB, so you should have a substantial number of formatted disks on hand before you start because you will need them to back up a large filesystem. Start the system administration shell with this command:

```
sysadmsh
```

Select *Backups→Create→Scheduled.* The program displays the *Create* form and immediately responds with the following message:

```
Executing command:
 /usr/lib/sysadmin/fsphoto


Level 0 backup of filesystem /dev/rroot, 16 Jun 90
         Floppy size     1200 Kb
         Floppy drive:   /dev/rfd096ds15
This floppy will be saved for 1 year, and is critical.

M)ounted volume, P)ostpone, C)heck or F)ormat volumes, R)etension, or H)elp: _
```

If for some reason you find that you are not ready to continue, type *P* and then press the Enter key to postpone the backup. Before returning you to the *Backups* form, the system administration shell will remind you that the backup has not been completed but should be. Otherwise, insert a blank, formatted disk in the boot drive, press the M key, and then press the Enter key. Soon you'll see a message like this one:

```
Level 0 backup of filesystem: /dev/root
Backing up all files

Generating a list of pathnames for backing up . . .

Reached end of medium on output.
Insert volume 2 and press <RETURN> to continue or 'q' to exit.
```

During the backup procedure, *sysadmsh* will prompt you to insert new disks as they are needed. When you remove the disks, number them sequentially, starting with 1. This numbering is important because the SCO UNIX *Restore* and *Backups* options refer to the disks by number.

When the backup is complete, you'll see the following message:

```
53140 blocks
Check critical volumes for format errors

M)ounted first volume, S)kip format check, or H)elp:
```

Press the S key and then press Enter to return to the *Backups* form.

> **NOTE:** *The backup disks created by using this option are created in the* cpio *format. If necessary, you can use the* cpio *command described in the* User's Reference *manual to read, write, or list files on these disks.*

If you want to ensure that the backup files are complete and undamaged on the disks, choose *Integrity* from the *Backups* form and follow the instructions on inserting the disks.

The following day, if you start the *sysadmsh* program and select the *Backups→ Create→Scheduled* option, the program will inform you that no backups are necessary (unless you have changed the default schedule). Thereafter, you should run the system administration shell every day and create the scheduled backups. The schedule will choose the proper type of backup and prompt for the disks as it needs them. The system administration shell indicates the level of backup that it has created, how long you should keep the disks, and how you should label them. With this system, you eventually will have a series of backups that cover a year. The most recent copy of a frequently used file will be two days old, and the oldest file will be one year old.

## Creating a list of backup files

Although information has been transferred to backup disks, you cannot tell which files have been backed up by looking at the backup disks, so part of your system procedure should include generating a list of the names of the files you've copied. You can do that with the *Backups→View* option of the *sysadmsh* program.

After you choose this option, *sysadmsh* prompts you for the backup media type and for a block size. You can usually accept the indicated block size. After you have filled in the fields with the appropriate values, press Enter to continue. The program prompts you to insert the first disk from the backup series you created. On this disk is a list of all the files you copied. The *sysadmsh* program reads the contents of the disk, and when the names of all the copied files have been read, *sysadmsh* displays a list of all the files on the *View* form. If, during the backup procedure, *sysadmsh* wrote the list of files on more than one disk, it will prompt you to insert the additional disk or disks as they are needed. You can use the direction keys to scroll down in the file if the file fills more than one screen.

## Restoring Files

The point of backing up files is that you need to be able to restore the files if information on your system's hard disk is lost. To do this, you need to start the system in multiuser mode if necessary so that files get the correct date and time when they are restored. You once again use *sysadmsh*, this time selecting option *Backups→Restore*. On this form, you can choose either *Partial* or *Full*. The *Partial* option lets you choose files from the backup disks; the *Full* option copies all the files from the backup disk onto the hard disk. When you choose the *Partial* option, you see a display like the following one:

```
                                                                        Partial

Press <F3> to choose from a list of available media

/                                                   Sunday June 17, 1990  10:18

┌──────────────────────────────Restore File───────────────────────────────┐
│                                                                          │
│      Media                  :    [_                            ]         │
│                                                                          │
│      File to restore        :    [                            ]         │
│                                                                          │
│      Directory to restore to :   [                            ]         │
│                                                                          │
│      Block size in Bytes    :    [10240    ]                            │
│                                                                          │
│                                                                          │
│      Press <Return> to restore the file or <ESC> to abandon             │
│                                                                          │
│                         [Restore]                                        │
│                                                                          │
└──────────────────────────────────────────────────────────────────────────┘
```

Press F3 to display a list of available devices. If you backed up on the 1.2-MB floppy disk drive, choose that one from the list. Next choose the file or files that you want to restore. If you looked at the list of files with the *View* option, enter the name as it appears in that list (without a leading slash). You can use wildcards to restore files with related names, such as *usr/danh/wp/*.doc*. In the field *Directory to restore to*, type the directory name (relative to the current working directory). If you need to find out your current working directory, enter *pwd* at the system prompt. In most cases, you will be in the root directory (/), and all files will be restored to this directory. In most cases, therefore, enter a dot (.), which stands for "here", as we saw earlier. In most cases, you can accept the default block size. Press Enter to continue with the restoration, and when *Restore* is highlighted, press Enter again. If you need to insert other volumes, the *Restore* option will prompt for them. After completion of the restoration, you will see a list of the restored files.

# Archiving with the *tar* Command

No matter how much time you schedule between backups, you'll encounter special circumstances that will require more frequent or less frequent backups. For example, if your accounting system is online, its files might need daily backup even though no other work does. To handle such a situation, you can use SCO UNIX's *tar* (tape archiver) utility. The *tar* utility copies files to other media in a special archive format.

Just as with the commands for administering the printer spooler, you have a choice between two ways of using *tar*. You can use the system administration shell (*sysadmsh*) to determine the correct options for the action you want and then execute *tar* with those options, or you can run *tar* as a separate command from the command line. The method you choose depends on your familiarity with the command and its options. We will start with the system administration shell and later discuss using *tar* from the command line.

## Copying files

Let's assume that your system has a user account called *accounts*. In keeping with our previous discussion of daily backups for heavily used files, we'll also assume that the account called *accounts* contains the only information on your system that requires a daily backup procedure. For the sake of speed, you can put the *accounts* directory on a separate floppy disk (or disks) by using *tar*. If you ever need to restore the *accounts* directory, you can do so quickly because *accounts* will be the only directory on the disk. If you examine a level 9 backup of your filesystem, you'll see that *sysadmsh* created a complete directory listing of the disk and marked most of the entries that had 0 length. Nonetheless, to restore from a backup disk, the *Restore* option needs to search through the complete list to find any files that you want to restore. This does not mean, however, that you should abandon the regularly scheduled backups using *Backups*. *Backups* will back up *all* files that change. With *tar*, you need to specify which files to back up.

To use the system administration shell to back up selected files, start the shell with the following command:

```
sysadmsh
```

Select *Media→Archive*. You will see the *Archive* form, as follows:

```
                                                          Archive
Press <F3> for a list of available media

/                                            Saturday June 16, 1990 10:18

                          ─────────Archive Files─────────
  ┌────────────────────────────────────────────────────────────────────┐
  │                                                                      │
  │    Media                  :  [_                                   ]  │
  │    Size (kilobytes)       :  [        ]                              │
  │    Blocking Factor (1-20) :  [  ]                                    │
  │                                                                      │
  │    Prevent splitting                                                 │
  │    files across media     :  Yes   [No]                             │
  │    (Size must be specified)                                          │
  │                                                                      │
  │                                                                      │
  │    Names of files and/or                                             │
  │    directories to archive :  [                                    ]  │
  │                                                                      │
  │                                                                      │
  └────────────────────────────────────────────────────────────────────┘
```

Press F3 to see a list of the devices that you can use with *tar*. If you are using the 1.2-MB floppy disk drive, select it from the list. If you choose the 1.2-MB floppy disk drive, the *Size* field will receive the value *1200*. You can ignore the *Blocking* field. In most cases, in the *Prevent splitting* field, you will want to select the default, *No*. However, if you want to ensure that an individual file is not split between two disks, select *Yes*.

In the field for the name of files, type the name of the file or directory you want to archive. In our example, type *./usr/accounts*. The *Archive* option then asks if you want to format the floppy disk that will receive the files. If the disk is already formatted, select *No*. When *Continue* is highlighted, press Enter to continue with the archiving process. The *Archive* option displays this message:

```
Executing command:
 tar cvfbk /dev/rfd096ds15 10 1200 ./user/accounts

Volume ends at 1199K, blocking factor = 5K
seek = 0k        a ./usr/accounts/.profile 1K
```

When *tar* has finished archiving the files on the floppy disk, it will prompt you to press any key to return to the *Archive* form.

> **NOTE:** *The* Archive *option passes to* tar *the filename in relation to the current working directory — that is, in relation to dot (.), or "here". This convention lets you restore files archived in this way to any directory.*

After the system has been running for a while, the cumulative size of the files in a directory you archive with the *tar* command might exceed the capacity of a single floppy disk.

## Listing the contents of a *tar* disk

You can use the system administration shell to list the contents of a *tar* disk. Start the shell with this command:

```
sysadmsh
```

Select *Media→List.* You will see the *List* form, as follows:

```
                                                                     List
Press <F3> for a list of available media.

/                                              Saturday June 16, 1990  9:15

┌─────────────────────────List Contents───────────────────────────┐
│                                                                   │
│      Media            :   [                        ]              │
│                                                                   │
│                                                                   │
│      Specify files                                                │
│      or directories  :   [all                      ]              │
│                                                                   │
│      Please make sure your media is in the drive and the          │
│      drive is ON LINE.  Press <Return> when everything is         │
│      in order or <ESC> to abandon command.                        │
│                     [Continue]                                    │
│                                                                   │
└───────────────────────────────────────────────────────────────────┘
```

Press F3 to see a list of the devices and select the 1.2-MB floppy disk drive. Press Enter to move the next field, and press Enter to list all the files on the drive. You will see a list similar to the following:

```
Executing command:
  tar tvf /dev/rf096ds15

tar: blocksize = 20
rw-r--r--200/50    53575 Jun  16 21:19 1990 ./usr/accounts/acct_pay
rw-r--r--200/50    43971 Jun  16 21:19 1990 ./usr/accounts/acct_rec
rw-r--r--200/50    28782 Jun  16 21:19 1990 ./usr/accounts/expense
```

# Restoring *tar* Files

To extract files from a *tar* archive, you can use the system administration shell. Using the system administration shell to extract files restores the files to the current directory. If the files listed with the *List* option show a pathname preceding the filename, the system administration shell will create those directories in the current directory if they don't exist. If they do exist, the shell will simply copy the files into the directory. For example, suppose your current working directory is root (/), and you are extracting *./usr/accounts/expense* from the *tar* disk. Because the directory */usr/accounts* already exists, the system administration shell simply extracts the file *expense* and puts it in that directory. Suppose, however, that your current directory is */tmp*. No *usr/accounts* subdirectory exists in */tmp*. If you extract the file *./usr/accounts/expense* while your current directory is */tmp*, however, the system administration shell will create the subdirectory */tmp/usr/accounts* and copy the file *expense* into that directory. In fact, you want to do that sometimes, rather than write over an existing file, so that you can compare them, for instance.

To extract files from a *tar* archive, start the shell with this command:

```
cd-/
```

```
sysadmsh
```

Select *Media→Extract*. You see the *Extract* form, as follows:

```
                                                           Extract
Press <F3> for a list of available media
/        ---------------------------------------Tuesday-June-19,-1990--10:18

                        ────────Extract Files────────
┌──────────────────────────────────────────────────────────────────────────┐
│                                                                            │
│         Media         :  [_                                       ]        │
│         Specify files                                                      │
│         or directories  :  [all                                   ]        │
│                                                                            │
│                                                                            │
│         Please make sure your media is in the drive and the               │
│         drive is ON LINE.  Press <Return> when everything is              │
│         in order or <ESC> to abandon command.                             │
│                                                                            │
│                        [Continue]                                          │
│                                                                            │
│                                                                            │
└──────────────────────────────────────────────────────────────────────────┘
```

Press F3 to see a list of devices, and select the 1.2-MB floppy disk drive. Type the name of the file to extract or several filenames separated by spaces. If you want to extract all the files, simply press Enter. You are asked to confirm your choices. When *Continue* is highlighted, press Enter. You see a message similar to this:

```
Executing command:
  tar xvf /dev/rfd096ds15

tar: blocksize = 20
x ./usr/accounts/acct_pay, 53575, 106 tape blocks
x ./usr/accounts/acct_rec, 43971, 86 tape blocks
x ./usr/accounts/expense, 28782, 56 tape blocks
```

The display lists all of the files extracted from the *tar* archive on the disk.

# Using *tar* from the Command Line

You can also use *tar* from the command line. To archive the files in */usr/accounts*, enter the following command:

```
tar cvfkb /dev/rfd0 1200 20 ./usr/accounts
```

Here is a breakdown of the command options and their corresponding arguments:

- The *tar* option list must begin with one (and only one) of the primary options. Here we used *c* to have *tar* create a new filesystem on the archive device.

- The *v* option places *tar* in verbose mode and prints the name of each file (and any additional information necessary) as it is copied.

- The *f* option and its argument (*/dev/rfd0*) name the archive device—here, a disk in the boot drive. The *tar* utility will accept either *rfd0* or *fd0*, but using *rfd0* is usually faster.

- The *k* option and its argument (*1200*) give the size of the archive device in kilobytes (1200). This is a standard high-density 1.2-MB drive.

- The *b* option and its argument of 20 specify a blocking factor of 10 KB.

- The pathname, */usr/accounts*, defines the source of the files to be transferred. When no more arguments are required by the options you listed, *tar* assumes that the next entry in the command line is the source pathname.

Note the order of the *f*, *k*, and *b* options and the corresponding order of the arguments in our command line. The option list could as easily have been entered as follows:

```
cvkfb
```

But in that case, the order of the arguments */dev/rfd0* and *1200* would have had to be reversed.

To list the files on the archive disk, you can use the following *tar* command:

```
tar tvnf /dev/rfd0
```

Finally, to extract all the files on the archive disk, use this command:

```
tar xvfn /dev/rfd0
```

## Including *tar* options

**NOTE:** *Before we discuss the* tar *command itself, note that all of the filename specifications you will see represent the superuser's point of reference. If you allow system users access to* tar, *be sure to instruct them to adjust their pathname usage accordingly.*

The *tar* utility was originally designed to work with tape storage, but several of its options are used to make floppy disk activity easier. We'll discuss these options here; for a complete list of *tar* options, you can refer to the *SCO UNIX User's Reference* portion of your documentation.

The general format of the *tar* command line is as follows:

```
tar primary_option secondary_option(s) secondary_option_argument(s) path
```

Note that in contrast to most SCO UNIX commands, the list of *tar* options is not preceded by a hyphen (-) because the hyphen has its own meaning in the *tar* command—it is used as a redirection symbol.

The two types of *tar* options are: primary, which tell *tar* what needs to be done, and secondary, which refine the command. The first (and possibly the only) option in a *tar* command must be a primary option.

The command line can include as many arguments as are required by the *tar* options you include. If you include several options and arguments, be sure to enter the arguments in the same order you enter the options that make them necessary.

The *tar* options for using disks as archive devices are described in the following table:

### Primary *tar* options

| | |
|---|---|
| c | Creates a new filesystem on the archive device; it overwrites any existing files. |
| t | Displays a list of the files on the archive device; depending on the arguments specified, it displays either all filenames or specified filenames if they are on that device. |
| u | Adds specified files to the archive device, if they are not already on the device or if they've been modified since they were last written. |

*(continued)*

*continued*

## Primary *tar* options

x     Extracts the named files from the archive device and writes them to the current working directory.

r     Writes the named files to the end of an archive; it preserves any existing files in the archive.

## Secondary options

f     Uses the argument corresponding to its position in the list of options as the archive device. If used with a disk, either the *k* or the *n* option must also be included, or *tar* will believe that the archive device is a tape.

k     Uses the argument corresponding to its position in the list of options as the size of the archive device in kilobytes (250-KB minimum). This option and its argument must be included if the archive device is a disk and the total size of all files being transferred exceeds the capacity of the disk. With this option, *tar* will prompt for new disks as required and continue the transfer. Without this option, *tar* will continue transferring files even when the disk is full, behaving as if the capacity of the disk were endless.

b     Specifies the blocking factor, a value originally intended for use with magnetic tape storage devices but also required with disks when transferred files require more than the storage capacity of a single disk. The argument of *b* is specified in number of blocks (one block equals approximately ½ KB). The value of *b* should always be 20 unless you have an unusual requirement for a different blocking factor. If this option is not included and files extend to more than one disk, SCO UNIX displays the *Can't open device device_name* message, and the backup operation stops even though the *tar* command prompts for a new disk.

n     Indicates that the archive device is not a tape device and, therefore, *tar* need not read sequentially through the files to arrive at those you've specified. (It would do so if the files were stored on magnetic tape.) Use of the *n* option speeds up the *t* option considerably. When it is included, this option must be accompanied by the *f* option. The *k* option can be added but is not essential unless the size of the files being transferred exceeds the capacity of the archive disk.

v     Places *tar* into verbose mode. The names of all transferred files are printed to the screen. (Normally, only error messages are displayed.) If this is used with the *t* option, filenames are displayed in verbose form, including the file sizes, modification dates, permissions, and owner and group identifications, as well as the filenames.

e     Instructs *tar* not to split files across separate volumes. If only a portion of the file fits on the disk, *tar* refrains from using the remaining space and begins the file on the next volume in the series. (You cannot use this option with a file that is larger than the capacity of a single disk.)

**NOTE:** *The* n *option can speed restoration by telling* tar *to use "random" rather than "sequential" access. Files in a* tar *archive are stored with a header that tells how big the file is. For example, assume that* tar *read the header for a file, determined the file size was 1000 bytes, and understood that it was a file you did not want to extract from the disk. This means* tar *should skip forward and look at the next file header, continuing in the same manner until it has found the file you want to restore to the hard disk. Because magnetic tapes are sequential-access devices, the only way the tape drive can skip ahead 1000 bytes is to read and count 1000 bytes of tape and then begin looking again at byte 1001. Modern disk drives, however, can read data stored on the disk simply by moving the read/write heads to the spot on the disk where the next header is located (the 1001st byte, in our example). This is generally much faster than sequential access. If you don't tell* tar *you are using a disk drive by specifying the* n *option, it assumes you are using a tape and reads each byte instead of skipping ahead.*

# MAINTAINING ADEQUATE OPERATING ROOM

Although *tar* and *sysadmsh* ensure the integrity of your system's files, you also need help in maintaining operating integrity of the system's hard disk. SCO UNIX operates most efficiently when at least 15 percent of the disk area is free. When available disk space drops below 15 percent, the system's responses begin to slow. If no space is available, many commands won't function.

## Determining Free Disk Space

Impress on your users that a multiuser environment such as SCO UNIX relies on a cooperative effort. Every time you shut the system down to do housekeeping, other users are denied access. Users can limit those periods of forced inactivity by keeping their own directories clean. And that's as simple as removing unneeded files or relegating seldom used files to floppy disk. (As you'll see later, you can always give users access to floppy disks when they need their files again.)

Several commands help you monitor system activity and the availability of disk space. One is the *df* (device free-space) command. Its syntax is as follows:

```
df -option device_file
```

The *df* command reports the number of blocks that are free on the named device. (Because a block is 512 bytes, divide the reported number of blocks by 2 for a rough estimate of the available space in kilobytes.)

The command gives additional information if it is used with the *v* option. To use this option to take a closer look at the hard disk itself, enter the following:

```
df -v
```

On our system, SCO UNIX responds:

```
# df -v
Mount Dir  Filesystem        blocks     used      free  %used
/          /dev/root          72074     49130     22944  68%
# _
```

To check the free space remaining on a disk in the boot drive, enter the following:

```
df -v /dev/fd0
```

(Note the use of *fd0* rather than *rfd0*).

If your report indicates the amount of free space is at or near 15 percent, you'll need to look at how your disk is being used and for what purposes. The most obvious places to look are the *mail* spool file and the printer spool file on the system and the *dead.letter*, *core*, and *mbox* files in each user account. All of these can become collections of unneeded or canceled files. In addition, if you've created a Micnet network (as described in Chapter 15), don't forget to check the Micnet *LOG* files.

## Determining Directory Usage

In ferreting out the files that clutter your system, you'll need assistance on the directory and data-file levels. The *du* (directory use) command can help. Used by itself on the command line, *du* generates a list of directories and subdirectories in the current directory, along with the number of blocks each occupies. Linked files are reported only once. The *du* command also includes the following options:

| | |
|---|---|
| s | Displays only the total number of blocks being used in the specified directory. |
| a | Displays information for all files as well as for all directories. |
| r | Displays error messages if it encounters files or directories that cannot be read. |
| u | Ignores files with more than one link. Normally files with more than one link are reported once. With this option they are not reported at all. |
| f | Reports only on the current directory entries. |

When you use the *du* command, look for large block counts. Data files or directory files that occupy a large amount of space are among the first places you should look for unneeded files.

# Finding Unused Files

Faced with a long list of files and directories belonging to other users, you might feel you have no basis for determining which are needed and which are not. In actuality, that's true; only a file's owner can ever tell you whether the file can be removed. However, on a systemwide basis, one criterion you can use to narrow the selection is file aging—how long a file has remained in storage without being used.

You can put SCO UNIX's *find* utility, with the *atime* (access time) option, to work here. The following command line will search the directory named */usr* for all files that have not been accessed in more than 15 days:

```
find /usr -atime +15 -print
```

It's reasonable to assume that a file not accessed for that length of time is no longer active. (Even so, of course, file aging remains a criterion, not a cause, for removal. You must still consult a file's owner before removing the file. You must also distinguish between system files—which you don't want to delete—and user files.)

When you include the *print* parameter, *find* displays the result on your screen. (Without *print*, it doesn't record the results anywhere.) If you want to send the results to a file, perhaps one called *oldfiles*, you can append an instruction that includes the following output redirection:

```
find /usr -atime +15 -print > oldfiles
```

(Note that you leave the *print* option intact.)

# Removing Old Files

After you determine which nonsystem files haven't been used for a certain length of time, you can send *mail* messages to the owners and ask them to remove the files or notify you of those (within reason) they want to keep. An easier approach, however, is to create a message that each user will see when he or she logs in.

### Modifying the daily message

When you first installed SCO UNIX, you were probably greeted with a line that read something like this:

```
Welcome to SCO System V/386

              From

The Santa Cruz Operation, Inc.
```

This message is stored in a text file called */etc/motd* (message of the day). Because it is a text file, you can use *vi* to load a copy and add your own message. You might, for example, add something like this about a week before your scheduled cleanup date:

```
All files not accessed since 8/15/86
will be removed on 9/15/86. Please mail root
if there are any exceptions.
```

When your message is complete, save the file on the disk and quit *vi*. From that point on, until you change the message, all users who log onto the system will see your note each time they log on.

## Saving Deleted Files

Even though you might want to clean house, don't simply delete files from user accounts. First use *tar* to archive the files on a disk and hold them for a few days. Even if you have received approval from the users, follow this procedure whenever you delete files other than your own. (In emergencies, bear in mind that even if you've disposed of the temporary copies you made, additional copies of the files still reside on your archive disks for some time.)

## Improving Disk Performance

After your system has been in use for some time, two factors can cause your hard disk to operate less efficiently. The first factor is disk fragmentation. The first time that a file is written on disk, it takes up sections of the disk next to one another, or contiguous sections. When users write other files, these files fill up the sections of the disk following the last existing file. If a user then adds to an existing file, the additions cannot be on a section of the file contiguous to the existing sections but must be noncontiguous. To read that file, the heads on the disk drive must travel farther and continually bridge that gap. A little fragmentation is not bad, and you probably would never notice it. On a heavily used system, after a year or so, all the users on the system might notice some performance loss.

The second factor that might affect disk performance for individual users is peak directory size. SCO UNIX has two thresholds for directory size: 30 entries and 286 entries. A directory with 30 entries or less is small, and the operating system can search it very quickly. A directory with up to 286 entries can still be searched quickly. More than 286 entries, however, can cause a significant increase in the search time for files in that directory. After files are created in that directory and the directory is expanded to hold those entries, the directory never shrinks below that size. In other words, if a user creates 287 files in a directory and then deletes 200 of them, the operating system still needs to search as if it had 287 files. This factor can be especially noticeable in login directories. If you notice a large number of files in any user directory that might be used as the user's current working directory, you might want to consult with the user and propose that the user change the directory structure for those files.

The solution for both types of inefficiencies is the same: Back up the files, remove the files from the hard disk, and then restore the files from the backup archive disks. To reduce disk fragmentation over the whole disk, you have to back up all the user files, remove all the user files from the filesystem, and then restore all the user files from the backup archive disks. The operating system writes files back onto the hard disk in contiguous sections. To fix a directory with a large number of files, you must back up the files in the directory (and all the subdirectories, if any exist) and then remove the directory. Next you need to create a sufficient number of new directories, subdirectories, or both to contain the backup files without exceeding the threshold. Finally you distribute the backed-up files among the new directories and subdirectories when you restore them. You might also need to modify shell scripts that refer to backed-up files.

> **NOTE:** *If you undertake either of these tasks, be certain that your backup disks are complete, accurate and readable.*

# ALTERNATIVE FILESYSTEMS

Your filesystem might benefit from having some users work from floppy disks rather than from the hard disk.

Providing floppy disk access is effective if a user is on the system infrequently. In fact, you can provide a whole series of users with one user account and a staggered login schedule, having them use no more than the minimum disk space necessary for that account.

In addition, if someone on the system is engaged in private or sensitive work, the safest way to protect a file is to make it totally unavailable to other users by keeping it on a floppy disk.

## Creating a Filesystem

In setting up floppy disk access for users, you begin with a formatted floppy disk, but you also need to create a filesystem on that disk. The *backup* and *tar* procedures do not require this step because the commands manage files in their own way. (That's the reason normal *ls* and *cp* commands won't work with *backup* and *tar* disks.)

To create a filesystem, you need four pieces of information about the disk: the device file that controls it, its block size, its gap, and its block number. The device file is one you've already used: */dev/fd0*. The other values, on IBM and compatible machines with 5.25-inch drives, are as follows:

| Equipment | Block size | Gap | Block number |
|-----------|-----------|-----|--------------|
| 386-compatibles | 1200 | 3 | 30 |

Thus, you place a formatted 5.25-inch disk in the boot drive and enter the following command:

```
mkfs /dev/fd0 1200 3 30
```

The *mkfs* (make filesystem) command examines the disk. If the disk is not freshly formatted, *mkfs* might find a filesystem already on the disk, and you'll see the following message:

```
# mkfs /dev/fd0 1200 3 30
mkfs: default type (AFS) used
mkfs: /dev/fd0 contains data. Overwrite? (y/n) _
```

This message might mean that the disk contains data files for a directory structure, a previously created filesystem, or some blank files but no actual data. If you respond *y* to this question, however, any files that do exist on the disk will be overwritten and thus become inaccessible to you. SCO UNIX offers you a way to check the disk later on. If you're uncertain of the disk's contents, it's best to answer *n* to the prompt, remove the disk, and use a newly formatted one.

## Mounting a Floppy Disk

After you create a filesystem on a floppy disk, you need to make SCO UNIX aware of the disk. At present, you cannot address the disk by its device filename. For example, if you used the following command, SCO UNIX would respond with a listing of the hard disk directory named */dev/fd0*, not with information on the disk in that disk drive:

```
ls /dev/fd0
```

To tell SCO UNIX to use the disk, you mount it as a directory by means of software in the system. After you do so, you can make the disk your working directory, create more directories on it, or run executable shell scripts from it. Whatever you can normally do within SCO UNIX to a file and a filesystem you can do to the contents of the disk itself, through the disk directory.

It isn't essential to create a directory specifically for your disk. If the directory name you specify happens to be an existing SCO UNIX directory, the contents of the directory remain unchanged and, while the disk is in use, inaccessible.

Mounting filesystems in this way, however, is not advisable. It's best to create an extra subdirectory in your home directory, giving it a descriptive name such as *Floppy*. To mount the disk onto that directory, you use the following command format:

```
/etc/mount .device  directory
```

Thus, the command to mount the disk to the *Floppy* directory for user *mikeh* would be as follows:

```
/etc/mount /dev/fd0 /usr/mikeh/Floppy
```

Note that you must use the leading slash with the directory name. You can also use the directory */mnt*, which SCO UNIX provides in the root directory for mounted filesystem use. However you do it, you must specify an existing directory when you use the *mount* command.

After you mount the disk, any work related to the *Floppy* directory will be performed with the disk in the */dev/fd0* directory. SCO UNIX uses the directory name as a gateway to that device.

The *mount* command cannot be used with *tar* disks or with disks created with the *Backups→Create* option of *sysadmsh*. The file structures are dissimilar. For example, you could pick any group of files in your *Floppy* directory, use the ordinary SCO UNIX copy command *cp filenames Floppy*, and then use either *lc Floppy* or *ls Floppy* to list the contents of the directory. The names of the files you just copied would appear. Recall that to list backed-up files, you could use the option *Backups→View*, the *Media→List* options of *sysadmsh*, or the *tf* or *tvf* options of the *tar* command.

## Unmounting a Floppy Disk

The complement of mounting a disk is, predictably enough, the *umount* (unmount) command, which takes the following form:

```
umount  device_name
```

Before a filesystem can be unmounted, all open files in the mount directory must be closed and all users must be out of the directory and any of its related files. To unmount the disk in the preceding example, the command would be as follows:

```
umount /dev/fd0
```

After unmounting, if you were to try listing the directory again when the shell prompt reappeared, you would no longer receive a listing of the filesystem on the floppy disk in the disk drive. However, unmounting a disk does not cause any work and files to disappear. If you remount the disk, you again have access to all the files on it.

Keeping SCO UNIX's treatment of mounted disks in mind, you can evaluate your system and available disk space in terms of your users. If a user needs absolute privacy for one or more tasks, you can mount a disk to take care of his or her needs—as long as that person understands that access to SCO UNIX will be limited to that disk at those times. Conversely, you can juggle a number of occasional SCO UNIX users, providing access to them on a staggered schedule and maintaining each person's work on a floppy disk. If you were to give each user two hours on the system per day, you could provide access for three additional people, each with a 1-MB filesystem area on a disk you can mount at the appointed time—and all using only a few extra bytes of storage space on your hard disk.

To back up data for people working from floppy disks, you need only copy the information to a temporary directory on the hard disk and then copy it back to a floppy disk. As long as such users' work never exceeds the capacity of one floppy disk, neither you nor they need be concerned about what means they use to access SCO UNIX.

# RECOVERING DISK ERRORS

Whether you're using the hard disk alone or in combination with floppy disks, you might at some point be informed of a disk error. The error can result from a circumstance as simple as an improperly closed file or as devastating as aging or corrupt media. (Neither floppy disks nor hard disks last forever.)

No matter what the cause, a disk error doesn't correct itself. And it can get worse if you leave it alone or try to ignore it. Hardware difficulties aside, if you or your users are having difficulty reading or writing files or if a disk won't mount properly, run the SCO UNIX *fsck* (filesystem check) utility. It's roughly equivalent to the MS-DOS Chkdsk program.

Because *fsck* checks on the filesystems on the hard disk, the argument to the command can take any of several forms, depending on the filesystems that you have on your system. For example, the correct *fsck* command for the disk in the boot drive is as follows:

```
fsck /dev/fd0
```

For the hard disk, it's as follows:

```
fsck /dev/root
```

The *fsck* command requires that you unmount a filesystem (with the exception of */dev/root*) before you attempt to clean it. The easiest way to deal with this requirement is to do all file cleaning and checking from system maintenance mode, before any file systems have been mounted. Using the *-n* option, you can also run *fsck* "read only" on mounted filesystems.

In all cases, as the program is running, you'll see this series of reports:

```
# fsck /dev/root

  /dev/root
  Fast File System:  Volume:

  ** Phase 1 - Check Blocks and Sizes
  ** Phase 2 - Check Pathnames
  ** Phase 3 - Check Connectivity
  ** Phase 4 - Check Reference Counts
  ** Phase 5 - Check Free List Bitmap
  2569 files 48000 blocks 22944 free
# _
```

If *fsck* encounters any problems, it will print appropriate messages to the screen and clean the system.

If *fsck* finds no problems, it will display a one-line report when it is finished. The report will show you the number of files in the system, the number of blocks used, and the number of free blocks remaining.

> **NOTE:** *As was mentioned before,* tar *and the archive disks created with the* Backups→Create *option of* sysadmsh *use a different file format. Because of this,* fsck *will always report problems with disks generated by one of those utilities, and any corrections you tell it to make* tar *and* Backups *disks will destroy the filestructure on those disks.*

# 15

# Networking for UNIX Computers

Although the benefits of networking a multiuser system might not be immediately apparent, networking actually expands the work you can do by bringing together the resources of other users and other machines. For example, networking is a logical choice if users of independent computing systems need access to each other and need access to work stored on separate computers. They might need to transfer program or data files, access large databases, or communicate through an electronic mail system. The modern computing environment offers a number of choices for networking computers. This chapter will help you sort out some of the considerations in choosing the right network for your computing needs.

## NETWORKS IN GENERAL

In a multiuser environment such as SCO UNIX, a single processor or computer serves the terminals, printers, and other devices connected to the system. Of necessity, the number of people who can access that system simultaneously is limited because the computer's time must be divided among the users. As more people make requests of the system at the same time, the computer's reaction to those requests slows.

On a network, two or more computers are linked together. No single computer bears the burden of serving all users, although some networks are designed so that one computer in the system does more work than the others.

A network in which all of the computers are in a single location is known as a *local area network*, or *LAN*. A network in which the computers are in widely separated locations is known as a *wide area network*, or *WAN*. The software and hardware for these two types of networks are different, even though the services they provide might be the same. In our discussion, we'll be focusing on LAN technology.

# Transmitting Information on Networks

Networks let users transmit information from one computer to another. The way in which each network transmits information is governed by a set of rules called a protocol. The protocol defines what kind of electrical signals travel on the cables connecting computers, how the computers are to be physically arranged on the network, how each computer can generate a signal on the network, how computers receive signals, and so on. To understand networks and network services, you need to understand protocols.

## The OSI Reference Model

The International Organization for Standardization (ISO) is, as its name implies, an international body whose task is to define standards in many fields. In the field of computer networking, the ISO has defined the Open Systems Interconnection (OSI) Reference Model. This reference model defines an ideal networking protocol—a set of rules for network services. The OSI protocol is a layered protocol. The layers in the protocol separate the different tasks required during network transmission, define what each task must be, and specify how the tasks relate to one another. These tasks are defined independently of any particular computer hardware or any particular computer application. This definition permits different types of computers to communicate on the same network, as long as they all conform to the requirements of the protocol. Not all protocols in current use conform to the OSI model—in some cases because they were developed before the model and in other cases because they were developed from other models. Most of them are also layered protocols, although the ways in which the tasks are distributed among the layers often are different from the OSI model. An OSI protocol set conforms exactly to the OSI model.

Figure 15-1 illustrates the OSI Reference Model.

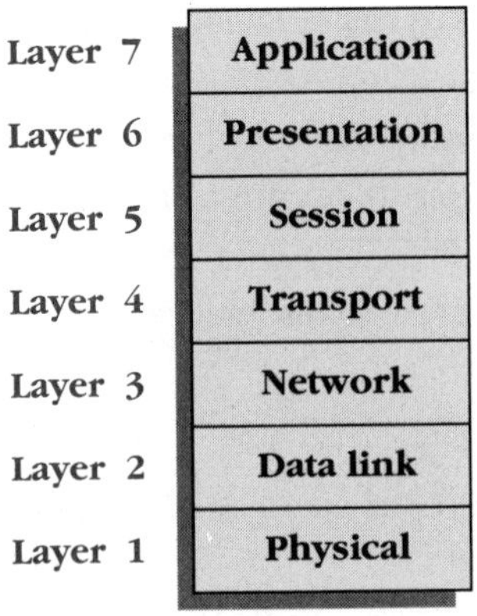

| Layer 7 | Application |
|---------|-------------|
| Layer 6 | Presentation |
| Layer 5 | Session |
| Layer 4 | Transport |
| Layer 3 | Network |
| Layer 2 | Data link |
| Layer 1 | Physical |

**Figure 15-1.** *The Open Systems Interconnection (OSI) Reference Model.*

Each layer in the protocol requests services from the layer below it; each layer in the protocol provides services to the layer above it. This structure permits programmers to develop all of the tasks independently. The only requirement is that each task conform to the protocol specifications for that level. In other words, a task must take into account exactly how the next higher layer will request a service from it and exactly how it must respond to that request. This requirement defines the interface between protocol levels. The application level is made up of programs, such as the SCO UNIX *mail* program, that you see on your display. The Data Link layer is made up of programs, such as an Ethernet Link program, that generate and receive signals on the attached cable.

In some ways, this layered network transmission resembles the movement of goods from manufacturers to retailers. Manufacturers produce goods, the goods are packed in cardboard boxes, the cardboard boxes are loaded aboard trucks, and the trucks travel across roadways to destinations. At the destinations the process is reversed: The boxes are unloaded from trucks, and the goods are taken out of the boxes, displayed by retailers, and sold. Within limits, the process doesn't depend on what kinds of packages are in the trucks—each truck can carry several kinds of packages. Likewise, the process doesn't depend on what kinds of trucks are traveling on the highways. As in other layered systems, the function of each layer is independent of the function of the other layers, yet each layer relies on the other layers for services.

In a computer network, because the layers and the function of each layer is intangible, confusion can arise. Asking whether a network should use NETBIOS or Ethernet is similar to a manufacturer asking whether he or she should use a cardboard box or a concrete highway. NETBIOS defines the interface between the session and the transport layers; Ethernet is the physical layer. Applications that use the NETBIOS interface can run on networks using Ethernet as the physical transmission medium. From another perspective, Ethernet networks can carry signals with information generated by applications that use the NETBIOS interface. In determining the services your network needs to offer and how to provide those services, keep in mind that in the myriad products available, some provide only certain layers of the network, some are complementary with others, some are independent of others, and some are dependent on others.

# Local Area Network Cabling

Local area networks can be laid out in any of several kinds of configurations, or topologies, and can be made up of any of several cable types. The topology you choose depends in many cases on the type of physical transmission protocol that you use. The type of cabling appropriate for your network also depends on the distances that your network must span and the cost of the cable.

## Network topologies

Any local area network exists in one of three basic topologies. These topologies are known as star, bus, and ring networks, and they describe the manner in which the elements of the network are physically connected. Individually, these topologies can be described as follows:

Star
: One computer is used as the communication node, or hub, of the network, and the others are connected directly to it. All communications between network components pass through this central machine. The topology is called a star system because the other computers radiate out from the one at the center of the group. Your multiuser SCO UNIX system, with terminals clustered around a central computer, resembles the star topology.

Bus
: The computers are connected to a linear cable, or bus. The bus itself has a definite starting point and ending point, but the network does not; no computer is actually defined as first or last—all are physically at the ends of the bus. Communications between network components are passed back and forth along the bus, with each machine capturing those transmissions that are intended for it.

Ring
: In a ring network, the computers are connected to a cable that forms a circle. Communications between network components are passed around the ring, with each machine capturing those transmissions that are intended for it. As with the other topologies, special internal rules govern the manner in which network communications occur.

To provide all the services your organization requires, you might need to connect your SCO UNIX computers to other types of computers on your network. This requirement might affect the type of network topology you need because the available networking software for that kind of network might use only one topology. For some types of computers, most of the available software might be only for a ring network. In other cases, you can choose between two topologies for the same type of network. For instance, Ethernet networks use two physical topologies. One is a bus topology using coaxial cable; the other is a star topology using twisted pair wires. Each topology has advantages and disadvantages. If transmission problems occur on a network using a star topology, you can disconnect one computer at a time from a central point and determine where the fault lies. In a bus topology, you might have to follow the cable wherever it leads—through walls and ceilings—checking cable connections and disconnecting computers to find the fault.

## Bridging the distance between computers

In networking computers, just as in installing terminals, you must consider the distance the computer signals must travel between devices. Computer signals are, simply, patterns of electrical signals representing the binary digits 0 and 1. A specific voltage (with a small plus or minus factor) is assigned to signify 1, and another is assigned to signify 0.

Under ideal conditions, the electrons in the signals transmitted through the computer cable would remain in motion and travel any distance between devices if they encounter no resistance of any sort. In the real world, however, the signals encounter resistance from the cable itself. As a result, as the signals travel along the cable between two devices, the resistance in the wires begins to lower the signal strength. Finally, exceeding the variance allowed, the signals become unrecognizable.

**Serial networks.** Allowing some margin for error, the maximum distance typically recommended between devices that communicate serially over unenhanced cable is 100 feet. (The quality of your cables will add to or detract from their overall effectiveness.) Beyond that, reliability becomes unpredictable.

However, SCO UNIX serial networks can and do extend well beyond the 100-foot range, so solutions to the distance problem exist. The Federal Communications Commission requires that, under certain conditions or with specified computer equipment, you must use shielded data cables. The shielding encases the wires in the cable and acts as a barrier that prevents the cable from "transmitting" interference— electrical noise. If shielding is mandatory for your network to prevent it from generating such interference, the equipment's manufacturer is required to say so in the manual.

Aside from FCC regulations, however, shielded cables might be essential for cable runs greater than 15 to 20 feet because the data traveling between two computers could be affected by other interference sources. As well as keeping noise in, shielded cables tend to prevent outside noise from entering your data line.

**Ethernet networks.** Ethernet networks have greater transmission speeds and provide for signal transmission over greater distances than serial lines. Computers on Ethernet networks require expansion cards designed for Ethernet transmission. Ethernet networks are bus networks that transmit 10 million bits per second (Mbps). Under the common protocol on serial lines when two computers are communicating, the receiving computer senses that a signal is approaching along the cable and then can establish contact. This protocol, known as handshaking, permits each computer in turn to send and receive on the line. Ethernet uses an access method known as Carrier Sense Multiple Access with Collision Detection (CSMA/CD). On an Ethernet network, all computers wanting to send a message monitor the cable to sense the carrier wave carrying the electrical signal. When a computer senses no carrier wave, it immediately begins its transmission. Because the signal travels on the cable at about 80 percent of the speed of light, there is a small delay in recognizing the state of the cable from one end to the other. Another computer wanting to transmit might begin a transmission a fraction of a second after the first, and the two simultaneous transmissions garble the signal. Both computers still monitor the cable, however, and when they recognize that both are trying to transmit at the same time, both stop transmitting. The two computers then wait for different random time intervals, after which they try to transmit again.

Standard Ethernet cable is half-inch diameter shielded coaxial cable, which permits transmission up to about 1700 feet. Each computer connects to standard Ethernet cable with a multistrand cable from the Ethernet expansion card to a transceiver on the coaxial Ethernet cable. Ethernet networks use two alternative cable types. Thin Ethernet cable permits transmission up to about 1000 feet. The thin Ethernet cable usually connects directly to a bayonet connector on the Ethernet expansion card in the computer. Both standard and thin Ethernet cable support 100 computers on a single network. Shielded twisted pair wiring can also be used for Ethernet networks. It also connects directly to the Ethernet expansion card, using an RJ-11 plug-in connector, which is similar to a standard wall jack for a telephone connection. The wires from each computer run to a concentrator, which transmit the signals on the wires. Physically, twisted pair cabling is like a star network, but logically it acts exactly like the bus network required for Ethernet transmission.

**Fiber-optic networks.** The Fiber Distributed Data Interface (FDDI) is an emerging standard from the American National Standards Institute (ANSI). FDDI uses fiber-optic cables to transmit data at 100 Mbps using light waves at the 1300 nanometer wavelength. This technology supports an FDDI network as long as approximately 125 miles. FDDI networks use a ring technology.

## Boosting computer signals

On many networks, computers are separated by distances that are greater than the maximum transmission distance that is specified for the network type. In most cases, however, ways exist to reproduce the signal on successive cable segments in order to span greater distances.

Even though, as was mentioned earlier, the maximum distance a cable can carry serial data is about 100 feet, this is not always a practical distance between SCO UNIX computers. Over longer distances, you can safeguard your data transmissions by using signal enhancers or short-haul modems.

If the cable on a serial network will run as far as 300 feet, you should consider installing signal enhancers (also known as line drivers) at 75-foot intervals. Signal enhancers are electronic devices that analyze the arriving signals, clean them of any noise, and restore the original voltage levels. You plug an incoming data cable into one end and the next segment of the cable into the other end.

Effective as they are, signal enhancers have two disadvantages in situations that require exceptionally long cables. Signal enhancers require power, so you must have an electrical outlet handy for the power supply at every signal enhancer. In addition, they are expensive. At current prices, three signal enhancers cost about as much as one short-haul modem.

Short-haul modems are convenient for boosting signals over distances in excess of 300 feet or so. They convert standard serial transmissions to a format that can be carried either by simple twisted pair cabling or by existing telephone lines. To use a short-haul modem, you attach one at each end of the connection. During transmission, the short-haul modem attached to the sending computer translates the signals into a format known as current loop. These modified signals can travel up to two miles or so. When the short-haul modem at the other end of the connection receives these signals, the modem retranslates them to the format readable by the serial port on the receiving SCO UNIX computer.

Within or between nearby office buildings, short-haul modems can enable you to use existing telephone lines to make the connection between SCO UNIX computers. (You'll need the permission of the telephone company to make use of their lines, and you'll probably be asked to pay a fee.)

On networks using Ethernet transmission, you can extend the reach of the network by using repeaters or bridges. A repeater is a device that receives electrical signals and reproduces them. A bridge is a device that operates on the lower two layers of the OSI Reference Model. It receives information in the form specified by the data link layer of the OSI model and interprets the information. It then reproduces the information and transmits it according to the specifications of the physical layer on the next segment of the Ethernet network.

## Costs of cabling

Providing all the cabling requirements for an extensive network spreading over even a modest physical space can be very expensive. In the case of a large office building in a big city, the cost to wire a local area network might be more than the cost to buy all the computers, other hardware, and software. In addition, maintaining the network cabling can be expensive. Adding computers and cable to expand a network can significantly increase costs.

# NETWORK SERVICES

The ultimate aim of a network is to provide services not locally available otherwise. Some types of services might require the users to make explicit connections to other machines. These terminal services provide a terminal connection to a distant machine, file transfer services, or electronic mail services. Other types of services might appear to the user to be provided locally, even though they are actually provided by some other machine across the network. The latter kinds of services are called server applications. A computer might provide other computers on the network with additional disk storage space. This machine is called a disk server. Other computers that access this disk space are called clients. The disk storage space on the disk server appears to them to be on their own computers, even though requests to read and write files are transmitted over the network, and the files themselves reside on the disk server. These network services are usually independent of the physical network type or the protocol used on the network. Not all services are available on all network types or with all protocols, however.

# Explicit Services

A number of networking products for SCO UNIX provide services at the application level of the OSI Reference Model: terminal emulation, file transfer, and electronic mail services. One set of products is based on the standard protocols developed under the auspices of the Defense Advanced Research Projects Agency (DARPA) for a prototype networking project called the ARPAnet. The ARPAnet subsequently evolved into a collection of interconnected networks called the Internet. The protocols developed for the Internet are generally known as TCP/IP for two of the protocols in the family: the Transmission Control Protocol (TCP) and the Internet Protocol (IP). These protocols are independent of any particular machine or manufacturer. They are very widespread because they are well suited to connecting different types of computers and are the standard of choice for connecting different local area networks to one another. Another set of products is based on the System Network Architecture (SNA) protocol from IBM and are used on networks for which connection to IBM mainframe computers is required. A third set is based on the OSI protocols, which are more common on networks outside the United States. Many governments also specify OSI protocols on the networks that they install or that must be compatible with their networks.

## Services based on TCP/IP

The services based on TCP/IP run across many kinds of physical networks and on many kinds of computers. Besides SCO, a number of other companies provide network services for SCO UNIX based on TCP/IP: Novell, Interlan, Communications Machinery Corporation (CMC), Network Research Corporation, and FTP Software. The most common utilities provided with TCP/IP implementations are *telnet*, *ftp*, and *mail*. The *telnet* utility is a remote terminal emulation program that lets you log onto a remote computer and access all its capabilities as if it were your local computer. The computer can be another computer running SCO UNIX or a computer running an entirely different operating system. The only requirement for making the remote connection is that the remote computer also must be using TCP/IP. To access the computer, you only need to have its Internet address. This address is usually presented as a series of four integers separated by dots (periods), such as *130.57.6.17*. This is called dotted decimal notation and represents an Internet address independent of any particular network type or hardware. The Internet Protocol uses this address to identify a particular computer on the network and to provide connections to it. As long as the host computer runs the appropriate programs based on the TCP/IP protocols, you can connect to it and use your computer as a terminal. In the case of *telnet*, the host computer needs to run *telnetd*, the *telnet* daemon. A daemon is a program that continually runs in the background on multiprocessing computer systems and waits for specific requests from computer users or other processes. The *ftp* utility is a file transfer program that lets you move files from a remote computer to your computer. The host computer must be running the *ftp* daemon, *ftpd*. After you connect to the computer using its Internet address, you can transfer files as binary files or as ASCII files, get directory listings, change directories, create directories, and accomplish other tasks. You can also transfer files between two remote computers. TCP/IP implementations also usually provide electronic mail services based on the Simple Mail Transfer Protocol (SMTP). SMTP specifies the format for electronic mail messages to be delivered to remote systems on the network and specifies the address formats for messages. Most implementations offer a variety of other services as well.

## Services based on SNA

SCO provides SCO uniPATH SNA-3270, a software product that connects networks of SCO UNIX computers to IBM SNA networks. A network of SCO UNIX computers can be based on the transport and network layers of TCP/IP, XNS, or OSI protocols. The computer running SCO uniPATH SNA-3270 functions as a gateway between the SCO UNIX network and the SNA network. A gateway is a computer that translates all of the layers in one set of protocols to the appropriate layers in another set of protocols. In this case, SCO uniPATH SNA-3270 converts protocols on the SCO UNIX network to the protocols on the SNA network. The gateway computer requires an expansion card for synchronous SNA transmission.

On the SNA network, the computer running SCO uniPATH SNA-3270 acts as a remote IBM 3274 communications controller, and the computers or terminals on the SCO UNIX network act like attached IBM 3278 display stations. This system provides sessions on the IBM mainframe host for each computer on the SCO UNIX network. SCO uniPATH SNA-3270 also provides the capability to transfer files between the computers on the network running SCO UNIX and the IBM host computer. Rabbit Software Corporation, SSI, and Cleo Software also provide connections based on SNA from SCO UNIX networks to IBM mainframe computers.

## Services based on OSI

The application services from SCO based on the OSI model include the VT (virtual terminal) login service and file transfer facilities based on the File Transfer and Access Method (FTAM) protocol. In addition, SCO provides an electronic mail program based on the OSI protocol for electronic mail services, X.400.

## Micnet serial networks

SCO UNIX is distributed with several programs that you can use to create a Micnet network based on serial transmissions. Creating a Micnet network essentially creates the transport and lower layers for the network, which permit the SCO UNIX *mail*, *rcp*, and *remote* programs to communicate over the network. In a Micnet network, serial lines from one computer's serial port to another computer's serial port make up the network transmission medium. You can lay out the network as a star network, as an inline network, or as a combination of the two topologies. In a star topology, all of the computers send their transmissions to the central computer, or hub, which then directs the transmissions to the correct destination computers. In an inline network, the computers are connected in a chain. The first computer is connected to a serial port on the second computer; the second computer is connected by one of its other serial ports to a serial port on the third computer in the network, and so on. When a computer in an inline network receives a transmission, it decides if the transmission was intended for it. If not, it retransmits the message to the next computer in the chain. (An inline network differs from a bus network in that each computer in an inline network always processes each transmission and retransmits it; each computer on a bus network processes a transmission only if it is the transmission's destination, and it never retransmits.) If you construct a network from a combination of star and inline topologies, you must ensure that the network doesn't form a ring at any point.

A Micnet network has the advantage of low cost. The software is included with SCO UNIX, and the hardware (serial port expansion cards and wiring) for serial networks is relatively inexpensive. Besides the relatively slow serial transmission speeds, the disadvantages of Micnet are that, in a star topology, the hub has to be provided with many serial ports, and handling network requests can take a large amount of processing time. In an inline topology, a transmission passing from one end of the network to the other can take a long time.

# Server Programs

Several server programs are available for SCO UNIX networks. Three are provided by SCO: SCO's implementation of LAN Manager for UNIX from Microsoft, SCO's implementation of Network File System (NFS), and SCO's Open Desktop implementation of the X Window System.

## LAN Manager for UNIX

The SCO implementation of LAN Manager for UNIX provides both client and server applications on a network. One of the principal services that LAN Manager for UNIX provides is file access through the Distributed File System (DFS). Each LAN Manager client can access all the files on any LAN Manager server on the network. The file system on each client begins with the root directory (/), and the first layer below the root directory consists of the names of the servers on the network. Under each machine name is a layer that includes all the files on that machine. The files on the servers appear to the client user as if they were on the client machine. Figure 15-2 on the following page shows the relationship between physical machines and the client directory structure.

**Physical layout**

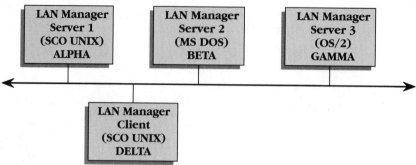

**Logical directory structure on machine DELTA**

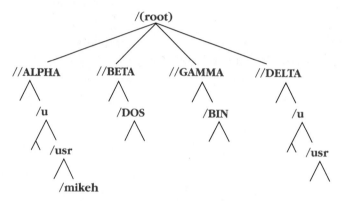

**Figure 15-2.** *The physical layout and client directory structure on a LAN Manager for UNIX network with machines ALPHA, BETA, GAMMA, and DELTA.*

From the client machine DELTA, the full pathname to reach the directory *mikeh* on the server ALPHA is *//ALPHA/u/usr/mikeh*. In a Distributed File System, the directory structure on the client machine begins with a machine name, followed by the rest of the directory structure on the server. The client "sees" all the LAN Manager for UNIX servers on the network as distinct entries in the client directory structure.

LAN Manager for UNIX provides other services as well, including remote login to other computers, access to printers and communications devices, and electronic mail.

LAN Manager for UNIX uses two protocols: the Server Message Based (SMB) protocol and NETBIOS. SMB defines an interface between the application and presentation layers of the OSI model. DFS uses SMB to access files on different machines. NETBIOS defines the interface between the session and transport layers of the OSI model. Its function is to pass transmissions to and from the underlying network transport protocols. These underlying transports can be based either on TCP/IP protocols or on OSI protocols. The transmission method on the network can be any method compatible with those protocols—Ethernet, for instance.

## File servers

SCO NFS, based on the Network File System (NFS) protocol from Sun Microsystems, provides servers that let clients on a network access files as if the files were on the client computers. This approach differs from the disk access provided by LAN Manager for UNIX in that remote filesystems are mounted on the filesystems of the client computers. Instead of starting file access from the root directory, beginning with the name of the computer on which the directory structure actually resides, NFS mounts the directory structure on the client computer so that the structure appears as if it were part of the client computer's directory structure. Figure 15-3 on the following page shows the relationship between physical machines and directory structures.

The directory *usr* from the NFS server DELTA is mounted remotely across the network on all the clients. The mount point in the diagram in Figure 15-3 for all the clients is the root directory (/). The directory *usr* appears to all the users on the client computers as if it were a part of the directory structures on their computers. Because NFS is designed to be independent of any specific computers or hardware, any computer attached to the network can be either a client or a server if it is running the appropriate NFS software compatible with the Sun NFS specification. In this example, the network has one MS-DOS client. The directory *usr* appears in its directory structure as well.

NFS has three protocol layers: NFS and the Remote Procedure Call (RPC) protocols at the application layers, the eXternal Data Representation (XDR) protocol at the presentation layer, and the RPC library at the session layer. The RPC library provides the interface to the transport layer. SCO NFS uses TCP/IP for its network transport.

## Graphics display servers

The Open Desktop graphics server program is based on the X Window System developed at the Massachusetts Institute of Technology. The X Window System provides graphics display services to remote client machines on a network. Each client can have its own window on the graphics display server. In this window, it can display the results of its calculations, its requests for data, and other of its activities. This approach provides users access to the graphics output of remote machines and lets remote machines use their processing units for computing rather than for updating graphics displays. For instance, let's suppose you want to use meteorological data to develop a weather forecast map, an activity that requires extremely large amounts of processing power. Let's further suppose that you are able to access such processing power because you are on a

**Physical layout**

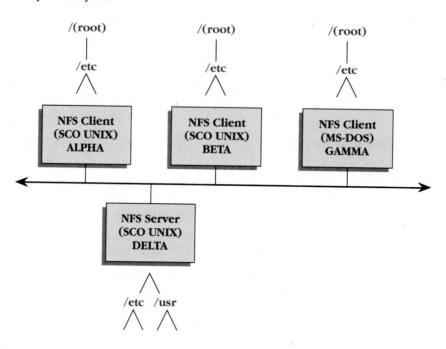

**Logical directory structures on client machines**

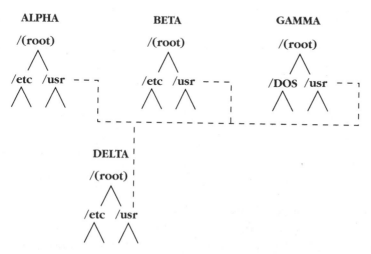

**Figure 15-3.** *The physical layout and directory structure on an SCO NFS network with machines ALPHA, BETA, GAMMA, and DELTA.*

network served by a Cray supercomputer. Using Open Desktop, you could start the programs necessary to make the forecast on the Cray but make the Cray computer a client of the graphic display server on your computer. Any time the Cray computer needed to update its weather map, it would send a request across the network to the graphics display server—the X Window System implemented in Open Desktop on your computer. The server would then display the transmitted data on your screen. Figure 15-4 shows the relationship between X Window System servers and clients.

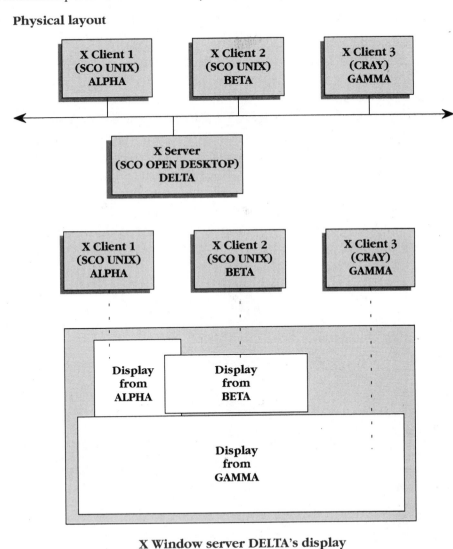

**Physical layout**

**X Window server DELTA's display**

**Figure 15-4.** *The physical layout and screen layout on an X Window System network with machines ALPHA, BETA, GAMMA, and DELTA.*

Because the X Window protocol is independent of any particular hardware or network, any X Window client can transmit any graphics information, and any X Window server can display that information. The display is not based on characters but is based on graphics information: pixels on the display screen.

The X Window System defines protocols at the application, presentation, and session layers. In SCO's Open Desktop, the network transport protocols are TCP/IP.

# THE FUTURE OF NETWORKING

Networking is an extremely broad field, and this survey barely scratches the surface of networking under SCO UNIX. Many software and hardware products beyond those mentioned here are currently available. No doubt an even wider variety of products will be available in the future. The underlying physical network technologies will almost certainly provide greater speeds and capacities, software will likely adopt standard protocols for network transmission, and more network protocols will strive for interoperability—the ability to operate transparently with all implementations of the same protocol. To prepare for the future, you should choose standard network protocols for implementing your current network. Doing so will ensure that the standards you use will be maintained into the future, providing access to future network technologies as they become available as well as providing access to paths for migration from current technologies to future ones.

# APPENDIXES

# A

# SCO UNIX Command Reference

This appendix provides a quick reference to SCO UNIX commands discussed in this book, but it is by no means complete. SCO UNIX offers a multitude of commands and command options. Use this listing as a memory aid to the form, options, or arguments for the most commonly used commands.

Commands are listed alphabetically, with references to the chapters in which they are discussed, unless they are commands you use through an SCO UNIX utility, such as *vi* or *mail*. These are discussed under the utility headings.

**NOTE:** *The system administration commands are, necessarily, described very briefly in this appendix. For more detail on system management, see the SCO UNIX manuals.*

**bc**. Starts the SCO UNIX calculator, which is useful for calculations ranging from addition and subtraction to the evaluation of complex mathematical expressions. Operators include + (addition), − (subtraction), * (multiplication), / (division), % (modulo, or remainder), and ∧ (exponentiation). Entries to be evaluated separately can be grouped within parentheses.

The order of evaluation is as follows:

| | |
|---|---|
| First level | Parentheses |
| Second level | Exponentiation |
| Third level | Multiplication, division, modulo |
| Fourth level | Addition, subtraction |

In the event of two operations of the same level, the expressions are evaluated from left to right. *Discussed in Chapter 2.*

**cal**. Displays a calendar for the specified year and, if requested, for the specified month. Syntax:

`cal month year`

The *month* option is a number between 1 and 12 or an unambiguous string of letters identifying the month—for example, *Jul*, rather than *Ju*. The *year* option must be a four-digit number for the years 1000 and above. For example, if you enter *86*, *cal* would interpret the year as 86, not 1986. If you don't specify a year, *cal* assumes the current year. If you don't specify a month, *cal* displays the current, prior, and coming months. *Discussed in Chapter 7.*

**calendar**. Represents a special SCO UNIX file that you can use to store appointments and other reminders that the system will automatically send through the *mail* system on the day before and the day of the date specified. You can append entries to the *calendar* file with the command *cat >> calendar*. Entries need not be in chronological order or in a particular date format. *Discussed in Chapter 7.*

**cat**. Displays files on the screen. Syntax:

`cat filename`

If you don't specify a filename, the command displays keyboard input.

When used with the redirection symbol(s) > or >>, *cat* creates or joins files under the filename specified. Syntax to create a file:

`cat > filename`

Syntax to join (>) or append (>>) files:

`cat filename(s) > filename`

Or:

`cat filename(s) >> filename`

*Warning:* Using a single redirection symbol (>) will overwrite the destination file. *Discussed in Chapter 4.*

**cd**. Changes the current (working) directory. Syntax:

`cd directory_name`

If you don't specify a directory, the user's home directory becomes the current directory. If you specify the directory as .. , the current directory moves up one level in the directory structure. *Discussed in Chapter 3.*

**chmod**. Changes access permissions for files or directories. Syntax:

`chmod who permission_level filename or directory_name`

You can specify *who* as the following:

| | |
|---|---|
| a | All users |
| g | The group |
| o | Others |
| u | The user |

Do not include blank spaces between items in the *who* and *permission_level* lists.

Permissions are set with + (to add permission), – (to remove permission), or = (to add indicated permissions and remove any others currently in effect). *Permission_level* can be the following:

| | |
|---|---|
| x | Execute |
| r | Read |
| w | Write |

*Discussed in Chapter 8.*

**copy**. Copies files or groups of files from one directory to another. Syntax:

`copy -(options) source destination`

The *source* can be any existing file or a directory. If the *destination* file or directory does not exist, it is created. Useful options include the following:

| | |
|---|---|
| a | Requests confirmation before making the copy |
| r | Copies recursively, including all subdirectories within the specified directory |
| v | Displays reports on the screen as the copy procedure is carried out |

*Discussed in Chapter 3.*

**cp**. Copies the contents of an existing file to another file or directory. Syntax:

`cp source destination`

If you copy a file to another file, the *source* and *destination* filenames cannot be the same. *Discussed in Chapter 4.*

**csh**. Starts the C shell. *C shell options and variables are discussed in Chapter 10.*

**date**. Displays the current day, date, time, and year. If you specify a date, it sets that date as the current date. (You must be a superuser to do this.) Syntax:

```
date mmddhhmmyy
```

The first *mm* option is the month (01 to 12); *dd* is the day of the month (01 to 31); *hh* is the hour (00 to 23); the second *mm* is the minute (00 to 59); and, optionally, *yy* is the last two digits of the current year (00 to 99). *Discussed in Chapter 2.*

# DOS COMMANDS

Nine SCO UNIX commands are available to handle MS-DOS text files. All commands require mounting a DOS floppy disk or accessing the DOS partition on the hard disk, and you must coordinate them through the system administrator to avoid unpredictable effects on the system. You can use the drive names A and B for any DOS disks placed in drives 0 and 1, respectively. In addition, you can use the drive name C: to access the DOS partition on your hard disk if one is installed or D: to access your second DOS disk drive. The DOS commands and syntax for each are as follows. (The *-r* option available with some of the commands displays the DOS file without newline conversions.)

| | |
|---|---|
| `doscat -r drive_name:filename` | Prints a DOS file to the screen. |
| `doscp -r drive_name:filename`<br>`    UNIX_filename` | Copies a DOS file onto an SCO UNIX disk, giving it the specified UNIX filename. |
| `doscp -r drive_name:filename`<br>`    UNIX_directory` | Copies the specified file(s) into the specified directory on an SCO UNIX disk. |
| `dosdir drive_name:DOS_directory` | Lists the contents of a DOS disk's directory in standard DOS format. |
| `dosformat -fqv drive_name:` | Formats a DOS disk. |
| `dosls drive_name:DOS_directory` | Lists the contents of a DOS disk's directory in UNIX format. |
| `dosmkdir drive_name:DOS_directory` | Creates a DOS directory on the specified DOS disk. |
| `dosrm drive_name:filename` | Removes the specified DOS file from a DOS disk. |
| `dosrmdir drive_name:DOS_directory` | Removes the specified DOS directory from a DOS disk. |

*Discussed in Chapter 8.*

**echo**. Displays the results of a command on the screen without actually carrying it out. Syntax:

```
echo command
```

In a script file, you can use *echo* to display text on the screen when used in the following format:

```
echo "text"
```

Or:

```
echo 'text'
```

*Discussed in Chapters 4, 9, and 10.*

**ed**. Starts the SCO UNIX line editor, *ed.* Syntax:

```
ed filename
```

If you specify a filename, the editor reads the file's contents into its buffer. Useful commands include the following:

a      Appends text. If you specify a line number, it appends after that line. To stop entering text, enter a period at the beginning of a new line.

w      Writes the contents of the buffer to disk using the current filename unless you specify another filename.

s      Substitutes one text string for another; used in the following format:

         `line_numbers /existing_text/replacement_text/`

         If you don't specify a line number, the command affects only the first occurrence of existing text on the current line. To substitute throughout a line, use the following format:

         `s/existing_text/replacement_text/g`

         To substitute throughout a document, use the following format:

         `1,$s/existing_text/replacement_text/g`

r      Reads in a specified file; used in the following format:

         `r filename`

p      Displays (prints) specified lines on the screen; use the following format:

         `number,numberp`

*Discussed in Chapter 4.*

**grep**. Searches a file for a specified pattern of characters. Syntax:

```
grep -(options) pattern filename(s)
```

When *grep* finds the pattern, it displays the entire line on the screen. You can search for exact matches by enclosing the search pattern in single quotation marks and, if appropriate, blank spaces. Actually, the following three SCO UNIX commands can search for patterns of characters:

| | |
|---|---|
| grep | Searches for patterns specified by pattern-matching characters; for example, *grep ' [a-z]at ' '* searches for any three-letter word that begins with the lowercase letters *a* through *z*, followed by *at*, with a blank space in front of and behind it. |
| egrep | Searches for multiple patterns; *egrep ' bat ¦ cat '*, for example, searches for all occurrences of *bat* or *cat*, or both, that exist with both leading and trailing blank spaces. |
| fgrep | Searches for multiple strings of characters separated by newline characters, but does not recognize characters that are used to match patterns; *fgrep ' [a-z]at '*, for example, searches for an exact match for *[a-z]at* and not for the possible words denoted in the range of characters that is specified in the regular expression *[a-z]*. |

Useful options include the following:

| | |
|---|---|
| v | Displays all except matching lines. |
| x | With *fgrep* only, displays lines that, in their entirety, exactly match the specified pattern. |
| c | Displays only the number of matching lines that were found. |
| l | Displays only the filenames containing matching lines. |
| n | Displays the relative line number of each matching line in the file. |
| y | With *grep* and *fgrep*, ignores case in searching for matches. |

*Discussed in Chapters 8 and 9.*

**head**. Displays the first few lines of files. Syntax:

```
head -number filename(s)
```

The *-number* option specifies the number of lines to be displayed. If you don't specify a number, it displays the first 10 lines. *Discussed in Chapter 4.*

**lc**. Lists the contents of directories in column format. If you enter *lc* without specifying a directory name, it lists the contents of the current directory. Syntax:

```
lc -(options) directory_name(s)
```

366

When used without any options, the command lists entries in alphabetic order. Useful options include the following:

| | |
|---|---|
| C | Maintains column format even when output is redirected to a file. |
| F | Places a slash (/) after each directory name and an asterisk (∗) after the name of each executable file. |
| R | Lists the contents of subdirectories within the specified directory. |
| a | Lists all files, including hidden files. |
| c | Lists files by time of creation. |
| d | Lists only the name of a specified directory, not its contents. |
| l | Lists entries in long format, showing file type and permissions, links, owner, group, file size, time of last change, and filename. |
| r | Lists entries in reverse order. |
| t | Lists entries according to the time they were last modified. |
| x | Displays entries across the screen rather than down columns. |

*Discussed in Chapter 4.*

**lp (or lpr)**. Prints a document on a line printer attached to the system. Syntax:

`lp -(options) filename(s)`

Files are printed in the order in which they are entered. Useful options include the following:

| | |
|---|---|
| d*destination* | Sends a file to the printer or class of printers specified; *see Chapter 13 for a discussion of printers and printer names.* |
| m | Sends notification through the *mail* system when a file has been printed. |
| n*number* | Prints the specified number of copies. |
| w | Displays (writes) on the user's screen a message announcing completion of printing. |

*Discussed in Chapters 7 and 13.*

**ls**. Lists the contents of a directory. Syntax:

`ls -(options) directory_name(s)`

If you enter *ls* without specifying a directory name, it lists the contents of the current directory alphabetically and in a single vertical column. If you specify directory names, the command lists the files in each directory in alphabetic order. Useful options include the following:

| | |
|---|---|
| a | Lists all entries, including hidden files. |
| d | Lists only the name of a directory, not its contents. |

| l | Lists entries in long format, showing file type and permissions, links, owner, group, file size, time of last change, and filename. |
|---|---|
| p | Places a slash (/) after the name of each directory. |
| r | Lists entries in reverse order. |
| t | Lists entries by time of last modification (latest first). |
| x | Displays entries in multiple-column format, across the screen. |

*Discussed in Chapter 3.*

**mail**. Starts the electronic mail utility used to send and receive messages between system users. The following commands are used within *mail*.

| ^ | Displays the oldest message in the list. |
|---|---|
| $ | Displays the newest message in the list. |
| alias *alias_name*<br>    *user_name(s)* | Enables sending a message to the specified users under a single alias name. When *alias* is used as a recipient, the message or a copy of the message is sent to all users within the group without typing each user name. An alias is temporary unless it is added to the *.mailrc* file. |
| d *message_number(s)* | Deletes the current message. If you specify message numbers, it deletes the messages specified. |
| d *start-end* | Deletes the range of messages specified. The complementary command, *u* (undelete), used in the same format, recovers messages deleted during the current session. The *u* command does not work after you exit *mail*. |
| F *message_number(s)*<br>    *user_name(s)* | Forwards messages in the same way as *fo*, but without the indentation. |
| fo *message_number(s)*<br>    *user_name(s)* | Forwards the specified message, list of messages, or range of messages to the user or users specified. If no message number is included, the current message is forwarded. Messages are indented one tab stop on the recipient's screen. |
| h *message_number(s)* | If you do not specify a message numbers, it displays a numbered list of message headers, with the most recent listed first. If you specify message numbers, it displays a list of the headers for the specified messages. |

| | |
|---|---|
| `h start-end` | Displays a list of the headers for the messages specified in the *start-end* range. Pressing Enter or + displays the first message following the current header list. Each subsequent time you press Enter or +, it displays the next message. |
| `ho message_number(s)` | Holds a specified message (or messages if you specify a list or a range) that you have marked for transfer during the current session, keeping them in the mailbox. |
| `l message_number(s) user_name` | Prints the specified message (or messages if you specify a list or a range) on the line printer attached to the system, or if *user_name* is included, the command prints all the letters sent by the specified user, ignoring any list or range specified. |
| `m user_name(s)` | Sends a message to the named recipients. After composing the message, press the Ctrl-D combination on a new line to send it. |
| `mb message_number(s)` | Transfers the specified mail to a mail-storage file named *mbox*, which is found in the home directory. |
| `p message_number(s)` | Displays a nonsequential series of messages specified in ascending order. |
| `p start-end user_name` | Displays a range of messages. If you specify a user name, it displays messages from the specified user. |
| `q` | Quits *mail* and returns you to the shell. Pressing Ctrl-D also quits *mail*. |
| `r message_number` | Replies to a message. Typed by itself after a message is displayed, *r* incorporates the lines you type until you press Ctrl-D at the beginning of a new line. Typed with a message number, *r* specifies a reply to a message other than the one currently displayed. |
| `s message_number(s) filename` | Saves the specified message (or messages if you specify a list or a range) in the file specified. Header lines are also saved. |
| `set option(s)` | Displays the current options settings in the *.mailrc* file. If you specify options, it lets you change settings. To restore the default options, use the *unset* command. |

| | |
|---|---|
| to *message_number(s)* | Displays the first five lines of each specified message. You can change the number of lines displayed with the *toplines* variable. |
| to *start-end* | Displays the first five lines of each message in the specified range. You can change the five-line default setting with the *toplines* command. |
| w *message_number(s) filename* | Saves the specified message (or messages if you specify a list or a range) in the file specified, but does not include the header lines. |
| x | Quits *mail*, but represents an abort command that leaves the contents of the mailbox unchanged. All transfers, deletions, and so on that were requested during the current session are ignored. |

**mail** compose-escape sequences. The *mail* facility includes the following useful compose-escape sequences.

| | |
|---|---|
| ~b *user_name(s)* | Includes the specified users in a *Bcc:* (blind-carbon-copy) line and sends a copy of the message to them without informing other recipients. |
| ~c *user_name(s)* | Includes the specified users in a *Cc:* (carbon-copy) line and sends a copy of the message to them. |
| ~h | Displays each header line in turn. You can edit each line or you can accept what is displayed by pressing Enter. |
| ~m *message_number(s)* | Includes the specified message, list of messages, or range of messages in the body of the message you are composing, indented one tab stop. |
| ~M *message_number(s)* | Includes one or more messages in the body of the message you are composing, but without the indentation. |
| ~p | Displays the current message, including header lines. |
| ~r *filename* | Reads the specified text file (for example, one created in *vi* or *ed*) into the message you are composing at that point. |
| ~s *subject* | Substitutes the new subject for the current subject. |
| ~t *user_name(s)* | Appends names of the specified users to the *To:* line of the header. |

~v
Starts the *vi* editor, which assigns a temporary file-name to existing text. You can then use *vi* to edit the body of the letter. When finished, exit *vi* and save the letter on disk with the *:x* command. When you do so, you're returned to the *mail* system with a message requesting that you continue.

*The* mail *system is discussed in Chapter 7.*

**mesg**. Sets the message permission status on your terminal. Syntax:

mesg y/n

Displays the current message permission status. The arguments *y* and *n* set the status to *yes* or *no*. If the status is set to *no*, users attempting to write to your terminal receive the message *Permission denied.*

**mkdir**. Creates a new directory. Syntax:

mkdir directory_name(s)

Directory names are limited to 14 characters. Unless specified with an absolute pathname, *directory_name* is created as a subdirectory of the current directory. To create more than one directory, separate the directory names with a space. *Discussed in Chapter 3.*

**more**. Displays one screenful of information at a time. The form *more filename* displays *filename* one screenful at a time, pausing between displays until you press the Enter key to request the next line, until you press the Spacebar to request the next screen, or until you press the Delete key to quit. *Discussed in Chapter 4.*

**mv**. Moves (renames) a file or directory. Syntax:

mv source destination

If you move a file to another directory containing a file with the same name, the existing file is overwritten. If the destination is a directory, the source files are moved to that directory. *Discussed in Chapter 3.*

**passwd**. Changes the current password. The command requires no arguments; SCO UNIX prompts for all required information. *Discussed in Chapters 2 and 12.*

**pr**. Starts the SCO UNIX print utility which, with its numerous options, you can use to emulate paper printing on the screen. Syntax:

```
pr -(options) filename(s)
```

Useful options include the following.

| | |
|---|---|
| `number` | Formats printing in *number* columns. |
| `+number` | Starts printing at page *number*, the default is 1. |
| `a` | Prints multiple-column output across the page; lines are alternated between the left and right. |
| `d` | Double-spaces printing. |
| `f` | Pauses for a formfeed to advance to next page. |
| `h` | Uses the next string of text (enclosed in quotation marks) as the page header; default is date, filename, and page number. |
| `m` | Merges and prints all files, one per column; negates the effects of *number* and *a*. |
| `n` | Prints each line with a line number; numbers are incremented by five. |
| `o number` | Indents each line *number* characters; the default is 0. |
| `p` | Pauses and rings a bell before displaying the next page; waits for a carriage return before continuing. |
| `t` | Suppresses the default five-line header and five-line footer at the top and bottom of each page. |
| `w number` | Sets the line width to *number* characters; the default is 72. |

*Discussed in Chapters 8 and 10.*

**pwd**. Prints the pathname of the current (working) directory. Syntax:

```
pwd
```

*Discussed in Chapter 2.*

**rm**. Removes one or more specified files. Syntax:

```
rm -(options) filename(s)
```

If you use wild cards to specify filenames, the *i* (interactive) option provides a safeguard against inadvertently removing wanted files by causing SCO UNIX to prompt for confirmation before each file is deleted. *Discussed in Chapter 4.*

**rmdir**. Removes one or more specified directories. Syntax:

```
rmdir -options directory_name(s)
```

Removes empty directories only. You must delete or transfer files within the directory to another directory before you carry out the *rmdir* command. *Discussed in Chapter 3.*

**sed**. Starts the SCO UNIX non-interactive stream editing utility. Syntax:

```
sed -(options) filename(s)
```

Options are as follows:

| | |
|---|---|
| n | Suppresses output; you can use it to test an editing script without sending the results to the screen or to a file. |
| e | Precedes script instructions that are written into the command line, instead of read from a separate file. |
| f | Precedes the name of the file from which *sed* should read its editing commands. |

*Discussed in Chapter 8.*

**sh**. Starts the Bourne shell.
*Bourne shell options and variables are discussed in Chapter 9.*

**sort**. Sorts the lines of one or more files. Syntax:

```
sort -(options) +number -number filename(s)
```

You can sort on more than one field by including *+number* and *−number*; *+number* begins the sort at the specified field (counting from 0 at the leftmost edge) and *−number*, restricts examination to the range of fields specified. The *sort* options include the following:

| | |
|---|---|
| b | Ignores leading blanks. |
| c | Checks to determine whether the file is already sorted according to any other options included in the command. If it is, another sort is not performed. |
| d | Sorts in dictionary order, ignoring punctuation and special symbols. |
| f | Interprets lowercase letters as uppercase, so case is not considered in sorting. |
| i | Considers only the ASCII characters in the decimal range 32 through 126 in non-numeric comparisons. |
| n | Sorts numbers according to their arithmetic value, not the ASCII value of each of their components. |
| o | Precedes the name of the output file in which the sorted data are to be stored. |
| r | Sorts in reverse (high to low) order. |
| t*character* | Recognizes *character* as the new field delimiter. |

*Discussed in Chapter 8.*

**spell**. Starts the SCO UNIX spelling checker. Syntax:

`spell -(options) +word_list filename(s)`

Unless redirected to another file, output is displayed on the screen. If you include *+word_list*, the document is checked against a user-created file of sorted and correctly spelled words. Useful *spell* options include the following:

| | |
|---|---|
| v | Displays assumptions in combining root words with prefixes and suffixes. |
| b | Checks British spelling. |

*Discussed in Chapter 6.*

**split**. Breaks one file into smaller segments. Syntax:

`split -lines_per_file filename new_name`

Breaks *filename* into the number of lines specified and gives the resulting files the new name, appending a two-letter suffix, beginning with *aa*, to the new filenames. *Discussed in Chapter 6.*

**tail**. Displays the last few lines of a file. Syntax:

`tail +!-number filename`

The *+number* option starts the display *number* of lines from the top of the file, and *−number* starts the display *number* of lines from the end of the file. If you don't specify a number, the last 10 lines are shown. *Discussed in Chapter 4.*

**test**. Evaluates conditions and returns a value of true or false. Syntax:

`test expression`
Useful expressions include the following:

| | |
|---|---|
| `-r filename` | Evaluates as true if *filename* is found and has read access. |
| `-w filename` | Evaluates as true if *filename* is found and has write access. |
| `-x filename` | Evaluates as true if *filename* is found and has executable access. |
| `-f filename` | Evaluates as true if *filename* is found and is a regular file. |
| `-d directory_name` | Evaluates as true if *directory_name* is found. |

| | |
|---|---|
| `-c filename` | Evaluates as true if *filename* is found and is a character-device file. |
| `-b filename` | Evaluates as true if *filename* is found and is a block-device file. |
| `-s filename` | Evaluates as true if *filename* is found and has a size greater than zero. |
| `-z string` | Evaluates as true if *string* has a length of zero. |
| `-n string` | Evaluates as true if *string* has a length other than zero. |
| `string_1 = string_2` | Evaluates as true if *string_1* is identical to *string_2*. |
| `string_1 != string_2` | Evaluates as true if *string_1* is not identical to *string_2*. |
| `string` | Evaluates as true if *string* is not a null string. |
| `integer_1 -eq integer_2` | Evaluates as true if *integer_1* is algebraically equal to *integer_2*. Other comparison operators that can be used are: *-ne*, not equal; *-gt*, greater than; *-ge*, greater than or equal to; *-lt*, less than; *-le*, less than or equal to. |

*Discussed in Chapter 9.*

**uniq**. Finds lines that are repeated in a file. Syntax:

`uniq -option +number -number input_file output_file`

Only one option can be included. Options are as follows:

| | |
|---|---|
| u | Copies only nonduplicated lines in the output. |
| d | Includes only one copy of each duplicated line in the output. |
| c | Includes one copy of each line in the source file, preceding the line with a number showing how many times the line is repeated in the file. |

If you include *+number*, the command skips the first *number* characters of each line; if you specify a field, the command skips the first *number* characters of the field. If you include *−number*, the command skips the first *number* fields of each line and begins the comparison at field *number+1*. *Discussed in Chapter 8.*

**vi**. Starts the visual text editor. When typed by itself, the command *vi* starts the editor without loading a file.

You can start *vi* in the following other ways:

| | |
|---|---|
| vi *filename* | Starts the editor and loads the specified file. |
| vi +*line_number filename* | Starts the editor with the cursor on the specified line of the specified file. |
| vi +/*word filename* | Starts the editor at the first occurrence of *word* in the specified file. |
| vi *filename(s)* | Starts the editor and queues the specified files. |
| vedit | Starts the editor and displays *INSERT MODE* on the status line during insert mode. |

Within *vi*, you have many options for entering text, moving the cursor, manipulating text, and working with files. The following table includes the commands for common tasks, arranged by task for ease of reference.

To enter text:

| | |
|---|---|
| a | Inserts text after the current cursor location; used with a new file, it has the same effect as *i.* |
| A | Inserts text after the last characters on the current line. |
| i | Inserts text, beginning at the space before the current cursor location. |
| I | Inserts text before the first character on the current line. |
| o | Opens a new, blank line immediately below the one containing the cursor. |
| O | Opens a new, blank line immediately above the one containing the cursor. |

To move the cursor:

| | |
|---|---|
| 0 (zero) | Moves to the beginning of the line. |
| $ | Moves to the end of the line. |
| *number*h | Moves left *number* characters. |
| F*character* | Moves left, stopping at the first occurrence (moving right to left) of *character.* |
| T*character* | Moves left, stopping at the character immediately to the right of the first occurrence (moving right to left) of *character.* |
| *number*l | Moves right *number* characters. |
| f*character* | Moves right, stopping at the first occurrence of *character.* |
| t*character* | Moves right, stopping at the character immediately to the left of the first occurrence of *character.* |
| *number*j | Moves down *number* lines. |
| *number*+ | Moves down *number* lines to the first character in that line. |
| *number*k | Moves up *number* lines. |
| *number*- | Moves up *number* lines to the first character in that line. |

| | |
|---|---|
| H | Moves to the upper left corner of the screen. |
| L | Moves to the lower left corner of the screen or to the lower left corner of the document, if less than a full screen. |

### To move the cursor to a word:

| | |
|---|---|
| *number*w | Moves *number* words to the right; counts punctuation marks as words. |
| *number*W | Moves *number* words to the right; does not count punctuation marks as words. |
| *number*b | Moves *number* words to the left; counts punctuation marks as words. |
| *number*B | Moves *number* words to the left; does not count punctuation marks as words. |

### To move to a line:

| | |
|---|---|
| G | Moves to the last line in a document. |
| *line_number* G | Moves to the first character of the line specified. |

### To move screen by screen:

| | |
|---|---|
| Ctrl-U | Scrolls up half a screen. |
| Ctrl-D | Scrolls down half a screen. |
| Ctrl-F | Scrolls one screen toward the end of the document. |
| Ctrl-B | Scrolls one screen toward the beginning of the document. |

### To number lines:

| | |
|---|---|
| :set number | Turns on line numbering. |
| :set nonumber | Turns off line numbering. |
| :*number,number*nu | Temporarily displays the numbers of the lines specified by *number,number*; entered by itself (*:nu*), it displays the current line and its number. |

### To rearrange line lengths:

| | |
|---|---|
| i  and press Enter | Breaks a line immediately to the left of the cursor location after you press Enter and enters insert mode. |
| J | Joins the line below to the end of the current line. |

### To specify a file:

| | |
|---|---|
| :r *filename* | Reads in the specified file. If no file is specified, the current one is read in. |

To edit a list of files:

| | |
|---|---|
| `:args` | Displays the names of queued files. |
| `:n` | Reads in the next file in the queue. |
| `:rew` | Reads in the first file in the queue. |
| `:e filename` | Reads in the specified file (not restricted to files in a queue). |
| `:e#` | Reads in the previously edited file. |

To delete text:

| | |
|---|---|
| `numberx` | Deletes *number* characters to the right, beginning at, and including, the current cursor location. |
| `numberX` | Deletes *number* characters to the left, beginning at, but not including, the current cursor location. |
| `numberdw` | Deletes *number* words to the right of the word containing the cursor. |
| `numberdd` | Deletes *number* lines below, beginning at and including the line containing the cursor. |
| `:start,end d` | Deletes the range of lines specified by the actual line numbers *start,end*. |

To undo an editing command:

| | |
|---|---|
| `u` | Undoes the last command issued. |

To copy and move text:

| | |
|---|---|
| `"buffer number_of_linesyy`<br>**NOTE:** Do not put a space between *buffer* and *number_of_lines*. The space here is for readability. | Yanks the specified number of lines to the insert buffer named by *buffer*. |
| `"BUFFER number_of_linesyy`<br>**NOTE:** Do not put a space between *BUFFER* and *number_of_lines*. The space here is for readability. | Yanks the specified number of lines and appends them to the current contents of the insert buffer named by *BUFFER*. |
| `mletter` | Marks the first line of text that is to be yanked with *letter*. |
| `"buffery'k` | Yanks lines from the line containing the cursor through the line marked with the *m* command. |
| `"bufferp` | Puts the contents of the specified buffer on the line(s) immediately below the current line. |
| `"bufferP` | Puts the contents of the specified buffer either above the current line or just before the current cursor location. |

| | |
|---|---|
| `:first,last co destination` | Duplicates the lines specified by *first,last* immediately below the *destination* line specified. |
| `:start,end m destination` | Moves the lines specified by *start,end* to immediately below the *destination* line specified. |

To search for text strings:

| | |
|---|---|
| `/search_text` | Searches forward (toward the end of the document) for the first occurrence of search_text. |
| `?search_text` | Searches backward (toward the beginning of the document) for the first occurrence of search_text. |
| `n` | Continues a search for the next occurrence of the text that is specified by / or ?. |
| `:set nowrapscan` | Stops a search at the end of the file, rather than wrapping back to the top of the file, even if the search text has not been found. |
| `:set wrapscan` | Wraps a search back to the top of the file if the search text has not been found when the end of the file is encountered. |
| `:set ignorecase` | Ignores case variations in a search. |
| `:set noignorecase` | Makes a search case-sensitive. |
| `:set nomagic` | Disables the editor's ability to recognize special characters (\ [ ] ~ $). |
| `:set magic` | Enables recognition of special characters. |

To replace text:

| | |
|---|---|
| `:gsearch_text/`<br>`s//replacement_text/options` | Searches every line of the file and substitutes the specified replacement text for the search text. The *options* include: *g* to replace search text whenever and wherever it occurs in the file; *gp* to print on the screen a copy of each line change; and *gc* to prompt for confirmation before the replacement. |

To save a file:

| | |
|---|---|
| `:w filename` | Saves (writes) the file on disk under the filename specified. If the command includes no filename, the file is written on disk under the current filename. |
| `:x filename` | Saves (writes) the file on disk under the specified or current filename and quits the editor. |

`:q`  Quits the editor. If unsaved changes exist, the command prompts with the message *No write since last change* (*:quit! overrides*). To abandon the document, type the absolute form of the command, *:q!*.

*The* vi *editor is discussed in Chapters 5 and 6.*

**who**. Lists the login names of users currently on the system. In addition, it shows the terminal identifier and the date and time of login for each user. Syntax:

`who -(options)`

Options include the following:

q  Shows only user names and the number of users currently logged in.

Typed as *who am i*, the command displays *who* information about the requesting user. *Discussed in Chapters 2, 7, and 9.*

**write**. Sends a message directly to the terminal of another user. Syntax:

`write user_name terminal_name <filename`

After you issue the *write* command, it sends all subsequent keyboard input to the recipient until transmission is ended by pressing Ctrl-D at the beginning of a new line.

You can include the *terminal_name* argument to write to only one of a number of users sharing a common user name.

You can include the *filename* argument to send the contents of a text file to the recipient if you use the redirection symbol (<).

# SYSTEM ADMINISTRATION

The following list gives some commands available to the system administrator in managing an SCO UNIX system:

**accept**. Causes an installed printer or class of printers to accept print requests; the printer must be activated with the *enable* command.

**df**. Reports available space, in blocks, on the specified device. Options include: $v$ to report percentage of blocks used; $t$, to report both free blocks and the total number allocated; and $i$, to report a complete summary. Can also be used by the superuser to check the */usr* and /directories. Syntax:

`df -(option) device_file`

**disable**. Deactivates a terminal; also removes a printer from service even if it is set to accept print requests.

**du**. Reports on disk usage by displaying a list of directories and subdirectories, along with the number of blocks occupied. Syntax:

```
du -(option) directory
```

Options include: *s*, to display the total number of blocks for the specified directory; *a*, to display information for all files, as well as all directories; *r*, to display error messages if files or directories cannot be read; *u*, to ignore files with more than one link; *f*, to report on current filesystem only. Can also be used by users to check */usr* and */*.

**enable**. Activates a terminal; also used to cause a printer to print documents.

**find**. Finds and displays the names of all files in the specified directory that satisfy (*options*). Can also be used by users to check */usr* and */*. Syntax:

```
find directory -(options)
```

**format**. Formats a floppy disk. Syntax:

```
format device_name
```

**fsck**. Checks on and cleans the filesystem specified; used in clearing up disk errors. Syntax:

```
fsck filesystem(s)
```

**haltsys**. Shuts down the system immediately; offers users no opportunity to clean up and save current work. Under normal circumstances, *shutdown* is preferable.

**lpstat**. Reports line printer status information. Syntax:

```
lpstat -(options)
```

Options include: *r*, to display data about the request scheduler; *d*, to display the default printer; and *t*, to display all status information.

**mount**. Mounts a disk onto the specified directory. Syntax:

```
mount device directory
```

**ps**. Reports the status of processes currently running.

**reject**. Causes an installed printer to reject print requests.

**/etc/shutdown**. Shuts down the system after a specified period of time (the default is one minute); prompts users to clean up and log out. You cannot terminate the command once you start it.

**sysadmsh**. Activates the system administrator shell. The system administration shell contains options to administer all facets of the system. You can use it to add printers to the system, to create backup disks of the entire filesystem, to copy files onto archive disks, to examine the system status, and to unlock user accounts or terminals, among other functions. You must use it to create, modify, and delete user accounts.

**tar**. Activates the tape archiver facility (used for backing up specified files). Syntax:

```
tar function modifiers modifier_arguments(s) files(s)
```

The functions are: *c*, to create a new file system on the archive device; *t*, to display a list of files on the archive device; *u*, to add specified files to the archive device; *x*, to extract specified files from the archive device; *r*, to write specified files to the end of an archive.

The modifiers include: *f*, to use the corresponding argument to name the archive device; *k*, to use the corresponding argument to specify the device's size; *b*, to specify a blocking factor (the default is 1); *n*, to indicate that the archive device is not a tape device; *v*, to display the names of all transferred files; *e*, to avoid splitting files across separate volumes (tapes or disks).

**umount**. Unmounts the specified disk. Syntax:

```
umount device_name
```

**/etc/wall**. Writes a message to the screens of all users logged in.
*SCO UNIX system administration commands and techniques are discussed in Chapters 12 through 14.*

# B

# Frequently Used SCO UNIX Files

The following files and directories are often used in the day-to-day tasks of SCO UNIX system administration and file handling. Before you make changes to them, consult the appropriate pages in this book or your SCO UNIX documentation, and save the original file under a different name. Then, if the changes that you make don't have the results that you intended, you can restore the original file.

## THE *root* (/) DIRECTORY

| | |
|---|---|
| /bin | An SCO UNIX command directory; contains most of the commonly used commands. |
| /dev | The special device directory; contains device files for the floppy and hard disk drives, attached terminals and printers, system boards, and a clock. |
| /etc | An additional program and data directory; contains many of the system-level commands. |
| /lib | A C program library directory. |
| /mnt | The mount directory; an empty directory reserved for mounted file systems. |
| /usr | The directory commonly containing users' home directories and additional user information. It also contains several other directories with additional SCO UNIX commands and data files. |
| /tmp | A temporary directory; reserved for temporary files created by programs; entire contents of this directory are automatically deleted every day. |

# COMMUNICATION

| | |
|---|---|
| /usr/lib/mail | The system *mail* directory; contains *mail* help messages, alias information, and system identification files. |
| /usr/spool/mail | The system mailbox directory; contains *mail* files for each user. |
| /usr/spool/lp | The system printer directory; contains printer programs and information. |
| /usr/spool/lp/model | The printer interface program directory. |
| /usr/spool/micnet/remote | The Micnet remote system directory; contains information about other machines in the network. |
| /etc/systemid | The system identification file used in the Micnet network. |
| /etc/inittab | The status file for the console and attached terminals. |
| /etc/ttytype | The terminal-type file for the console and attached terminals. |
| /etc/gettydefs | The default communication-parameter and login-prompt lists for the console and attached terminals. |
| /etc/termcap | The communication-parameter database for attached terminals; contains information for most terminals currently available. |

# SCO UNIX STARTUP FILES

| | |
|---|---|
| /etc/rc2 | Command file containing shell scripts used to boot the system. |
| /etc/inittab | File containing the instructions for the system to use when it changes from one state to another (for instance, from single-user maintenance mode to multiuser mode). |
| /.profile | Startup file for the superuser; contains custom shell instructions. |
| /usr/*/.profile | Startup file for Bourne shell users; found in the home directory. (Replace * with your user name.) |
| /usr/*/.login | Startup file for the C shell; found in the home directory of accounts for which the login shell is the C shell. (Replace * with your user name.) |

`/usr/*/.cshrc`  Additional startup file for the C shell, also found in the home directory of accounts for which the login shell is the C shell. Can be used by any user to set the environment on entering the C shell. (Replace * with your user name.)

`/usr/ad/messages`  Message file; contains various system messages, including errors generated by the system upon startup.

`/etc/motd`  Message-of-the-day text file; contents are displayed on each user's monitor at each time of login.

# INDEX

**NOTE:** *Italicized page numbers refer to figures and illustrations.*

## Special Characters

! (exclamation point)
   in absolute commands 80, 88
   in C shell 191, 196
   as escape command 112, 139
   in *test* command 183
" (double quotation marks) 98, 110, 181
# (pound sign) 200–201, 270, 308
$ (dollar sign)
   in Bourne shell 20, 22–23
   in scripts 160
   as wildcard 52, 85, 88
% (percent sign)
   in C shell 20, 22, 189
   as modulo operator 361
& (ampersand) 117, 233, 361
' (single quotation mark) 146–47
( ) (parentheses) 361
* (asterisk)
   in *mail* system 132–33
   as multiplication operator 25, 361
   as wildcard 42–43, 53–54, 181
+ (plus sign) 124, 361
- (hyphen)
   in command options 45, 62
   in *mail* system 124
   as subtraction operator 361
. (dot) 138, 184, 219, 308. *See also* dot (.)
      command; dot (.) indicator
.. (dot dot) 38–39, 219. *See also* dot dot (..)
      indicator
/ (slash)
   as division operator 25, 361
   in *ed* 51
   in pathnames 26–27, 35, 232, 241
   in *vi* 107
: (colon)
   as prompt 28, 246, 270
   in *vi* commands 78, 79–80
;; (double semicolon) 179
< (redirection symbol) 168, 380
= (equal sign) 183
> (greater than sign)
   as redirection symbol 59, 115–16, 168, 362
   in *mail* system 123
   as secondary prompt 170

>> (redirection symbol) 59, 116, 145, 146,
      168, 362
? (question mark) 43, 54, 108
[] (square brackets) 28, 54–55
\ (backslash) 110, 190, 191, 232
^ (caret)
   in C shell 197
   as exponentiation operator 361
   in scripts 160
   in *vi* searches 108–9
¦ (vertical bar) 168–69
~ (tilde) 74, 134, 194

## A

absolute commands 80
absolute pathnames 39
*accept* command 293, 380
access permissions 44, 66, 172, 185–86,
      231, 252
   changing 147–49
   displaying 234
activation key 251
addition operator (+) 361
*alias* command 137–38, 139, 198–99
aliases 197–98
   creating 137–38, 198–99
   deleting 199
   *flipd* 198
   listing 200
   *popd* 197
   *pushd* 197
   *swapd* 197
Alpha Lock key 17
ampersand (&) 117, 233
appending text 50, 75
appointments 142–43
arguments 173. *See also argv* variable
*argv* variable 200, 202
ARPAnet 351
ASCII codes 55
*askcc* option 139
assembly language 6, 7
asterisk (*)
   in *mail* system 132–33
   as multiplication symbol 25, 361
   as wildcard 42–43, 53–54, 181

## Joanne Woodcock

Joanne Woodcock is currently a Master Writer/Editor for Microsoft Press. She is the coauthor of *Microsoft Word Style Sheets*, published by Microsoft Press.

## Michael Halvorson

Michael Halvorson received his B.A. in computer science from Pacific Lutheran University in 1985 and has been employed as a programmer, technical editor, and community college instructor. He is currently an acquisitions editor for Microsoft Press. Halvorson coauthored *Learn Basic Now*, published in 1989 by Microsoft Press.

## Robert Ackerman

Robert Ackerman has been writing for various software companies and computer magazines, including *Programmer's Journal*, for the past six years. Previously, he was managing editor for *Home Computer Magazine*. Ackerman has a B.S. in Computer Science. He lives in San Jose, California.

The manuscript for this book was prepared and submitted to Microsoft Press in electronic form. Text files were processed and formatted using Microsoft Word.

Principal word processor: Debbie Kem
Principal proofreader: Cynthia Riskin
Principal typographer: Carolyn A. Magruder
Interior text designer: Darcie S. Furlan
Principal illustrator: Rebecca Geisler-Johnson
Cover designer: Thomas A. Draper
Cover color separator: Rainier Color

Text composition by Microsoft Press in Garamond Light with display in Garamond Bold, using the Magna composition system and the Linotronic 300 laser imagesetter.

*Printed on recycled paper stock.*

# Other Titles from Microsoft Press

## MICROSOFT® LAN MANAGER
### A Programmer's Guide
*Ralph Ryan*

This is the first book to give an insider's view of Microsoft LAN Manager version 2. Ralph Ryan provides a richly detailed overview of the goals and design theory behind LAN Manager architecture and of fundamental LAN Manager programming principles. This is an ideal reference for experienced developers who want to write distributed applications (based on OS/2, DOS, or UNIX) that use the features of LAN Manager, programmers who want to write administration programs for LAN Manager, and network administrators who want to learn more about how the system works. Ryan includes a wealth of information on the Applications Programming Interface (API), accompanied by scores of real-world sample programs that are practical as well as instructive. Special information—not found in any user manual—covers creating and debugging network-aware programs. Although this book focuses on version 2, everything you learn here will still be true for later versions.

**537 pages, softcover**          $7^{3}/_{8}$ x $9^{1}/_{4}$          **$29.95**          **Order Code LAMA**

## THE *NEW* PETER NORTON PROGRAMMER'S GUIDE TO THE IBM® PC & PS/2®
### The Ultimate Reference Guide to the *Entire* Family of IBM Personal Computers
*Peter Norton and Richard Wilton*

To be a real power programmer, you must understand the design concepts, architecture, and technical details of your PC. That's where THE *NEW* PETER NORTON PROGRAMMER'S GUIDE TO THE IBM PC & PS/2 comes in. This clearly written reference and how-to book provides the knowledge, skills, and concepts you need to master your computer, sharpen your programming skills, and write clean, effective programs. Norton and Wilton include updated material on the 80286 and 80386 micro-processors; the enhanced keyboard, interrupts, device drivers, and video programming; the VGA and MCGA; DOS basics, interrupts, and functions (through version 4); the PS/2 ROM BIOS; programming in C, Microsoft QuickBASIC, and Turbo Pascal; and more. Accept no substitutes—this is the book to have.

**528 pages, softcover**          $7^{3}/_{8}$ x $9^{1}/_{4}$          **$22.95**   **Order Code NEPEN2**

## HARD DISK MANAGEMENT: MICROSOFT® QUICK REFERENCE
### Now with Information on Version 4 and the DOS Shell
*Van Wolverton*

If you own an IBM PC, PS/2, or compatible computer, and you want the efficiency of a well-managed hard disk but don't have the time to read a full-length hard disk management book, this handy reference guide is for you. From the author of the classic *Running MS-DOS*, here is all the core information you need to configure MS-DOS for your system, format your hard disk, organize your files and directories, create timesaving batch files, and back up and maintain your hard disk. Dozens of great examples help you take control of your hard disk.

**128 pages, softcover**          $4^{3}/_{4}$ x 8          **$7.95**   **Order Code QRHADR**

## MICROSOFT® MOUSE PROGRAMMER'S REFERENCE

*Microsoft Press and the Hardware Division of Microsoft Corporation*

MICROSOFT MOUSE PROGRAMMER'S REFERENCE—from the hardware experts at Microsoft—is a complete guide to providing mouse support in all your MS-DOS programs. Both an essential reference to the mouse programming interface and a handbook for writing functional mouse menus, this one-of-a-kind guide includes

- Ready-to-run mouse menu programs
- A complete reference to the mouse function calls
- Specifics on writing mouse programs for IBM EGA modes
- The Microsoft InPort technical specifications

Two 5 1/4-inch companion disks include sample mouse menus, MOUSE.LIB and EGA.LIB, interpreted BASIC, Microsoft QuickC, Microsoft C, Microsoft Macro Assembler, and FORTRAN. MICROSOFT MOUSE PROGRAMMER'S REFERENCE is your complete technical resource for mouse support.

**336 pages, softcover, with two 5 1/4-inch disks**      7 3/8 x 9 1/4      **$29.95**
**Order Code MOPRRE**

## LEARN C NOW

*Augie Hansen*

Learn how to program in C, quickly and painlessly, with LEARN C NOW. This completely integrated system is designed to make C programming fun and easy to learn on any microcomputer running MS-DOS. This unique package includes three 5 1/4-inch disks and a companion book and gives you everything you need to learn C at your own pace before purchasing expensive programming tools. The disks contain

- Lessons in C programming
- Information on using the Learn C Compiler
- The Learn C in-memory compiler, based on Microsoft QuickC and featuring a full screen editor, debugger, online task-specific help, and blazing 7000 line-per-minute compiler speed
- Scores of sample programs

Complementing the online information, Hansen's companion book provides lessons in C programming, question-and-answer sections, and helpful recommendations for getting the most out of this excellent course. And with your copy of LEARN C NOW, you'll also receive a special discount coupon for the full-strength Microsoft QuickC Compiler with Microsoft QuickAssembler.

**384 pages, softcover, with three 5 1/4-inch disks**      7 3/8 x 9 1/4      **$39.95**
**Order Code LECNO**

*Microsoft Press® books are available wherever quality computer books are sold, or credit card orders can be placed by calling 1-800-MSPRESS. Please refer to BBK.*